Macroeconomic Analysis for Economic Growth

Edited by Musa Jega Ibrahim

Published in London, United Kingdom

IntechOpen

Supporting open minds since 2005

Macroeconomic Analysis for Economic Growth
http://dx.doi.org/10.5772/intechopen.95670
Edited by Musa Jega Ibrahim

Contributors
Tonprebofa Waikumo Okotori, Gbalam Peter Eze, Kehinde Mary Bello, David Oluseun Olayungbo, Benjamin Ayodele Folorunso, Meng Sun, Nemer Badwan, Wasseem Mina, Ayşegül Aytaç Emin, Maria Letizia Bertotti, Karl Farmer, Richard Sendi, John Bbale Mayanja, Enock Nyorekwa, Ombeswa Ralarala, Masenkane Happiness Makwala, Olfa Frini, Musa Jega Ibrahim

First published in London, United Kingdom, 2022 by IntechOpen
IntechOpen is the global imprint of INTECHOPEN LIMITED, registered in England and Wales, registration number: 11086078, 5 Princes Gate Court, London, SW7 2QJ, United Kingdom
Printed in Croatia

British Library Cataloguing-in-Publication Data
A catalogue record for this book is available from the British Library

Additional hard and PDF copies can be obtained from orders@intechopen.com

Macroeconomic Analysis for Economic Growth
Edited by Musa Jega Ibrahim
p. cm.
Print ISBN 978-1-83969-881-1
Online ISBN 978-1-83969-882-8
eBook (PDF) ISBN 978-1-83969-883-5

Meet the editor

Dr. Ibrahim obtained an MSc in Economics from the University of Edinburgh, United Kingdom, and a Ph.D. in Economics from the University of Strathclyde, United Kingdom. He also obtained a BSc and MSc in Economics from Ahmadu Bello University, Nigeria. He began his working career in 1992 as a lecturer in Economics at Ahmadu Bello University and worked as an associate lecturer and research fellow at the University of Strathclyde while he was on a study fellowship between 2001 and 2007. In 2007, Dr. Ibrahim joined the Islamic Development Bank (IsDB) with headquarters in Jeddah Saudi Arabia as an economist and subsequently rose to his current position as a lead economist. During his 15 years at the IsDB, he has been involved in various research- and operation-related activities on international development financing and coordinated the preparation and publishing of the IsDB Annual Report between 2018 and 2021. In his current position as a lead economist, he undertakes high-level macroeconomic research to highlight economic and social development challenges to development financing activities for achieving strong economic growth and sustainable development.

Contents

Preface XI

Section 1
Macroeconomics of Economic Growth 1

Chapter 1 3
Introductory Chapter: Macroeconomic Policy Perspectives of Economic Growth
by Musa Jega Ibrahim

Chapter 2 11
Determinants of Economic Growth: An Empirical Evaluation of the Ugandan Economy
by Richard Sendi, John Bbale Mayanja and Enock Nyorekwa

Chapter 3 35
The Life Cycle Hypothesis and Uncertainty: Analyzing Aging Savings Relationship in Tunisia
by Olfa Frini

Chapter 4 59
Foreign Direct Divestment Phenomenon in Selected Sub-Saharan African Countries
by Ombeswa Ralarala and Masenkane Happiness Makwala

Chapter 5 77
Taxation and Redistribution against Inequality: A Mathematical Model
by Maria Letizia Bertotti

Section 2
Labour Market and Employment 91

Chapter 6 93
Labor Markets
by Meng Sun

Chapter 7 109
Involuntary Unemployment in Diamond-Type Overlapping Generations Models
by Karl Farmer

Chapter 8 127
Youth Unemployment and Productivity-Pay in the GCC Countries
by Wasseem Mina

Section 3
The Financial System and Macroeconomic Performance 143

Chapter 9 145
Perspective Chapter: International Financial Markets and Financial Capital Flows - Forms, Factors and Assessment Tools
by Nemer Badwan

Chapter 10 181
Indicators of Banking Fragility of Participation Banks in Turkey
by Ayşegül Aytaç Emin

Chapter 11 203
Exchange Rate Volatility and Monetary Policy Shocks
by Gbalam Peter Eze and Tonprebofa Waikumo Okotori

Chapter 12 225
Exchange Rate Volatility and Macroeconomic Performance in Nigeria
by Kehinde Mary Bello, David Oluseun Olayungbo and Benjamin Ayodele Folorunso

Preface

Macroeconomic analysis is a potent tool for stimulating strong economic growth and sustainable development. It generates insights into understanding the intricacies of national and global economic trends and issues that arise from the policy choices of governments. The core principles of macroeconomics are about activities that determine the performance of the economy based on the intricate interaction of variables relating to the components of the economic system. Economic growth is about relationships among such factors as competitive behaviour and equilibrium dynamics, diminishing returns and the accumulation of physical and human capital, the interplay between per capita income and the population growth rate, and the effects of technological progress on the capabilities of factors of production in the discovery of new goods and methods of production.

The relationship between production and consumption is the bedrock upon which all other factors revolve in driving economic growth. Hence, macroeconomic policies for generating growth require effective coordination of production and consumption, the intensity of which leads to discoveries of more sophisticated methods of production through which technological progress occur to accelerate economic growth. Technological progress enhances the productivity of factors of production thereby increasing the absorptive capacity of the economy. Through inter-sectoral linkages and response to incentives, sectors of the economy expand production by mutually self-perpetuating processes to create opportunities for economies of scale that translate into the lower per-unit cost of production.

Effective governance, resource endowments, and demography are critical factors that need to be properly harnessed along with sound economic principles to underpin strong economic growth. The efficacy of regulatory framework to create enabling conditions for nurturing and bolstering robust value-adding production structures anchored on appropriate macroeconomic management are the fundamental building blocks of strong economic growth. In accordance with these essential principles that elucidate the essence of macroeconomics in achieving strong economic growth, this book brings together a collection of chapters by experts in the field. Macroeconomic Analysis for Economic Growth examines different aspects of macroeconomics that are germane to achieving strong economic growth.

Section 1, "Macroeconomics of Economic Growth," begins with an introductory chapter that discusses the analytical convergence of various economic growth models with macroeconomic policy insights emanating from them. Chapter 2 presents an investigation into the key factors behind the impressive growth of the Ugandan economy, revealing that government consumption and investment have been crucial determinants of the strong growth trajectory overshadowing such drawback variables as inflation, foreign aid, and structural adjustment disruptions. Chapter 3 is an empirical evaluation of the theory of life-cycle hypothesis in Tunisia based on the uncertainties that becloud the ageing population with inadequate savings amid employment challenges, concluding that without employment the life-cycle expectation is untenable. Chapter 4 argues that instead of foreign direct investment (FDI), Sub-Saharan African (SSA) countries are facing the challenge of foreign direct divestment (FDD), both of which are determined by similar factors such as lending rates, urbanisation, and trade openness. Chapter 5 discusses the use of taxation as a tool for reducing inequality, which is crucial for improving welfare through redistribution and ensuring that more people benefit from the proceeds of economic growth.

Section 2, "Labour Market and Employment," begins with Chapter 6, which explains the dynamics of the labour market in terms of the supply of labour by workers and the demand for labour by firms. It illustrates the backwards-bending nature of the labour supply curve and the downward-sloping nature of the labour demand curve with the equilibrium in a perfectly competitive labour market, concluding with policy recommendations for achieving favourable labour market equilibrium. Chapter 7 discusses the possible occurrence of involuntary unemployment in the overlapping generations model of economic growth, concluding that aggregate demand failures with sticky prices tend to weaken investments. Chapter 8 discusses the implication of the relatively low rate of the youth unemployment rate, which is higher among females compared to males, in the Gulf Cooperation Council (GCC) countries. It reveals that the gender disparity in youth unemployment is caused by policies that reflect the social and cultural realities of the GCC countries and concludes that linking pay to productivity is likely to reduce the total and female youth unemployment rates.

Section 3, "The Financial System and Macroeconomic Performance," begins with Chapter 9, which examines anatomized financial markets and the pattern of financial capital flows into developing and developed countries in mobilizing domestic savings and attracting foreign investments to finance development activities. Chapter 10 reports the findings from an investigation of factors underlying banking fragility in Turkey and reveals that asset growth, capital adequacy ratio, financing-to-total deposits ratio, return on asset, and cost-to-income ratio are significant banking-level indicators of the banking fragility of participation banks in Turkey. Chapter 11 reports the outcome of an evaluation of the impact of innovative monetary policies on exchange rate volatility in Nigeria and shows that the implementation of managed exchange rate instruments has the desired effect of moderating exchange rate volatility, leading to inflationary spikes in the Nigerian economy. Chapter 12 examines the asymmetric relationship between exchange rate volatility and macroeconomic performance in Nigeria between 1986 and 2019 and shows that exchange rate volatility exhibited a significant effect on the inflation rate. The chapter authors recommend that monetary policy should focus on regulating the exchange rate to control the general price level in the economy.

The topics, issues, and findings that make up the twelve chapters of this book provide insights to guide macroeconomic policy formulation implementation to stimulate and drive strong economic growth. Even though all the chapters are relevant to all economies at various stages of development, some are more relevant to economies at certain specific stages.

Musa Jega Ibrahim
Islamic Development Bank,
Jeddah, Saudi Arabia

Section 1

Macroeconomics of Economic Growth

Chapter 1

Introductory Chapter: Macroeconomic Policy Perspectives of Economic Growth

Musa Jega Ibrahim

1. Introduction

Macroeconomic policy formulation and implementation are crucial for creating the enabling environment for wide-ranging economic activities to drive economic growth, which manifests into increase in the outputs of major sectors of an economy. A multiple sector positive performance is essential for the growth of the overall economy, but a sector of the economy that attracts large spectrum of economic activities can stimulate the productivity of other sectors to achieve strong sustainable growth of the economy. It is assumed that if an economy is not achieving high growth as expected, it is due to market imperfections, likely coming from economic distortions that emanate from such sources as government tax policies, human capital externalities and information spill overs. The distortions prevent the best use of economic resources (i.e., efficiency) by hindering the free flow of economic activities, thus the economy performs at levels far below its potential.

Based on the balanced growth path principles of the standard growth analysis, which assumes that economic growth on balanced path is equal to the rate of asset accumulation, growth is a function of the difference between the expected returns to asset accumulation and the opportunity cost of investing those assets from the perspective of private economic agents. Low growth rate is due to low social returns or high cost of capital (investment) or both. Increase in private investment leads to increase in capital accumulation to stimulate growth of the economy. Therefore, holding all things constant, economies with high level of private investments tend to achieve high growth and vice versa, but distortions could lead to high cost to discourage investments, thereby stifling growth even with high investments.

Different economies have peculiar conditions and therefore likely to have different critical growth determinants and constraints even though certain factors such as property rights, the rule of law, market-oriented incentives, sound money and sustainable public finance are universally applicable to all economies. The purpose of this introductory chapter is to generate insights into salient issues from standard economic growth analysis to develop macroeconomic policy perspectives therefrom. In subsequent sections, the convergence of standard growth analysis is presented, followed by macroeconomic policy implications and completing with a section on summary and conclusions.

IntechOpen

2. Convergence of standard economic growth analysis

Economic growth analysis illuminates the essence of the effective use of factors of production as the mechanism for attaining economic growth. A given level of natural resource requires the use of labour, capital and the 'effectiveness of labour' (technology) to spring up a production process. The imperative of household consumption is the main activity, which is a veritable source of demand that facilitates production. In turn, the household is the source of labour input for production activities that leads to output of goods and services.

Through persistent production activities to meet growing demand, endogenous process of 'learning-by-doing' facilitates technological progress to underpin strong and sustainable growth of the economy. In the context of classical theory with exogenous technology effect, the economy convergences towards a balanced growth path, implying that the rate of growth cannot be influenced by the activities within the economy. Consumers' preferences, production processes and policy changes within the economy cannot influence the growth rate of the economy with capital, output and consumption per unit of effective labour being constant.

The economy grows through the effective use value-adding capabilities of factors of production to adapt to the effect of existing technology. Based on assumption of constant saving rate, the capital stock does not exceed its golden rule level, such that even if shocks occur, it will eventually adjust to the golden rule value. However, it is difficult to determine a desirable level of saving rate due to the notion that it will be inefficient for the saving rate to exceed the golden-rule level forever because higher quantities of per capita consumption could be attained at all points in time by reducing the saving rate (see, for instance, [1]). The neoclassical growth analysis tends to either suggest the same growth rate for all economies or that growth rates are determined by unexplained factors, but experience has shown that different economies have maintained different per capita growth rates over a long period of time.

Transitional growth rates will differ among economies based on differences in the ratios of capital to effective labour. The assertion of convergence principle implies that if all economies have the same parameters for taste, technology and population growth rate, then they should have the same steady-state level of per capita income. Accordingly, low-income economies will grow more rapidly than high-income economies, and per capita income levels of different economies will converge to a common level.[1] Economies with lower ratios of capital to effective labour relative to the steady-state values will grow faster. Variation in countries' growth rates is as result of variations in distances from steady state and by the rate of decrease of returns to capital. As a country approaches steady-state level of capital per unit of effective labour, diminishing returns to investment will cause a decline in growth rate.

Dowrick and Rogers [3], argued in line with Bernard and Jones [4], that technology transfer and catch-up race among economies could be adduced as explanation for the convergence prediction of the neoclassical models. However, this logic is overshadowed by differences in human capital, external benefits of human capital and capital market imperfections, which renders the prediction of catch-up and a convergence of all economies on a steady-state growth path untenable. Economies

[1] This convergence principle is based on a condition of equal parameters, which does not exist *ipso facto*; hence it is more appropriately termed conditional convergence. McCallum [2] provides a technical and detailed analysis of this convergence condition, further stressing that average growth rates among countries tend to be positively correlated with shares of total income devoted to investment, rather than consumption as espoused by the neoclassical models.

with inherent demand and supply distortions tend to stultify growth in a sustained manner and lead to a cyclical trend of slow growth of such economies. In an empirical cross-country study, Salai-Martin et al. [5] discovered, among several variables tested, that the ones that are significantly related to economic growth are human capital development, average price of investment goods, the initial level of per capita GDP and fraction of GDP in mining.

In endogenous growth analysis, the arbitrary assumption of constant returns with respect to the producible inputs reflects a "knife-edge" character in that slight increasing returns would lead to explosive growth and a slight decreasing return leads to shrinking growth. Both the capital accumulation and the technological progress models subscribe to this knife-edge principle. According to Groth and Schou [6], this is an indication that the models are not amenable to endogenous variables and as such lack robustness. In the absence of population growth, the strictly endogenous models transform into instability problems which give credence to the weakly endogenous growth or semi-endogenous growth in terms of growth in per capita consumption in the long run at a constant positive rate. In strict endogenous context, even without any exogenous technological change and discounting increasing returns and population growth, a stable positive per capita growth and constant growth rate of per capita consumption will occur in the long run.

The attainment of never-ending growth requires never-ending increase in human capital, but human capital is not monolithic, since human skills are peculiar and cannot be automatically transferred to succeeding generations. The assumption of scale effect is therefore mundane, without a discernible analysis of human capital and stock of knowledge that is owned by society in general. Knowledge in use, not human capital per se, can provide a basis for never-ending growth through incentives for Research and Development (R&D) and spill over effects that lead to chain of innovations over time in quality and variety. Li [7], in consonance with Jones [8], argued that the possibility of inter-R&D knowledge spill overs leads to semi-endogenous growth where technological change, which requires real resources, is endogenous while long-run growth is exogenous as in the neoclassical models, which weakens the impact of scale effects.

Natural resources have a double-edge effect on economic growth, the intensity of utilisation of such resources increases total output of the economy but also leads to higher depletion rate of such resources. Given that natural resources are essential in production, growth rate can be constant only through mechanism for maintaining constant level of output. A combination of Hartwick rule of investing the rents derived from efficient extraction, the Hotelling's rule of efficient intertemporal resource extraction and the acquisition of backstop technology has been emphasised as means by which adverse effects of resource depletion can be alleviated. The principle of maximising the utilitarian social utility is a basis for obtaining optimal resource utilisation. The backbone of these expositions is the constant returns to scale assumption relative to technology, which brings the analysis close to endogenous growth models.[2] According to Groth and Schou [6], a one-sector model including non-renewable resource as production inputs does not generate endogenous growth because the strain of extracting successfully smaller amounts of the resource can offset the impact of increasing returns to producible inputs to lead to instability.

According to the 'leading sector' strategy of economic growth [9], a sector with intrinsic potential for large-scale economic activities but strangulated by

[2] Allyn Young conceives economic growth based on increasing returns to scale and cumulative causation that leads to self-sustaining growth due to market size which provides opportunities and incentives for innovation.

institutional and related policies can be liberated to spring up and stimulate strong economic growth. In this context, it is more effective to increase overall growth of the economy in terms of output and employment by removing barriers or provide incentives to investment in sectors in which there is a large but latent demand that can be exploited, so that an increase in investment and consequent output can find a market without resulting in distortions in prices and incomes in the sector. Without removing this barrier, standard growth policies such as propping aggregate demand, spontaneous innovations, cost reductions, tax incentives or direct government investment in general would be less effective. Two main characteristics of a 'lead sector' are the existence of latent demand, the size of which must be large enough to have significant impact on the whole economy if it is actualised; and secondly, an increase in the sector's growth can be exogenous and occur independently of the current overall rate of growth of the economy.

The existence of industrial production, on the one hand, and demand for the products of the industries, on the other hand, create opportunities for market expansion, competition and specialisation. Through a favourable 'forward linkage' effect, an endogenous self-perpetuating process of growth emerges and feeds on it almost automatically. By the prompting of internal and external economies of scale, the process of industrial production evolves into higher and more sophisticated levels of production, giving rise to further specialisation, new products and quality improvements, leading to technological acquisition and economic growth. Adaptation to a growing market, widened by international trade, stimulates industrial production and provides additional impetus to the attainment of strong and sustainable economic growth.

Inter-industry linkages facilitate economic growth by increasing the absorptive capacity of industries through interdependence for goods and services produced by the cluster of existing industries. As each producing sector uses a given level of inputs to produce, it creates demand for products of other sectors. The interdependence of sectors of the economy leads to expansion in production due to increasing demand for goods and services by all sectors. The intensity of this interdependence generates high level of learning by doing, motivates innovation and R&D activities to lead to positive technological change to underpin strong and sustainable growth of the economy.

3. Macroeconomic policy implications

The most significant deduction from economic growth analysis is the convergence of the role of technology as the catalyst for economic growth through facilitating relationship between production and consumption. Production is meant to provide for consumption, which originates from the urge of the household to consume to attain welfare. Since utility is a function of quantity and quality, the motivation to improve on the variety (quantity and quality) of consumption leads to discoveries of more sophisticated methods of production. A co-ordinated institutional motivation for effective utilisation of resources is therefore a fundamental condition for generating strong and sustainable growth path. This implies that, in a situation where consumption is not significantly linked to the process of production, technological progress will be undermined and economic growth, measured by increase in per capita output induced by the enhanced value-adding capabilities of factors of production (technology), will be weak.

For natural resource abundant economies, temptation for rent seeking could facilitate complacent consumption to the detriment of production, thereby crippling value-adding capability of factors of production. The absence of 'backward and forward linkages' and learning-by-doing effects will result into socially inefficient economic structure to adversely affect the growth prospects of the economy. A strategy that ensures optimal utilisation of resources requires providing incentives for investments that makes use of natural resources as intermediate goods to be transformed into finished goods through manufacturing production and inter-industry linkages. Rents from natural resource extraction need to be deployed to build requisite institutional and infrastructure that create opportunities for value-adding production investments. This process will enhance the value-adding capabilities of factors of production, facilitate learning-by-doing complemented by R&D and lead to technological progress that will underpin strong and sustainable growth of the economy.

As the pivotal role of government is crucial in the implementation of appropriate macroeconomic policies in terms of fiscal and monetary policies as well as other aspects of governance, public expenditure pattern needs to align with allocation priority and efficiency of implementating projects and programmes. Production activities in sectors of the economy take place effectively under enabling conditions such as infrastructure and the rule of law that guarantees property rights (patents and copy right laws) along with robust human capital. These are the core pillars that propel economic activities to drive strong economic growth as they are essential to both firms (businesses) and households. However, their non-excludability character, on the one hand, and the competitive profit-making objectives of firms, on the other, prevent firms from engaging in the provision of these services.

Furthermore, given the significant relationship between consumption and production and input-output mechanism needed to drive this relationship, an effective coordination is necessary to generate expansionary economic activities, which is by default expected from the government in accordance with its non-profit and welfare responsibility. Thus, without the ability of government to perform its welfare and coordination functions, all the building blocks of economic growth analysis ('effectiveness of labour', capital, technological change, R&D, etc.) will not be able to contribute adequately to value-adding production activities. Furthermore, natural resource sectors, which are the roots of economic activities, require legal and institutional framework of operations, and this can only be provided by government institutions. Effective governance, through the proper functioning of institutions and the implementation of robust policies, is therefore a crucial prerequisite to the attainment of economic growth.

Two significant interrelated issues arise. One is that the assumption of a responsible government appreciating its crucial role and discharging its functions in accordance with perfect objectivity and rationality may be untenable. Secondly, the possibility of trade-off between the implementation of economic growth enhancing policies on the one hand and the social welfare and intergenerational equity policies on the other give rise to difficult policy choices. A properly balanced combination of the equity-economic growth policy implementation then becomes the fundamental challenge of governance.

A robust macroeconomic policy framework is critical to the size of policy multipliers. However, as modern economies are connected to global economic trends, the most effective strategy is to implement market-oriented policies with indirect government participation to align fiscal policies. It is important to formulate a macroeconomic framework that is contingent upon the core pillars of economic growth with strong institutional arrangements to ensure sustainability. This implies the need to establish a strong fiscal system with public expenditure pattern that invests significantly in human capital development and economic infrastructure while ensuring that core governance issues such as rule of law and property rights are adequately enforced. Economic growth will emanate from strategic macroeconomic policies that provide incentives for investments in key sectors of the economy to expand manufacturing value-added production activities by removing institutional bottlenecks to supply responses and expand the demand for goods and services from the strategic sectors of the economy.

4. Summary and conclusions

The fundamental convergence of various strand of economic growth analysis is that technological progress is the critical factor for achieving strong and sustainable growth of the economy. However, economic growth process is hinged on strong relationship between consumption and production driven by effectiveness of factors of production. Sectoral interdependence based on input-output principles is vital for expanding economic activities to enhance the capability of factors of production that could lead to technological progress through application and adaptation to exogenous technology that is amplified by endogenous technological change made possible by 'learning-by-doing' and further enhanced by R&D activities.

Production activities by all sectors of the economy are possible only if basic infrastructures and the rule of law that guarantees property rights (patents and copy right laws) are in existence. In addition, human capital formation, which is the bedrock upon which all aspects of economic growth processes are hinged, requires to be nurtured by services that are provided by non-profit-making principles. Effective governance in the performance of welfare and coordination functions, through the proper functioning of institutions and the implementation of robust policies, is a fundamental enabling condition for robust economic activities to enhance the effectiveness of factors of production (labour, capital, land) for technological progress to occur for a strong and sustainable growth of the economy to be achieved.

Inter-industry linkages are essential for achieving economic growth through facilitation absorptive capacity of industries through interdependence for goods and services produced by the cluster of existing industries. The intensity of this interdependence generates high level of learning by doing, prompts the need for innovation, which leads to R&D activities and positive technological change occurs to accelerate economic growth.

It follows therefore that, in general, macroeconomic policies for achieving strong and sustainable growth need to focus on value-adding investments that could expand economic activities to develop a strong household sector to emerge as a source of demand for goods and services on the one hand and source of quality labour input on the other hand to facilitate inter-industry linkages. It is crucial to develop robust manufacturing value-added sector as the core of economic growth strategy to take advantage of high value-adding and inter-industry linkages potential of manufacturing activities to drive strong economic growth.

In conclusion, it is fundamental to implement far-reaching policies for achieving inter-generational equity by investing significantly in social and economic services such as education and health anchored on sound and efficient macroeconomic management.

Author details

Musa Jega Ibrahim
Islamic Development Bank, Jeddah, Saudi Arabia

*Address all correspondence to: mjega@isdb.org

References

[1] Barro R, Sala-i-Martin X. Economic Growth. New York: McGraw Hill; 1995

[2] McCallum BT. Neoclassical vs. Endogenous Growth Analysis: An Overview. Cambridge, Massachusetts, United States: National Bureau of Economic Research, Inc.; 1996

[3] Dowrick S, Rogers M. Classical and technological convergence: Beyond the Solow-Swan growth model. Oxford Economic Papers. 2002;**54**:369-385

[4] Bernard BB, Jones CI. Productivity across industries and countries: Time series theory and evidence. Review of Economics and Statistics. 1996;**78**(1): 135-146

[5] Sala-I-Martin X, Doppelhofer G, Miller RI. Determinants of long-term growth: A Bayesian averaging of classical estimates (BACE) approach. American Economic Review. 2004;**94**(4):813-835

[6] Groth C, Schou P. Can non-renewable resources alleviate the knife-edge character of endogenous growth? Oxford Economic Papers. 2002;**54**:386-411

[7] Li CW. Growth and scale effects: The role of knowledge spillovers. Economic Letters. 2001;**74**(2):177-185

[8] Jones CI. R&D-based models of economic growth. Journal of Political Economy. 1995;**103**:759-784

[9] Currie L. The 'leading sector' model of growth in developing countries. Journal of Economic Studies. 1974;**1**(1):1-11

Chapter 2

Determinants of Economic Growth: An Empirical Evaluation of the Ugandan Economy

Richard Sendi, John Bbale Mayanja and Enock Nyorekwa

Abstract

This paper investigated the determinants of economic growth in Uganda for the period 1982–2015 using the autoregressive distributed lag (ARDL) mode. The paper was motivated by the impressive economic performance of Uganda since 1986 that made her graduate from a "failed state" to a "mature reformer" in a short time. The paper established that while the initial level of GDP growth, government consumption and investment positively affected Uganda's economic growth in the short run, inflation, foreign aid and a policy dummy variable representing structural adjustment programmes negatively impacted GDP growth. The results revealed that in the long run, trade openness, population growth, government consumption and investment positively influenced GDP growth in Uganda. The results failed to show a significant relationship between trade openness, population growth and human capital accumulation and economic growth in the short run. The study also failed to show a significant relationship between inflation, human capital and foreign aid and economic growth in the long run. The paper recommends policies that enhances sound macroeconomic fundamentals such as price stability, investment promotion, trade openness, increased government consumption, increased population growth and effective foreign aid.

Keywords: Uganda, Economic growth, Auto Regressive Distribute Lag Model

1. Introduction

"Once one starts to think about the human welfare consequences of economic growth, it is hard to think about anything else" [1]. Economic growth is the basis for increased prosperity, and its importance cannot be overstated. Barro and Sala-i-Martin [2] argue that continuous and sustained economic growth is important for improving the welfare of individuals and that aggregate growth is probably the single most important factor affecting individual levels of income. Due to the importance of economic growth, attainment of high economic growth rates is a major national objective of any country. It is, however, puzzling and at the same time worrisome that the riches of the world are so unequally shared among countries [3].

Over the years, growth performance has varied notably across regions and countries. In some economies, it has experienced major shifts over time. A few developing countries have experienced rapid growth yet some other countries have grown at only a stagnant rate. This discrepancy in economic growth among numerous countries and the dynamics of growth have become provocative research targets. The main questions are why some countries are rich while others are poor, and what determines the rate of growth? Rosa notes that it seems certain that there is no all-encompassing theory of economic growth, but different sources of economic growth can be observed to be relevant for different stages of economic development.

Several reasons have been provided that explain the differences, key among them being the fact that initial conditions differ greatly. Isaksson [4] asserts that some, if not many, of the differences in income per capita are human-created. He asserts that how a society and its production are organized can significantly explain the observed income divergence since the industrial revolution.

In the case of Uganda, the last five decades have been difficult in terms of overall economic growth and stability, let alone the first eight years after independence and the last three decades, when episodes of high yet unstable economic growth occurred, especially from the late 1980s to the late 2000s. Economic growth was impressive for the first eight years after independence, but by 1986, the economy had descended into a deep recession owing to poor governance from the early 1970s to that time. Since 1986, the country has undergone a major transformation from a "failed state" to one of the fastest-growing economies in the world. As early as 1993, Uganda started implementing structural adjustment programmes (SAPS) and other economic policies and programmes such as; economic recovery programme (ERP), medium-term expenditure framework, Plan for Modernization of Agriculture (PMA), and Poverty Eradication Action Plan (PEAP), among others all aimed at poverty reduction and attaining higher levels of economic growth in Uganda. The reforms ushered in relatively high economic growth rates based on incentives for private production. Between 1990 and 2010, GDP growth averaged 7.3 percent per annum, placing Uganda among the fastest-growing economies in the world and creating momentum for take-off. This growth was higher than the Sub-Saharan African growth rate, which averaged approximately 2.1 and was close to that of the East Asian and Pacific region of 7.9 and 6.6 percent, respectively.

To consolidate and accelerate this growth process, the Ugandan government approved the Comprehensive National Development Planning Framework Policy in 2007 which provided the developmental agenda for a 30-year vision to be implemented through three 10-year plans and six 5-year national development plans (NDPs), among other operational plans. However, data shows that Uganda's growth has been mostly unstable; it has been described as unsustainable because it has been sustained partly by significant aid inflows and only a few tradable commodities, such as coffee, flowers and fish. The government of Uganda, like many other governments elsewhere continues to target improving GDP growth. The key to achieving this improvement has been the careful development and implementation of policies and programmes to improve capital stock, labour stock, price stability and productivity and competitiveness as major drivers of economic growth [5].

Uganda has set its Vision 2040 as a guiding framework for transforming the country from "a peasant to a modern and prosperous country with a per capita income of USD 9,500 from the base figure of USD 506 in the year 2010 by the year 2040". For the country to achieve this transformation, Uganda Vision 2040 projects that Uganda's real GDP will have to grow at an average of 8.2 percent, while the IMF forecasts approximately 9 percent growth rate as necessary for the remaining period. However, the achievement of Vision 2040 has been threatened not only by lower-than-targeted rates of annual GDP growth since the inception of the vision but also by a recent slump from the average GDP growth rate of approximately 6.8 percent that was posted in the last half of the 2000s to an average of 4.6 percent between 2010 and 2015.

To achieve the Vision, understanding the determinants of past growth, removing the constraints on present growth and maximizing the prospects for future growth are key. It is important to note that inferring the determinants of growth faces considerable uncertainty due to the existence of multiple overlapping theories that emphasize different channels of growth over time. Therefore, this paper aims at providing more robust and targeted policy interventions to generate higher and more sustainable economic growth by examining the determinants of economic growth in Uganda using the ARDL frameworks.

2. A review of empirical literature

A wide range of studies have investigated the factors underlying economic growth in different countries. Using differing conceptual and methodological viewpoints, studies have identified different factors that explain economic growth world over [6]. However, existing literature has not yet reached a consensus about a typical set of variables that may affect economic growth.

The accumulation of physical capital (investment) is one of the most fundamental determinants of economic growth identified in the literature per the neoclassical and endogenous growth models and much empirical work has been performed on the subject [7–9]. It has been found to be robust to most specifications and sample size changes [10]. The impact of several types of investment has been studied over time and varying levels of significance have been attached to varying types of investment. Gross capital formation affects economic growth by either directly increasing the physical capital stock in the domestic economy [11] or indirectly promoting technology [12]. Other researchers have investigated the impact of private and public investment on economic growth and have found significant variations. Khan and Kumar [13] found private investment to be more productive than public investment. In this paper, investment is represented by physical capital accumulation and it is expected to have a positive and statistically significant relationship with economic growth.

Exports are another factor identified by both the neoclassical and endogenous growth models in explaining economic growth variations. Awokuse [14] notes that linking exports to economic growth is pied when he found that there is a flow of Granger cause from real exports to real GDP. There is also a strand of studies that find no conclusive evidence of the causal relationship between exports and GDP growth. Ruiz-Nápoles [15] argues that even in cases where increasing exports has a positive effect on production expansion, such an effect may be limited and offset by increasing manufacturing imports displacing domestic production. Fouad Abou-Stait [16] found that time series studies find fewer conclusive associations between exports and growth, whereas cross-sectional studies appear to support the positive relationship.

Closely related to exports is trade openness with mixed results. A large part of the literature find that economies that are more open grow more rapidly [17–20]. Baliamoune [21] finds that trade openness is closely associated with positive effects in higher-income and negative effects in lower-income African countries. Arezki and Gylfason [22] find that trade openness has a positive and statistically significant impact on non-resource GDP growth. Several scholars have however criticized the robustness of these findings, especially on methodological and measurement grounds (see, [23, 24]). Vamvakidis [24] and Wong [25] find a negative relationship between openness to international trade and economic growth. Fowe finds no significant effect of openness to trade on economic growth in SSA.

Several endogenous growth models and extensions of the neoclassical growth model find human capital and/or knowledge to be a major source of growth [26]. A large number of studies find evidence suggesting that an educated population is a key determinant of economic growth (see [8, 27, 28]). However, other scholars find mixed results while others question studies that have found a positive relationships

[29, 30]. Some empirical findings have shown that human capital accumulation plays only a small role in economic growth [31]. Studies by Bils and Klenow [32], Pritchett [29], Easterly and Levine [33] found that the evidence was weak, absent or even pointed to a negative impact.

Population growth rate is another important variable in economic growth literature. The relationship between population and economic growth is mixed and varies between countries [34]. Some empirical studies have found a negative relationship between population and economic growth [35, 36]; and in others there was a positive association with economic growth [37, 38]. Another factor influencing economic growth is population growth rate [36, 39, 40]. High population growth, for example, could have a negative impact on economic growth, influencing the dependency ratio, investment and saving behavior and quality of human capital countries [41]. However, the findings are again inconclusive since there some studies have reported no (strong) correlation between economic growth and demographic trends (e.g., [29, 42]).

Foreign Aid has received renewed political interest in economic growth discourse resulting into numerous studies. There is however little evidence of a significant positive effect of aid on the long-term growth of poor countries [43, 44]. Andersson and Karlsson, C. [45] finds support for the basic idea that an increase in aid flows strengthens economic growth in poor countries when the policy environment is conducive. Collier and Dehn [46] find that well-timed aid alleviates effects of negative export shocks while Collier and Hoeffler [47] find that aid works particularly well in good policy environments a few years after a conflict has ended. Other scholars argue that aid spurs economic growth unconditionally (see, [37, 48]), or in certain macroeconomic environments that it is growth-neutral [49]. In contrast, some studies have argued that aid has historically been ineffective in promoting growth [50, 51]. Rajan and Subramanian [43] provide evidence that total aid is ineffective at promoting growth.

The relationship between government consumption expenditure and economic growth has attracted a great deal of interest among policymakers and economists. Empirical work on this subject has also provided mixed results. On one side, there are Keynesian economists who consider consumption expenditure as a dependable function of income and on the other side there are substantial numbers of economists who believe that higher consumption can stimulate economic growth [52, 53]. Other studies have found that small to moderate government sizes are positively associated with economic growth while large government sizes impede economic growth [54, 55].

It is argued that inflation is a good macroeconomic indicator of how the government manages the economy [55–57]. Although the empirical evidence has strongly supported a negative relationship between inflation and growth, especially through the impact of inflation on capital intensity [58], other studies have found that inflation exhibits threshold effects on economic growth [59, 60]. Khan and Senhadji, [60] explore this issue and reach several conclusions. In particular, medium and high inflation hamper economic growth due to the adverse impact on the efficient distribution of resources by changing relative prices [57].

3. Analytical framework and data

3.1 Theoretical framework

Based on the foregoing literature, we assume a Cobb–Douglas production function with labour-augmenting (Harrod-Neutral) technological progress following Mankiw, et al. [27] and Acikgoz and Mert [61].

$$Y = K^{\alpha} (A L)^{\beta}; < \alpha, \beta < 1 \text{ Such that } \alpha + \beta = 1 \quad (1)$$

where Y, K and L indicate the levels of output, capital stock and, labour respectively, and A indicates the level of technology. But Economists have long stressed the importance of human capital to the process of economic growth. Following Mankiw, et al. [27], the augmented classic Solow model takes the following form:

$$Y_t = K_t^{\alpha} HC_t^{\beta} (A_t L_t)^{1-\alpha-\beta} \quad (2)$$

where HC is human capital, and all other variables are defined as before. Following Mankiw, et al. [27], Acikgoz and Mert [61], and Chirwa and Odhiambo [17], the aggregate Cobb–Douglas production function is assumed to take the following form:

$$Y_t = K_t^{\alpha} HC_t^{\beta} (A_t\{GC_t, AID_t, INF_t, TRD_t\}L_t)^{1-\alpha-\beta} \quad (3)$$

where α and β represent the partial elasticity of output with respect to physical capital and human capital respectively. Per the literature, technological progress (A_t) is assumed to be labour augmenting and the function therefore denotes a skill-adjusted measure of the labour input.

Several efficiency variables have been identified in the literature to provide a link to how policy variables influence the aggregate production function [55, 57]. The variables selected for this study consist of the accumulation of physical capital (investment); human capital (total school enrolment); population; and policy variables (efficiency factors) that include government consumption share in GDP, inflation, foreign aid as a share of GDP and international trade. The efficiency factors, similar to population growth, are assumed to grow exogenously (see [27, 62]).

3.2 Estimation techniques

Auto Regressive Distributed Lag (ARDL) bounds testing approach developed by Pesaran and Shin [63], Pesaran, Shin and Smith [64] was employed. The modeling approach allows us to capture the short and long run dynamics as well as the speed of adjustment between the independent variables and the dependent variable. The embedded Error Correlation Model (ECM) is a restricted representation that has cointegration restrictions built into the specification so that it is designed for use with non-stationary series that are known to be cointegrated. The ECM specification restricts the long run behavior of the endogenous variables to converge to their cointegrating relationships while allowing a wide range of short run dynamics. Choice of the ARDL model was taken based on the following reasons: (1) the variables were found to be integrated of different orders i.e. (I(0) and I(1) and ARDL can be applied even when variables are not integrated of the same order; (2) ARDL performs better than other co-integration tests in small and finite data samples [65]. The two stage ARDL approach effectively corrects for any possible endogeneity in the regressors [61, 66]; (3) According to [67, 68] the ARDL model also allows for different optimal lags among the different variables to capture the data-generating process as a general-to-specific modeling framework [68, 69], (4) ARDL is known to have information about the structural break in time series data and lastly Pesaran and Shin [63] contented that appropriate modification of the orders of the ARDL model is sufficient to simultaneously correct for residual serial correlation and the problem of endogenous variables. The only drawback being that ARDI approach collapses when variables are integrated of order two (i.e I(2)).

The ARDL representation of the empirical model for this study is expressed as follows:

$$\begin{aligned}\Delta LGDP_t = {} & \alpha_0 + \sum_{i=1}^{p} \alpha_{1i}\Delta LGDP_{t-1} + \sum_{i=0}^{p} \alpha_{2i}\Delta LTRO_{t-1} + \sum_{i=0}^{p} \alpha_{3i}\Delta LTSE_{t-1} \\ & + \sum_{i=0}^{p} \alpha_{4i}\Delta LPOPN_{t-1} + \sum_{i=0}^{p} \alpha_{5i}\Delta LGGC_{t-1} + \sum_{i=0}^{p} \alpha_{6i}\Delta LGFCF_{t-1} \\ & + \sum_{i=0}^{p} \alpha_{7i}\Delta LCPI_{t-1} + \sum_{i=0}^{p} \alpha_{8i}\Delta LAID_{t-1} + \beta_1 LGDP_{t-1} + \beta_2 LTRO_{t-1} \\ & + \beta_3 LTSE_{t-1} + \beta_4 LPOPN_{t-1} + \beta_5 LGGC_{t-1} + \beta_6 LGFCF_{t-1} + \beta_7 LCPI_{t-1} \\ & + \varepsilon_{it}\end{aligned} \tag{4}$$

where Δ is the difference operator, α_0 is the drift component, p is the lag length, α_{1i} is the short-run coefficient and β_{1i} is the corresponding long-run multiplier and ε_{it} is the white-noise error term of the underlying ARDL model.

Two steps are involved in estimating an ARDL model. First, the long-run equilibrium relationship between the variables is tested using the upper and lower bounds; then, the short-run and long-run causalities are estimated. The ARDL bounds test is based mainly on the joint F-statistic in which its asymptotic distribution is non-standard under the null hypothesis of no co-integration [70].

In Eq. 4 above, the null hypothesis of no co-integration relationship, defined as $H_0 : \emptyset_1 = \emptyset_2 = \emptyset_3 = \emptyset_4 = \emptyset_5 = \emptyset_6 = \emptyset_7 = \emptyset_8 = 0$, is tested against the alternative of the existence of a co-integration relationship as H_1: $\emptyset_1 \neq \emptyset_2 \neq \emptyset_3 \neq \emptyset_4 \neq \emptyset_5 \neq \emptyset_6 \neq \emptyset_7 \neq \emptyset_8 \neq 0$ for $i = 1, 2, 3, 4, 5, 6, 7, 8$. The hypothesis is tested using the mean of the computed F-statistic. According to Pesaran et al. [64], given that the model takes the form of ARDL (p, q), two sets of critical values for a given significance level are then determined because p and q need not be integrated of the same order.

Using the Wald test, the computed F-statistic is then compared with the lower and upper asymptotic critical bounds values, as reported in Pesaran et al. [64]. The lower-bound critical value assumes that all the regressors are I(0), while the upper-bound critical value assumes that they are I(l). We reject the null hypothesis of no co-integration if the computed test statistic exceeds the upper-bound critical value, and we do not reject the null hypothesis if the F-statistic is lower than the lower-bound critical value. The test is, however, inconclusive if the computed F-statistic lies between the lower-bound and upper-bound critical values. In this context, unit root tests should be conducted to ascertain the order of integration of the variables. If all the variables are found to be I(1), then the decision is made on the basis of the upper-bound critical value. On the other hand, if all the variables are I(0), then the decision is based on the lower-bound critical value. To test for the long-run relationship between the variables, we exclude the lagged-level variables from Eq. (4). Once the presence of co-integration is confirmed, we estimate the long-run coefficients of the growth model and the associated ARDL of the ECM for the short-run coefficients.

The ARDL method estimates $(p + 1)^k$ number of regressions to obtain the optimal lags for each variable, where p is the maximum number of lags to be used and k is the number of variables in the equation [71]. The model is selected based on the Schwartz-Bayesian criterion (SBC) or the Akaike information criterion (AIC).

3.2.1 Estimation of the error correction-based ARDL model

ARDL estimation provides both the short run (model) and long run estimation results. The ECM is specified as follows:

$$\Delta LGDP_t = \alpha_0 + \sum_{i=1}^{p} \alpha_{1i}\Delta LGDP_{t-1} + \sum_{i=0}^{p} \alpha_{2i}\Delta LTRO_{t-1} + \sum_{i=0}^{p} \alpha_{3i}\Delta LTSE_{t-1} + + \sum_{i=0}^{p} \alpha_{4i}\Delta LPOPN_{t-1} + \sum_{i=0}^{p} \alpha_{5i}\Delta LGGC_{t-1} + \sum_{i=0}^{p} \alpha_{6i}\Delta LGFCF_{t-1} + \sum_{i=0}^{p} \alpha_{7i}\Delta LCPI_{t-1} + \sum_{i=0}^{p} \alpha_{8i}\Delta LAID_{t-1}\, \beta_{9i}ECT_{t-1} + \varepsilon_t \quad (5)$$

where β_{9i} is the coefficient of the one-lag error correction model, which measures the short-run speed of adjustment to restore equilibrium in the dynamic model following a disturbance [72]. This implies that the coefficient of the error correction should be negative and statistically significant and that the magnitude of this coefficient should be less than one.

3.3 Data type and sources

Annual time series data for the period 1982–2015, that was obtained from World Bank Development Indicators [73, 74] was used in this study. The following variables were used: Real GDP (expressed in 2010 U.S. dollars.) at purchaser's prices; Investment (proxied by gross fixed capital formation as a share of GDP); Inflation (measured by the consumer price index); General government expenditure as a share in GDP (General government expenditure as a share in GDP); Human Capital (representing knowledge spill over effects) was proxied by Human capital index[3], based on years of schooling and returns to education); Demography (proxied by total population); Trade openness (measured by the sum of exports and imports as a proportion of GDP); and Foreign Aid as a proportion to GDP (measured by net official development assistance and official aid received as a share of real GDP). Eviews 9.5 software was used to conduct the empirical analysis.

3.4 Analysis and discussion of results

3.4.1 Unit root tests

Unit roots/stationarity tests were conducted because this is a prime requirement for any co-integration and causality tests. The augmented Dickey-Fuller test (ADF: [75]) was used to establish the order of integration. The ADF test results were augmented with the Phillips-Perron (PP: [76]) test. **Table 1** presents the results of the unit root tests.

The ADF test results with trend and intercept at level in part A indicate that GDP, GGC, and GFCF were stationary at the 5 percent level of significance, whereas CPI was stationary at the 1 percent level of significance. The researcher thus carried out stationarity tests for all series in first difference with constant and trend, as indicated in part B (ADF test), and the variables, except CPI, became stationary.

The variables were also tested for stationarity using the Phillips-Perron test. The PP test results at level with constant and trend were found to be non-stationary except for GDP and GGC, which were found to be stationary at 10 percent and 5 percent levels of significance, respectively. The variables were tested for stationarity in first difference, and they all became stationary except CPI.

3.4.2 ARDL bounds tests for co-integration results

We tested for co-integration among the variables to establish whether they had a long-run relationship. From a statistical point of view, a long-run relationship

Variables	Augmented Dickey Fuller	Phillips-Perron test
	Constant + trend	Constant + trend
Part A: Level		
Log Real Gross Domestic Product	−3.48*	−3.48*
Log Trade Openness	−2.81	−2.62
Log Human Capital	−2.84	−2.26
Log Population Growth	−0.06	−1.72
Log Gross Government Final Consumption (% GDP)	−1.77	−1.71
Log Gross Fixed Capital Formation	−3.95**	−2.89
Log Inflation Rate	−5.28***	−2.22
Log Aid	−2.24	−2.18
Log Total School Enrolment, Primary	−1.85	−1.74
Log Imports	3.41*	−2.43
Log Exports	−2.86	−3.21
Part B: First difference		
Log Real Gross Domestic Product	−3.38*	−3.38*
Log Trade Openness	−4.51***	−4.37***
Log Human Capital	−3.80	−3.85*
Log Population Growth	−3.80**	−2.35
Log Gross Government Final Consumption (percent) GDP)	−4.92***	−6.02***
Log Gross Fixed Capital Formation	−4.33***	−5.24***
Log Inflation Rate	−2.05	−2.30
Log Aid	−6.41***	−7.56***
Log Total School Enrolment, Primary	−6.91***	7.08***
Log Imports	−3.77**	−3.40*
Log Exports	−6.49***	−6.49***

****, **, and * denote rejection of the null hypothesis of unit root at the 1 percent, 5 percent and 10 percent significance levels, respectively.*

Table 1.
Unit root test at level and in first difference.

implies that variables move together over time and that short-term disturbances arising from the long-term trend are corrected. Co-integration is necessary because a valid ARDL requires the presence of a co-integrating set of variables. The ARDL method allows us to test both short- and long-run relationships between the dependent and independent variables in a multivariate framework. The critical value bounds are computed by stochastic simulations using 20,000 replications [66].

The variables are jointly tested if they are equal to zero. That is:

H0: They are jointly equal to zero.
H1: They are not jointly equal to zero.

Once the test statistic is computed, it is compared to two asymptotic critical values corresponding to polar cases of all variables being purely I(0) or purely I(1). When the test statistic is below the lower-bound critical value, the null hypothesis is not rejected, and co-integration is not possible. In contrast, when the test statistic is above the upper-bound critical value, the null hypothesis is rejected, and co-integration is indeed possible. Alternatively, should the test statistic fall between the lower-bound and upper-bound critical values, the test results are inconclusive, and knowledge of the co-integration rank is required to proceed further.

The Akaike information criterion was employed to determine the appropriate lag length for the estimated ARDL equation. This method was chosen because it tends to over-fit the model of interest, given that the optimal lag length for the growth model is up to 2 lags. The optimal lag length is chosen based on the number of dynamic regressors included in the model and the sample size. The optimal lag-length selection criteria are based on the lowest AIC obtained. For this growth equation, (regression I), the optimal ARDL model selected was the ARDL (2, 1, 0, 1, 0, 1, 0, 0, 2) model with restricted intercept and trend, while for regression II, the optimal ARDL model selected was the ARDL (2, 0, 2, 0, 1, 0, 0, 1, 0, 2) model with restricted intercept and trend. **Table 2** reports the Pesaran et al. [64] bounds test for level relationships for the selected equation.

As illustrated in **Table 2**, regression I, the computed ?-statistic is 5.47, and it is statistically significant at the 1 percent upper-bound critical value, meaning that the null hypothesis of no co-integration is rejected at the 1 percent significance level. In regression II, the computed ?-statistic is 3.909, and it is statistically significant at the 5 percent upper-bound critical value, meaning that the null hypothesis of no co-integration is rejected at the 5 percent significance level. In summary, the bounds test of co-integration relationships using the Pesaran et al. [64] approach confirms the existence of long-run level relationships between the dependent variable and the set of covariates in both regressions. The study results also reveal that the underlying ARDL model is a good fit, represented by an estimated $R-$squared value of 0.84 and an adjusted $R-$squared value of 0.67.

ARDL bounds test	**Regression I**		**Regression II**	
Included observations: 32 after adjustments				
Null hypothesis: no long-run relationships exist				
Test statistic	**Value**	**k**	**Value**	**K**
F-statistic	5.47***	8	3.909**	9
Critical Value Bounds				
Significance	I0 Bound	I1 Bound	I0 Bound	I1 Bound
10 percent	1.95	3.06	1.88	2.99
5 percent	2.22	3.39	2.14	3.3
2.5 percent	2.48	3.7	2.37	3.6
1 percent	2.79	4.1	2.65	3.97
R-squared	0.845152		0.852168	
Adjusted R-squared	0.699981		0.672657	

****, **, and * denote 1 percent, 5 percent and 10 percent significance levels, respectively.*

Table 2.
Results of ARDL bounds test for co-integration.

3.4.3 Relative superiority of the selected models

Using the ARDL model, the researcher selected the overall best model from the 20 best selected ARDL models. As shown in **Figure 1**, the selected model in regression I is ARDL (2, 1, 0, 1, 0, 0, 1, 0, 0, 2), and the selected model in the second regression is ARDL (2, 0, 2, 0, 1, 0, 0, 1, 0, 2). These two models were significantly superior to the second-best models in each case [66].

3.4.4 Empirical results of the ARDL models

The short and long run elasticities for the ARDL model were estimated. **Table 3**, part A presents the short-run ARDL results (including the ECM representation), while part B pre-sets the long-run results of the ARDL models.

Part A of **Table 3** reports the estimated short-run coefficients, while Part B reports the estimated long-run coefficients. Two different regressions were estimated. Regression I was the "benchmark" regression, while regression II was used for sensitivity/options analysis. Among other variables, regression II used a different proxy for trade openness, which is a fundamental variable for GDP growth, according to the literature. Specifically, instead of using trade openness, we used exports and imports to examine the effect of trade on GDP growth.

As shown in part A, the short-run dynamics and the adjustment towards the long-run equilibrium path are measured by the error correction term (ECT) [77]. In the short run, deviations from the long-run equilibrium can occur due to shocks in any of the variables in the model; thus, all the short-run coefficients show the dynamic adjustments of all variables to their long-run equilibrium [70]. If the coefficient is significant, it implies that past equilibrium errors play a role in determining the outcomes of the current period. The ECT measures the speed of adjustment to restore equilibrium in the dynamic model after a disturbance. For the coefficient to be significant, it is required that the error correction term (ECT) must be negative and significant. A highly significant ECT is further proof of a stable long-run relationship [78].

From **Table 3**, part A, regression I, the ECT estimation results show that the estimated coefficient of the error correction term has the expected sign (negative) and is statistically significant. This reinforces the finding of a long-run relationship in the co-integration equation. The results show that a 1 percent deviation from the equilibrium path is corrected in the next period at a rate of 59.5 percent and is statistically significant at the 1 percent significance level. This confirms the

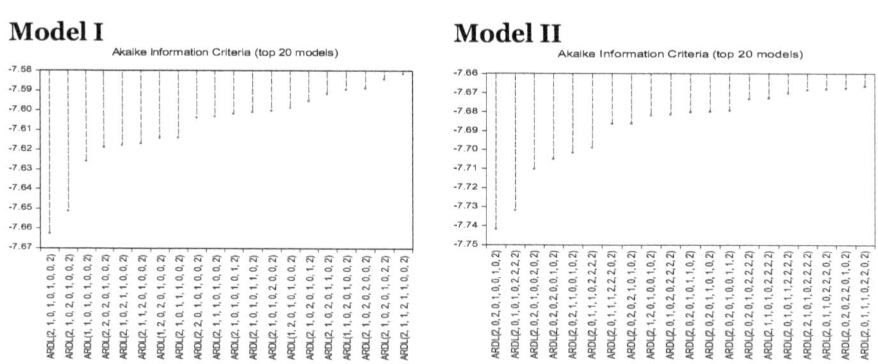

Figure 1.
Relative superiority of the selected models.

ARDL co-integration and long-run form		
Dependent variable: LRGDP		
Part A		
Co-integration form		
Selected Model: Included observations: 32	ARDL (2,1,0,1,0,1,0,0,2)	ARDL (2,0,2,0,1,0,0,1,0,2)
Co-integration Form	Regression I	Regression II
Variable	Coefficient(Prob.)	Coefficient (Prob.)
D(Log Real Gross Domestic Product (−1))	0.179(0.049)**	0.279(0.003)***
D(Log Trade Openness)	0.036(0.190)	
D(Log Population Growth)	0.481(0.784)	0.126(0.941)
D(Log Inflation Rate)	−0.085(0.000)**	−0.086(0.000)*
D(Log Human Capital)	0.240(0.507)	0.619(0.109)
D(Log Gross Government Consumption)	0.061(0.001)***	0.066(0.000)***
D(Log Gross Fixed Capital Formation)	0.192(0.000)***	0.145(0.000)***
D(Log Aid)	−0.033(0.022)**	−0.021(0.111)
D(Log Exports)		0.027(0.047)**
D(Log Imports)		0.056(0.178)
D(Dummy for Structural Adjustment)	−0.008(0.092)*	−0.018(0.007)***
C	0.185(0.001)***	2.786(0.000)***
Coint Eq (−1)	−0.595(0.00)***	−0.646 (0.000)***
PART B		
Long-Run Coefficients		
Variable	**Coefficient**	
Log Trade Openness	0.295(0.002)***	
Log Population Growth	1.008(0.090)*	0.334(0.605)
Log Inflation Rate	−0.009(0.624)	−0.018(0.361)
Log Human Capital	0.293(0.639)	0.848(0.244)
Log Gross Government Consumption (percent, GDP)	0.198(0.001)***	0.159(0.007)***
Log Gross Fixed Capital Formation	0.316(0.003)***	0.220(0.029)**
Log Aid	−0.053(0.227)	−0.032(0.399)
Log Exports		0.121(0.007)***
Log Imports		0.090(0.244)
D(Dummy for Structural Adjustment)	−0.007(0.003)***	−0.071(0.003)***

****, **, and * denote 1 percent, 5 percent and 10 percent significance levels, respectively.*

Table 3.
Short-run and long-run ARDL results.

presence of a long-run level equilibrium path between real GDP and the selected regressors (trade openness, human capital, population, government consumption, investment, inflation, foreign aid and a policy dummy (structural adjustment programme). The regression results for the ARDL model reveal a good fit represented by an estimated *R*-squared value of 0.85 and an adjusted *R*-squared value of 0.70, as shown in **Table 3**.

Part B, regression I of **Table 3** presents the long-run coefficient estimates. The results reveal that the key macroeconomic determinants that are significantly associated with long-run economic growth in Uganda include trade openness, population growth, government consumption, investment, and the policy dummy variable for the structural adjustment programmes (SAPs).

In the long run, the relationship between trade openness and real GDP is positive and statistically significant at the 1 percent significance level. The results reveal that a 1 percent increase in trade openness in the long run leads to a 0.295 percent increase in the level of real GDP. These findings are supported by previous studies that have found a positive and significant relationship between trade openness and economic growth (e.g. [17, 19, 20]).

The study reveals that population growth is positively and significantly associated with the growth of real GDP in Uganda at the 10 percent level of significance. It shows that a 1 percent increase in population leads to a 1.01 percent increase in real GDP. These results are supported by similar studies conducted in developing countries that have found a positive relationship between investment and economic growth in the long run (e.g., [41, 79]).

The study reveals a positive relationship between government consumption and the growth of real GDP at the 1 percent significance level in the long run. A 1 percent increase in government consumption results in a 0.20 percent increase in the level of real GDP. These results are supported by similar studies conducted in developing countries that have found a positive relationship between government consumption and economic growth in the long run (e.g., [17]).

The results confirm the widely established empirical estimation finding that investment and growth in GDP have a positive relationship. A 1 percent increase in the level of investment results in a 0.32 percent increase in the level of real GDP. These results are supported by similar studies conducted in developing countries that have found a positive relationship between investment and economic growth in the long run (e.g., [10, 54, 80–82]).

The study results did not reveal a significant association between inflation, human capital and foreign aid and the long-run level of GDP growth.

The short-run results presented in Part A of **Table 3** reveal that the key macroeconomic determinants that are significantly associated with the growth of real GDP in the short run are initial GDP, inflation, government consumption (percent of GDP), investment, foreign aid, and the policy dummy. The results show that a 1 percent increase in initial real GDP leads to a 0.18 percent increase in real GDP. Meaning that the level of and sign of initial GDP has a positive relationship with current GDP.

The results reveal a negative association between inflation and economic growth. A 1 percent increase in inflation leads to a 0.90 reduction in GDP. These results are supported by a number of empirical growth studies that have also found a negative association between inflation and economic growth in developing countries (e.g., [56, 57, 83–86]).

The results show that government consumption is positively and significantly associated with the growth of real GDP at the 1 percent significance level. A 1 percent change in government consumption leads to a 0.06 percent increase in the growth of GDP. The positive relationship found between government consumption and economic growth is supported by similar studies in the empirical growth literature that have found a positive relationship between trade openness and economic growth (e.g., [17, 87]).

There is a positive and significant relationship between investment and economic growth at the 1 percent level of significance. A 1 percent increase in investment leads to a 0.19 percent increase in GDP. The results are consistent with existing empirical growth studies that have found a positive relationship between investment and economic growth (e.g., [10, 17, 88]).

The results show that foreign aid is negatively and significantly associated with the growth of real GDP, and the results are statistically significant at the 5 percent significance level. A 1 percent change in foreign aid leads to a 0.03 percent reduction in the growth of GDP. The negative relationship found between foreign aid and economic growth is supported by similar studies in the empirical growth literature (e.g., [10]).

The study results did not reveal a significant association between trade openness, population growth, human capital, and real GDP growth in the short run.

Sensitivity analysis was carried out to examine the significance of other variables or proxies for the variables used in regression II. This analysis was carried out bearing in mind theory, certain empirical studies and the nature of the Ugandan economy. Key variables/proxies were imports and exports as proxies for trade openness. Exports were found to be positively and significantly associated with GDP at the 1 percent level of significance, while imports were found to be non-significant.

From **Table 3**, Part A, regression II above, the ECT estimation results show that the estimated coefficient of the error correction term has the expected sign (negative) and is statistically significant. The ECT shows that a 1 percent deviation from the equilibrium path is corrected in the next period at a rate of -0.65 percent and is statistically significant at the 1 percent significance level. This confirms the presence of a long-run level equilibrium path between real GDP and the selected regressors (total school enrolment, primary; real exchange rate; population; government consumption; investment; inflation; foreign aid; imports; and exports). The regression results for the ARDL model reveal a good fit represented by an estimated R-squared value of 0.85 and an adjusted R-squared value of 0.67, as shown in **Table 3**.

Part B, regression II of **Table 3** presents the long-run coefficient estimates. The results reveal that the key macroeconomic determinants that are significantly associated with long-run GDP growth in Uganda are government consumption, investment, exports and the policy dummy.

The study reveals a positive relationship between government consumption and real GDP growth at the 1 percent significance level in the long run. A 1 percent increase in government consumption results in a 0.20 percent increase in the level of real GDP. These results are supported by Doppelhofer and Weeks [89] who find a positive relationship between government consumption and economic growth in the long run in developing countries.

The study reveals a positive relationship between investment and real GDP growth at the 1 percent significance level in the long run. A 1 percent increase in the level of investment results in a 0.22 percent increase in the level of real GDP. These results are supported by similar studies conducted in developing countries that have found a positive relationship between investment and economic growth in the long run (e.g., [10, 17, 54, 81, 82]).

There is a positive and significant relationship between GDP and exports in the long run at the 1 percent level of significance. A 1 percent increase in exports leads to a 0.12 percent increase in GDP growth (see [14, 16]).

There is also a negative and significant relationship between GDP and the policy dummy for SAPs in Uganda, as a 1 percent increase in implementation of the SAPs leads to a 0.07 percent reduction in real GDP growth.

The study results did not reveal a significant association between population growth, inflation human capital and foreign aid, imports and GDP growth in the long run.

The short-run results for the sensitivity/option analysis are shown in Part A, regression II of **Table 3** above. The key macroeconomic determinants that are significantly associated with the growth of real GDP in the short run are initial GDP, inflation, government consumption (percent, GDP), investment, exports, and the policy dummy in both the current and the previous period.

The results show that a 1 percent increase in initial real GDP leads to a 0.28 percent increase in real GDP.

The results reveal a negative association between inflation and economic growth. A 1 percent increase in inflation leads to a 0.90 percent reduction in GDP. These results are supported by a number of empirical growth studies that have also found a negative association between inflation and economic growth in developing countries (e.g., [55–57, 83–86]).

The results show that government consumption is positively and significantly associated with the growth of real GDP at the 1 percent significance level. A 1 percent change in government consumption leads to a 0.07 percent increase in the growth of GDP. The positive relationship found between government consumption and economic growth is supported by similar studies in the empirical growth literature that have found a positive relationship between trade openness and economic growth (e.g., [17]).

There is a positive and significant relationship between investment and economic growth at the 1 percent level of significance. A 1 percent increase in investment leads to a 0.15 percent increase in GDP. The results are consistent with the existing empirical growth studies that have found a positive relationship between investment and economic growth (e.g., [10, 17, 88]).

The results show that exports are positively and significantly associated with the growth of real GDP at the 5 percent significance level. A 1 percent change in exports leads to a 0.03 percent increase in GDP growth. The positive relationship found between exports and GDP growth is supported by similar studies in the empirical growth literature (e.g., [14, 90]).

There was a negative and significant relationship between the implementation of the structural adjustment programmes and GDP growth in the current period. A 1 percent increase in the implementation of the SAPs led to a 0.1 reduction in GDP.

The results indicate that in the short run, policy variables contributed to economic growth more than factor accumulation, while in the long run, a mixture of factor accumulation and policy variables was the major driver of economic growth.

3.5 Post-estimation diagnostic tests

The regressions were tested to ascertain their applicability and robustness. Robustness was confirmed by the Breusch-Godfrey serial correlation LM test, Jarque-Bera normality test, recursive stability tests, and Breusch-Pagan-Godfrey heteroscedasticity test. This means that the model has the desired econometric properties of time series data.

Recursive Tests were done using a visual examination of the graphs of the recursive parameter estimates. Additionally, a formal statistical test to test the null hypothesis of model stability was undertaken using the CUSUM test [91]. **Figure 2** regression I and regression II illustrate the CUSUM and CUSUMSQ at the 5 percent significance level.

As illustrated in **Figure 2**, the CUSUM test reveals parameter stability, while the results of the CUSUMQ test reveal variance stability given that the residuals for both tests are within the 5 percent critical lines. According to these tests, our ARDL model is stable and has no serial correlation.

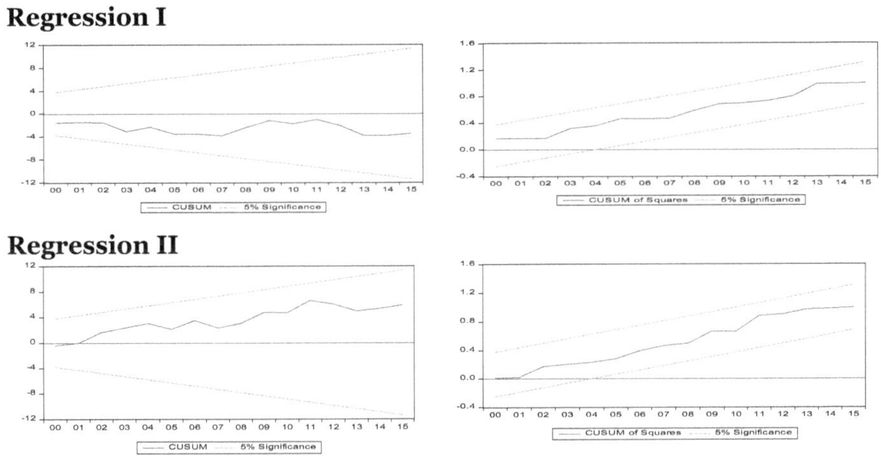

Figure 2.
CUSUM and CUSUMSQ results for the estimated growth equation.

3.5.1 Serial correlation tests of residuals

Serial correlation was undertaken to test whether the residual is correlated with its own lagged values using the Breusch-Godfrey LM test for serial correlation, and the results are presented in **Table 4** below.

The Breusch-Godfrey serial correlation test statistic for the null hypothesis of no serial correlation (**Table 4**) for regression I has a probability value of 0.2739, which is greater than 5 percent. Thus, we fail to reject the null hypothesis, which indicates that there is no serial correlation in the residuals.

3.5.2 Heteroscedasticity test

The Breusch-Pagan-Godfrey tests for heteroscedasticity statistic for the null hypothesis of no heteroscedasticity in regressions I and II have probability values of 0.6996 and 0.0612, respectively, which are greater than 5 percent. Thus, we fail to reject the null hypothesis, which indicates that there is no heteroscedasticity in the residuals (**Table 5**).

Breusch-Godfrey serial correlation LM test			**Regression I**	**Regression II**
F-statistic	1.332638	Prob. F(3,13)	0.2739	0.0223
Obs*R-squared	7.526409	Prob. Chi-Square(3)	0.1921	0.0004

Table 4.
The Breusch-Godfrey test for serial correlation in the residuals of the regression.

Heteroscedasticity test: Breusch-Pagan-Godfrey			**Model I (probability)**	**Model II**
F-statistic	0.760385	Prob. F(15,16)	0.6996	0.0612
Obs*R-squared	13.31781	Prob.Chi-Square(15)	0.5778	0.1320
Scaled Explained SS	2.325347	Prob.Chi-Square(15)	0.9999	0.9945

Table 5.
Breusch-Pagan-Godfrey test for heteroscedasticity results.

3.5.3 Normality test

The ARDL model assumes that the residuals are normally distributed. The Jarque-Bera statistic is assumed to have a *chi-square* ($\chi2$) distribution with two degrees of freedom, and the null hypothesis assumes that the errors are normally distributed [92–94].

As indicated in **Figure 3**, in regression I, the probability value for the Jarque-Bera statistic is 0.49 with a probability value of 0.782, which is more than 5 percent; hence, the residuals are normally distributed. In regression II, the probability value for the Jarque-Bera statistic is 0.647 with a probability value of 0.724, which is more than 5 percent; hence, the residuals are normally distributed. This means that statistical tests for inference on regression coefficients are reliable, since these tests require that the dependent variable (and hence the residuals) follows a normal distribution.

3.5.4 Ramsey rest test for the functional form

Specification errors can be errors in the specification of the functional form that the equation should take in describing the relationship between the variable. If the F test statistic is greater than the F critical value, we reject the null hypothesis that the true specification is greater than the F critical value, hence reject the null hypothesis that the true specification is linear (which implies that the true specification is non-linear). If we are unable to reject the null, then the results suggest that the true specification is linear and the equation passes the Ramsey Reset test (**Table 6**).

The probability values from the Ramsey rest test for the T and F statistics are greater than 0.05 level of significance, meaning that the estimated model is free from specification errors.

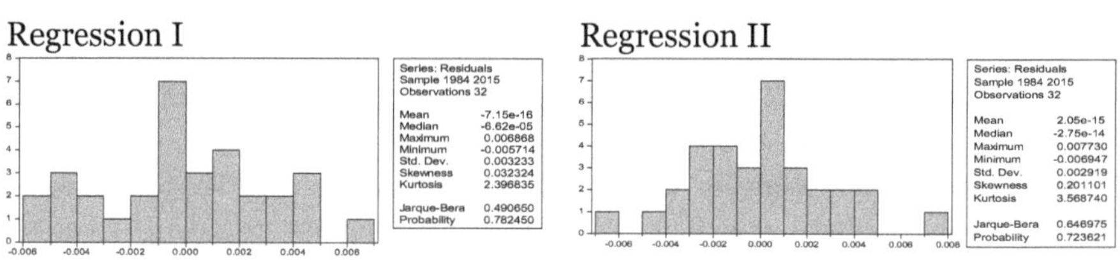

Figure 3.
Histogram normality test model I.

Ramsey RESET Test			
Equation: UNTITLED			
Specification: LRGDP LRGDP(−1) LTRO LTRO(−1) LPOPN LINF LINF(−1) LHC LHC(−1) LHC(−2) LGGC LGGC(−1) LGFCF LAID C			
Omitted variables: squares of fitted values			
	Value	**df**	**Probability**
t-statistic	0.326505	17	0.7481
F-statistic	0.106606	(1, 17)	0.7480

Table 6.
Ramsey rest test for the functional form test results.

3.6 Conclusion

Attaining high and sustainable economic growth is a major policy objective for any country especially among developing countries. In this paper, we examined the macroeconomic determinants of economic growth in Uganda using the factor accumulation framework for the period 1982–2015.

The autoregressive distributed lag (ARDL) approach to co-integration was used to estimate both the short- and long-run elasticities of the selected macroeconomic determinants. The ARDL bounds testing approach to co-integration in the benchmark regression indicated that the key determinants that are positively associated with growth in GDP in the short run are the initial level of real GDP growth, government consumption and investment, while foreign aid, inflation and a dummy for SAPs were negatively and significantly associated with real GDP growth. The results failed to show that trade openness, population growth and human capital accumulation were significantly associated with real GDP growth in the short run [95–98].

The study revealed that in the long run, trade openness, population growth and government consumption and investment were positively and significantly associated with GDP growth, while the policy dummy on SAPs was negatively and significantly associated with GDP. In the long run, the study failed to show that inflation, human capital and foreign aid were significantly associated with GDP growth. It can be concluded that in the short run, policy variables contributed to economic growth more than factor accumulation (physical and human capital), while in the long run, a mixture of both factor accumulation and policy variables was the major driver of economic growth.

The study results have significant policy implications for Uganda. They show that investment and population have are significantly associated with economic growth both in the short and long run. Thus, it is recommended that the economic strategies to be adopted should include those that create incentives to attract investment—with an emphasis on the adoption of labour–intensive technologies, on quality–based human capital development. In the short run trade openness, government consumption, foreign aid and inflation are positively and significantly associated with economic growth meaning that the country should pursue policies that enhance trade, government effectiveness, aid effectiveness and economic management.

The study found that the key determinants that were positively associated with growth in GDP in the short run were the initial level of GDP growth, government consumption, investment and a dummy for SAPs, while foreign aid and inflation were negatively associated with GDP growth. The results failed to show that trade openness, population growth and human capital accumulation were significantly associated with GDP growth in the short run. In the long run, the study revealed that trade openness, population growth, government consumption and investment were positively associated with GDP, while the policy dummy on SAPs was negatively associated with GDP growth. In the long run, the study failed to show that inflation, human capital and foreign aid were significantly associated with growth in GDP.

These results have significant policy implications for Uganda, both in the short and long run. In the short run it is recommended that economic strategies that would spur accumulation of physical capital/Investment, increase government consumption, improve price stability be pursued while in the long run, strategies that improve trade openness, population growth, government consumption and investment should be pursued.

Acknowledgements

We would like to acknowledge Prof John Dumba Ssentamu and Associate Professor Eria Hisali, for their insurmountable technical contribution to this paper through their reviews and comments.

Author details

Richard Sendi[1*], John Bbale Mayanja[2] and Enock Nyorekwa[3]

1 Ministry of Works and Transport, Kampala, Uganda

2 Makerere University College of Business and Management Sciences, Kampala, Uganda

3 The Sustainable Development Goals Center for Africa (SDGC/A), Africa

*Address all correspondence to: sendirichard@yahoo.com

References

[1] Lucas Jr, R. E. (1988). On the mechanics of economic development. Journal of monetary economics, *22*(1), 3-42.

[2] Barro, R. J., & Sala-i-Martin, X. (2004). Economic Growth: MIT Press. *Cambridge, Massachusettes*.

[3] Durlauf, S. N., Johnson, P. A., & Temple, J. R. (2005). Growth econometrics. Handbook of economic growth, *1*, 555-677.

[4] Isaksson, A. (2007). Determinants of total factor productivity: a literature review. *Research and Statistics Branch, UNIDO*.

[5] NPA (2010). National Development Plan 20210/11-2014/15.

[6] Lensink, R., & Morrissey, O. (2006). Foreign direct investment: Flows, volatility, and the impact on growth. *Review of International Economics*, *14*(3), 478-493.

[7] Abou-Ali, H., & Kheir-El-Din, H. (2009). Inflation and Growth in Egypt: is there a Threshold Effect?. *Middle East Development Journal*, *1*(1), 59-78.

[8] Barro, R., & Sala-i-Martin, X. (1995). Economic growth. ed.

[9] Fowowe, B. (2008). Financial liberalization policies and economic growth: panel data evidence from Sub-Saharan Africa. *African Development Review*, *20*(3), 549-574.

[10] Anyanwu, J. C. (2014). Factors affecting economic growth in Africa: Are there any lessons from China?. *African Development Review*, *26*(3), 468.

[11] Plosser, C. I. (1992, August). The search for growth. In *A Symposium Sponsored By The Federal Reserve Bank Of Kansas City, Policies For Long-Run Economic Growth* (pp. 57-86).

[12] Levine, R., & Renelt, D. (1992). A sensitivity analysis of cross-country growth regressions. The American economic review, 942-963.

[13] Khan, M. S., & Kumar, M. S. (1997). Public and private investment and the growth process in developing countries. *Oxford bulletin of economics and statistics*, *59*(1), 69-88.

[14] Awokuse, T. O. (2003). Is the export-led growth hypothesis valid for Canada?. *Canadian Journal of Economics/Revue canadienne d'économique*, *36*(1), 126-136.

[15] Ruiz-Nápoles, P. (2001). Liberalisation, Exports and Growth in Mexico 1978-94: A structural analysis. *International review of applied economics*, *15*(2), 163-180.

[16] Abou-Stait, F. (2005a). *Working Paper 76-Are Exports the Engine of Economic Growth? An Application of Cointegration and Causality Analysis for Egypt, 1977-2003* (No. 211).

[17] Chirwa, T. G., & Odhiambo, N. M. (2016). Macroeconomic determinants of economic growth: A review of international literature. *South East European Journal of Economics and Business*, *11*(2), 33-47.

[18] Khungwa, M. (2007). Determinants of economic growth in Malawi. *Abstract Retrieved April14, 2009, from UNPANO261pdf*.

[19] Uwatt, B. U. (2003). Capital and Economic Growth: The African Experience. In *Proceedings of the Nigerian Economic Society Annual Conference*.

[20] Yavari, K., & Mohseni, R. (2012). Trade liberalization and economic

growth: A case study of Iran. *Journal of Economic Policy Reform*, *15*(1), 13-23.

[21] Baliamoune-Lutz, M., & Mavrotas, G. (2009). Aid effectiveness: looking at the aid–social capital–growth nexus. *Review of Development Economics*, *13*(3), 510-525.

[22] Arezki, R., & Gylfason, T. (2011). *Commodity Price Volatility, Democracy, and Economic Growth*. Emerald Group Publishing Limited.

[23] Rodrik, D. (1999). Where did all the growth go? External shocks, social conflict, and growth collapses. Journal of economic growth, *4*(4), 385-412.

[24] Vamvakidis, A. (2002). How robust is the growth-openness connection? Historical evidence. *Journal of Economic Growth*, *7*(1), 57-80.

[25] Wang, M., & Wong, M. S. (2009). Foreign direct investment and economic growth: The growth accounting perspective. Economic Inquiry, *47*(4), 701-710.

[26] Romer, D. (2001). [Is Growth Exogenous? Taking Mankiw, Romer, and Weil Seriously]: Comment. NBER Macroeconomics Annual, *16*, 62-70.

[27] Mankiw, N. G., Romer, D., & Weil, D. N. (1992). A contribution to the empirics of economic growth. The quarterly journal of economics, *107*(2), 407-437.

[28] Fayissa, B., & Nsiah, C. (2010). The impact of remittances on economic growth and development in Africa. *The American Economist*, *55*(2), 92-103.

[29] Pritchett, L. (2001). Where has all the education gone?. *The world bank economic review*, *15*(3), 367-391.

[30] Krueger, Alan B., and Mikael Lindahl. "Education for growth: Why and for whom?." *Journal of economic literature* 39, no. 4 (2001): 1101-1136.

[31] Temple, J. (2002). Growth effects of education and social capital in the OECD countries. *Historical Social Research/ Historische Sozialforschung*, 5-46.

[32] Bils, M., & Klenow, P. J. (2000). Does schooling cause growth?. *American economic review*, *90*(5), 1160-1183.

[33] Easterly, W., & Levine, R. (2002). *It's not factor accumulation: stylized facts and growth models* (Vol. 6, pp. 061-114). Central Bank of Chile.

[34] Warr, P. (2004). Globalization, growth, and poverty reduction in Thailand. ASEAN Economic Bulletin, *21* (1), 1-18.

[35] Most, S. J., & De Berg, H. V. (1996). Growth in Africa: Does the source of investment financing matter?. Applied Economics, *28*(11), 1427-1433.

[36] Kalemli-Ozcan, S. (2002). Does the mortality decline promote economic growth?. *Journal of Economic Growth*, *7* (4), 411-439.

[37] Radelet, S., Clemens, M., & Bhavnani, R. (2004). Aid and growth: The current debate and some new evidence. *Center for Global Development*.

[38] Sachs, J. D., & Warner, A. M. (1997). Sources of slow growth in African economies. *Journal of African economies*, *6*(3), 335-376.

[39] Bloom, D. E., & Williamson, J. G. (1998). Demographic transitions and economic miracles in emerging Asia. *The World Bank Economic Review*, *12*(3), 419-455.

[40] Kelley, A. C., & Schmidt, R. M. (1995). Aggregate population and economic growth correlations: the role of the components of demographic change. *Demography*, *32*(4), 543-555.

[41] Petrakos, G., Arvanitidis, P., & Pavleas, S. (2007a, March). Determinants of economic growth: the experts' view. In *2nd Workshop of DYNREG in Athens* (Vol. 2, No. 1, pp. 9-10).

[42] Grier, K. B., & Tullock, G. (1989). An empirical analysis of cross-national economic growth, 1951–1980. *Journal of monetary economics*, *24*(2), 259-276.

[43] Rajan, R., & Subramanian, A. (2005). What undermines aid's impact on growth?.

[44] Sachs, J. (2005). The End of Poverty: Economic possibilities for our time. *International Journal*, *60*(3), 849.

[45] Andersson, M., & Karlsson, C. (2007). Knowledge in regional economic growth—the role of knowledge accessibility. *Industry and innovation*, *14*(2), 129-149.

[46] Collier, P., & Dehn, J. (2001). *Aid, shocks, and growth* (Vol. 2688). World Bank Publications.

[47] Collier, P., & Hoeffler, A. (2004). Aid, policy and growth in post-conflict societies. *European economic review*, *48* (5), 1125-1145.

[48] Anyanwu, J. C. (2011). *Determinants of foreign direct investment inflows to Africa, 1980-2007* (pp. 1-32). African Development Bank Group.

[49] Easterly, W., Levine, R., & Roodman, D. (2004). Aid, policies, and growth: comment. American economic review, *94*(3), 774-780.

[50] Easterly, W. (2007a). Was development assistance a mistake?. American Economic Review, *97*(2), 328-332.

[51] Bobba, M., & Powell, A. (2007). *Aid effectiveness: politics matters* (No. 601). Working Paper.

[52] SakibBin-Amin 2011; (2011). Causal Relationship between Consumption Expenditure and Economic Growth in Banglade.

[53] Dobronogov, A., & Iqbal, F. (2007). Economic growth in Egypt: Constraints and determinants. *Journal of African Development*, *9*(1), 31-66.

[54] Anaman, K. A. (2004). Determinants of economic growth in Brunei Darussalam. Journal of Asian Economics, *15*(4), 777-796.

[55] Barro, R. J. (2003). Determinants of economic growth in a panel of countries. Annals of economics and finance, *4*, 231-274.

[56] Fischer, S. (1992). Macroeconomic stability and growth. Cuadernos de Economía, *29*(87), 171-186.

[57] Fischer, S. (1993). The role of macroeconomic factors in growth. Journal of monetary economics, *32*(3), 485-512.

[58] Manamperi, N. (2014). The short and long-run dynamics between inflation and economic growth in BRICS. Applied Economics Letters, *21* (2), 140-145.

[59] Kasidi, F., & Mwakanemela, K. (2013). Impact of inflation on economic growth: A case study of Tanzania.

[60] Khan, M. S., Senhadji, A., & Smith, B. D. (2001). Inflation and financial depth.

[61] Acikgoz, S., & Mert, M. (2014). Sources of Growth Revisited: The importance of the nature of technological progress. *Journal of Applied Economics*, *17*(1), 31-62.

[62] Nonneman, W., & Vanhoudt, P. (1996). A further augmentation of the Solow model and the empirics of economic growth for OECD countries.

The Quarterly Journal of Economics, *111* (3), 943-953.

[63] Pesaran, M. H., & Shin, Y. (1995). An autoregressive distributed lag modelling approach to cointegration analysis.

[64] Pesaran, M. H., Shin, Y., & Smith, R. J. (2001). Bounds testing approaches to the analysis of level relationships. Journal of applied econometrics, *16*(3), 289-326.

[65] Haug, A.A., 2002. Temporal aggregation and the power of cointegration tests: A monte carlo study. xford Bulletin of Economics and Statistics, 64(4): 399-412.

[66] Pesaran, M. H., & Shin, Y. (1998). An autoregressive distributed-lag modelling approach to cointegration analysis. Econometric Society Monographs, *31*, 371-413.

[67] Jayaraman, T. K., Choong, C. K., & Kumar, R. R. (2011). Financial sector development and remittances in Pacific island economies: how do they help the world's two most recipient-dependent countries?. *Perspectives on Global Development and Technology*, *10*(3-4), 386-405.

[68] Laurenceson, J., & Chai, J. C. (2003). *Financial reform and economic development in China*. Edward Elgar Publishing.

[69] Hirnissa, M. T., Habibullah, M. S., & Baharom, A. H. (2009). Military expenditure and economic growth in Asean-5 countries. Journal of sustainable development, *2*(2), 192.

[70] Dritsakis, N. (2011). Demand for money in Hungary: an ARDL approach. *Review of Economics and Finance*, (5).

[71] Shrestha, M.B. and Chowdhury K. (2005), 'ARDL modelling approach to testing the financial liberalization hypothesis', Economics Working Paper Series 2005, University of Wollongong.

[72] Collier, P., & Goderis, B. (2012). Commodity prices and growth: An empirical investigation. European Economic Review, *56*(6), 1241-1260.

[73] Penn World Tables 9.0 Real GDP, Employment and PopulationLevels; https://fred.stlouisfed.org/

[74] World Bank 2016, WDI Data bank, https://data.worldbank.org/indicator/ NY.GDP. PCAP.KD.ZG? end=2019& start=1961&view=chart

[75] Dickey, D. A., & Fuller, W. A. (1981). Likelihood ratio statistics for autoregressive time series with a unit root. Econometrica: journal of the Econometric Society, 1057-1072.

[76] Phillips, P. C., & Perron, P. (1988). Testing for a unit root in time series regression. Biometrika, *75*(2), 335-346.

[77] Narayan, P. K., & Smyth, R. (2008). Energy consumption and real GDP in G7 countries: new evidence from panel cointegration with structural breaks. *Energy Economics*, *30*(5), 2331-2341.

[78] Verma, R. (2007). Savings, investment and growth in India: An application of the ARDL bounds testing approach. *South Asia Economic Journal*, *8* (1), 87-98.

[79] Tolo, W. B. J. (2011). The determinants of economic growth in the Philippines: A new look. *IMF Working Papers*, 1-24.

[80] Abu-Bader, S., & Abu-Qarn, A. S. (2008). Financial development and economic growth: empirical evidence from six MENA countries. *Review of Development Economics*, *12*(4), 803-817.

[81] Asheghian, Parviz. "Determinants of economic growth in Japan: The role of

foreign direct investment." *Global Economy Journal* 9.3 (2009): 1850171.

[82] Bleaney, M., Gemmell, N., & Kneller, R. (2001). Testing the endogenous growth model: public expenditure, taxation, and growth over the long run. *Canadian Journal of Economics/Revue canadienne d'économique*, *34*(1), 36-57.

[83] Barro, R. J. (1999). Determinants of economic growth: implications of the global evidence for Chile. Cuadernos de economía, 443-478.

[84] Bayraktar, B. (2006). Investigation on sources of growth for Turkey. Canadian Journal of Development Studies/Revue canadienne d'études du développement, *27*(1), 25-38.

[85] Rao, B. B., & Hassan, G. (2011). Determinants of the long-run growth rate of Bangladesh. Applied Economics Letters, *18*(7), 655-658.

[86] Burnside, C., & Dollar, D. (2000). Aid, policies, and growth. *American economic review*, *90*(4), 847-868.

[87] Parjiono, Beg, A. R. A., & Monypenny, R. (2013). The driving forces of the level and the growth rate of real per capita income in Indonesia. *Applied Economics*, *45*(17), 2389-2400.

[88] Freire-Seren, M. J. (2002). On the relationship between human capital accumulation and economic growth. Applied Economics Letters, *9*(12), 805-808.

[89] Doppelhofer, G., & Weeks, M. (2011). Robust growth determinants.

[90] Ahmad, J., & Harnhirun, S. (1996). Cointegration and causality between exports and economic growth: evidence from the ASEAN countries. *The Canadian Journal of Economics/ Revue canadienne d'Economique*, *29*, S413-S416.

[91] Studenmund, A. H., & Econometrics, H. U. (2001). *Using econometrics:* A Practical Guide. Addison-Wesley Educational Publishers.

[92] Jarque, C. M., & Bera, A. K. (1980). Efficient tests for normality, homoscedasticity and serial independence of regression residuals. *Economics letters*, *6*(3), 255-259.

[93] Jarque, C. M., & Bera, A. K. (1987). A test for normality of observations and regression residuals. *International Statistical Review/Revue Internationale de Statistique*, 163-172.

[94] Bera, A. K., & Jarque, C. M. (1981). Efficient tests for normality, homoscedasticity and serial independence of regression residuals: Monte Carlo evidence. *Economics letters*, *7*(4), 313-318.

[95] Capolupo, R. (2009). The new growth theories and their empirics after twenty years. *Economics*, *3*(1).

[96] Havi, E. D. K., Enu, P., Osei-Gyimah, F., Attah-Obeng, P., & Opoku, C. D. K. (2013). Macroeconomic determinants of economic growth in Ghana: Cointegration approach. *European Scientific Journal*, *9*(19).

[97] Steven, R., Jeffrey, S., & Jong-Wha, L. (2001). The determinants and prospects of economic growth in Asia. *International Economic Journal*, *15*(3), 1-29.

[98] Veiderpass, A., & Andersson, P. (2007). Foreign aid, economic growth and efficiency development. *Swedish Agency for Development Evaluation*.

Chapter 3

The Life Cycle Hypothesis and Uncertainty: Analyzing Aging Savings Relationship in Tunisia

Olfa Frini

Abstract

This research empirically checks the effect of uncertainty on aging-saving link that is indirectly captured by an auxiliary variable: the unemployment. It looks at the nexus population aging and savings by bringing out the unemployment context importance in determination saving behavior notably in a setting of unavailability of unemployment allowance. To better estimate population aging, it considers the old-age dependency ratio besides the total dependency one, which is the usually indicator used. Applying the Structural VAR model, the variance decomposition technique and the response impulse function, on Tunisia during 1970–2019, it puts on show that elderly do not dissave in a context of enduring unemployment and unavailability of unemployment allowance. Unemployment is an important factor able to shaping the saving behavior and to distort the life cycle hypothesis's prediction. Consequently, the life cycle hypothesis cannot be validated under uncertainty. Hence, aging does not to alter savings systematically. The nature of aging-saving relationship is upon to social and economic context.

Keywords: Aging, Unemployment, Saving, life cycle hypothesis, SVAR, Tunisia

1. Introduction

There is a great concern about the increase of elderly proportion follow-up the aging population process over the world. It is likely to create important macroeconomic issues and involve new policies challenges as it will put downward pressure on saving according to the life cycle hypothesis (LCH) prediction formulated by Modigliani and Brumberg [1]. Indeed, the saving decline is well recognized to be associated with lower rates of capital accumulation and growth in the economy. Saving is crucial for investment and the maintenance of strong and sustainable economic growth. In addition, saving is one of the essential aspects of building wealth and having a secure financial future. It gives a way out from uncertainties of life and enjoy a quality of life.

Hence, it is of great interest to look at the demographic changes impact on saving in order to seek how to prevent saving from such an eventual decline. The empirical studies in the topic, generally, have relied on the life cycle model; as it better explains the varying rates of savings in societies with relatively younger or older populations. However, the LCH's prediction was not often empirically validated to argue that saving will be automatically depressed consequence of the population aging process. There is evidence that the social and economic conditions limit the scope of the LCH.

This study reviews the LCH to emphasize the most significant factors that may distort its prediction. It focuses on the uncertainty to explain the aging-saving relationship. It tries to check empirically whether uncertainty consideration may distort the LCH. Thereby the aging population do not put a down pressure on saving systematically.

However, given the difficulty to directly and objectively estimate uncertainty extent on saving behavior, we indirectly capture by an auxiliary variable the unemployment. We seek to highlight the influence of the precautionary motive related to the risk of unemployment. Thus, we try to give information about the transmission mechanism between aging population and saving considering the unemployment savings pattern as a determinant of saving behavior in a setting of unavailability of unemployment allowance. So, we draw attention that unemployment is an important factor up to distort the life cycle model's prediction.

Unlike previous studies, we build our estimates not only on the total dependency ratio (the proportion of population aged less than 15 years and aged 60 years or more versus the proportion aged 15–59) as an aging indicator, but also on the old-age dependency ratio (the proportion of population aged 60 years or more versus the proportion aged 15–59). This will allow us to make comparison and to deduce the effect of the child dependency ratio (the proportion of population aged less than 15 years versus the proportion aged 15–59). Besides, we focus on national saving to avoid narrowing the population aging impacts since the corporate and the government saving are sensitive to population aging as the household saving.

In addition, given the lack of researches on this issue on developing countries (which economic and social environment greatly differ from the developed countries) we devote our study to Tunisian case. Tunisia is an interesting case of study because it is a well advanced in the aging process. As well, it suffers from an enduring and high unemployment rate and an inefficient pension system (as detailed in Section 3). Furthermore, it is characterized by a strong altruistic familial intergenerational relationship [2–4].

To check out the relationship between aging, unemployment, national saving and economic growth we apply a time series modeling approach over the period 1970–2019. We carry out a Structural VAR model, as defined by Sims [5]. We analyze the impulse response functions (IRFs) of different shocks for all variable's fluctuations. We also apply the bootstrap methods to construct the confidence intervals of the IRFs. Additionally, we complete our dynamic analysis by the variance decomposition.

This study represents the first attempt to model the Tunisian aggregate national saving by considering both the impact of demographic changes and of unemployment.

In what follows, we give, in Section 2, an overview of the life cycle hypothesis and its bounds. In Section 3 we give some sight of the demographic change and the saving evolution occurred in Tunisia. In Section 4, we specify the econometric model and in Section 5 we discuss the results found. Finally, we end, in Section 6, with the main findings and policy recommendations.

2. Life cycle pattern overview

In this section we state the life cycle's savings to emphasize the social and economic conditions that may constrain its validation.

2.1 Life cycle hypothesis

The life cycle theory pinpoints the intertemporal allocation of time, effort and money. In its simple form, the standard life cycle hypothesis's (LCH) formulated by Modigliani and Brumberg [6], suggests that individuals save during working life for their consumption needs when they retire, dissave after retirement, and die without wealth. Hence, individuals will smooth consumption over their lifetime regard to the expected lifetime resources. They accumulate wealth during the pre-retirement period by consuming less than their disposable income. So, during retirement, they de-cumulates wealth to finance its consumption. That is, the saving rate should follow a hump-shaped over the life cycle as shown by the **Figure 1** (in the Appendix).

Therefore, one very important implication of the LCH is that the demographic profile of a population should be an important factor influencing the aggregate saving rate. Given that population aging is defined as a shift in the population age distribution towards old age, so a change of the balance between youth and elderly proportion (defined in the following as a person aged over 60 years-old) causes society to age and subsequently to affect the saving pattern.[1] Such a change may change the savers proportion in the economy and diminish the aggregate saving rate according to the LCH.

If there is a large proportion of the population working, then, the saving rate should be high. However, if there is a large population proportion over retirement age or very young, the saving rate would be low. This suggests that aggregate saving rate should be negatively correlated with total dependency ratio.

Even though the theoretical conclusion of the life cycle model is clear, the empirical evidence is not often proved and stays controversial until today as it was decades ago. There is evidence that elderly may not dissave, at least not to the extend hypothesis suggested by the pure life cycle model which abstracts a number of factors that would complicate its prediction.

2.2 The life cycle hypothesis bounds

The Life cycle theoretical conclusion is understandable given its simplifying assumptions such as no uncertainty, a finite decision horizon, no inheritance and perfect financial market with no credit constraint [7]. According to the LCH, individual takes decisions basically depending to events and fact that are known with certainty in each period of life (such future income, death date, and interest rate). Nevertheless, these assumptions are considered too restrictive. Indeed, events are uncertain [8, 9] and financial market is imperfect with credit constraint. Uncertainty affects consumption and savings behavior as consumers are generally cautious. Moreover, according to the Kotlikoff [10] dynastic model of savings, individuals do not act in a finite horizon, but in an infinite one. In addition, they have a dynastic behavior characterized by a strong preference to let, at their death, a very limited capital de-cumulation [11–13]. Thus, parents, having an altruistic motive, seek to not decumulate wealth to leave inheritance to their children. Consequently, the population aging may not automatically depress national saving. Kotlikoff and Summers [14] conclude that the "life cycle saving" cannot account for more than 20 percent of U.S. capital formation, and the intergenerational transfers

[1] Population aging arises from two demographic phenomena the birth and the mortality decline. As for declining fertility, it reduces the number of children, which is generally considered a main explanation of growing aging. For mortality decline, it increases the longevity and the number of elderly.

play a dominant role in wealth accumulation, accounting for 80 percent or more of observed wealth.

Additionally, it is worth noting that the conflicting evidence on the life cycle saving may also be due to the econometric approaches used and the aging indicator chosen. Indeed, the micro econometric analysis invalidates life cycle model's prediction to support the Kotilkoff hypothesis but their results are difficult to aggregate because of severe problem of heterogeneous behavior at the household level. Conversely, studies based on macro data for a country generally support the prediction. However, most of them refer to developed societies while in developing societies people face different economic challenges and social conditions, which may lead to different evidences. In that way, these studies could not be very useful for understanding saving behavior in developing countries. The difference through countries is in the design of pension systems and health care, taxes and transfers as well as labour market conditions, which are unavoidably depend to the population age distribution. As well, they may alter individual economic behavior and so could be the origin of the inconsistency LCH's evidences.

Also, the choice of the population aging indicator to estimate is crucial. The total dependency ratio which is generally used does not accurately reflect the aged population since it composed of both the old and the child dependency ratio. It is more fitting to use the old-age dependency ratio to explicitly consider the effect of aged population on savings rate [15]. With more cautious in the aging indicator use, the life cycle model's prediction is likely to be endorsed also in macroeconomic approach.

2.3 The life cycle hypothesis and uncertainty

The LCH analysis has been gradually enriched, to focus on three reasons for accumulation: the foresight for retirement, the intergenerational altruism and inheritance and the wariness of the saver face to risk (of income, health and lifetime span). In this work, we focus more on the third reason of accumulation by looking at how uncertainty, about future income affects the behavior of the individual' saving. Uncertainty consideration has made it possible to highlight precautionary behavior as the future work income is random; consumption (otherwise savings) depends not only on expectation, but also on the variance of the expected income. A risk-averse or aware consumer will save more. In fact, savings play an insurance role against the hazards affecting the household, especially the hazards related to income (unemployment, loss of wages, etc.) [16]. Thus, uncertainty about future income affects the behavior of the individual 'saving by increasing the demand for precautionary assets, and hence savings amount.

As well, there is precautionary behavior as to face health care expenditure at advanced aged when the risk of health problems is potentially great; notably in the context of inefficient health care system [17]. As a result, households are saving not only to offset lower future income, but also to insure against all sorts of risks.

However, empirically it is not easy to estimate uncertainty extent on saving behavior. It is difficult to quantify this relationship given the difficulty to directly and objectively estimate uncertainty. Empirically there are no quantitative measurements of uncertainty that could be used directly. In the case studies, income uncertainty is usually measured indirectly by auxiliary variables such as inflation rate, unemployment rate or a derivative of these variables. In this case of study, we focus on unemployment as an income uncertainty indicator to better understand the aging impact on saving and to find an answer to the crucial question: do population aging depress savings?

Unemployment inevitably alters the savings behavior by its two aspects: (1) a high rate and (2) an increase in the average age of unemployed [18].

(1) The high and persistent unemployment rate weights on household confidence, prompting them to increase their precautionary savings. Such behavior is accentuated in a setting of unavailability of unemployment allowance (like in Tunisia) [19]. Thus, for precautionary reasons and to finance unexpected income losses, unemployment is viewed as an income uncertainty given the probability to become unemployed alters the savings behavior. Faure et al. [20] shown that unemployment and the deterioration of household confidence accounted for almost 20% of the aggregate consumption decline.

(2) The increase of the unemployed average age implies that the working population becomes occupied at advanced age. Consequently, they would save a less amount of wealth and they would form a low retirement pension. To offset at this lack of savings they do not immediately dissave at the beginning of the retirement. They would even compensate their low pension by working further after retirement, mainly at the beginning of the period (as long as they stay in better health) to face the future' uncertainties. Also, given the granting difficulties for credit liquidity at the retirement period, this insufficient pension nudges them to continue to save to keep up a certain level of consumption. It increases, in addition, the need for retirement savings from private sources.

Furthermore, the high and enduring unemployment increases inter-vivos transfers, which represents a form of precautionary saving [21]. With a dynastic behavior (which is ignored by the LCH) the old generation (parents) saves more throughout the life cycle to help the young generation (their offspring) to facing uncertainty and hard-economic conditions related for instance to unemployment's conditions. Thus, if intergenerational transfers (by purely altruistic incentive or following a kind of implicit contract between parents and children) are an important motive for savings; elderly rarely decumulate their wealth.

Henceforth, given uncertainty about the future income and lifespan, liquidity constraints, and the wish to leave bequests (a dynastic savings) population aging would not drive the decrease of savings. Therefore, aging economic impact on the household saving and so on the cumulative and on national saving, may not be large [22].

Hence, for our empirical evaluation of the life cycle hypothesis, we analyze the aging-savings relationship in a developing country, in particular, Tunisia. It greatly differs, economically and socially, from the developed countries, by its altruistic familial intergenerational relationship, the enduring and high unemployment rate and the inefficient pension system; as detailed in the section below.

3. The Tunisian demographic and economic setting

3.1 Demographic shifts and age structure evolution

Tunisia after has shortly ended its demographic transition regime, it has well undertaken the population aging process. During the period 1960–2019, the mortality rate fell from 35 to 40 per thousand to a low rate 5.9. Likewise, fertility which was nearby 8 children per woman fell to 2.17. Thus, the life expectancy has attained an average close to that of developed countries 75.4 years (78.1 years for woman and 74.5 years for man) in 2017.

Accordingly, the population age distribution has shifted towards aging. This fertility decline has narrowed the bottom of the age pyramid by the decline of the younger generation size, while the mortality decline has enlarged the top of the pyramid through the life expectancy gain. Thus, the age range proportion less than 15 years-old becomes less important (passing from 46.5 percent to 24.7) and it is likely to continue its decline. In the contrary, a remarkable increase is recorded for the proportion of person aged over 60 years-old (from 5.5 percent to 12.6) and is expected to increase by 10 points over the future three decades. Therefore, during 1966–2019, the child dependency ratio has sharply declined (from 96.27 percent to 39.36) while the old-age dependency ratio has increased (from 11.60 percent to 20.08). Consequently, the total dependency ratio has decreased (from 107.86 percent to 59.44).

3.2 Economic setting

Tunisian economy recorded a high and enduring unemployment. Over the period 1966–2000, it has increased by 6.1 points to pass from 12.5 percent to 18.6, and then fell slightly to stabilize during the last two decades (2000–2019) around 15.3 percent. Additionally, aging has hit the age composition of the unemployed. Indeed, the modal age range of the unemployed population has moved from less than 25 years-old (by about 29 percent) to 25–29 years-old (by about 34.2 percent) during 2005–2011. It is worth noting here that Tunisian authorities do not distribute any unemployment allowance.[2]

For the national saving, it has evolved with some fluctuations. During the period 1970–2010, the national saving rate (of gross national disposable income) was relatively stable around an average of 22.8 percent then progressively fell to achieve 9.3 in 2019, mainly due to a steady loss of purchasing power.[3]

According to the Islamic Development Bank, the behavior of Tunisian investors appears to be driven by factors related to consumer demand and/or the income effect [23]. The financial changes in interest rates have more effect on the savings structure than on its volume. Indeed, the financial liberalization policy adopted (since the structural adjustment plan in 1986) has not succeeded to stimulate private savings through the increasing of the real interest rates [24]. In Tunisia, saving behavior seems to comply more to the Keynesian approach.

However, an interest for the long-term financial savings is recorded. During 2010–2017, the listed companies increase from 56 to 81 with a broad sectors diversification. Likewise, the life insurance, as a long-term saving vehicle, has undergone an important increase; the average annual growth rate was 18 percent in 2017. Its share in the insurance market has climbed from 12.05 percent in 2009 to 20.2 in 2017; however, it remains far from the international standards (about 56.2 percent).

This interest for the long-term savings is explained by the failure of the pension system the pay-as-you-go system and the bankruptcy of the provident fund as well as the authority's future intention to withhold a proportion of the retirement pension.[4] Thus, the insured people are driven to form a complementary retirement pension under others retirement savings forms through voluntarily paying into saving schemes in private financial institutions. This savings form is encouraged by the financial authority through the establishment of tax benefits.

Concerning the non-financial savings, it is allocated to buy housing, jewelry or land by household and productive assets by individual corporate. Household saving is particularly oriented to housing savings which has experienced a growth rate of about 5.5 percent during 2000–2017.

---

[2] Source: NIS employment 1966, 2005, 2007, 2010, 2011.

[3] During 2011–2019 inflation rate has passed from 3.7 percent to 6.2.

[4] For instance, during 2010–2017, the overall financial situation of the three funds of the social security recorded a very serious drop going from 40MD in 2010 to −1326 MD.

4. Econometric model and data specification

To look at the relationship between population aging and savings in an unemployment context in Tunisia over the period 1970–2019, we apply a structural VAR model, as defined by Sims [25]. This enables us to approach a multivariate causal setting allowing the coexistence of both short and long-term forces derived from the aging influences on saving decisions. Finally, we deepen our dynamic analysis by application the techniques of impulse response functions (IRFs) of different shocks for all variable's fluctuations and of the variance decomposition (VDC).

4.1 Data specification

To undertake the aggregate saving model estimating, we use as an independent variable the national savings rate unlike previous studies, which generally referred to the household savings rate. National saving is important as it is a source of investment and one of the major determinants of macroeconomic growth. Also, as it is closely related to the demand for financial and real assets and it may affect asset price formation. In addition, we seek to avoid narrowing the aging impact as its takes into account companies and public sector saving (related to social sector, health, education and pensions). On another side, the household savings refers to survey measure which undervalues personal income as it provides information related to expenditure than to income sources. Likewise, it does not capture the same share of total saving for persons at different ages, so the estimate of relationship between savings and age may be fallacious.

As a definition, between the two known alternative measures of savings (S) we adopt that of national account (as income minus consumption expenditure) given data availability.[5] Explicitly, we use the savings rate with respect to the gross national income disposable income[6].

For independent variables, we refer to the main population aging indicators. We consider the mortality rate (MR) and fertility rate (FR) to capture demographic changes and its impact on the age structure composition, and likewise on the dependency ratio. We consider the old-age dependency ratio (EDR) to accurately look at the effect of aging besides the broadly used the total dependency ratio (TDR). Then, we could deduce if the aging impact is due to the fertility decline or to the longevity increase.

Concerning economic variables, we include three macroeconomic variables. (1) Basing to the neoclassical approach we introduce the interest rate (MMR) in particular the money market rate as a driver of the real interest rate (credit and debit). (2) As a one quantitative measure of aggregate income uncertainty we consider the aggregate unemployment rate (U). (3) In order to check the economic effect of saving, we examine the economic growth (G) measured by the GDP per capita at constant domestic prices. It is computed by dividing GDP per capita at current domestic prices by the consumption price index (base 1990). Hence, the inflation rate is indirectly considered.

---

[5] The second defines savings as the changes in net wealth. Net wealth accumulation includes capital gains and losses, adjusted for general inflation, and is more relevant for purposes of measuring changes individual's economic well-being.

[6] Gross national income equal to the gross national income minus the current transfers (current taxes on income and wealth, social security contributions, social security benefits) paid to non-residents units plus the current transfers received from the rest of the world by the residents.

The main statistical characteristics of these variables used are summarized in **Table 1** (in the Appendix). Data are drawn from the Central Bank of Tunisia (CBT), the National Institution of Statistics (NIS) and Tunisian Institute of competitively and quantitative study (ITCQS).

4.2 Econometric models

Our analysis is based on the identification and estimation of structural vector autoregressive (SVAR). The SVAR model is used in macroeconomic analysis in order to check the effect of exogenous shocks (of the demographic change, for instance) on macroeconomic variables.

Our basic model VAR is the following:

$$Y_t = \Gamma(L)\, Y_t + \nu_t \tag{1}$$

where Y_t is a column vector of stationary variables considered in the estimate.

The selection and order of independent variables are essential in the SVAR estimate. Thus, the independent demographic variables are introduced with caution following the demographic transition theory. As mortality decline brings that of fertility, so we first introduce the mortality rate (MR) followed by the fertility rate (FR). Then, we integrate the dependency ratio as an indicator of the population aging and the age structure change following the demographic transition.

After what, we consider the economic variable exogenous effect on saving. So, we insert the interest rate (MMR) as a saving determinant and the aggregate unemployment rate (U) as a measure of aggregate income uncertainty. Lastly, we introduce the national savings rate (S) followed by the economic growth (G) to check the aging impact on economic growth through the savings evolution.

As we use two dependency ratios, we estimate two distinct vectors autoregression. A vector includes the total dependency ratio which reflects the effect of both the mortality and fertility evolution as a result of the demographic policy as follows (MR_t, FR_t, TDR_t, U_t, MMR_t, S_t, G_t).

The second vector includes the old-age dependency ratio and takes the mortality choc as the main cause of the elderly proportion evolution as follows (MR_t, EDR_t, U_t, MMR_t, S_t, G_t).

Otherwise, $\Gamma(L) = \Gamma_1 L^1 + \Gamma_2 L^2 + \dots + \Gamma p.\ L^P$ is a lag operator in the form of polynomial matrix and ν_t is a vector of idiosyncratic errors, where $\nu_t = (\mu^1{}_t, \dots, \mu^5{}_t)'$. These errors are not auto correlated and are homoscedastic. Then, the representation (1) can be written in the form of a moving average of infinite order VMA (∞) (representation theorem of Wald):

$$Y_t = C(L)\, v_t \tag{2}$$

where $C(L) = [I - \Gamma(L)]^{-1}$.

The structural form (SF) of the model (1) can be written as follows:

$$Y_t = A(L)\, \varepsilon_t \tag{3}$$

where $A(L) = C(L)\, H$ is the coefficient matrix (a_{ij}) of (7×7 or 6×6 for the two vectors respectively) size, and more precisely it represents the impulse response functions of the elements of Y_t following the various shocks. Moreover, H is the transition matrix and ε is the vector of structural shocks where $E(\varepsilon_t \varepsilon_t') = I_N$.

However, the identification of these shocks requires the Cholesky decomposition in the order to identify the structure of the shocks. As a result, the decomposition of the variance covariance matrix of the reduced form residuals is written in a lower triangular matrix A(L). The number of constraints imposed on A (L) is equal to 21 i.e. n × (n-1) / 2 with n = 7 variables and where some of the structural shocks do not have contemporaneous impact on other variables.

Additionally, the Cholesky decomposition assumes that series listed earlier in the VAR order impact the others variables contemporaneously. But series listed later in the VAR order impact those listed earlier only with lag. Therefore, the variables listed early in the VAR order are considered more exogenous. As mentioned above, the order of endogenous variables is central to the identification of structural shocks, i.e. it determines the structure of the shocks. More precisely, the first variable has impacts on all the variables that are below it, but it does not receive any impacts from these variables. This rule applies to all subsequent variables. For instance, the triangular matrix A(L), for the case of n = 7 variables, is as follows.

$$\mathrm{A(L)} = \begin{pmatrix} 1 & 0 & 0 & 0 & 0 & 0 & 0 \\ C21 & 1 & 0 & 0 & 0 & 0 & 0 \\ C31 & C32 & 1 & 0 & 0 & 0 & 0 \\ C41 & C42 & C43 & 1 & 0 & 0 & 0 \\ C51 & C52 & C53 & C54 & 1 & 0 & 0 \\ C61 & C62 & C63 & C64 & C65 & 1 & 0 \\ C71 & C72 & C73 & C74 & C75 & C76 & 1 \end{pmatrix} \tag{4}$$

Henceforth, we have to estimate four matrixes: a matrix (Alt1) for the total dependency ratio and one for the old-age dependency ratio (Alt2). Two others matrixes are also estimates as a robustness test by omitting the unemployment rate, respectively the matrixes (Alt3) and (Alt4).

To undertake the SVAR estimate model, we first study the stationarity of all variables using the Phillips-Perron test [26]. As reported in **Table 2** (in the Appendix) all the considered variables are I(0) suggesting that a long-run (cointegration) relationship could exist between the considered variables.

Then we determine the order p of the VAR process to remember. To do this, we consider various processes for VAR lag orders p ranging from 1 to 4. For each model, we calculate the Akaike information criteria (AIC) and Schwarz (SC), and the log-likelihood (LV) to hold the p lag (=4) that minimizes these criteria as indicated in **Table 3** (in the Appendix).

Accordingly, four alternatives are estimated, respectively with the identification of cointegration relationships by using the cointegration test of Johansen [27] as well as the structural factorization (with 500 iterations).

Finally, to examine the dynamic of the model, we refer to the impulse response function (IRF). It helps us to judge and to appreciate the channel(s) of population age structure change transmission. It allows to see if there is really a robust, stable and predictable relationship between aging and savings. In this respect, we will identify the different responses of all the variables in the model to various shocks. It should be noted that we focused on the effects of the shock on 10 periods and that errors are generated by Monte Carlo with 100 repetitions. Such analysis is strengthened with the variance decomposition analysis (VDC), which however, indicates the proportion of the variable changes due to own shocks versus shocks on the other variables. Namely, the variance of the forecast error of the change in savings rate is partitioned among the contributions of the innovations in each variable of the system.

5. Results interpretation

Interestingly, results put forward that the LCH prediction is not automatically confirmed, but it is up to the economic uncertainty extent. Indeed, the LCH is not validated in the unemployment setting, which is considered in our study as an indirect measure of income uncertainty.

5.1 The SVAR results interpretation

The SVAR's estimate results (reported in **Table 4** in the Appendix) points out that uncertainty encourages saving. Indeed, for the two aging indicators used (TDR and EDR) the LCH prediction is not validated once unemployment is introduced unlike Ahmedova's [28] findings. As we note from matrixes Alt1 and Alt2, the two indicators present a significant positive effect on savings rate in the context of enduring unemployment without allowance, like in Frini' work [29]. However, this effect is found more significant for old-age dependency ratio, unlike in Wong and Tang [30] and Loumrhari's [31] findings.

In contrast, the LCH prediction is validated by the estimate omitting the unemployment rate, however, for only the total dependency ratio. Indeed, a significant negative effect is found in the matrix Alt3.

Such results confirm that the demographic changes impact on saving depends on the perception of the economic context and the confidence towards future. Furthermore, the LCH's validation appears to be, as well, empirically related to the aging indicator used in the estimate. This confirms our proposal that the old-age dependency ratio indicator seems more efficient to explicitly check the effect of aging.

The unemployment which hints uncertainty about future income pushes the savers to keep up savings. It reduces confidence and intensifies incentives for precautionary saving so that, it prevents savings from decline. Indeed, the unemployment rate displays a significant and positive coefficient. The weight of the future uncertainty boosts the employed population to form a precautionary savings. This precautionary saving is important to offset the small amount of wealth accumulated after an enduring unemployment without any allocation benefit. When enduring a long unemployment period and facing great difficulties for credit liquidity at old age, elderly try to continue to save to keep up a certain level of consumption. Such behavior is very pronounced in Tunisia since retired do not benefit from a sufficient pension in a distressed pay-as-you-go system. The insufficiency of pension and medical care benefits entails the elderly saving's behavior adjustment by continuing to work and to save at the beginning of the retirement period (as long as they remain in better health). As pointed out by Frini [32, 33] the new retirees or the youngest elderly (which share, generally, weighs more than that of the old retirees or the old elderly) maintain their savings mainly for precautionary motives in high uncertainty economic environment.

This Tunisian elderly saving behavior may in part be strengthened by the intentional transfers motivation of the old generation towards the young one. Indeed, Tunisian families, as stressed by Mahfoud [34] and Frini [35, 36], are strongly linked and directed by an intergenerational altruistic motive. So, the old generation do not seek to cut savings so as to help the young generation to face uncertain environment and hard economic conditions.

As expected, mortality drop induces a fertility decline, putting on show the demographic transition theory. This fertility decline increases the savings rate. It seems that the youth share decrease outweighs the small increase in the elderly share since the aggregate savings rate increases. Household with fewer children are likely to incur less expenditure in respect to their income for looking after them and then would save more. In addition, a reduced family size leads to a competition between children as a mean of transferring income from present to future and as a financial asset.[7] Henceforth, by the fall of fertility rate, the demand of financial and capital market as a substitute of youth assurance service will increase and thus savings. Additionally, the decline of government expenditures for youth (given their share decline), seems to make up or even more the government expenditures increase for elderly (due to their share increase) to not lead savings decrease.

Considering uncertainty, mortality evolution positively influences savings rate when considering the economic and social facts, but negatively when they are neglected. The increase of mortality risk and health problem intensifies precautionary behavior to face health care expenditure at old age.

The uncertainty related to interest rate affects positively the savings rate. An increase in interest rate will make saving more attractive. Finally, like in AbuAl-Foul's [37] work results show that no long-run relationship exists between saving and GDP growth. This in part due to that saving is, generally, done in real estate, which is known as a small creator of wealth with a small ripple effect.

5.2 The IRF's and VDC's results interpretation

Likewise, the IRF's and VDC's results underline that population aging on savings evolution changes respect to the economic uncertainty context. Savings positively respond to age structure changes once unemployment is taken into account. The different graphs of impulse responses (**Figure 2** in the Appendix) show that savings respond quickly to demographic changes (mortality rate, fertility rate and dependency ratio jointly), but weakly to the shock of the money market rate. The response due to unemployment rate shock can be judged as significant with a return to equilibrium in the long-term. The saving response to economic growth innovations is, however, slow and limited. This analysis is corroborated out by the variance decomposition as displayed in **Table 5** (in the Appendix).[8] In detail, a relatively constant proportion of the change in savings rate variance is recorded for both ratios. The total dependency ratio shock is by about 3.75 percent for Alt1 and by 4.26 percent for Alt3 after three years. The old-age dependency ratio shocks are, however, of a less proportion by 1.42 percent for Alt2 and 0.16 percent for Alt4 over ten years. The noteworthy result is that savings evolution follow-up a shock of the total dependency ratio is more significant (by three times more) than of the elderly one. This fact is also proved by the dynamic response path. Fewer children lower the dependent population and consumption without contribution to income. The decrease of the youth dependent proportion out weights the increase of the elderly dependent in the proportion, which limits saving rate depression. This brings up the role of relative weight of the youth share to the elderly share on savings evolution. Further, the increase of elderly proportion appears not to cut savings rate. Thus, savings rises when fertility declines and longevity increases, but less intensively. In the contrary, to the LCH prediction, the old-age dependency ratio shock instantaneously and positively affects saving rate, however, more weakly than the total dependency ratio.

---

[7] Children is treated as pure capital goods and a kind of safety assets which returns are "elderly assurance".

[8] The VDC indicates the proportion of the variable changes due to own shocks versus shocks on the other variables. The Cholesky decomposition method is used in orthogonalizing the innovations across equation. Percentage of forecast variances is explained by innovations.

Remarkably, once we ignore the labour market unbalance (or uncertainty) of the estimates the relationship between aging and savings becomes consistent with the LCH prediction. The total dependency ratio shocks present a negative short-term impact on saving to disappear at long-run (after eight years). However, no impact is found for the old-age dependency ratio. This discrepancy in estimated magnitude through the two dependency ratios used refers back to our assumption that aging impact may be sensitive to the measurement used to describe it.

Moreover, demographic indicators shocks trace the variance of savings innovations. Mortality rate explains saving variance by almost the same small proportion (by about 2.30 percent) for all alternatives in the variance decomposition, but relatively less without the unemployment rate. In the impulse function graph, a negligible positive impact is found of mortality shock. Hence, with the rise of longevity and elderly proportion savings may not decline. Fertility decline significantly contributes in the savings change variance (by about 5.16 percent in Alt1) and even much more when forsaking the unemployment rate (by about 17.79 percent in Alt3). The corresponding impulse function displays a negative influence over six years to reverse positively after.

However, saving is less sensitive to interest rate shock. Money market rate contribution is more pronounced for the total dependency ratio than the elderly one. The same evidence is observed through the impulse function graph shown a very small positive influence which disappears in the long-term. This small impact of the real interest rate on saving may hide the offsetting of its two effects (of income and substitution). In other hand, it may be related to the Tunisian household's behavior which seems to comply more with the Keynesian approach.

Finally, in the long-term, savings shocks seem to produce an effect on economic growth, but weakly when the imbalance labour market is considered (as reported in **Table 6** in the Appendix). As mapped out by the response functions this dynamic is non-instantaneous. In contrast, a very small 'feed-back' seems to be produced of economic growth over three years on saving.

6. Conclusion

This study puts on show that the life cycle prediction of a downward pressure on saving by aging population could not be proved under uncertainty. Population aging is, on contrast, found to exert a long-term upward pressure on saving in an unemployment context. The economic environment's uncertainty (such income uncertainty) quantified, in our case of study, by the unemployment phenomenon, looks to be an essential factor of the change in the life cycle pattern of savings. It is able to shaping the saving behavior and to distort the LCH. The impact of the demographic change seems strongly related to the economic confidence factors. Accordingly, the social and economic conditions limit the scope of the LCH. Thus, population aging will not necessarily spell disaster on national saving. Consequently, studies' findings on developed countries could not be representative of saving behavioral in developing countries; where pension and medical insurance schemes are less developed and the persistent unemployment is without unemployment allowance benefit. Furthermore, it seems that the empirical findings checking the LCH depend on the aging indicator used. In fact, the use of the total dependency ratio could not validate the LCH, but it is validated by the old-age dependency ratio use. So, with more caution on the population aging measure, the evidence that elderly do not dissave may be found and the life cycle prediction may not be endorsed. Henceforth, the life cycle hypothesis may not be validated in macroeconomic approach as in the micro-econometric approach.

Finally, as policy implications, several measures are needed to sustain saving rate or to prevent it from an eventual decline. In addition to the strategy applied lately to postponing the retirement age to 62 years-old, Tunisian Policy-makers have to accelerate the move from the pay-as-you-ago public pension system towards the funded pension system to cut costs of increasing old-age benefits. As well, to mobilize more savings, they should shift the liquid savings towards long-term products. Accordingly, it is important to reconsider the long-term savings strategy to meet the household's needs as well as the huge potential investment's needs. Therefore, major economic and financial reforms should be undertaken to restructure public corporates and the partial openness of their capital, to strengthen the pension plans, to develop the insurance sector and promote life insurance, and to improve the framework of the stock market and the bond market and diversify product of savings.

Appendix

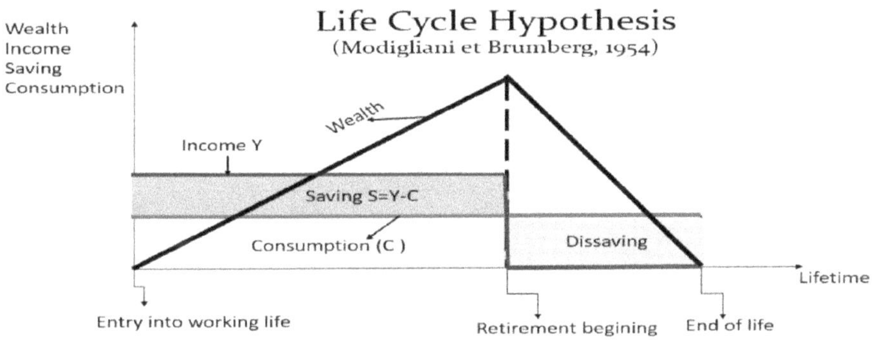

Figure 1.
Consumption,consumer income, wealth and saving over the life cycle.

	S	MR	FR	EDR	TDR	G	U	TMM
Mean	20.73	0.68	3.55	14.21	75.70	4.52	15.28	6.85
Median	21.75	0.59	3.01	14.35	77.05	4.67	15.60	6.40
Maximum	26.40	1.34	6.29	20.08	108.69	17.74	18.30	11.79
Minimum	9.40	0.55	2.00	11.15	50.51	−1.92	12.40	3.00
Std. Dev.	3.94	0.19	1.51	1.93	18.76	3.35	0.86	2.34
Observations	50	50	50	50	50	50	50	50

Table 1.
Descriptive statistics variables.

Series	level	1st difference
MR	0.06*	0.00*
FR	0.34	0.00*
TDR	0.80	0.00*
EDR	0.52	0.00*
U	0.01*	0.00*
TMM	0.19	0.00*
S	0. 02*	0.00**
G	0.04*	0.00**

Note: The null hypothesis for the ADF test is that the series are non-stationary i.e. there is presence of unit root. The values in the table indicate the p-values of this test. Using the Phillips-Perron test, the results were the same.
** and **denotes that the null hypothesis of unit root is rejected at the 5% level and 10% level respectively.*

Table 2.
Unit root test of ADF.

The lag number p	AIC	SC	LV
Alternative 1 (MR_t,FR_t, TDR_t, U_t, MMR_t, S_t, G_t)			
1	4.56	5.62*	−36. 29
2	3.98	8.43	25.03
3	3.61	10.30	80.48
4	−1.48*	7.69	211.19*
Alternative 2 (MR_t, EDR_t, U_t, TMM_t, S_t, G_t)			
1	1.73	3.03*	31.44
2	0.18	4.51	94.32
3	−0.75	5.33	165.21
4	−3.84*	4.64	266.06*
Alternative 3 (MR_t,FR_t, TDR_t, TMM_t, S_t, G_t)			
1	2.22	3.48*	0.35
2	1.34	4.27	47.13
3	1.12	6.74	86.61
4	−0.87*	6.67	187.23*
Alternative 4 (MR_t, EDR_t, TMM_t, S_t, G_t)			
1	1.36	0.89*	68.74
2	−2.34	1.58	118.97
3	−2.89	2.72	166.54
4	−4.62*	1.85	225.99*

Note: LV denotes the log-likelihood; the asterisk indicates P order to retain according to the criterion used.

Table 3.
Choice of the lag number of VAR (p) process.

$$
Alt1(L)=\begin{bmatrix}
1 & 0 & 0 & 0 & 0 & 0 & 0 \\
0.87^{***} & 1 & 0 & 0 & 0 & 0 & 0 \\
-0.44 & 3.62^{***} & 1 & 0 & 0 & 0 & 0 \\
0.67 & -5.85^{***} & -0.79^{***} & 1 & 0 & 0 & 0 \\
1.32^{***} & 0.70^{***} & 0.32^{**} & -0.44 & 1 & 0 & 0 \\
3.23^{***} & -1.63^{***} & 0.52^{*} & 0.56^{**} & 0.72^{**} & 1 & 0 \\
0.10 & 0.12 & -0.00 & 0.01 & 0.00 & -0.00 & 1
\end{bmatrix}
$$

Vector autoregressive estimated is: MR_t, FR_t, TDR_t, U_t, MMR_t, S_t, G_t.

$$
Alt2(L)=\begin{bmatrix}
1 & 0 & 0 & 0 & 0 & 0 \\
-0.85^{***} & 1 & 0 & 0 & 0 & 0 \\
0.27 & -1.79^{***} & 1 & 0 & 0 & 0 \\
1.86^{***} & 1.32^{***} & -0.44 & 1 & 0 & 0 \\
3.53^{***} & 1.42^{*} & 0.56^{**} & 0.72^{**} & 1 & 0 \\
0.10 & -0.00 & 0.01 & 0.00 & -0.00 & 1
\end{bmatrix}
$$

Vector autoregressive estimated is: MR_t, EDR_t, U_t, MMR_t , S_t, G_t)

$$
Alt3(L)=\begin{bmatrix}
1 & 0 & 0 & 0 & 0 & 0 \\
0.78^{***} & 1 & 0 & 0 & 0 & 0 \\
5.76^{***} & -0.86^{***} & 1 & 0 & 0 & 0 \\
0.23 & -0.59^{***} & 0.02 & 1 & 0 & 0 \\
-6.36^{***} & -1.12^{*} & -1.34^{***} & 2.52 & 1 & 0 \\
0.00 & 0.06 & -0.00 & 0.00 & 0.04 & 1
\end{bmatrix}
$$

Vector autoregressive estimated is: MR_t, FR_t, TDR_t, MMR_t, S_t, G_t.

$$
Alt4(L)=\begin{bmatrix}
1 & 0 & 0 & 0 & 0 \\
-0.35 & 1 & 0 & 0 & 0 \\
-0.45 & 0.07 & 1 & 0 & 0 \\
-6.21 & 3.25^{***} & 2.44^{***} & 1 & 0 \\
0.03 & -0.05 & 0.06 & 0.01 & 1
\end{bmatrix}
$$

Vector autoregressive estimated is: MR_t, EDR_t, MMR_t , S_t, G_t.

*** $p<0.01$, ** $p<0.05$, * $p<0.1$

Table 4.
SVAR estimates results for the four alternatives.

Alt1								
Period	S.E.	MR	D(FR)	D(TDR)	U	D(MMR)	S	G
1	1.82	0.04	0.50	1.58	29.01	1.00	67.63	0.00
2	2.39	2.03	5.90	1.10	24.92	1.23	61.03	3.75
3	2.71	1.83	6.76	2.93	21.94	1.85	61.39	3.27
4	2.78	1.75	8.16	3.32	21.51	2.06	59.98	3.18
5	2.86	1.77	7.53	3.07	29.72	1.94	53.01	2.93
6	3.17	1.97	6.57	3.77	35.50	1.68	47.87	2.60
7	3.48	2.12	5.44	3.77	42.08	1.51	42.85	2.20
8	3.68	2.27	4.98	3.89	42.84	1.65	42.32	2.01
9	3.70	2.36	4.90	3.83	42.67	1.88	42.43	1.89
10	3.86	2.39	5.16	3.75	41.77	2.06	42.98	1.851

Alt2							
Period	S.E.	MR	D(EDR)	U	D(MMR)	S	G
1	1.94	0.11	0.11	28.54	2.95	67.59	0.00
2	2.43	1.44	0.28	26.42	1.95	60.16	5.58
3	2.58	1.38	0.89	24.00	2.00	60.68	5.15
4	2.66	1.87	1.42	24.84	1.89	57.50	5.03
5	2.81	2.04	1.60	30.82	1.75	51.97	4.66
6	2.97	2.27	1.56	35.23	1.56	48.47	4.49
7	3.11	2.28	1.48	37.45	1.46	47.10	4.36
8	3.19	2.30	1.43	37.67	1.44	47.07	4.34
9	3.21	2.30	1.41	37.34	1.45	47.31	4.349
10	3.22	2.29	1.42	37.24	1.46	47.25	4.33

Alt3							
Period	S.E.	MR	D(FR)	D(TDR)	D(MMR)	S	G
1	1.74	0.00	0.20	0.91	4.79	94.08	0.00
2	2.35	2.18	6.64	0.64	4.72	81.92	3.87
3	2.68	1.94	9.56	4.19	5.43	75.81	3.04
4	2.84	1.88	13.29	3.86	6.08	72.04	2.81
5	2.95	1.92	15.14	4.39	6.51	69.28	2.72
6	3.00	1.93	16.46	4.28	6.89	67.74	2.66
7	3.02	1.94	17.15	4.31	7.08	66.81	2.68
8	3.04	1.93	17.53	4.27	7.16	66.38	2.69
9	3.05	1.93	17.71	4.27	7.20	66.17	2.70
10	3.05	1.92	17.79	4.26	7.22	66.07	2.71

Alt4						
Period	S.E.	MR	D(EDR)	D(MMR)	S	G
1	1.89	0.10	0.19	6.90	92.75	0.00
2	2.47	1.14	0.13	4.28	82.12	5.97
3	2.71	1.01	0.15	4.22	79.41	5.21

			Alt4			
Period	**S.E.**	**MR**	**D(EDR)**	**D(MMR)**	**S**	**G**
4	2.81	0.94	0.15	4.06	76.99	4.85
5	2.85	0.94	0.15	4.02	75.79	4.75
6	2.85	0.93	0.16	4.03	75.35	4.74
7	2.86	0.93	0.16	4.03	75.29	4.77
8	2.86	0.94	0.16	4.02	75.29	4.81
9	2.86	0.96	0.16	4.02	75.26	4.83
10	2.87	0.98	0.16	4.02	75.21	4.84

Notes: Cholesky ordering follow that of the four alternatives. The second column (S.E) shows the forecast error of the variable at the given forecast horizon. The source of this forecast error is the variation in the current and future values of the innovations to each endogenous variable in the VAR. The other columns give the percentage of the forecast variance due to each innovation.

Table 5.
Variance decomposition of saving rates (Cholesky ordering).

Alt1	Alt2	Alt3	Alt4
23.54	29.50	27.41	33.20
22.72	27.47	27.69	32.28
20.20	24.18	25.27	31.54
21.88	26.15	25.43	32.72
21.19	26.48	25.37	32.70
21.56	26.46	25.37	32.63
21.75	26.38	25.35	32.60
22.03	26.29	25.35	32.60
21.97	26.22	25.35	32.61
21.74	26.21	25.34	32.

Table 6.
Variance decomposition of economic growth to saving rates.

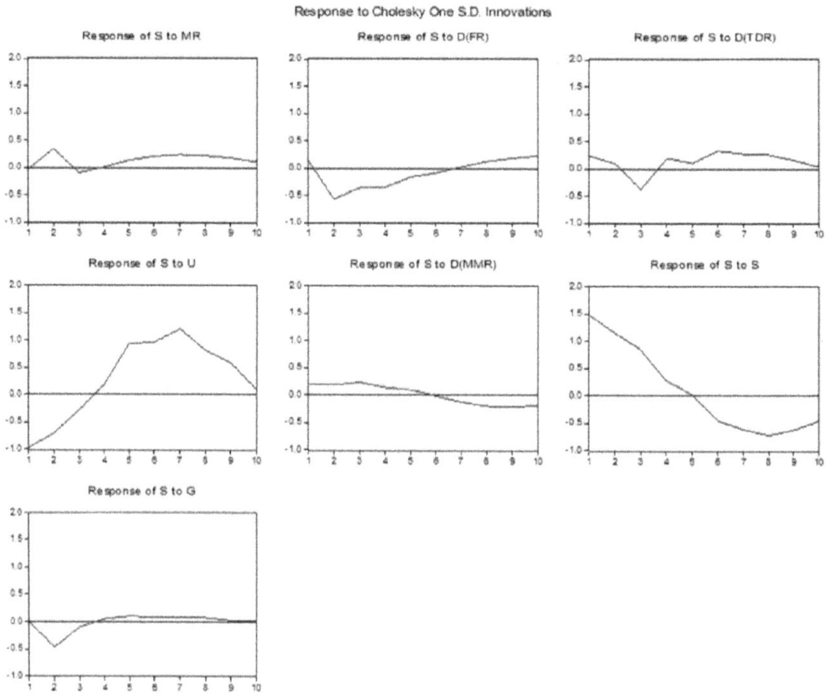
Response to Cholesky One S.D. Innovations
Response of S to MR
Response of S to D(FR)
Response of S to D(TDR)
Response of S to U
Response of S to D(MMR)
Response of S to S
Response of S to G

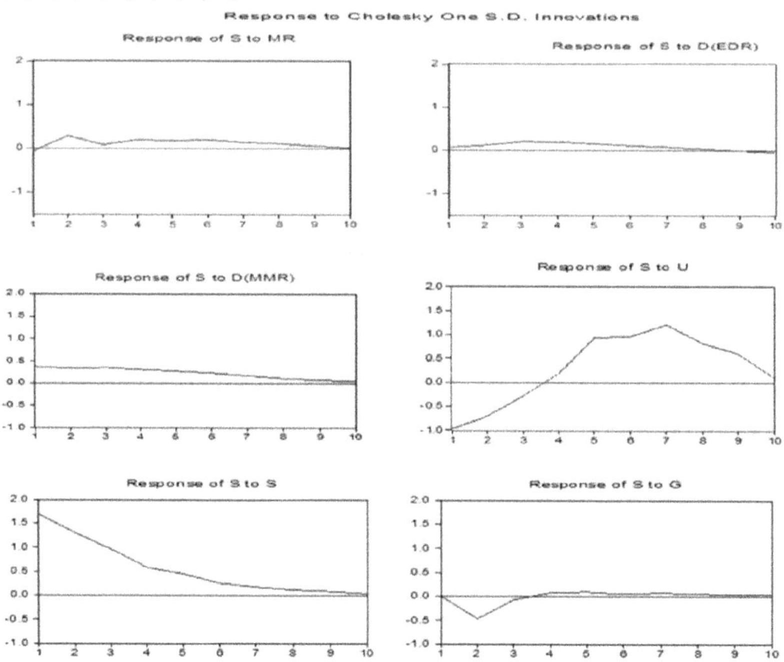
Response to Cholesky One S.D. Innovations
Response of S to MR
Response of S to D(EDR)
Response of S to D(MMR)
Response of S to U
Response of S to S
Response of S to G

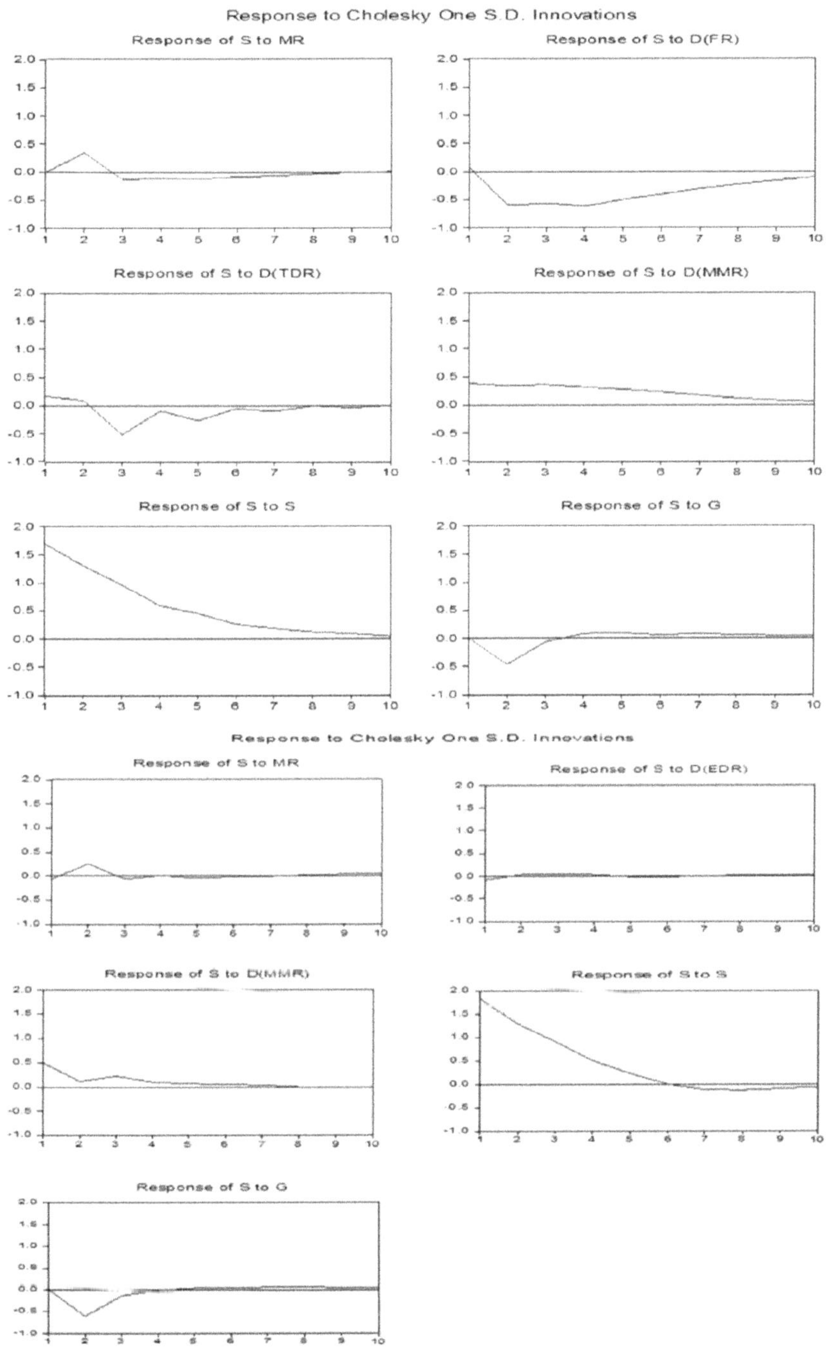

Figure 2.
Estimated impulse response functions. Response to Cholesky one S.D. innovations.

Classifications

JEL Classifications: J1, E2, C3

Author details

Olfa Frini[1,2]

1 ISCAE, University of Manouba, Tunisia

2 ECSTRA Lab, Carthage University, Tunisia

*Address all correspondence to: frini.olfa@planet.tn

References

[1] Modigliani, F. & Brumberg, R. (1954). *Utility Analysis and the Consumption Function: An Interpretation of Cross-section Data' Post Keynesian Economics*, ed Kenneth K. Kurihara. New Brunswick: Rutgers University Press.

[2] Frini, O. (1996). *Le transfert intergénérationnel et accumulation du capital humain: cas de la Tunisie.* A search dissertation.

[3] Frini, O. (2014). The Familial Network Influence on Fertility Behaviour in Tunisia. Journal of Economic and Social Research, 16(1–2), 33-61

[4] Mahfoud Draoui, D. (2006). Entraide familiale et nouvelles formes de solidarité', 2ème table ronde des cercles de la population et de la santé de la reproduction; "dynamiques familiales et solidarités intergenérationnelles" ONFP, Tunis 24 February 2006.

[5] Sims, C (2002). Solving Linear Rational Expectations Models. Computational Economics 20, 1–20.

[6] Modigliani, F. & Brumberg, R. (1954). *Utility Analysis and the Consumption Function: An Interpretation of Cross-section Data' Post Keynesian Economics*, ed Kenneth K. Kurihara. New Brunswick: Rutgers University Press.

[7] Attanasio, O. & Weber, G. (2010). Consumption and Saving: Models intertemporal Allocation and their implication for Public Policy. Journal of Economic Literature, 48(3), 693-751. h ttp://www.nber.org/papers/w15756.pdf

[8] Leland, H. (1968). Savings and Uncertainty: The Precautionary Demand for Savings. The Quarterly Journal of Economics 82, 465-473.

[9] Nagatani, K. (1972). Life Cycle Savings: Theory and Fact, American Economic Review 62(1), 344-353.

[10] Kotlikoff, L. (1988). Intergenerational Transfers and Savings, Journal of Economic Perspectives 2, 41-58. DOI: 10.1257/jep.2.2.41.

[11] Ameriks J., A., Laufer, C., S. & Van Nieuwerburgh, S. (2011). The Joy of Giving or Assisted Living ? Using Strategic Surveys to Separate Public Care Aversion from Bequest Motives. The Journal of Finance, 66(2), 519-561. https://doi.org/10.1111/j.1540-6261.2010.01641.x

[12] Lockwood, L. (2016). Incidental Bequests: Bequest Motives and the Choice to Self-Insure Late-Life Risks. *NBER Working Paper* No. 20745.

[13] De Nardi, M., French, E., & French, J. (2016). Medicaid Insurance in Old Age. The American Economic Review, 106(11), 3480-3520. http://dx.doi.org/10.1257/aer.20140015.

[14] Kotlikoff, L. J. & Summers, L. H. (1981). The Role of Intergenerational Transfers in Aggregate Capital Accumulation, Journal of Political Economy 89 (4), 706-732.

[15] Ahmedova, D. (2011). The impact of population Ageing on Private Savings Rate: Empirical Evidence from the OCDE Members Countries. Department of Economic, Central European University.

[16] Antonin, C. (2018). *Les liens entre taux d'épargne, revenu et incertitude. Une illustration sur données françaises.* Documents de Travail de l'OFCE 2018-19. Observatoire Français des Conjonctures Economiques.

[17] De Nardi, M., French, E., & Jones, J. (2010). Why Do the Elderly Save? The Role of Medical Expenses', Journal of Political Economy, 118(1), 39-75. DOI: 10.1086/651674.

[18] Kessler, D., Perelman, S., & Pestieau, P. (1993). Savings behavior in 17 OECD countries. Review of Income and Wealth Series, 39, (1)

[19] Engen, E. M., & Gruber, J. (2001). Unemployment insurance and precautionary saving. Journal of Monetary Economics, 47 (3), 545-579.

[20] Faure, M-E., Soual, H., & Clovis, K. (2012). La consommation des ménages dans la crise. Note de Conjoncture : 23–37.

[21] Kotlikoff, L.J., & Spivak, A. (1981). The Family as an Incomplete Annuities Market. Journal of Political Economy, 89 (2), 372-391.

[22] Yamauchi, N. (1996). The effects of Aging on National Saving and Asset Accumulation. *National Bureau of Ec onomic Research (NBER)*, Inc, 131-151.

[23] BID, Thomson Reuters, IIRF and CIBAFI (2013) *Tunisie prudemment optimiste* Rapport pays sur la finance islamique, Retrieved from : http://www.irti.org/irj/go/km/docs/documents/IDBDevelopments/Internet/English/IRTI/CM/downloads/Reports/Tunisia_Islamic_Finance_Country_Report_Cautiously_Optimistic_Fr.pdf/

[24] Tunisian Professional Association of Banks and Financial Institutions (2005) 'L'épargne', Retrieved from: http://www.apbt.org.tn/upload/telechargement/

[25] Sims, C (2002). Solving Linear Rational Expectations Models. Computational Economics 20, 1–20.

[26] Phillips, P. C. B., & Perron, P. (1988), Testing for a Unit Root in Time Series Regression, Biometrika, 75, 335-346.

[27] Johansen, S (1988) Statistical analysis of cointegration vectors, Journal of Economic Dynamics and Control 12, 231-254.

[28] Ahmedova, D. (2011). The impact of population Ageing on Private Savings Rate: Empirical Evidence from the OCDE Members Countries. Department of Economic, Central European University.

[29] Frini, O. (2021). The relationship aging of the population and saving in an unemployment context: Empirical evidence using an autoregressive distributed lag bounds testing approach. Australian Economic Papers, 60(1), 98-121. DOI:10.1111/1467-8454.12195.

[30] Wong, B. & Tang, K.K. (2013). Do Ageing Economies Save Less? Evidence from OECD Data, International Journal of Social Economics, 40(6), 591-605.

[31] Loumrhari, G. (2014). Ageing, Longevity and Savings: The Case of Morocco, *International Journal of Economics and Financial Issues*. 4, 344-352.

[32] Frini, O. (2018). Do elderly really dissave? Empirical analysis using ARDL and NARDL bounds approach'4èmes Journées Economiques et Financières Appliquées; Mahdia Tunisia 11 - 12 May 2018.

[33] Frini, O. (2021). The relationship aging of the population and saving in an unemployment context: Empirical evidence using an autoregressive distributed lag bounds testing approach. Australian Economic Papers, 60(1), 98-121. DOI: 10.1111/1467-8454.12195.

[34] Mahfoud Draoui, D. (2006). Entraide familiale et nouvelles formes de solidarité', 2ème table ronde des cercles de la population et de la santé de la reproduction; "dynamiques familiales et solidarités intergenérationnelles" ONFP, Tunis 24 February 2006.

[35] Frini, O. (1996). *Le transfert intergénérationnel et accumulation du capital humain: cas de la Tunisie.* A search dissertation.

[36] Frini, O. (2014). The Familial Network Influence on Fertility Behaviour in Tunisia. Journal of Economic and Social Research, 16(1–2), 33-61.

[37] AbuAl-Foul, B. (2010). The Causal Relation between Savings and Economic Growth: Some Evidence from MENA Countries', *The 30ThMEEA Meeting Atlanta*.

Chapter 4

Foreign Direct Divestment Phenomenon in Selected Sub-Saharan African Countries

Ombeswa Ralarala and Masenkane Happiness Makwala

Abstract

Foreign direct divestment can occur for either external or internal factors. The determinants of FDI are also the same determinants for FDD. FDD might lead to numerous negative economic factors such as a decline in economic development, reduction in employment and might also cripple the facilitation in technology transfers. In this paper, the FDD concept in the Sub-Saharan African countries was investigated using annual data spanning from 1998 to 2018. The panel autoregressive distributive lag was used to develop the FDD model. The findings of the panel ARDL long run equation revealed that lending rates and urbanisation have a negative and significant influence on foreign direct investment. Further, the findings revealed an insignificant influence of real gross domestic product per capita on FDI. Finally, trade openness showed a positive significant impact on foreign direct investment. We recommend policies that increase FDI through the cost of borrowing since increasing this results in foreign direct divestment. Real gross domestic product per capita cannot be used for policy making purposes in the study. Trade openness makes a country more accessible on the world market and thus, policies that promote foreign trade such as exporting complex and sophisticated products, trade liberalisation, free trade agreements and open trade systems could help reduce the presence of foreign direct divestment in the selected countries. Finally, urbanisation deter foreign direct investment, therefore countries should invest more on infrastructure and reduce poverty in rural areas to transform them into urban areas to decrease urbanisation.

Keywords: foreign direct divestment, panel autoregressive distributive lag, Sub-Saharan African countries

1. Introduction

Foreign investment and foreign trade remain interesting subject matters for most researchers, economists and governments owing to their prestigious impact on a country's aggregate economy and its sectors. With that being mentioned, notably less attention has been given to foreign direct divestment (FDD). FDD seems to be the most neglected area of research and it seems as if there is not much literature regarding this phenomenon. This study aims to address the FDD concept in selected Sub-Saharan African countries. Foreign direct divestment is a concept involving an adjustment in the ownership of a business that involves the partial or full disposal of an asset or a business unit [1]. Also, when there is an increase in the general prices of goods, it is referred to as inflation and the opposite as deflation. The same concept also applies when there is an increase in investment inflows from foreign nationals to a domestic economy, it is referred to as FDI inflows for the host economy and the opposite is referred to as FDD. This implies that foreign direct divestment occurs when there is a decrease in foreign direct investment. Most researchers, policy makers and governments seem to be mostly concerned about the trends in FDI while totally neglecting putting measures that may reduce or sidestep FDD to have consistent and stable FDI inflows and outflows.

FDD can occur for either external or internal factors. García-Bolívar [1] suggests that weak business climate seemingly contributes to a decision to divest as much as there is no proven direct correlation. FDD might lead to numerous negative economic factors such as a decline in economic development, reduction in employment and might also cripple the facilitation in technology transfers. Among other reasons, this might be because most developing and Sub-Saharan African countries use FDI to fill the gap between domestic investment and savings due to their low levels income. According to literature, the determinants of foreign direct investment are the same for foreign direct divestment but with the opposite sign. However, no consensus seems to have been reached regarding the determinants of FDI according to past studies [2].

Boddewyn found that foreign direct divestment is the opposite of FDI. Before divestment, there must be investment and there are also several studies across the globe on foreign direct investment, such as studies by Kumari and Sharma [2]; Tahmad and Adow [3].

Most studies have already established that there is investment but tend to pay little or no attention to the concept of divestment. This paper therefore aims to fill research gaps in literature by attempting to find any occurrences of foreign direct divestment during the period 1998–2018. The limited availability of data restricted the study from including all developing and all Sub-Saharan African countries. The countries under investigation are Botswana, Egypt, India, Namibia, Nigeria and South Africa. This study attempted to find variables that are most likely to cause foreign direct divestment. The chosen variables are real gross domestic product, trade openness, lending rates and urbanisation. The rest of the paper is therefore organised as follows, following the introductory section is Section 2 which presents the trends of FDI in the selected Sub-Saharan, developing and emerging countries. Section 3 presents the theoretical analysis of the macroeconomics of FDI and FDD. Section 4 gives a brief review of literature followed by Section 5 which discusses the methodology of the study. Section 6 focuses on the discussion of the empirical results and the last section concludes the study and provides recommendations.

2. FDI trends in the selected Sub-Saharan, developing and emerging economies

Figure 1 shows the trends of FDI inflows as a percentage of GDP for six countries from 1998 to 2018. The trends give an idea whether these countries are failing to attract FDI or it is merely investors losing interest. In the year 1999, Namibia was experiencing better inflows reaching a peak of roughly 11% than all other countries until it rapidly dropped in the year 2001. In South Africa, FDI inflows increased rapidly from 0.71% in 2000 to 6% and then significantly dropped within a year and this occurrence of foreign direct divestment was highly perceptible.

Botswana's vulnerability to external economic shocks was experienced during the global financial crisis of 2008. FDI inflows declined as signposted by [5] due

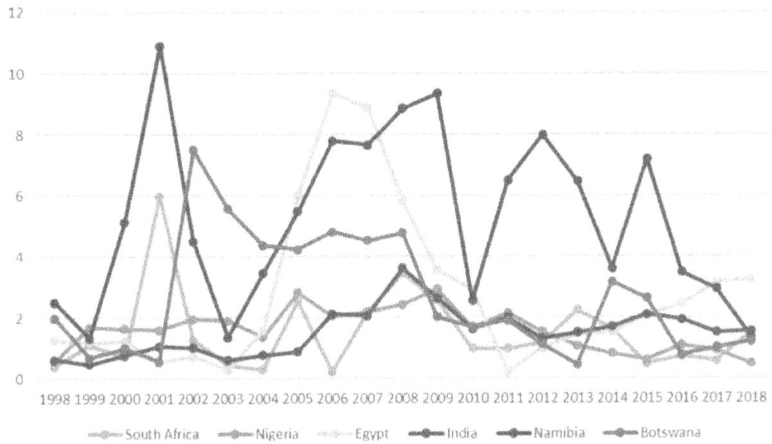

Figure 1.
FDI inflows as a percentage of GDP for the 1998 to 2018 period [4].

to the low global demand for minerals, which led to a sharp decline in commodity prices and volumes traded and this translated into provisional closures of diamond mines, and possible job losses. The country's dependence on minerals which are finite left it more susceptible to external economic shocks and this further entails that the country is nothing without its diamond mining. Also, evidence pointed out that Botswana has gone from being low-income nation to an upper-middle income country after the discovery of the diamond mine, with an increased real GDP averaged at 4.6% between 1994 and 2011 [5].

All countries experienced a foreign direct divestment after the world financial crisis in 2008 of which Namibia and Egypt mostly recovered in 2010 and 2011 respectively. This was the most severe financial crisis the world economy has ever faced since the Great Depression. These countries need to find ways that attract foreign investment to earn foreign currency and bring employment opportunities to their respective economies. In addition, Namibia's inflows seem to be upward trending over the years moving away from the mean average, say 1.5%. However, FDI inflows to developing countries remained quite stable since 2004 with an increase of roughly two percent relative to a decrease of 27 percent for developed economies [6].

The world recession owing to the global financial crisis was highly perceptible in 2008 as shown in **Figure 2**. This occurrence of foreign direct divestment was not

Figure 2.
World FDI inflows (US$ trillion) for the 1998 to 2018 period [4].

only experienced by developing and emerging economies as discussed earlier in **Figure 1** but the world economy as well. The world economy experienced another fall in FDI inflows from 2016 and this decline seem to be noticeable again in 2018 onward. In addition, world FDI flows continuously declined by 13 percent in 2018. This decline was due to United States (US) intercontinental enterprises through returns at US of tax reforms and foreign earnings [7].

The occurrence of foreign direct divestment in 2018 could also have been induced by the spillover effects of the US-China trade wars which could have affected the world economy through trade openness (measured by the sum of imports and exports) and made it difficult for some countries (particularly developing countries) to be accessible in the world market. US has since imposed tariffs of around $436 billion on Chinese goods since July 2008 until July 2019 and this trade war was significant and most likely to effect in some economic displacements [8]. The spillover effect of the US-China trade war is that both these countries affect any significant trade, economic and investment links and any direct foreign investment links with their respective trading partners [8].

3. The macroeconomics of foreign direct investment and foreign direct divestment: theoretical analyisis

The FDI trends discussed earlier in Section 2 have precisely shown the movement of foreign direct investment changing its direction heading to foreign direct divestment. This was due to the global financial crisis and the spillover effects of the US-China trade wars. That said, Maček [9] postulated that the dynamic economic progresses in the flow of economic and financial crisis have shown the likelihood of foreign direct investment changing its course resulting to FDD. This implies that FDI and FDD cannot occur simultaneously in a single economy, but each may occur in either South Africa, Nigeria, Egypt etc. The determinants of FDD are said to reciprocate those of FDI but with the opposite sign as suggested by Boddewyn [10]. This theory was developed from Dunning's theory of FDI. This implies that theoretical analysis of FDI concept also applies to FDD but in reverse. There are various studies that paid too much attention on FDI discussions but ignore the other side of the coin. This is like a detective who focuses on how to catch criminals but does not investigate the reasons for crime and how to prevent it. Here is what theory says concerning the rationale for both foreign direct investment and foreign direct divestment:

3.1 Dunning's FDI theory

There are three basic conditions that must be met for FDI to take place as postulated by Dunning [11]. (i) a firm has net competitive exclusive advantages in relation to other countries in serving specific markets. That said, these exclusive advantages are at least for a period notably to the firm or country owning them and mostly take form of the ownership of tangible assets. (ii) Assuming that the first condition is met, the firm owning these advantages must benefit when utilising them on its own relative to leasing or selling them to foreign firms. This implies that it must benefit through internalisation from its own activities in rather than externalising them through contracts and or licencing to foreign firms. (iii) If condition (i) and (ii) are assumed to have been satisfied, the firm must be profitable when utilising these advantages in alignment with a minimum of one factor input (natural resources included) outside its geographical borders. If not, Dunning stated that domestic markets would be served solely by domestic production and foreign markets by exports.

These three conditions explain the rationale for a firm to engage in FDI and international production activities if it has more ownership advantages, the better the incentive it holds to internalise them and the more it finds it more profitable to exploit them beyond its geographical boundaries [11]. This implies that these conditions are interrelated and must be satisfied simultaneously, and if not, FDI activities are more likely to change direction to divestment.

3.2 Boddewyn's FDD theory

Boddewyn's [10] used Dunning's theory of FDI to develop the foreign direct divestment concept. Boddewyn stated that violating at least one of Dunning's conditions of FDI would lead to foreign direct divestment. FDD occurs when: (i) a firm no longer has net competitive advantages over firms of other countries; (ii) or if it has the net competitive advantages, they are no longer beneficial for self-use rather than renting or selling them to foreign firms; (iii) or the firm no longer realise profits from using its internalised net competitive advantages beyond its national boundaries (i.e., the firm now finds it profitable to produce locally to domestic markets and export the surplus to foreign markets). This theory is quite simple and straightforward since it was adopted from Dunning's FDI theory. If one pays close attention, the differences between these theories is the opposite sign and the keywords "and" and "or" for the FDI and FDD theories, respectively. As mentioned earlier, Dunning's theory requires all the conditions to be met, hence the word "and" while Boddewyn's theory requires at least one condition [10]. Also, violating at least one of the Dunning's conditions to FDI leads to FDD. Therefore, these two theories extensively explain the rationale for both FDD and FDI to take place.

4. Literature review

This section is divided into theoretical (which adds to the theories already discussed in Section 3) and empirical literature reviewed by the study.

4.1 Theoretical review

4.1.1 The eclectic paradigm theory

Based on Dunning's three conditions in the Eclectic Paradigm, Boddewyn [10] found that foreign direct divestment occurs when a firm no longer enjoys the net competitive advantages over firms of other economies; or when it has competitive advantages but is not profitable to adopt these advantages; or it no longer benefits or enjoys less benefits to remain in other foreign markets through this mode as discussed earlier. In other words, Boddewyn [10] found that foreign direct divestment is the opposite of FDI, which entails that before divestment, there must be investment. According to the eclectic paradigm, multi-national corporations engage in foreign direct investment based on three advantages: ownership, location and internalisation advantages.

4.1.2 Strategic motivations of foreign direct investment

Strategic Motivations of Foreign Direct Investment was also adopted by the study. This theory was established by Knickerbocker [12] and later advanced by Graham [13, 14]. The distinguished feature of the strategic approach to FDI is that it believes that an initial inflow of FDI into a country will produce a reaction form the local producers in that country, so that FDI is a dynamic process. Dunning [15] explains that the process from the domestic producers can either be aggressive or defensive in nature. An aggressive response would be a price war or entry into the foreign firm's home market while a defensive response would be an acquisition or merger of other domestic producers to reinforce market power.

4.2 Empirical review

The influence of trade openness and real gross domestic product (GDP) per capita on FDI is controversial and little or no attention has been paid on FDD. It also seems as if there is no data available for the FDD proxy. However, Chen and Wu [16] add that the determinants of foreign direct investment are also the determinants for foreign direct divestment but with the opposite sign. Therefore, the study will review theoretical and empirical literature on foreign direct investment.

On utmost occasions, it is common that countries seek to attract FDI for several reasons, with various beliefs that FDI allows for more variety of positive societal activities that enable the flow of capital across nations. The variables found to be the most significant determinants of foreign direct investment are openness, market share, return on investment, infrastructure, market size, human capital, real labour costs, exchange rates, political risks, agglomeration and government incentives [2].

Past experiences provide an abundant clarification that FDI encourages exports and allows domestic firms and infant industries to enter the world markets while operating resourcefully by adopting latest technologies and attempt to be competitive, which highlights economic freedom worth to attracting FDI [17] and confirms the cause-and-effect mechanism for exports. Lipsey [18] defines the macroeconomic view as perceiving foreign direct investment as a specific system capital flow across national borders, from home economies to host economies, measured in statistics of balance-of-payments. These flows give rise to a precise form of capital stocks in host economies, precisely the value of home economy investment in entities, such as corporations, regulated by a home-country owner, or where home-country owner has a certain share of voting rights.

The Keynesian theory of investment by Keynes and Fisher as supported by Baddeley [19] and Alchian [20] state that speculations are made until the present estimation of future expected incomes at the margin equal to the opportunity cost of capital. Further, the return on speculation equals to Fisher's internal rate of return and Keynes' nominal productivity of capital. The theory highlights the significance of interest rates for investment decisions. A decrease in the interest rates amount to a decrease in the cost of investment in relation to the possible returns. According to this theory, a firm will only invest if the discounted return exceeds the cost of the project. Keynes yet believed that savings do not rely on interest rate but on level of income [21].

Khamis, Mohd and Muhammad [22] attempted to find the influence of inflation rate and GDP per capita on FDI inflows in United Arab Emirates during 1980 to 2013. The study used the ARDL model to examine the long-run relationships between the dependent and independent variables. The findings of the study revealed that inflation has no significant influence on FDI inflows. However GDP per capita proxy used for market size was found to have a significant positive effect on FDI inflows.

There are empirical studies such as those by Edwards [23], Gastanaga, Nugent and Pashamiva [24], Asiedu [25], Na and Lightfoot [26], Cevis and Çamurdan [27], Rogmans and Ebbers [28], Bagli and Adhikary [29], Donghui, Yasin, Zaman and Imran [30] found that FDI was positively related to trade openness of any economy. Musyoka and Ocharo [31] attempted to find the effect of real exchange rate, competitiveness and inflation on foreign direct investment in Kenya using time series data for the 1970 to 2016 period. The study used ordinary least squares regression technique for the variables in study. The findings of the study concluded that competitiveness has a positive and significant influence on FDI inflows, inflation was insignificant for the studied period which concur with the findings of Khamis *et al.* [22], and lastly real interest rates and exchange rates were found to have a negative significant impact on FDI inflows in Kenya. The study recommended that there is need for favourable interest rates, desirable exchange rates and trade liberalisation over comprehensive programmes to trade reforms, aimed to open the economy and increase its competitiveness, and government must encourage freedom of foreign capital transactions and competition in the local markets.

Kumari and Sharma [2] identified key determinants of FDI inflows in developing countries using unbalanced panel data for the 1990 to 2012 period. The study selected 20 developing countries from the South, East and South-East Asia. Using seven explanatory variables (market size, infrastructure, trade openness, interest rate, inflation, human capital and research and development), the study attempted to find the best fit model from the two models in consideration (fixed effect model and random effect model) with the help of Hausman test. The findings have shown that fixed effect estimation confirms that interest rates, market size, trade openness and human capital yield significant coefficients relative to FDI inflow for the panel of developing countries under study. In addition, findings revealed that market size was the most significant determinant of FDI inflow. The authors recommend than interest rates and inflation must be controlled and monitored since they have an influence on FDI.

Tahmad and Adow [3] investigated the long-run equilibrium relationship of trade openness and foreign direct investment in Sudan by sector during the 1990 to 2017 period. The study used the Johansson co-integration technique and the findings revealed that there is a long-run equilibrium co-integration between trade openness and FDI inflows estimated at negative 0.53 for the aggregate economy when trade openness is measured in terms of the sum of exports and imports over GDP. The degree of openness was estimated at positive values of 0.55, 0.17, and 0.9 for the industrial sector, the aggregate economy and the agricultural sector respectively. The findings indicated that for the studied period, FDI flows for the aggregate economy by sector are influenced by the extent of trade openness in terms of their combined measurement. Furthermore, the greatness of the extent of the industrial trade openness model is a strong one and the government must prioritise this sector regarding exports. The government must also encourage the manufacturing sector, thus promoting attentiveness of FDI in the country's production sectors and developing infrastructure, particularly those which support the paradigm that Sudan, like various Sub-Saharan African countries, should promote its primary exports to convert from a developing country to a developed one. The study suggests that, according to size of industrial sector trade openness degree, government should use more energy for it to expand and detect this sector as a leading sector utilising trade efficiently and therefore prioritise it in the export.

5. Methodology

This section discusses the methodology used in the study which was inspired by the FDI theory and the interest rates and investment theory. The study adopts an econometric model by using the panel ARDL procedure to examine occurrence of foreign direct divestment in Sub-Saharan countries [32].

5.1 Data

The study used panel annual data of six countries in the Sub-Saharan economies, emerging and developing economies from 1998 to 2018 due to availability of data and these countries were randomly selected to avoid any biases. The selected countries are South Africa, India, Nigeria, Italy, Egypt and Botswana. The secondary data for the following variables: foreign direct investment, trade openness, lending rates, real gross domestic product per capita and urbanisation was obtained from the World Bank.

$$FDI_{it} = \propto + \beta_1 LOPENNESS_{it} + \beta_2 LR_{it} + \beta_3 LRGDP_{it} + \beta_4 URB_{it} + \varepsilon_{it} \quad (1)$$

where ∝ = represents the constant parameter, LOPENNESS = log of trade openness measured by the sum of imports and exports. Trade openness is expected to have a positive influence on foreign direct investment according to the FDI theory. LR = lending rates which represents the cost of borrowing. Lending rates are expected to have a negative impact on foreign direct investment according to the inverse relationship between interest rates and investment theory. LRGDP = log of real gross domestic product per capita proxy for market size. URB = urbanisation as a percentage of total population.

5.2 Empirical analysis

The following econometric measures are undertaken to investigate the existence of foreign direct divestment in the Sub-Saharan, developing and emerging economies.

5.2.1 The panel unit root test

Before testing for long run cointegration among variables, the study used several tests for stationarity. The panel unit root test is conducted to determine the order of integration among variables which helps in identifying the best suitable model for the data used in the study. The several approaches to unit root testing used in the study for the panel data were Levin, Lin and Chu (2002) (LLC) test; Im, Pesaran, Shin (2003) (IPS) test and the Fisher- Augmented Dickey-Fuller (ADF) test as supported by Maddala and Wu [33].

5.2.2 The panel cointegration test

The panel cointegration test is useful when examining the existence of long run relationships between the regressors and the regressed variables. The Kao panel cointegration test which follows the same basic approach as the Pedroni test extends the Engle-Granger [34] framework to panel cointegration test. The distinct feature of the Kao test from the Pedroni test is that it typically stipulates the cross sections exact intercept and similar coefficients of regressors on the early stage. Also, the Kao and the Pedroni panel cointegration tests are generally used to examine the long run relationship between variables used in a study [35]. The Johansen-Fisher cointegration test uses the findings of the individual independent tests [36]. The Johansen-Fisher panel cointegration pioneered by Maddala and Wu [33] to examine the cointegration in panel data by incorporating the test from individual cross sections to get a test statistic for the whole panel. Say the π_i is the p-value from the distinct cointegration test for cross section i, under the null hypothesis of the panel.

$$-2\sum_{i-1}^{N} \log\left(x^2 \pi_i\right) \rightarrow x^2 2N \quad (2)$$

Therefore, the value of x^2 is built upon the MacKinnon-Haug-Michelis p-values for Johansen's cointegration trace test and maximum eigenvalue test.

5.2.3 The panel autoregressive distributed lag procedure

The autoregressive distributed lag (ARDL) procedure supported by Pesaran et al. [32] which combines lags of both explained and explanatory variables as regressors is used in the study. The ARDL model is used owing to its ability to join small sample size data and yet generating useful findings [34, 37]. Johansen and Juselius [37] point that the traditional cointegration technique have fewer advantages compared to ARDL that has several advantages. First, it requires small sample size, with variables that are pure I(1), purely I(0) or integrated at different orders of integration but not I(2) [37]. Secondly, it does not require variables to be integrated in the same order compared to the Johansen cointegration approach. Thirdly, ARDL approach caters for any structural breaks in a time series. And lastly, this approach carries a method of measuring the long run and short run findings of one variable on the other and as well distinct both once an appropriate selection of order of the ARDL model is made [38]. Regardless of these advantages, the study employed this model due to its small sample sized panel data and the variables used are integrated at different orders of integration.

6. Results and discussion

Levin, Lin & Chu, Im, Pesaran and Chin W-stat and Augmented Dickey Fuller – Fisher Chi-square tests were employed to perform the panel unit root test and it was discovered that the variables are integrated at different orders of integration [$I(0)$ and $I(1)$] and none of which are $I(2)$. This gave justification to use panel ARDL. For instance, foreign direct investment was stationary at level, $I(0)$ for all tests. Trade openness was stationary at $I(1)$ for IPS and Fisher-ADF. Further, lending rates became stationary at 1%, 5% and 10% level of significance for all tests after first differencing. Gross domestic product was stationary at $I(1)$ for LLC at 10% level of significance and IPS and Fisher-ADF at 5% respectively. Finally, urbanisation was stationary at $I(1)$ for all tests (**Table 1**).

Having established the order of integration for the panel series, the next step is to examine the probability of long-run association between variables. The study will begin with the Kao panel cointegration test. The p-value of 0.004 in the ADF test is less than 0.05 and thus the null hypothesis of no cointegration is rejected and fail to reject the alternative hypothesis of cointegration between the variables. Therefore, the variables have a long run relationship according to the Kao panel cointegration test (**Table 2**).

The test results of the Johansen Fisher panel cointegration with linear deterministic trend test are shown in **Table 3**. Johansen Fisher panel cointegration test results indicate that the trace statistic has five cointegrating equations and the Fisher

Variables	Tests	Test equations	P-value [level]	P-value [1st difference]
FDI	LLC	Individual & intercept	0.0177	–
		Individual, intercept & trend	0.0113	–
	IPS	Individual & intercept	0.0053	–
		Individual, intercept & trend	0.0812	–
	Fisher-ADF	Individual & intercept	0.0051	–
		Individual, intercept & trend	0.0888	–
LOPENNESS	LLC	Individual & intercept	0.028	0.0022
		Individual, intercept & trend	0.5713	0.1015
	IPS	Individual & intercept	0.0511	0.0011
		Individual, intercept & trend	0.5015	0.0682
	Fisher-ADF	Individual & intercept	0.1048	0.0028
		Individual, intercept & trend	0.5017	0.0996
LR	LLC	Individual & intercept	0.2676	0.0000
		Individual, intercept & trend	0.1315	0.0000
	IPS	Individual & intercept	0.1922	0.0000
		Individual, intercept & trend	0.0743	0.0000
	Fisher-ADF	Individual & intercept	0.1903	0.0000
		Individual, intercept & trend	0.0856	0.0000
LRGDP	LLC	Individual & intercept	0.3227	0.0974
		Individual, intercept & trend	0.4345	0.0782
	IPS	Individual & intercept	0.9084	0.0117
		Individual, intercept & trend	0.6837	0.0309
	Fisher-ADF	Individual & intercept	0.5518	0.0160
		Individual, intercept & trend	0.2319	0.0428
URB	LLC	Individual & intercept	0.0829	0.0000
		Individual, intercept & trend	0.0039	0.0000
	IPS	Individual & intercept	0.9798	0.0000
		Individual, intercept & trend	0.0009	0.0000
	Fisher-ADF	Individual & intercept	0.6535	0.0000
		Individual, intercept & trend	0.0002	0.0007

Source: Author's compilation from E-views.

Table 1.
Summary of panel unit root test results.

maximum-eigen test also shows five cointegrating equations at a 10%, 5% and 1% significance level. The first four equations shows that all p-values are statistically significant at 10%, 5% and 1% level of significance respectively (only one equation at 10%) thus rejecting the null hypothesis of no cointegration. This indicates that there is long run relationship between the variables.

In **Table 4**, the test results of Johansen Fisher panel cointegration with no deterministic trend test indicates that all p-values are significant at 10%, 5% and 1% level of significance respectively (only the last equation at 10%). Therefore, the

Variable	t-Statistic	P-value
ADF	−3.385868	0.0004
Residual variance	3.624602	
HAC variance	1.520078	

Table 2.
Kao panel cointegration test results.

Hypothesised no. of CE(s)	Fisher stat.* (from trace test)	Prob.	Fisher stat.* (from max-eigen test)	Prob.
None	187.9***	0.0000	128.2***	0.0000
At most 1	91.75***	0.0000	57.50***	0.0000
At most 2	44.24***	0.0000	35.63***	0.0004
At most 3	19.57*	0.0756	18.73*	0.0953
At most 4	14.56	0.2664	14.56	0.2664

*Note: *, **, and *** indicate that the p-values are significant at 10%, 5% and 1% level of significance respectively. The Fisher's test applies regardless of the dependent variable.*

Table 3.
Johansen Fisher panel cointegration with linear deterministic trend test.

Hypothesised no. of CE(s)	Fisher stat.* (from trace test)	Prob.	Fisher stat.* (from max-eigen test)	Prob.
None	192.5***	0.0000	105.9***	0.0000
At most 1	108.7***	0.0000	62.16***	0.0000
At most 2	62.58***	0.0000	40.67***	0.0001
At most 3	37.08***	0.0002	32.36***	0.0012
At most 4	19.05*	0.0874	19.05*	0.0874

*Note: *, **, and *** indicate that the p-values are significant at 10%, 5% and 1% level of significance respectively. The Fisher's test applies regardless of the dependent variable.*

Table 4.
Johansen Fisher panel cointegration with no deterministic trend test.

null hypothesis of no cointegration is rejected, indicating that there is a long run relationship between the variables.

Table 5 shows the test results of the Johansen Fisher panel cointegration with Quadratic deterministic trend test. The results indicate that all p-values are significant at 10%, 5% and 1% level of significance, meaning that the null hypothesis of no cointegration is rejected. This indicates that the variables are cointegrated in the long run.

Table 6a and **b** show the Autoregressive Distributive Lag Short Run and Long Run Results. The long run results indicated that there is an insignificant long run relationship between gross domestic product and FDI (dependent variable) and cannot be used for policy making purposes in this study. These findings contradicts with the findings of Pegkas [39] with FDI as an independent variable. Further, the results showed that lending rates coefficient had a negative significant long run impact on FDI at 5% level of significance. This indicates that if lending rates were to increase by one percent, FDI for the panel six Sub-Saharan and developing economies would

Hypothesised no. of CE(s)	Fisher stat.* (from trace test)	Prob.	Fisher stat.* (from max-eigen test)	Prob.
None	283***	0.0000	387.1***	0.0000
At most 1	102.2***	0.0000	64.2***	0.0000
At most 2	54.83***	0.0000	26.8***	0.0083
At most 3	40.32***	0.0001	28.75***	0.0043
At most 4	35.46***	0.0004	35.46***	0.0004

*Note: *, **, and *** indicate that the p-values are significant at 10%, 5% and 1% level of significance.*

Table 5.
Johansen Fisher panel cointegration with quadratic deterministic trend test.

Variable	Coefficient	Std. Error	t-Statistic	P-value
(a) Long run results				
LRGDP	−1.411786	8.392655	−0.168217	0.8669
LR	−0.167845	0.080281	−2.090724	0.0400
LOPENNESS	20.6322	1.689844	12.20953	0.0000
URB	−2.236179	0.49482	−4.519181	0.0000
(b) Short run results				
ECT(−1)	−0.925834	0.33952	−2.726895	0.0080
D(FDI(−1))	0.131771	0.23861	0.552243	0.5824
D(LRGDP)	−1.231988	32.44146	−0.037976	0.9698
D(LR)	0.308568	0.138535	2.227367	0.0290
D(LOPENNESS)	−4.313282	4.535335	−0.951039	0.3447
D(URB)	−4.99435	2.965234	−1.684302	0.0963
C	69.30302	26.85282	2.580847	0.0118

Notes: D-denotes differenced results for short run.

Table 6.
(a and b) Autoregressive distributed lag short run and long run results.

decrease by 16.7845%. The findings are in line with Musyoka and Ocharo [31] who discovered that real interest rates have a negative significant impact on foreign direct investment inflows. This further implies that increasing the cost of borrowing will lead to foreign direct divestment in the countries, thus resulting in a decline in inflows. This also indicates that FDI is particularly sensitive to increase in cost of borrowing as suggested by theory on interest rates and investment.

Trade openness had a positive significant long run relationship with FDI at 10%, 5% and 1% level. This concur with the findings of Kumari and Sharma [2] which revealed that trade openness was significant at 10% level. Furthermore, these findings supports the FDI theory that states that for investment purposes, degree of openness indicates the ease with which a host country is accessible in the world market. Finally, urbanisation showed a negative significant long run relationship with FDI at 10%, 5% and 1% level of significance.

The relationship between the coefficients in **Table 6** can also be represented in an equation to further understand their meaning and their influence on FDI. Lending rates and urbanisation both had a significant negative influence on foreign direct investment indicating that an increase in these variables would lead to what we refer to as foreign direct divestment for these selected Sub-Saharan and developing economies. Trade openness showed a positive significant influence on FDI, implying increasing trade openness increases FDI and a decrease leads to foreign direct divestment.

$$FDI_{it} = \propto +20.6322LOPENNES_{it} + 20.6322LR_{it} + -1.4117LRGDP_{it} + -2.2362URB_{it} + \varepsilon_{it} \tag{3}$$

In the short run, the critical part of the analysis is the error correction term (ECT), which must always be negative according to theory otherwise the model will be explosive and may never return to equilibrium if it is positive. ECT is also referred to the speed of adjustment which shows whether the estimated economic models will be able to return to equilibrium or not and at what speed.

The estimated speed of adjustment, which is at −0.925834, has a negative sign and it is significant at 1% level of significance, as expected by theory. A highly significant speed of adjustment also confirms the existence of cointegration among the variables and a stable long run relationship. This indicates that there is a long-run causality running from the independent variables to the dependent variable and that approximately 93 percent of disequilibrium is corrected each year. It will take 93 percent each year for foreign direct investment activity to return to equilibrium, which is not a slow movement back to equilibrium.

7. Conclusion and recommendations

The aim of the study was to investigate the presence of any noticeable foreign direct divestment, that is any perceptible rapid drop of FDI inflows in the Sub-Saharan African countries using annual panel data from 1998 to 2018. The FDI inflows trends established that there was a rapid decline of FDI inflows for all selected countries after the 2008 global financial crisis and the spillover effects US-China trade war. The study used panel autoregressive distributed lag to determine long run and short run equation for variables that are likely to influence foreign direct investment. The study began by testing for unit root using Levin, Lin & Chu, Im, Pesaran and Chin W-stat and Augmented Dickey Fuller – Fisher Chi-square tests and it was discovered that the variables are integrated at different orders of integration [I(0) and I(1)] and none of which are I(2). The Kao and the Johansen Fisher panel cointegration tests confirmed the long run cointegration among the variables.

The findings of the long run equation revealed that lending rates and urbanisation have a negative and significant influence on foreign direct investment. Further, the findings revealed an insignificant influence of real gross domestic product per capita on FDI. Finally, trade openness showed a positive significant impact on foreign direct investment. This was in line with the FDI theory that states that for investment purposes, degree of openness indicates the ease with which a host coun try is accessible in the world market. The error correction model also divulged that approximately 93% of disequilibrium will converge towards equilibrium annually.

Like any quantitative or econometrics research, this study also had some limitations. For instance, the period of study ended in 2018 due to unavailability of data for some countries. Lack of data and literature on foreign direct divestment and the absence of data on key variables such as corruption, political risks, labour costs, natural resources and exchange rates may be perceived as limitations. Also, controlling variables such as corruption, exchange rate, political risk and labor cost could make significant improvements to this study. The study also have practical and significant implications for researchers, scholars, governments, policy makers, managers and notably foreign investors.

We recommend policies that increase FDI through cost of borrowing since increasing interest rates result in foreign direct divestment. Real gross domestic product per capita (market size) cannot be used for policy making purposes in the study. Trade openness makes a country accessible on the world market, therefore, policies that promote foreign trade such as exporting complex products, shifting production capabilities from raw materials to more sophisticated products and services, reduce dependence on the primary sector, trade liberalisation, free trade agreements and open trade systems could help reduce the presence of foreign direct divestment in the selected countries. Finally, urbanisation deter foreign direct investment, therefore countries should invest on infrastructure and reduce poverty in rural areas to transform them into urban areas to reduce urbanisation.

JEL classification

E20; F20; F17

Author details

Ombeswa Ralarala* and Masenkane Happiness Makwala
University of Limpopo, Polokwane, South Africa

*Address all correspondence to: ombeswa.ralarala@ul.ac.za

References

[1] García-Bolívar, O.E., 2020. Business Climate: When Weakness Means Foreign Direct Divestment. In Foreign Direct Investment Perspective Through Foreign Direct Divestment. IntechOpen.

[2] Kumari, R. and Sharma, A.K., 2017. Determinants of foreign direct investment in developing countries: a panel data study. *International Journal of Emerging Markets*.

[3] Tahmad, A.M.I. and Adow, A.H., 2018. The impact of trade openness on foreign direct investment in Sudan by sector in the 1990-2017 period: an empirical analysis. Economic annals-XXI, (172), pp. 14-22.

[4] World Bank (2020). World Development Indicators 2020. Washington, D.C.: World Bank.

[5] Makoni, P.L., 2015. Foreign Direct Investment–The Case of Botswana. Acta Universitatis Danubius. Œconomica, 11(4), pp. 160-173.

[6] UNCTAD. 2019. World Investment Report (WIR) 2019.

[7] Ren, Y., Sankara, J. and Trimble, M., 2020. The Impact of the Tax Cuts and Jobs Act's Repatriation Tax on Financial Statements. The CPA Journal, *90*(1), pp. 34-39

[8] Ajami, RA. 2020. US-China Trade War: The Spillover Effect, Journal of Asia-Pacific Business, 21:1, 1-3, DOI: 10.1080/10599231.2020.1708227

[9] Maček, A. ed., 2021. *Foreign Direct Investment Perspective through Foreign Direct Divestment*. BoD–Books on Demand.

[10] Boddewyn, J.J. 1983. "Foreign direct divestment theory: is it the reverse of FDI theory?", Review of World Economics, vol. 119, no. 2, pp. 345-355.

[11] Dunning, J.H., 1979. Explaining changing patterns of international production: in defence of the eclectic theory. Oxford bulletin of economics and statistics, 41(4), pp. 269-295.

[12] Knickerbocker, F.T., 1973. Oligopolistic reaction and multinational enterprise. The International Executive, 15(2), pp. 7-9.

[13] Graham, E.M., 1978. Transatlantic investment by multinational firms: a rivalistic phenomenon?. Journal of post Keynesian economics, 1(1), pp. 82-99.

[14] Graham, E.M., 1998. Market structure and the multinational enterprise: a game-theoretic approach. Journal of International Business Studies, 29(1), pp. 67-83.

[15] Dunning, J.H., 1996. The geographical sources of the competitiveness of firms: some results of a new survey. Reading: University of Reading, Department of Economics.

[16] Chen, T.J. and Wu, G., 1996. Determinants of divestment of FDI in Taiwan. Weltwirtschaftliches Archiv, *132*(1), pp. 172-184.

[17] Apergis, N., Lyroudi, K. and Vamvakidis, A., 2008. The relationship between foreign direct investment and economic growth: evidence from transition countries. Transition Studies Review, 15(1), pp. 37-51.

[18] Lipsey, R.E. 2004. "Home-and host-country effects of foreign direct investment" in Challenges to globalization: *Analyzing the economics University of Chicago Press*, pp. 333-382.

[19] Baddeley, M.C. 2003. *Investment Theory and* Analysis, Palgrave Macmillan, New York.Central Bank of Kenya (2015). Monetary Policy

[20] Alchian, A. A. 1955. The Rate of Interest, Fisher's Rate of Return over Cost, and Keynes' Internal Rate of Return, *American Economic Review*, Vol. 45no. 5,938-943.

[21] Eklund E.J. 2013. "Theories of investment: A Theoretical Review with Empirical Applications", *Swedish Entrepreneurship Forum.*

[22] Khamis, H A., Mohd, RH. and Muhammad A. 2015. The impact of inflation and GDP per capita on foreign direct investment: the case of United Arab Emirates. Investment Management and Financial Innovations, 12(3-1), 132-141.

[23] Edwards, S. 1990, "Capital flows, foreign direct investment, and debt-equity swaps in developing countries", No. w3497, National Bureau of Economic Research.

[24] Gastanaga, V.M., Nugent, J.B. and Pashamova, B. 1998., "Host country reforms and FDI inflows: how much difference do they make?", World Development, Vol. 26 No. 7, pp. 1299-1314.

[25] Asiedu, E. 2002. "On the determinants of foreign direct investment to developing countries: is Africa different?", World Development, Vol. 30 No. 1, pp. 107-119.

[26] Na, L. and Lightfoot, W.S., 2006. Determinants of foreign direct investment at the regional level in China. Journal of Technology Management in China.

[27] Cevis, I. and Çamurdan, B. 2007. "The economic determinants of foreign direct investment in developing countries and transition economies", The Pakistan Development Review, Vol. 46 No. 3, pp. 285-299.

[28] Rogmans, T. and Ebbers, H. 2013. "The determinants of foreign direct investment in the Middle East North Africa region", International Journal of Emerging Markets, Vol. 8 No. 3, pp. 240-257.

[29] Bagli, S. and Adhikary, M. 2014, "FDI inflow and economic growth in India an empirical analysis", Economic Affairs, Vol. 59 No. 1, pp. 23-33.

[30] Donghui, Z., Yasin, G., Zaman, S. and Imran, M., 2018. Trade Openness and FDI Inflows: A Comparative Study of Asian Countries. *European Online Journal of Natural and Social Sciences*, *7*(2), pp. pp-386.

[31] Musyoka, N. and Ocharo, K.N., 2018. Real interest rate, inflation, exchange rate, competitiveness and foreign direct investment in Kenya. American journal of economics, *3*(1), pp. 1-18.

[32] Pesaran, M., Shin, Y., & Smith, R. 2001. Bounds Testing Approaches to the Analysis of Level Relationships. Journal of Applied Econometrics, *16*(3), 289-326.

[33] Maddala, G. S. and Wu, S. 1999. 'A comparative study of unit root tests with panel data and a new simple test', Oxford Bulletin of Economics and Statistics, 61(S1), pp. 631-652.

[34] Engle, R. F., & Granger, C. W. J. 1987. Co-integration and error correction: representation estimation and testing, Econometrica, 55(2) 251-276

[35] Ahmad, F. 2015. Determinants of savings behavior in Pakistan: Long run-short run association and causality. Timisoara Journal of Economics and Business, 8 (1), 103- 136.

[36] Fisher, R. A. 1932. Statistical Methods for Research Workers, 4th Edition. Oliver & Boyd: Edinburgh.

[37] Johansen, S., & Juselius, K. 1990. Maximum likelihood estimation and

DOI: http://dx.doi.org/10.5772/intechopen.100304

inference on cointegration with application to the demand for money. Oxford bulletin of economics and statistics, 3(52) 169-210.

[38] Bentzen, J and Engsted, T. 2001. A Revival of the ARDL Model in Estimating Energy Demand Relationship (Cointegration: Bounds Testing Approah). Vol. 26.

[39] Pegkas, P., 2015. The impact of FDI on economic growth in Eurozone countries. The Journal of Economic Asymmetries, 12(2), pp. 124-132.

Chapter 5

Taxation and Redistribution against Inequality: A Mathematical Model

Maria Letizia Bertotti

Abstract

Reducing inequality is a tremendously important sustainable development goal. Albeit providing stylised frames for modelling, also mathematics can contribute to understanding and explaining the emergence of collective patterns in complex socio-economic systems. It can then effectively help to identify actions and measures to be taken and support policy-makers towards adoption of conceivable welfare measures aimed at halting the growth of inequality. Based on these assumptions, we here discuss some variants of a mathematical "micro-to-macro" model for the dynamics of taxation and redistribution processes in a closed trading market society. The model has an exploratory character resulting from possible tuning of various parameters involved: through its analysis, one can foresee the consequences on the long-run income distributions of different fiscal policies and differently weighted welfare policies, interventions, and subsidy provision, as well as the impact of the extent of tax evasion. In short, the model shows that in the long term redistributive policy results in a lower level of economic inequality in society.

Keywords: taxation and redistribution, welfare, income distribution, economic inequality, mathematical models

1. Introduction

Income disparities and economic inequality are all but recent problems. They are, however, becoming worryingly and increasingly significant (for a few references in this regard see e.g. [1–7]). In fact, reducing inequality within and between countries is one of the sustainable development goals included in the 2030 Agenda of by the United Nations General Assembly. Certainly, such an objective is, as least in the first instance, a main responsibility and competence of economists and policy-makers. Nonetheless, mathematics can provide some hints and contributions towards it.

The goal of this chapter is to provide a brief illustration of the role that mathematics can play in this regard. By way of example, we will recall an elementary (first approximation) model first proposed by Bertotti in [8], together with some variants and extensions of it, developed and investigated in a series of other studies by Bertotti et al. [9–13].

The approach of this model can be seen as a contribution attempt in the spirit of complexity economics. This paradigm, which began to take shape in the late 1980s, looks at the economy as an evolving system, not in equilibrium, and puts emphasis on the process through which structures and patterns emerge from the micro-interactions (see e.g. [14–16]). Similarly, the perspective of the model here discussed is to put the interactions among heterogeneous individuals at the very heart of the question. These interactions lead to self-organised collective features and macro-observables, which emerge from the system as a whole.

It should be noted here that during the last two/three decades a research line has been developing, not only but mostly among the physicist's community, which addresses socio-economic questions and phenomena using ideas, methods and tools, which have their roots in statistical mechanics and the kinetic theory of gases. An explanation for that comes from the existing analogy, for example, between complex systems composed by a number of individuals who interact exchanging money with each other (may be participating in a financial market) and physical systems consisting of a huge number of particles (atoms or molecules), which interact with each other undergoing collisions.

A variety of tools and techniques, including for example Boltzmann type equations, Fokker-Planck type equations, Ising type models and agent-based simulations, have been adapted and employed in this connection. See for example references [17–21] and the survey papers [22, 23] that offer an interesting historical perspective and also contain extensive bibliographies.

The model developed in the paper [8] and then further generalised and explored in subsequent work [9–13] differs to a great extent from those we know belonging to the mentioned literature strand. The motivation behind [8] was precisely to understand how the taxation process and diverse fiscal systems could affect the income distribution of a population. Aiming at modelling a fiscal system with taxes on personal income levied at a finite number of progressive rates, with high-income earners expected to pay more than low-income earners, as in the case of the Italian IRPEF (Imposta sul Reddito delle Persone Fisiche), the most natural approach seemed to be one dividing a population into a finite number of income classes. This is the reason behind the construction of a discrete framework, suitable for the formulation of the model, which will be briefly recalled in the next section. Albeit expressed using a system of ordinary differential equations (ODE)—as many as the income classes in the society—the model incorporates stochastic and probabilistic components. In a nutshell, the ODE system governs the evolution in time of the income distribution, generated by a whole of money exchanges expressing binary individual interactions, and a whole of withdrawals and earnings of the individuals, due to taxation and redistribution. Specifically, each differential equation in the system describes the variation in time of the fraction of individuals belonging to a certain class. As we will see in the next section, the framework allows possible tuning of various parameters (the frequencies with which the interactions are supposed to occur, the probability that in an encounter between two individuals the one who pays is one or the other, the tax rates or other) that give it an exploratory character.

The study of the dynamics of the model, supported by some analytical results and, inevitably, largely pursued through numerical simulations (performed using Mathematica software [24]), focuses on the asymptotic behaviour of the system. What all simulations suggest is that after a sufficiently long time the solutions of the equations reach a stationary state corresponding to an income distribution, which depends on the total wealth and the interaction parameters, but not on the specific initial distribution. This stationary state represents in fact a macro-observable feature. At the micro-individual level, the economic exchanges continue to take place and the situation is a non-equilibrium one.

The interest is to find and compare one with the other different shapes of the asymptotic income distributions corresponding to different fiscal policies. In this connection, the model shows that over time redistributive policy leads to a reduction of economic inequality.

The rest of the chapter is organised as follows:

In Section 2, we recall the framework of the original model.

In Section 3, we revisit some insights and extensions of the model discussed in previous work. The issues include the following:

- the occurrence of fat tails of the asymptotic income distribution in cases with a high number of classes;
- the existence of a very good fit of certain asymptotic income distributions with cases (characterised by suitable parameters) of the κ-generalised distribution introduced by Kaniadakis [25] and then analysed in connection with real data in the works [26, 27];
- the incorporation in the model of an additional welfare form;
- the analysis of the negative correlation between economic inequality and social mobility predicted by the model;
- the effect of tax evasion.

In Section 4, a novel application of the model is developed, which shows the impact of different fiscal policies.

Section 5 contains concluding considerations.

2. General framework

Referring the reader to the paper [8] for further explanations and details on the mechanism behind the formulation of the proposed framework, we recall here that, if n denotes the number of income classes of a population, characterised by their average incomes $r_1 < r_2 < \ldots < r_n$, and $x_i(t)$, with $x_i : \mathbf{R} \to [0, +\infty)$ for $i = 1, 2, \ldots, n$ denotes the fraction at the time t of individuals belonging to the i-th class (with the normalisation $\sum_{i=1}^{n} x_i = 1$), the variation in time of the quantities $x_i(t)$ may be thought to obey a system of differential equations of the form

$$dx_i dt = \sum_{h=1}^{n} \sum_{k=1}^{n} \left(C_{hk}^{i} + T_{[hk]}^{i}(x) \right) x_h x_k - x_i \sum_{k=1}^{n} x_k, \qquad i = 1, 2, \ldots, n. \tag{1}$$

The coefficients C_{hk}^{i}'s and the continuous functions $T_{[hk]}^{i}$'s in (Eq. (1)) incorporate the instructions for the variation of the fraction of individuals (i.e. the movement of individuals) from one class to another. They keep into account "impoverishment and enrichment" due both to direct money exchanges taking place between pairs of individuals and to the (small) withdrawals and earnings of each individual, due to taxation and redistribution, processes that are here considered as occurring in correspondence to each transaction. More precisely, $C_{hk}^{i} \in [0, +\infty)$ expresses the probability density that an individual of the h-th class will belong to the i-th class after a direct interaction with an individual of the k-th class. Accordingly, the identity $\sum_{i=1}^{n} C_{hk}^{i} = 1$ has to be satisfied for any fixed h and k;

- $T^i_{[hk]} : \mathbf{R}^n \to \mathbf{R}$ expresses the variation density in the i-th class due to an interaction between an individual of the h-th class with an individual of the k-th class. The functions $T^i_{[hk]}$ are required to satisfy $\sum_{i=1}^{n} T^i_{[hk]}(x) = 0$ for any fixed h, k and $x \in \mathbf{R}^n$.

Specific expressions for these quantities have to be carefully calibrated if we want, as is the case in the model at hand, to treat a case in which the total amount of money is constant. Towards this, let

- S denote a fixed minimum amount of money that individuals may exchange;
- $p_{h,k}$ (for $h, k = 1, 2, \dots, n$) denote the probability that in an interaction between an individual of the h-th class with an individual of the k-th class, the one who pays is the former one. In principle, no interaction may occur between individuals of two classes, and thus, the $p_{h,k}$ are required to satisfy $0 \leq p_{h,k} \leq 1$ and $p_{h,k} + p_{k,h} \leq 1$;
- $0 \leq \tau_1 \leq \tau_2 \leq \dots \leq \tau_n \leq 1$ denote the tax rates relative to the n income classes.

The ratio for the definition of C^i_{hk} and $T^i_{[hk]}$ is that when an individual of the h-th class pays a quantity S to an individual of the k-th class, this one in turn has to pay a tax $S\tau_k$. The government, for its part, redistributes to the entire population the revenue collected by all taxes and this one in particular (this redistribution may be interpreted as public expenditure in health, education, security and defence, transports and so on). From a practical standpoint, the effect of a payment of S from an h-individual to a k-individual can be thought, bypassing the government, as the same of a payment of $S(1-\tau_k)$ from the h-individual to the k-individual and payment of $S\tau_k$ from the h-individual to the entire population.

Skipping here some technical details, we recall that the expressions proposed in paper [8] for C^i_{hk} and $T^i_{[hk]}$ are as follows: each C^i_{hk} can be written as $C^i_{hk} = a^i_{hk} + b^i_{hk}$, where the only nonzero elements a^i_{hk} are $a^i_{ij} = 1$ for $i, j = 1, 2, \dots, n$ and the only possibly nonzero elements b^i_{hk} are those of the form

$$\begin{aligned} b^i_{i+1,k} &= p_{i+1,k} S \frac{1-\tau_k}{r_{i+1} - r_i}, \\ b^i_{i,k} &= -p_{k,i} S \frac{1-\tau_i}{r_{i+1} - r_i} - p_{i,k} S \frac{1-\tau_k}{r_i - r_{i-1}}, \\ b^i_{i-1,k} &= p_{k,i-1} S \frac{1-\tau_{i-1}}{r_i - r_{i-1}}, \end{aligned} \tag{2}$$

whereas $T^i_{[hk]}(x) = U^i_{[hk]}(x) + V^i_{[hk]}(x)$, with

$$U^i_{[hk]}(x) = \frac{p_{h,k} S \tau_k}{\sum_{j=1}^{n} x_j} \left(\frac{x_{i-1}}{r_i - r_{i-1}} - \frac{x_i}{r_{i+1} - r_i} \right), \tag{3}$$

and

$$V^i_{[hk]}(x) = p_{h,k} S \tau_k \left(\frac{\delta_{h,i+1}}{r_h - r_i} - \frac{\delta_{h,i}}{r_h - r_{i-1}} \right) \frac{\sum_{j=1}^{n-1} x_j}{\sum_{j=1}^{n} x_j}. \tag{4}$$

In particular, $U^i_{[hk]}(x)$ keeps track of the advancement from a class to the subsequent one, due to the benefit of tax revenue redistribution and $V^i_{[hk]}(x)$ of the retrocession from a class to the preceding one, due to the payment of some tax. The symbol $\delta_{h,k}$ denotes the *Kronecker delta* and all expressions are to be thought as present only for meaningful values of the indices.

Well-posedness of the equation system (Eq. (1)) is proved in [8]: in correspondence to any initial condition $x_0 = (x_{01}, \dots, x_{0n})$ with $x_{0i} \geq 0$ for all $i = 1, 2, \dots, n$ and $\sum_{i=1}^n x_{0i} = 1$, a unique solution $x(t) = (x_1(t), \dots, x_n(t))$ of (Eq. (1)), satisfying $x(0) = x_0$, exists, defined for all $t \in [0, +\infty)$, and such that for all $t \geq 0$, both $x_i(t) \geq 0$ for $i = 1, 2, \dots, n$ and $\sum_{i=1}^n x_i(t) = 1$ hold true. Hence, the solutions of (Eq. (1)) are distribution functions. Also, the expressions of $U^i_{[hk]}(x)$ and $V^i_{[hk]}(x)$ above simplify becoming linear in the variables x_j and the right-hand sides of (Eq. (1)) turn out to be polynomials of degree three.

A second result proved in [8] is that the scalar function $\mu(x) = \sum_{i=1}^n r_i x_i$, expressing the global income (total amount of money) and, due to the population normalisation, also the mean income, is a first integral for the system (Eq. (1)).

Also, the following empirical fact (not analytically proved) is recognised to be true according to a large number of numerical simulations. If the parameters in the model are fixed, for any fixed value of the global income μ, a unique asymptotic stationary solution of (Eq. (1)) exists to which all solutions $x(t) = (x_1(t), \dots, x_n(t))$ satisfying $x(0) = x_0$ with $\mu(x_0) = \mu$ (i.e. all solutions evolving from initial conditions which share the same value μ of the global income) tend as $t \to \infty$.

As already emphasised, a great freedom remains for the choice of various parameters, namely the average incomes $r_1, r_2, \dots, r_n$, the tax rates $\tau_1, \tau_2, \dots, \tau_n$, and the $p_{h,k}$ for $h, k = 1, 2, \dots, n$. Different cases were already considered in [8].

3. Properties of the model and its variants

The first result of interest from a socio-economic point of view, which is discussed in [8] is that for fixed parameters $r_1, r_2, \dots, r_n$ and $p_{h,k}$ $(h, k = 1, 2, \dots, n)$ and fixed growth laws of the tax rates $0 \leq \tau_1 \leq \tau_2 \leq \dots < \tau_n \leq 1$, the effect of an increase of the difference $\tau_n - \tau_1$ between the maximum and the minimum tax rate in correspondence to the stationary income distribution is an increase of the fraction of individuals belonging to the middle classes, accompanied by a decrease of the fraction of individuals belonging to the poorest and the richest classes. We remark that only five income classes were considered in [8], the motivation being that the number of different tax rates generally foreseen in real world is similarly small (in Italy the number of the IRPEF tax rates relative to different income ranges is exactly five).

To try and see whether the model allows to obtain long-time stationary income distributions with shapes exhibiting fat tails as it occurs in real world, a larger number of classes in the model were considered in the work by Bertotti et al. [9]. Various choices of the parameters were evaluated. The purpose was to deal with cases as realistic as possible, and initial distributions of the population were chosen with a majority of individuals in lower-income classes and only a minority in higher income classes. In this way, stationary income distributions with Pareto-like behaviour were found.

Among other aspects to be explored, the curiosity remained to see whether one can find an analytic expression of a distribution, to which the stationary solutions of the model suit. A focus of the paper [10] by Bertotti et al. is on the search for such an analytic expression. Several parameter choices as well as various distributions proposed in the literature are considered in that paper. What is found is that an excellent fitting can be obtained between distributions arising from numerical simulations of the model and the κ-generalised distribution proposed by Kaniadakis in [25]. And it is worth pointing out that, in turn, the κ-generalised distribution has proved to greatly perform when considered in connection with empirical data: for example, its agreement with data on personal income of Germany, Italy and the United Kingdom is discussed by Kaniadakis et al. in [26] and that one with data on personal income of Australia and the United States by Kaniadakis et al. in [27].

In real life, welfare policies provide benefits, in particular to the lowest income classes, in connection with health care, education, home, to help improve living conditions. To simulate a policy of this kind, a modified version of the model is treated in the paper by Bertotti et al. [11], where also the contribution of what can be considered as a welfare form is incorporated. This is achieved through some weights that differently measure the amount of tax revenue redistributed among classes. In the same paper, also a comparison is established between different ways to fight economic inequality. A specific result therein obtained is that, at least under certain hypotheses, inequality reduction is more efficiently reached by a policy of reduction of the welfare and subsidies for the rich classes than by an enlargement of the tax rate difference $\tau_n - \tau_1$ aimed at taxing rich people much more than poor ones.

A further issue on which the model was tested relates to social mobility. Empirical data relative to several countries show the general existence of a negative correlation between economic inequality and mobility (a reference for that being e.g. the article by Corak [1]). This relevant topic is dealt with in the paper by Bertotti et al. [12]. Certainly, in the model at hand, one cannot distinguish different generations. Nonetheless, some indicators are introduced, useful to quantify mobility, which is meant here as a probability for individuals of a given class to climb up [respectively, down] the income ladder and pass to an upper [respectively, lower] class. Without entering technical details, we emphasise that a negative correlation between economic inequality and upward mobility turns out to be in fact a feature of the model.

Finally, the question of tax evasion, occurring as a matter of fact in a stronger or weaker form in several countries, can be and was investigated in the context of the model under consideration. In the work by Bertotti et al. [13], for instance, also the co-existence of different evasion levels among individuals was postulated and its consequences were explored. In particular, it was shown there that, besides leading to a reduction in tax revenue, the evasion misbehaviour too contributes to an increase of economic inequality.

4. The impact of different fiscal policies towards economic inequality

To give a further illustration of the impact of different fiscal policies on the shape of income distribution and economic inequality as suggested by the model, we develop in this section a novel application.

To solve numerically the differential equations, we have to fix the parameters that are so far free. We choose for example

- the number of income classes in which the population is divided to be equal to $n = 15$,
- the unitary amount of money that can be exchanged in each transaction to be given by $S = 1$,

- the average incomes of the classes to be linearly growing according to

$$r_j = 25j, \tag{5}$$

- the tax rates relative to the different income classes to be of the form

$$\tau_j = \tau_{min} + \frac{j-1}{n-1}(\tau_{max} - \tau_{min}), \tag{6}$$

for $j = 1, \dots, n$, with τ_{min} rand τ_{max} respectively denoting the minimum and maximum tax rate.

Finally,

- with the purpose to define reasonable heterogeneous transaction and payment probabilities, we assume the coefficients $p_{h,k}$ to be given by

$$p_{h,k} = \min\{r_h, r_k\}/4r_n, \tag{7}$$

except for the terms

$$\begin{aligned} p_{j,j} &= r_j/2r_n \quad \text{for} \quad j = 2, \dots, n-1, \\ p_{h,1} &= r_1/2r_n \quad \text{for} \quad h = 2, \dots, n, \\ p_{n,k} &= r_k/2r_n \quad \text{for} \quad k = 1, \dots, n-1, \\ p_{1,k} &= 0 \quad \text{for} \quad k = 1, \dots, n, \\ p_{h,n} &= 0 \quad \text{for} \quad h = 1, \dots, n. \end{aligned} \tag{8}$$

Such a choice stands for the belief that poorer individuals usually spend and earn less than richer ones. The requirements for the coefficients with $h, k = 1$ or n are of a technical nature, due to constraints on the extreme classes.

According to the empirical result recalled at the end of Section 2, for a specific given model (i.e. once parameters are fixed), the solutions of (Eq. (1)) evolving from all initial conditions x_0 with the same global income tend to a same asymptotic equilibrium.

The application we are going to discuss here includes four steps and is constructed as follows:

- Step (i): Starting from a quasi-random initial condition x_0 (the only requirement for realism being that the majority of individuals occupy the lowest income classes), we assume that in the closed society at hand no taxation exists. Accordingly, we put $\tau_{min} = 0$ and $\tau_{max} = 0$. Making to evolve the equations (Eq. (1)) for a sufficiently long time, we obtain an "asymptotic" stationary solution corresponding to a first income distribution, which is displayed in Panel (i) in **Figure 1**.

- Step (ii): We postulate at this point the introduction of a taxation system that provides the same tax rate for each income class. Towards this and to fix ideas, we choose $\tau_{min} = \tau_{max} = 20\%$. Then, we take the asymptotic stationary solution of step (i) as the initial condition, and we make the equations (Eq. (1)) (which are of course different from those in the previous step) evolve. After a sufficiently long time, a new "asymptotic" stationary solution is reached, which represents a second income distribution. It is that one displayed in Panel (ii) in **Figure 1**.

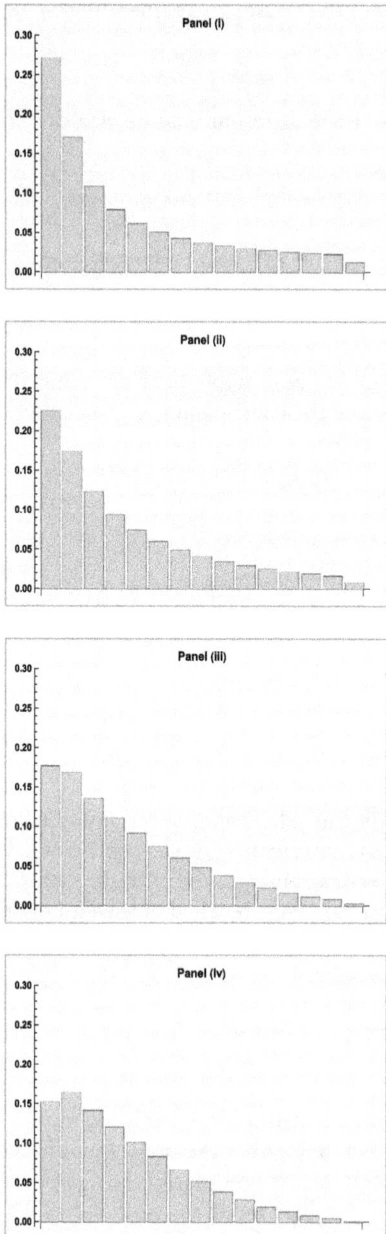

Figure 1.
The four panels display the stationary income distributions in correspondence to the same given global income for the four different fiscal policies described in steps (i), (ii), (iii), and (iv). Even a simple look provides evidence of the fact that in passing from each panel to the next one the fraction of individuals in the poorest as well as in the richest class decreases while increasing in the intermediate classes. Correspondingly, economic inequality decreases.

- Step (iii): To simulate the implementation of a more targeted fiscal policy, we now introduce another change amounting to the choice of a progressive taxation. Equivalently, we fix different tax rates, lower for low-income earners and higher for high-income earners. Specifically, we choose here $\tau_{min} = 20\%$ and $\tau_{max} = 50\%$. The "asymptotic" stationary solution obtained in correspondence to an initial condition coinciding with the asymptotic stationary solution of step (ii) is displayed in Panel (iii) in **Figure 1**.

- Step (iv): As a further focused fiscal policy, we also incorporate in the taxation algorithm what can be thought of as an addition of welfare provision. From a technical point of view, this can be achieved through the introduction of suitable weights in the terms $U^i_{[hk]}(x)$ and $V^i_{[hk]}(x)$ in system (Eq. (1)). Such weights allow to differently measure the portion of redistributed tax revenue to individuals of different income classes. A formula able to realise this is given in [11], and we refer to that paper for further details. What is of interest here is the final "asymptotic" income distribution relative to the equations, which include this modification and to an initial condition coinciding with the asymptotic stationary solution of step (iii). This income distribution is shown in Panel (iv) in **Figure 1**.

Already a simple look at the panels in **Figure 1** provides evidence of the fact that the effect in the long run of each of the different fiscal policies adopted throughout the steps (i), (ii), (iii), and (iv) is to modify the income distribution over the population so as to lower the number of individuals in the poorest as well as in the richest classes, simultaneously increasing this number in the intermediate classes. Also, an alternative, unified representation of the four stationary income distributions corresponding to the four different taxation system fiscal policies (i), (ii), (iii), and (iv) is given in **Figure 2**. Lastly, in **Figure 3** the evolution in time of the fraction of individuals in the 15 income classes is displayed. Once again, together with others, one may notice that the fractions of individuals that are initially the largest and the smallest (fractions to which the poorest and the richest individuals belong) are both non-increasing in time.

We emphasise that economic inequality decreases in passing from the income distribution displayed in Panel (i) of **Figure 1** to the income distributions in Panel (ii). The same holds true in passing from the distribution in Panel (ii) to that one in Panel (iii), and from the distribution in Panel (ii) to that one in Panel (iv).

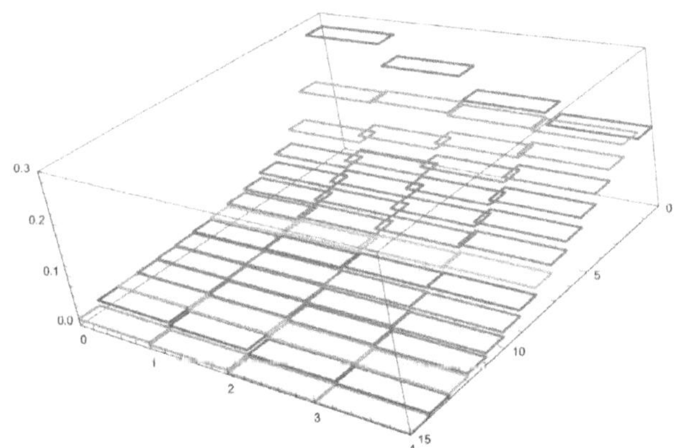

Figure 2.
An alternative representation of the stationary income distributions in correspondence to a given global income for the four different taxation systems fiscal policies described in steps (i), (ii), (iii), and (iv). One clearly notices that the fraction of the poorest and the fraction of the richest individuals decrease when passing from the distribution for step (i) (corresponding to the strip [0,1]) to the distribution for step (iv) (corresponding to the strip [3, 4]).

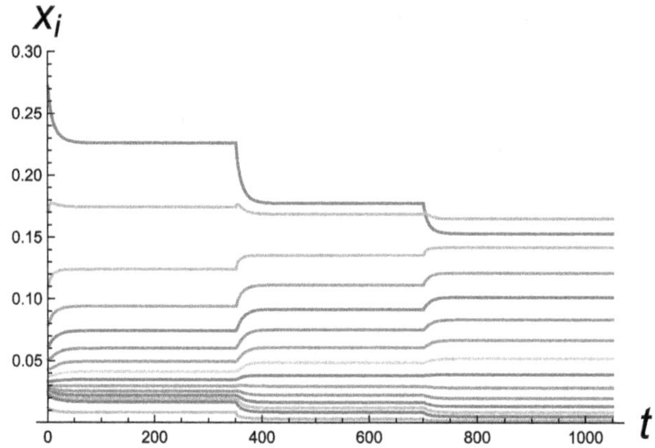

Figure 3.
The evolution in time of the fraction of individuals in the 15 income classes for the model with fiscal policies as in steps (ii), (iii), and (iv). One may notice, in particular, that the fractions of individuals which are initially (in the stationary distribution reached in absence of taxes) the largest and the smallest—fractions to which the poorest and the richest individuals belong—are both non-increasing in time.

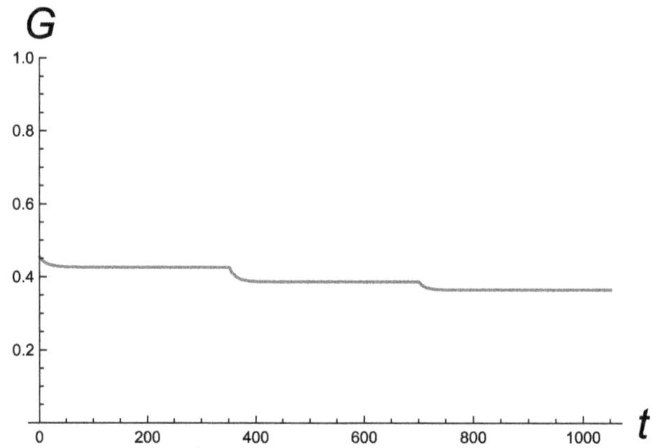

Figure 4.
The graph of the Gini coefficient as a function of time in correspondence to the application in the sequence of the three different fiscal policies adopted throughout the steps (ii), (iii), and (iv).

A quantitative measure of economic inequality is given by the Gini coefficient G (named after the Italian statistician and economist C. Gini who introduced it in the early twentieth century, see [28]), whose definition we recall next: if the Lorenz curve expresses on the y-axis, the cumulative percentage of the total income of a population earned by the bottom percentage of individuals (represented, in turn, on the x-axis), denote A_1 the area between the Lorenz curve of the distribution at hand and the line of perfect equality $y = x$, characterising a uniform distribution; also, denote A_2 the total area under the line of perfect equality. The Gini coefficient is defined as the ratio A_1/A_2 and takes values in the interval $[0, 1]$. The extreme values 0 and 1 of G respectively represent complete equality and complete inequality.

The Gini coefficients relative to the income distributions in the Panels (i), (ii), (iii), and (iv) in **Figure 1** are

$$G = 0.453551, \quad G = 0.426308, \quad G = 0.386833, \quad G = 0.365182 \tag{9}$$

respectively.

Time t	G for (ii)[a]	G for (iii)[b]	G for (iv)[c]
500	0.4474	0.4170	0.3812
1000	0.4430	0.4102	0.3771
2500	0.4349	0.3978	0.3703
5000	0.4292	0.3899	0.3665
10,000	0.4266	0.3871	0.3653
25,000	0.4263	0.3868	0.3652
55,000	0.4263	0.3868	0.3652

[a]*refers the solution at time t of the equation system with coefficients as in step (ii),*
[b]*refers to the solution at time t of the equation system with coefficients as in step (iii),*
[c]*refers to the solution at time t of the equation system with coefficients as in step (iv).*

Table 1.
In this table, the Gini coefficients G relative to the income distributions are evaluated in correspondence of a finite number of times for the model systems described in steps (ii), (iii), and (iv). One sees here that each of the solutions G decreases. Accordingly, economic inequality is decreasing for each of the three models (ii), (iii), and (iv), models characterised respectively by the existence of a taxation system with a unique tax rate, the existence of a progressive taxation system with different tax rates, the existence of a taxation system integrated by welfare.

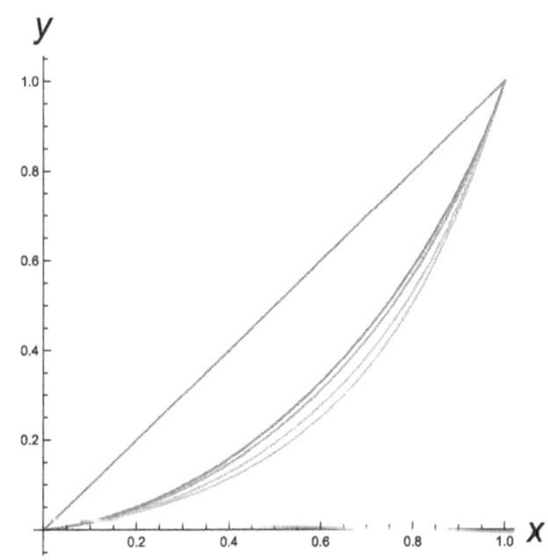

Figure 5.
The Lorenz curves corresponding to the stationary income distributions reached at the end of steps (i), (ii), (ii), and (iv). The variable on the x-axis denotes the bottom percentage of individuals and the variable on the y-axis is the cumulative percentage of the total income earned by the corresponding percentage of individuals. The Lorenz curves referring to the final distribution relative to steps (i), (ii), (ii), and (iv) are ordered from the lowest to the highest. Accordingly, in passing from step (i) to step (ii) to step (iii) to step (iv) the Gini coefficient decreases.

It is also worth noting that the Gini coefficient decreases along with the solutions of the equation systems relative to the three models defined in steps (ii), (iii), and (iv). In particular, in **Table 1** some values of G are reported, relative to the income distributions in a finite number of instants during the evolution of the three dynamical systems. An overall picture of this behaviour is contained in **Figure 4**: there, the graph of the Gini coefficient as a function of time is shown, in correspondence to the application in the sequence of the three different fiscal policies adopted throughout the steps (ii), (iii), and (iv). Lastly, **Figure 5** displays the Lorenz curves corresponding to the stationary income distributions reached at the end of steps (i), (ii), (ii), and (iv).

5. Conclusions

In this chapter, we have revisited, also discussing a novel application of it, a mathematical "micro-to-macro" model suitable for the study of the aggregate formation of the income distribution in a closed market society out of a whole of economic interactions including taxation and redistribution. The model, originally proposed by Bertotti in [8], was further developed and analysed in various papers by Bertotti et al. [9–13]. We have shown that it can be adapted to analyse issues related to economic inequality. In particular, the model identifies in redistributive policy a driver towards economic inequality reduction. The theme is complex and requires a broad spectrum of skills, knowledge, real data, ideas. The model encompasses (as is inevitable) great simplifications and probably a naive approach, and cannot offer magical solutions to the problems it addresses. Nonetheless, thanks to the considerable flexibility it enjoys and to its ability to make predictions in the presence of different conditions and policies, it could hopefully contribute to providing some insight towards forecasting of possible outcomes and behaviours, in this way serving as an inspiration and source of suggestions for policy-makers.

Author details

Maria Letizia Bertotti
Free University of Bozen-Bolzano, Bolzano, Italy

*Address all correspondence to: marialetizia.bertotti@unibz.it

References

[1] Corak M. Income inequality, equality of opportunity, and intergenerational mobility. Journal of Economic Perspectives. 2013;**27**:79-102. DOI: 10.1257/jep.27.3.79

[2] Piketty T, Saez E. Inequality in the long run. Science. 2014;**344**:838-843. DOI: 10.1126/science.1251936

[3] Stiglitz JE. The Price of Inequality: How Today's Divided Society Endangers Our Future. New York: W.W. Norton & Company; 2012

[4] Deaton A. The Great Escape: Health, Wealth, and the Origins of Inequality. Princeton: Princeton University Press; 2013

[5] Atkinson AB. Inequality: What Can Be Done? Cambridge: Harvard University Press; 2015

[6] Milanovic B. Global Inequality. A New Approach for the Age of Globalization. Cambridge: Harvard University Press; 2016

[7] World Inequality Database: Home—WID. Available from: https://wid.world [Accessed: 05 August 2021]

[8] Bertotti ML. Modelling taxation and redistribution: A discrete active particle kinetic approach. Applied Mathematics and Computation. 2010;**217**:752-762. DOI: 10.1016/j.amc.2010.06.013

[9] Bertotti ML, Modanese G. From microscopic taxation and redistribution models to macroscopic income distributions. Physica A. 2011;**390**: 3782-3793. DOI: 10.1016/j.physa.2011.06.008

[10] Bertotti ML, Modanese G. Exploiting the flexibility of a family of models for taxation and redistribution. European Physical Journal B. 2012;**85**: 261. DOI: 10.1140/epjb/e2012-30239-3

[11] Bertotti ML, Modanese G. Microscopic models for welfare measures addressing a reduction of economic inequality. Complexity. 2016; **21**:89-98. DOI: 10.1002/cplx.21669

[12] Bertotti ML, Modanese G. Economic inequality and mobility in kinetic models for social sciences. European Physical Journal Special Topics. 2016; **225**:1945-1958. DOI: 10.1140/epjst/e2015-50117-8

[13] Bertotti ML, Modanese G. Mathematical models describing the effects of different tax evasion behaviors. Journal of Economic Interaction and Coordination. 2018;**13**: 351-363. DOI: 10.1007/s11403-016-0185-9

[14] Arthur WB, Durlauf S, Lane DA. Process and the emergence in the economy. In: Arthur WB, Durlauf S, Lane DA, editors. The Economy as an Evolving Complex System II. Reading: Addison-Wesley; 1997. pp. 2-14

[15] Kirman A. Complex Economics: Individual and Collective Rationality. London: Routledge; 2010

[16] Arthur WB. Complexity and the Economy. Oxford: Oxford University Press; 2014

[17] Yakovenko VM, Rosser JB Jr. Colloquium: Statistical mechanics of money, wealth, and income. Reviews of Modern Physics. 2009;**81**:1703-1725. DOI: 10.1103/RevModPhys.81.1703

[18] Chatterjee A, Chakrabarti BK, Manna SS. Pareto law in a kinetic model of market with random saving propensity. Physica A. 2004;**335**: 155-163. DOI: 10.1016/j.physa.2003.11.014

[19] Cordier S, Pareschi L, Toscani G. On a kinetic model for a simple market

economy. Journal of Statistical Physics. 2005;**120**:253-277. DOI: 10.1007/s10955-005-5456-0

[20] Matthes D, Toscani G. On steady distributions of kinetic models of conservative economies. Journal of Statistical Physics. 2008;**130**:1087-1117. DOI: 10.1007/s10955-007-9462-2

[21] Chakrabarti BK, Chakraborti A, Chakravarty SR, Chatterjee A. Econophysics of Income and Wealth Distributions. Cambridge: Cambridge University Press; 2013

[22] Lux T. Applications of statistical physics to finance and economics. In: Rosser JB Jr, editor. Handbook of Research on Complexity. Edward Elgar Publishing: Cheltenham; 2009. pp. 213-258

[23] Kutner R, Ausloos M, Grech D, Di Matteo T, Schinckus C, Stanley HE. Econophysics and sociophysics: Their milestones & challenges. Physica A. 2019;**516**:240-253. DOI: 10.1016/j.physa.2018.10.019

[24] Wolfram Research, Inc. Mathematica, Version 12.3.0.0. Champaign, IL: Wolfram Research, Inc.; 2021

[25] Kaniadakis G. Non-linear kinetics underlying generalized statistics. Physica A. 2001;**296**:405-425. DOI: 10.1016/S0378-4371(01)00184-4

[26] Clementi F, Gallegati M, Kaniadakis G κ-generalized statistics in personal income distribution. European Physical Journal B. 2007; 52: 187-193. DOI: 10.1140/epjb/e2007-00120-9

[27] Clementi F, Di Matteo T, Gallegati M, Kaniadakis G. The κ-generalized distribution: A new descriptive model for the size distribution of incomes. Physica A. 2008;**387**:3201-3208. DOI: 10.1016/j.physa.2008.01.109

[28] Gini C. Variabilità e mutabilità. Contributo allo studio delle distribuzioni e delle relazioni statistiche. Bologna: Tipografia di Paolo Cuppini; 1912

Section 2

Labour Market and Employment

Chapter 6

Labor Markets

Meng Sun

Abstract

What is the labor market? Like the goods and services markets, a labor market consists of the supply and demand sides. In the labor market, while workers supply labor, firms demand labor. This chapter studies the backward-bending nature of the labor supply curve and the downward-sloping nature of the labor demand curve. We also analyze the labor market equilibrium in a perfectly competitive labor market. Several policies such as immigration and minimum wage will be introduced to illustrate how government policies affect the labor market equilibrium.

Keywords: labor market, labor demand, labor supply, labor market equilibrium, policies

1. Introduction

Just like the goods and services markets, the labor market has supply and demand. Although the labor market works similar to the goods and services markets, the stories behind the demand and supply are different. In the labor market, workers supply labor, the valuable services they contribute to producing goods and services because they need money for food, rent, and other activities. On the other hand, firms who hire labor are the demanders for labor. Without workers, firms could not produce goods and services and earn profits. For this reason, the "product" in the labor market is labor, and the "price" of the labor is the wage rate.

Modern labor markets are complex. Companies from all over the world hire many different occupations such as engineers, business analysts, construction workers, designers. Today, over 3 billion people are either working or looking for jobs in the labor market, and each of these people has different skills and experiences. How do companies decide which employee to hire and at what wage rate? How do the workers decide which company they want to work for? To answer these questions, we follow the economist's approach: simplify the problem by using a model.

In this chapter, we will construct the competitive labor market model. We will discuss the backward-bending nature of the labor supply curve and the downward-sloping nature of the labor demand curve. We then will look at how workers and firms interact in the labor market to determine how many workers to hire and at what wage rate? Immigration and minimum wage policies will be introduced, and we will discuss how these policies affect the labor market equilibrium.

2. Key assumptions of the competitive labor market model

Competitive labor markets are similar to competitive goods and services markets. **Table 1** compares the assumptions in competitive labor markets and

Goods and services markets	Labor markets
Large number of sellers and buyers	Large number of workers and firms
Sellers produce homogenous product	Workers are homogenous
Sellers and buyers have perfect information	Workers and firms have perfect information

Table 1.
The key assumptions in competitive labor markets and competitive goods and services market.

competitive goods and services markets. There are four key assumptions we need to make in order to simplify our analysis:

1. **Workers are homogenous.** It means the workers in a competitive labor market are identical and equally productive. Therefore, firms have no preference toward one worker over another.

2. **Workers and firms share complete and accurate information in the labor market.** Every worker has the same information on wage, and every firm knows how productive a worker is. This assumption is a natural extension of the homogenous-workers assumption, which also implies no negotiation between firms and workers.

3. **There are many workers and firms in the labor market.** This assumption implies that no worker or firm has the market power to affect the wage. In other words, the wage is determined by the labor demand and supply, and everyone in the market is a "price (wage) -taker."

Notice that those simplifying assumptions of the competitive labor market model are not (entirely) realistic. For example, in reality, workers have different training, level of skills, and experiences. Therefore, they are not homogenous, especially in terms of productivity. The information in the labor market is also not likely to be perfect. It is challenging for firms to evaluate a work's productivity during the interview. Moreover, workers are also not likely to know the wage a firm is willing to offer. Nevertheless, the model provides a good description of how the labor market work. It can help us to focus on and understand the essential labor market mechanism.

3. The supply of labor

3.1 Work and leisure

An individual needs to decide how to allocate time between market and nonmarket activities.

Market activity: activities that include financial transactions and done with intention of earning money or profit [1]:

- Work (for pay)

Nonmarket activity: activities that do not include any financial transactions and done without any intention of earning money or profit [1]:

- Leisure

- Household production (raising children, cooking, home repair, growing vegetables, etc.)
- Investing in "human capital" (i.e., acquiring skills/knowledge that increase future earning capacity)

For the sake of simplicity, we divide an individual's activities into: *work and leisure*. Note that *leisure* here includes all activities that are not *work*.

3.2 Utility function

Assume that an individual can allocate his/her time between two activities: *work and leisure*. Assume that the total time the individual can allocate a day is T. Let I denote the hours of leisure the individual spends. The individual's hours of work are $T - I$. Choosing to work $T - I$ hours at a given wage is equivalent to consuming I hours of leisure. Therefore, we can model either the individual's leisure demand or the individual's labor supply. We will model the individual's leisure demand here.

Assume there are two categories of goods that an individual can consume: *leisure and consumption goods*. We can describe the individual's preferences by an utility function

$$U = U(C, I) \tag{1}$$

where C is the quantity of the consumption goods. The utility function measures the individual's satisfaction or happiness at any quantities of the consumption goods and the individual's leisure hours. In addition, we assume that buying more consumption goods or having more leisure hours both increase the individual's utility. **Figure 1** shows a typical indifference curve.

3.3 Indifference curves

Suppose that an individual consumes \$100 worth of consumption goods and 2 hours of leisure a day (point A in **Figure 1**). Combining the \$100 worth of consumption and 2 hours of leisure give the individual 60 units of happiness. If the individual only consumes \$60 worth of consumption goods and 5 hours of leisure (point B in **Figure 1**), the individual receives the same level of happiness.

Suppose that the individual is still consuming \$100 worth of consumer goods. At the same time, he/she spends 5 hours on leisure instead of 2 hours (point C in **Figure 1**). Combining the \$100 worth of consumption and 5 hours of leisure give the individual 90 units of happiness. The indifference curves are the graphical representation of the utility function.[1]

3.4 The budget constraint

An individual's income consist of two parts: earned income and unearned income. **Earned income** is the money you make in exchange for the work you do. For most people, almost all the money they make is earned income. Any money earned in professional wages or fees—including tips—counts as earned income. Reimbursements from your employer for travel expenses, including meals, accommodations,

[1] Indifference curves have five important properties: 1. indifference curves are strictly downward sloping; 2. indifference curves are convex to the origin; 3. indifference curves never cross; 4. higher indifference curves mean higher levels of utility; 5. indifference curves are continuous, with no gaps.

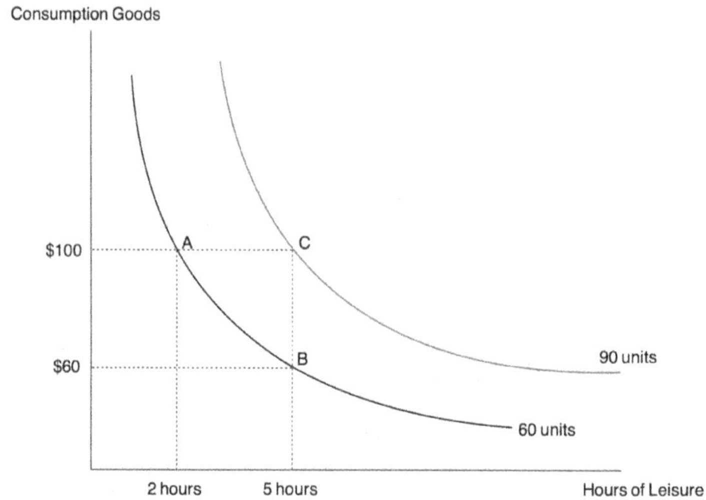

Figure 1.
Consumption-leisure indifference curves.

and transportation, also count as earned income. Unearned income involves the money you make without having performed a professional service. **Unearned income** includes money-making sources that involve interest, dividends, and capital gains. Additional forms of unearned income include retirement account distributions, annuities, unemployment compensation, social security benefits, and gambling winnings. Other forms of income, such as money from an estate, trust, or partnership, may also be considered unearned income [2].

Let K denote an individual's unearned income. Let L be the number of hours the individual works and w be the hourly wage rate. C is the quantity of the consumption goods. The individual's budget constraint can be written as

$$C = wL + K \tag{2}$$

Eq. (2) means the expenditures on the consumption goods equals to the sum of earned income and unearned income.

Since the total time the individual can allocate a day is T and the individual can only allocate his/her time between two activities: *work (L) and leisure (I)*, we have $T = L + I$. Thus, $L = T - I$. We can then rewrite the budget constraint as

$$C = w(T - I) + K \tag{3}$$

Rearrange Eq. (3)

$$C = (wT + K) - wI \tag{4}$$

Figure 2 shows the consumption-leisure budget line. If the individual chooses to spend all of his/her time on leisure, the individual's expenditure on the consumption goods is K, which is his/her unearned income (point D in **Figure 2**). If the individual chooses to spend all of his/her time on work, the individual's expenditure on the consumption goods is $wT + K$, which is the sum of his/her earned income and unearned income (point E in **Figure 2**). Moreover, the slope of the consumption-leisure budget line is $-w$.

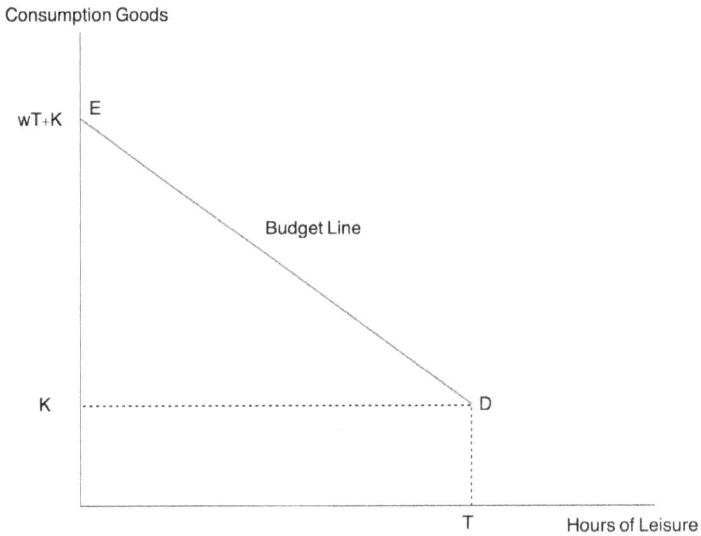

Figure 2.
Consumption-leisure budget line.

3.5 Worker's optimal choice

The budget line shows the combinations of the consumption goods and the hours of leisure that the individual can afford. Notice that the individual can choose any combination of the consumption goods and leisure hours on the budget line or in the area below the budget line. We want to determine which combination within the budget gives the individual the highest level of utility. **Figure 3** illustrates the solution to this problem.

Combinations that lie on indifference curves above the budget line, such as point E, are not in the budget set. Even though the individual prefers point E to point A or B, he/she cannot afford the combination of the consumption goods and the hours of leisure at point E.

Although the individual can afford any combination inside the budget line, such as point B, he/she can always find a better affordable combination such as point D. Thus, the individual will not choose any combination of the consumption goods and leisure hours in the area below the budget line.

Points A and C lie on the budget line as point D. However, the indifference curve that passes through point D is higher than the indifference curve that pass through points A and C. Therefore, the combination of the consumption goods and leisure hours at point D gives the individual higher level of utility (higher indifference curves mean higher levels of utility). In fact, the point where an indifference curve is tangent to the budget line is the affordable combination of the consumption goods and leisure hours that gives the individual the highest level of utility.

3.6 Substitution and income effects

Figure 3 demonstrates the optimal combination of the consumption goods and leisure hours an individual will choose given the hourly wage rage at w. What happens if the wage rate increases? Would the individual choose more work and less leisure because he/she can earn more per hour? Or would the individual choose less

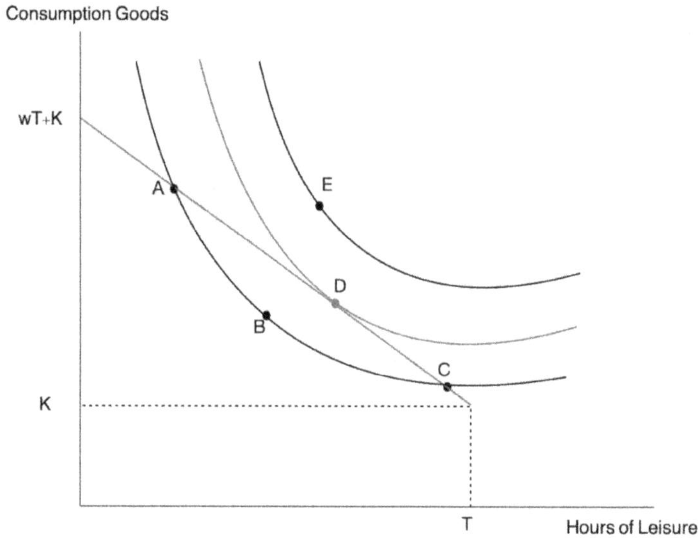

Figure 3.
Worker's optimal choice of the combination of the consumption goods and leisure hours.

work and more leisure because he/she has a higher income to maintain the same standard of living by working less?

- **Substitution effect:** When an individual earns a higher wage rate, the opportunity cost of leisure increases. In other words, leisure is more expensive and the quantity demanded for leisure decreases.
- **Income effect:** When an individual earns a higher wage rate, the income of the individual increases. Since leisure is a normal good, the demand for leisure increases.

Both the substitution and income effects are present for all individuals. When the substitution effect dominates the income effect, a higher wage reduces leisure hours and, therefore, increases work hours. On the other hand, when the income effect dominates the substitution effect, higher wage increases the hours of leisure and, therefore, decreases work hours.

- If substitution effect > income effect: wage $\uparrow \Rightarrow$ hours of leisure $\downarrow \Rightarrow$ hours of work $\uparrow$ (**Figure 4 (a)**).
- If substitution effect < income effect: wage $\uparrow \Rightarrow$ hours of leisure $\uparrow \Rightarrow$ hours of work $\downarrow$ (**Figure 4 (b)**).

3.7 Individual labor supply curve

Figure 5 shows a typical individual labor supply curve. When the hourly wage rate is w_1, the individual is willing to work L_1 hours and spends $T - L_1$ on leisure activities. When the hourly wage rate rises from w_1 to w_2, the individual increases his/her hours of work from L_1 to L_2. The substitution effect dominates the income effect, and the individual is substituting leisure with work. When the hourly wage rate rises from w_2 to w_3, the individual reduces his/her hours of work from L_2 to L_3.

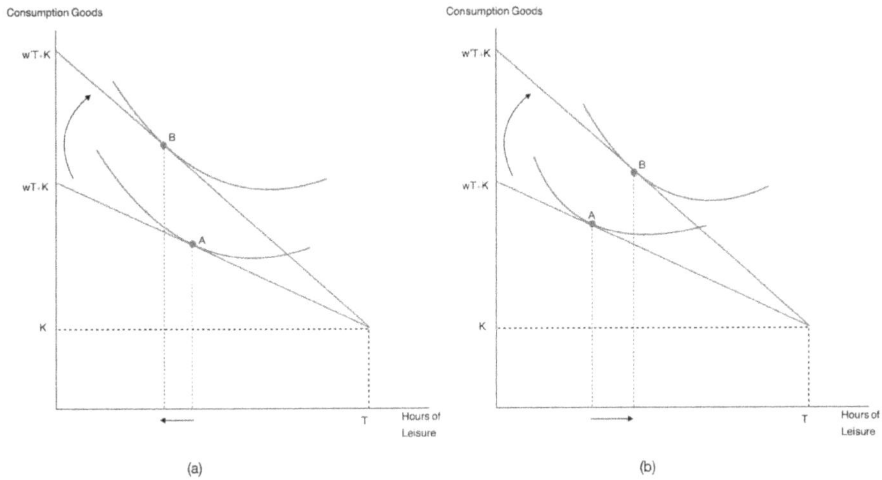

Figure 4.
Substitution and income effects. (a) the substitution effect dominates the income effect, (b) the income effect dominates the substitution effect.

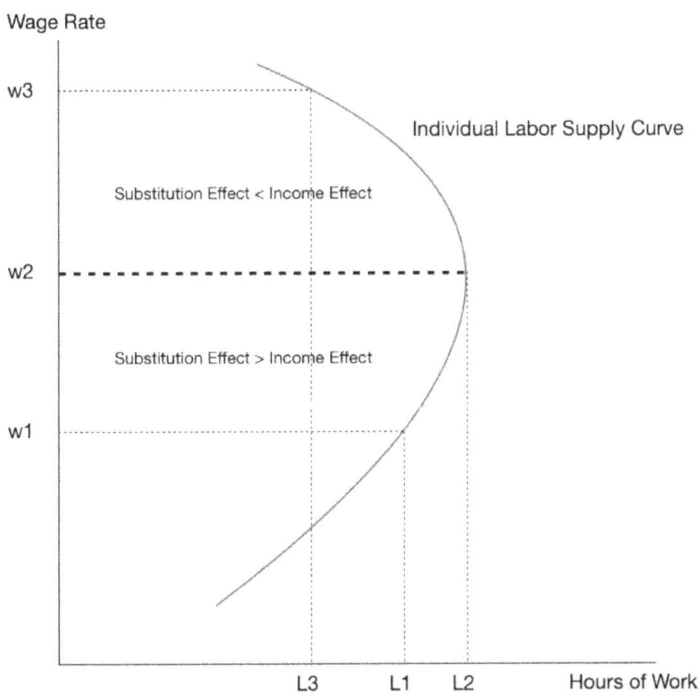

Figure 5.
Individual labor supply curve.

The income effect dominates the substitution effect, and the individual is "buying" more leisure hours.

The substitution effect of a higher wage encourages the individual to work more, while the income effect encourages the individual to work less. Therefore, the individual labor supply curve is *backward-bending*.

Wage rate	Individual 1 (hours of work)	Individual 2 (hours of work)	Individual 3 (hours of work)	Market (hours of work)
$6	5	5	5	15
$12	8	9	9	26
$15	10	7	11	28

Table 2.
Individual and market labor supply.

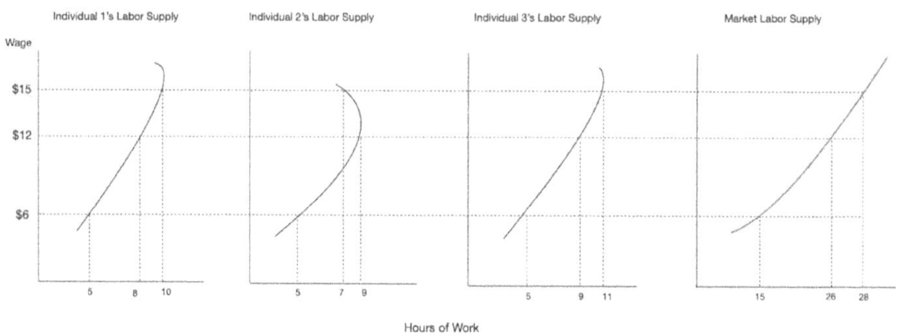

Figure 6.
From the individual labor supply curves to the market labor supply curve.

3.8 Market labor supply curve

The individual labor supply can tell us how many hours an individual is willing to work given different wages. We can add together all the labor supply curves of the individuals to obtain the market labor supply curve.

Table 2 shows the hours of work three different individuals are willing to supply under different wage rates. When the hourly wage rate is $6, all three individuals are willing to work for 5 hours. Thus, the market's supply of work hours is $5 + 5 + 5 = 15$ hours. When the hourly wage rate is $12, all three individuals increase their work hours. The market's supply of work hours is $8 + 9 + 9 = 26$ hours. When the hourly wage rate increases to $15, individuals 1 and 3 increase their work hours, while individual 2 reduces work hours because his income effect dominates the substitution effect. The market's supply of work hours is $10 + 7 + 11 = 28$. The market's supply of work hours is still increasing even individual 2 reduces his work hours.

Figure 6 shows the individual labor supply curves of individuals 1, 2, and 3. We get the market labor supply curve by horizontally adding up all the individual labor supply curves at any wage rate. Although an individual?s labor supply curve is backward-bending, the market labor supply curves usually are upward sloping, as shown in **Figure 6**. Just like the goods and services markets, higher wages mean a higher quantity supplied of labor.

4. The demand of labor

In this section, we will focus on the behavior of the firms. Firms demand labor to use it as an input to produce output. For example, the demand for App developers is linked to the need to develop new smartphone software. Therefore, unlike goods and services, the demand for labor is a "derived demand."[2]

4.1 Short run vs. long run

We first need to distinguish between the "short-run" and "long-run." However, how short is short, and how long is long? In the study of economics, the short run and the long run do not refer to a specific period, such as 3 months versus 3 years. Instead, they depend on the number of variable and/or fixed inputs that affect the production output [4].

- **The short run** is a period of time in which the quantity of at least one input is fixed and the quantities of the other inputs can be varied [5].
- **The long run** is a period of time in which the quantities of all inputs can be varied [5].

Here, we assume that capital is fixed, while labor is variable. Extra shifts, overtime, and hiring can be relatively easily arranged when more labor is needed. However, it will not be able to employ more capital in the same time frame as capital acquisition takes time.

4.2 Short-run labor demand curve

Imagine a firm in the short run. The capital inputs are fixed. The firm needs to decide how many workers to hire. Hiring an additional worker increases the firm's output and therefore revenue. The output the additional worker contributes is the **marginal product of labor**, MP_L.[3] The revenue by selling the output contributed by the additional worker is the **marginal revenue product of labor**, MRP_L. We assume that the final goods and services markets are perfectly competitive, and the market price of the firm's product is P. Thus,

$$MRP_L = MP_L \times P \tag{5}$$

While hiring the additional worker raises the revenue, the firm has to pay the wage to the worker. The cost of hiring one additional worker is the **marginal wage cost**, MWC. We assume that the labor market is perfectly competitive, and the wage rate is w. Thus,

$$MWC = w \tag{6}$$

If $MRP_L > MWC$, the firm wants to hire more workers because the benefit from hiring an additional worker is greater than the cost. On the other hand, if $MRP_L < MWC$, the firm does not want to hire because the cost from hiring an additional worker is greater than the benefit the firm can receive. The firm has the optimal amount of labor when

$$MRP_L = MWC \tag{7}$$

---

[2] Derived demand is the demand for intermediate goods that is derived from the demand for the final goods [3].

[3] A firm's production exhibits diminishing marginal product of labor.

or

$$MP_L \times P = w \quad (8)$$

Table 3 assumes that the firm can sell its output at \$50 in a competitive market. When the firm hires the first worker, the worker produces 10 units of output, resulting in a marginal product of labor of 10 units. The marginal revenue product of labor is, therefore, $MPL \times P = \$500$. If the market-determined wage rate is $w = \$500$, the firm will hire one worker.

Assume that the market-determined wage rate is $w = \$300$. The gain from hiring the second worker is \$450, while the cost is \$300. Therefore, the firm will hire a second worker. Similarly, the gain from hiring the third worker is \$400, while the cost is \$300. Therefore, the firm will hire a third worker. In fact, the firm will continue hiring until the gain equals the cost. It results in hiring five workers at $w = \$300$.

By plotting the number of labor (column (1)) on the horizontal axis and wage (column (5)) on the vertical axis, we have a downward sloping short-run labor demand curve (**Figure** 7).

4.3 Long-run labor demand curve

In long run, both labor and capital are variable. Suppose wage increases. How would a firm respond to the increase in wage?

- **Substitution effect:** An increase in wage increases the cost of labor. Since labor is now more expensive relative to capital and assuming that labor and capital are substitutes in production, the firm will use less labor and more capital to produce any output level.

- **Scale effect:** Again, an increase in wage increases the cost of labor, which increases the cost of production. Since a competitive firm sells its product at a market-determined price, a higher production cost reduces its output level. Therefore, the firm will use less labor and capital.

Number of labor	Quantity of output	MP_L	Price of output	$MRP_L = w$
0	0	—	\$50	—
1	10	10	\$50	\$500
2	19	9	\$50	\$450
3	27	8	\$50	\$400
4	34	7	\$50	\$350
5	40	6	\$50	\$300
6	45	5	\$50	\$250
7	49	4	\$50	\$200
8	52	3	\$50	\$150
9	54	2	\$50	\$100
10	55	1	\$50	\$50

Table 3.
Firm's short-run hiring decision.

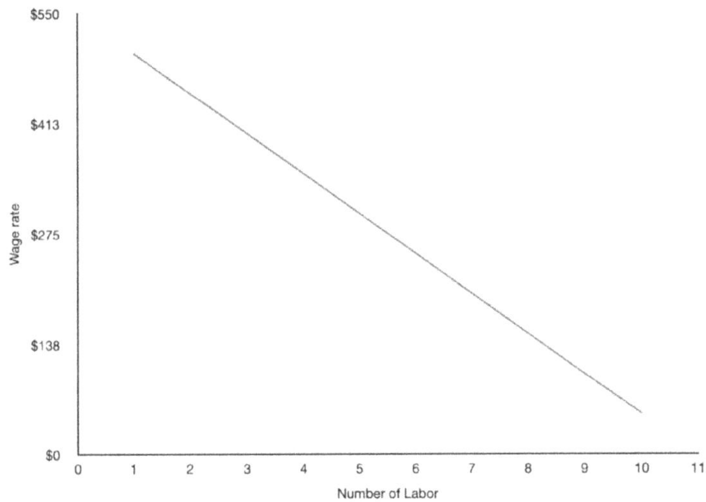

Figure 7.
Short-run labor demand curve.

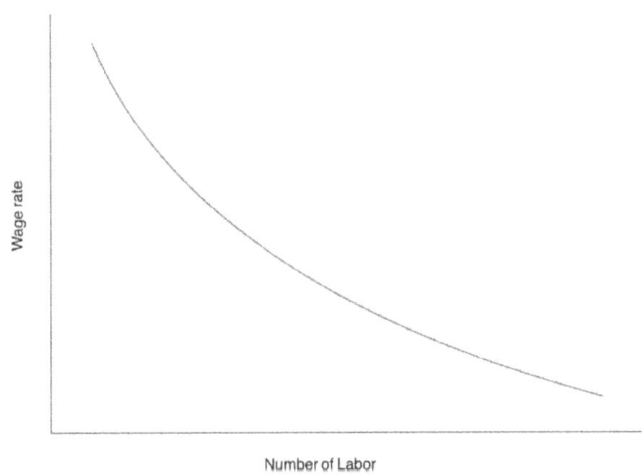

Figure 8.
Long-run labor demand curve.

When wage increases, both the substitution effect and scale effect cause the demand for labor to decrease. Thus, wage and demand for labor are negatively related in the long run, which means the long-run labor demand curve is also downward sloping (**Figure 8**).

5. Competitive labor market equilibrium

One of the most important implications of the perfectly competitive assumptions is that buyers and sellers are price takers. In other words, all the firms (buyers of labor) and workers (sellers of labor) in a perfectly competitive labor market accept the market price (wage) as given. No firm and worker has any influence over the market wage.

However, if all the firms and workers cannot influence the wage, who sets the wage? In fact, in a perfectly competitive market, the demand and supply of labor together determine the market wage and the trading quantity of labor (employment).

When a competitive labor market is in equilibrium, the quantity supplied for labor equals the quantity demanded for labor at the market wage. **Figure 9** combines the supply and demand for labor in a perfectly competitive labor market. In **Figure 9**, the competitive labor market equilibrium is where the labor supply and demand curves cross. The equilibrium wage is $20 per hour, and the equilibrium employment level is 300 workers.

If the wage rate is above $20, as shown in **Figure 10 (a)**, the quantity supplied for labor is greater than the quantity demanded. The excess supply is known as a surplus. It means some of the workers cannot find a job. In order to find a job, those workers would accept a lower wage rate. As wage falls, the quantity demanded for labor rises and the quantity supplied falls until the market reaches equilibrium at point E.

If the wage rate is below $20, as shown in **Figure 10 (b)**, the quantity demanded for labor is greater than the quantity supplied. The excess demand is known as a shortage. It means some of the firms cannot find workers. In order to find workers,

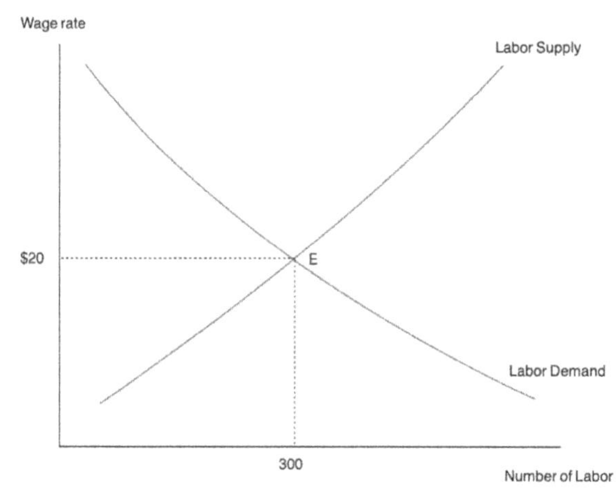

Figure 9.
Competitive labor market equilibrium.

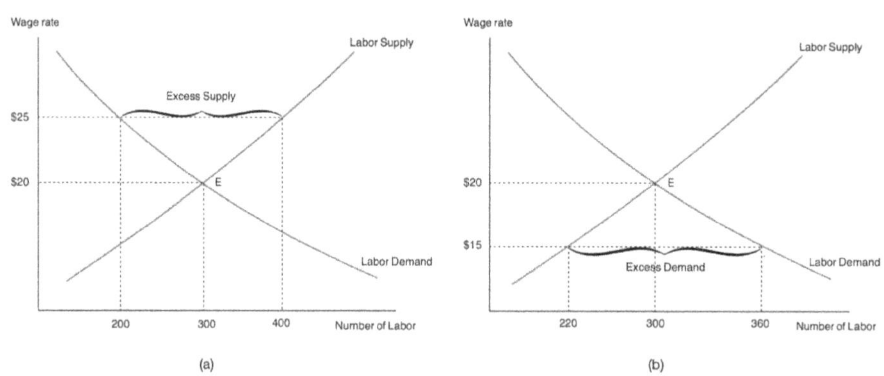

Figure 10.
Why the intersection of the labor supply and demand is the equilibrium. (a) the quantity supplied for labor is greater than the quantity demanded (b) the quantity supplied for labor is less than the quantity demanded.

those firms would offer a higher wage rate. As wage rises, the quantity demanded for labor falls and the quantity supplied rises until the market reaches equilibrium at point E.

Notice that both the supply and the demand together bring the wage back to $20 per hour. When the wage is at $20 per hour, no worker has an incentive to accept a lower wage, and no firm has an incentive to offer a higher wage. Therefore, the equilibrium wage is $20 per hour.

6. Policy application: Immigration

Immigrant workers can either be substitutes for native-born workers or complements to them. When immigrant workers are perfect substitutes for native-born workers, they have the same skills and compete for the same jobs. Thus, an influx of immigrant workers increases the labor supply, shifting the labor supply curve to the right.

The impact of immigration on the labor market when immigrant workers are substitutes for native-born workers is illustrated in **Figure 11 (a)**. As the immigrants enter the labor market, the labor supply curve shifts to the right, increasing the total employment from 300 to 320. In addition, the hourly wage rate decreases from $20 to $18. Because many immigrants are low-skilled workers, economic studies have found that an influx of immigrants depresses wages for low-skilled native-born workers in the short run. And, because many immigrants are also high-skilled, a similar substitution effect occurs for some high-skilled workers [6]. Since native workers are less likely to accept the lower wage, the employment of native workers decreases.

However, when workers are complementary, an influx of immigrant workers can increase the productivity of the native workers. Thus, an increase in immigrant labor can raise the demand for native workers.

The impact of immigration on the labor market when immigrant workers are complements for native-born workers is illustrated in **Figure 11 (b)**. As the immigrants enter the labor market, the labor demand curve for native workers shifts to the right, increasing the total employment of native workers from 300 to 330. In addition, the hourly wage rate of native workers also increases from $20 to $23.

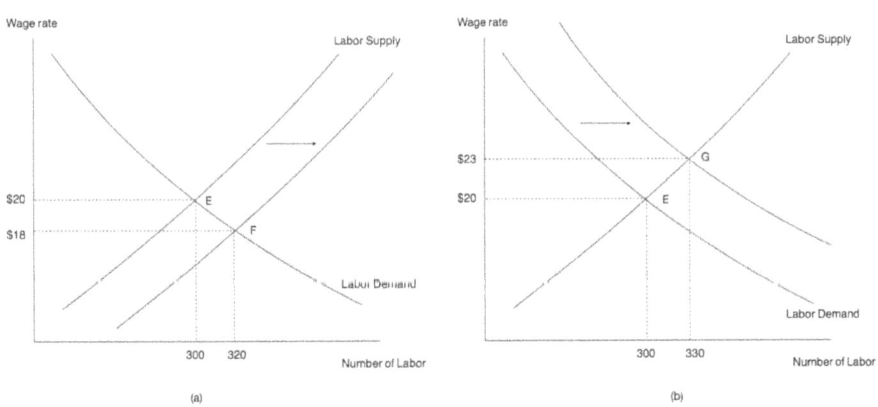

Figure 11.
The impacts of immigration on labor market. (a) the impact of immigration on the labor market when immigrant workers are substitutes for native-born workers, (b) the impact of immigration on the labor market when immigrant workers are complements for native-born workers.

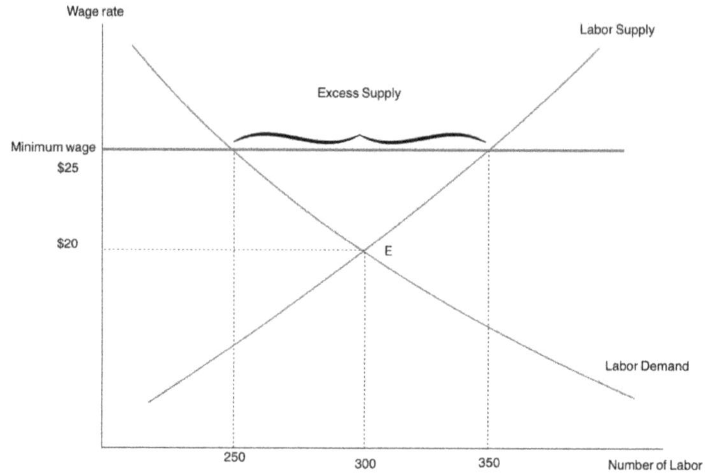

Figure 12.
The impacts of minimum wage on labor market.

7. Policy application: Minimum wage

Minimum wage is a government-mandated lowest wage rate an employer can pay an employee. If the minimum wage is below the market equilibrium wage, it is not binding and will not impact the market equilibrium. When the minimum wage is above the market equilibrium wage, the hourly wage rate cannot legally fall below the minimum wage rate.

Figure 12 shows the economic impact of the minimum wage. Before the minimum wage, the equilibrium wage rate is $20 per hour, and the total employment is 300. When the government implements the minimum wage, the lowest wage rate the firms can offer is $25 per hour. The workers are willing to supply 350 hours at the mandated minimum wage the firms only demand 250 hours. That is, there is an excess supply of labor in the labor market.

8. Conclusion

In this chapter, we have studied the labor market. Just like the goods and services markets, the labor market consists of supply and demand. We saw that the backward-bending nature of the labor supply curve arises from people's decisions between work and leisure. We also learned that the downward-sloping nature of the labor demand curve arises from the fixed amount of capital. The interaction of labor supply with demand determines the market equilibrium wage and total employment. Using this perfectly competitive labor market model, we examined the impacts of immigration and minimum wage on the labor market. Although the labor market, in reality, can be very complicated, the simplified model can assist us in understanding the core of the labor market.

Author details

Meng Sun
Department of Economics, School of Business and Economics, Thompson Rivers University, Kamloops, Canada

*Address all correspondence to: msun@tru.ca

References

[1] Oli H. Towards a definition of non-market activities. Review of Income and Wealth. 1977;**23**(1):79-96. DOI: 10.1111/j.1475-4991.1977.tb00005.x

[2] Earned vs. Unearned Income: What's the Difference [Internet]? 2020. Available from: https://www.mdtaxattorney.com/resources/determining-income-type-earned-and-unearned/ [Accessed: November 03, 2021]

[3] Whitaker JK. Derived demand. In: Palgrave Macmillan, editor. The New Palgrave Dictionary of Economics. London: Palgrave Macmillan; 2008. DOI: 10.1057/978-1-349-95121-5

[4] Moffatt M. The Short Run vs. the Long Run in Microeconomics [Internet]. 2018. Available from: https://www.thoughtco.com/the-short-run-vs-long-run-1146343 [Accessed: November 03, 2021]

[5] Bade R, Parkin M. Derived Demand. Essential Foundations of Economics. Canada: Pearson Education; 2009

[6] Wolla SA. The Economics of Immigration: A Story of Substitutes and Complements. St Louis: Page One Economics®; 2014

Chapter 7

Involuntary Unemployment in Diamond-Type Overlapping Generations Models

Karl Farmer

Abstract

Thus far involuntary unemployment does not occur in Diamond-type Overlapping Generations models. In line with Keynesian macroeconomics, involuntary unemployment is traced back to aggregate demand failures. While macroeconomists majority refers aggregate demand failures to sticky prices, a minority attributes lacking aggregate demand to not perfectly flexible aggregate investment. The chapter investigates how an independent aggregate investment function causes involuntary unemployment under perfectly flexible competitive wage and interest rates in a Diamond-type neoclassical growth model with public debt and human capital accumulation. Moreover, it is shown that a higher public debt to output ratio enhances output growth and reduces involuntary unemployment.

Keywords: involuntary unemployment, overlapping generations models, inflexible aggregate investment, public debt, human capital accumulation

1. Introduction

Involuntary unemployment in Diamond-type Overlapping Generations (OLG) models seem to be a contradiction in terms. As in Solow [1]'s neoclassical growth model, Diamond assumed full employment of the workforce for the OLG economy with production and capital accumulation. Thus, in this economy, unemployment is purely voluntary. Moreover, fiscal policy does not impact the steady-state growth rate of gross domestic product (GDP) since the output growth is exogenously determined. Both, voluntary unemployment and growth ineffectiveness of fiscal policy, do not accord well with the current state of the pandemic-affected world economy which is characterized by high involuntary unemployment and enormous government expenditures to compensate lockdown-related private losses. To be capable to address the effectiveness of fiscal policy to reduce involuntary unemployment, an additional extension of Diamond [2]'s seminal OLG model towards endogenous growth becomes inevitable.

As is well-known, involuntary unemployment is usually associated with Keynesian macroeconomics [3, 4]. Involuntary unemployment is traced back to lacking aggregate demand. But on the reasons why aggregate demand remains below full employment output in a perfectly functioning market economy, there is no consensus among mainstream macro-economists to this date. The majority view follows the New-Keynesian approach in which prices and wages adapt sluggishly to market imbalances due to imperfect competition and other market failures (for a survey see [5]). In contradistinction to the majority view, a macroeconomists' minority follows [6] and more recently [7] who trace back aggregate demand failures to inflexible aggregate investment demand governed by (pessimistic) "animal spirits" of investors independently from aggregate savings of households. In contrast to the imperfectly flexible-price approach, [6, 7] presume perfectly flexible and perfectly competitive output prices, wage rates and interest rates. Despite this perfect-market setting employees do not become fully employed because an independent investment function makes the general equilibrium equations' system over-determinate. Over-determinacy disappears only if at least one market-clearing condition is cancelled, and it is the labor market clearing condition that is deleted.

Magnani [7] without noting precursor Morishima [6] incorporates a macro-founded investment function into Solow [1]'s neoclassical growth model without public debt. Since the chapter intends to study the effects of public debt on private capital accumulation, GDP growth and unemployment in the long run, the present author switches to Diamond [2]'s OLG model with non-neutral internal public debt. Long-run GDP growth in Diamond [2]'s OLG model is, however, exogenous precluding the analysis of how larger public debt impacts GDP growth and unemployment. Hence, there is a need for a mechanism that endogenizes GDP growth. To this end, we stick to human capital accumulation à la [8, 9].

This chapter pursues several purposes: Firstly, it will be shown how in a log-linear utility and Cobb–Douglas production function version of Diamond [2]'s OLG model with internal public debt, the intertemporal equilibrium dynamics based on household's and firm's first-order conditions, on government's budget constraint and intertemporal market-clearing conditions is modified when aggregate investment demand is governed by a savings-independent investment function. Transcending [7] we secondly intend to rigorously prove the existence and dynamic stability of a steady-state of the equilibrium dynamics in a model which closely follows Farmer [10]'s model setting. Our third purpose is to investigate the effects of a higher public debt to output ratio on the output growth rate, on the capital-output ratio, on the interest factor and on the wage tax rate in a steady state of the Diamond OLG model extended by human capital accumulation which is financed by public human capital investment expenditures as in Farmer [11] and in Lin [9]. In extending [9, 11] by an independent aggregate investment function we are capable of exploring analytically and numerically the steady-state effects of a higher public debt to output ratio on the unemployment rate. In particular, we will demonstrate on which factors it depends whether a higher public debt to output ratio raises the output growth rate and decreases the unemployment rate. In contradistinction to the author's contributions in Farmer [10] and Farmer [12] this chapter exhibits the OLG model presented there more completely and succeeds in deriving the steady-state effects of larger public debt more succinctly. This chapter together with Farmer and Farmer [10, 12] can be seen as our contribution to the recent macroeconomic literature.

The structure of the chapter is as follows. In the next section (2.) the model set-up will be presented. In section 3, temporary equilibrium relations and the intertemporal equilibrium dynamics are derived from intertemporal utility maximization, atemporal profit maximization, government's budget constraint and the market-clearing condition in each period. In section 4, the existence of a steady-state solution of the equilibrium dynamics and its local dynamic stability is investigated. Section 5, is devoted to the analysis of the comparative steady-state effects of larger public debt. Section 6, concludes.

2. The model set-up

As in Farmer and Farmer [10, 12], we consider an economy of the infinite horizon which is composed of infinitely lived firms, finitely lived households and an infinitely lived government. In each period $t = 0, 1, 2, \ldots$ a new generation, called generation t, enters the economy. A continuum of $L_t > 0$ units of identical agents comprise generation t.

As mentioned above, to be able to address the question of how fiscal policy impacts long-run growth we extend Diamond [2]'s basic OLG model by introducing human capital accumulation. To point out the growth-enhancing effects of human capital accumulation most clearly, it is assumed here that there is no population growth g^L, i.e. $g^L = 0 \Leftrightarrow G^L = 1$, and no exogenous growth in labor efficiency denoted as g^a, i.e.$g^a = 0 \Leftrightarrow G^a = 1$. As a result of the first assumption, the number of households, L_t, remains constant over time: $L_t = L_{t-1} = L$.

Each household consists of one agent and the agent acts intergenerationally egoistic: The old agent does not take care of the young agent and the young agent does not take care of the old agent. They live two periods long, namely youth (adult) and old age. In youth age, each household starts with human capital h_t, accumulated by the household in period $t-1$. Individual human capital is inelastically supplied to firms that remunerate the real wage rate w_t in exchange for the labor supply. The former denotes the units of the produced good per efficiency unit of labor. In contradistinction to the original [2] OLG model, not the total labor supply is employed but only $(1-u_t)L_t$, where $0 \le u_t < 1$ denotes the unemployment rate. The number of unemployed people is thus $u_t L_t$. The government collects taxes on wages, quoted as a fixed proportion of wage income, $\tau_t w_t h_t$, $0 < \tau_t < 1$. The unemployed do not pay any taxes. Young, employed agents, denoted by superscript E, split the net wage income $(1-\tau_t)w_t h_t$ each period between current consumption $c_t^{1,E}$ and savings s_t^E. Savings of the employed are invested in real capital in period t per employed capita, $I_t^D/L_t(1-u_t)$, which is demanded by employed households in youth, and in real government bonds per employed capita, $B_{t+1}^D/L_t(1-u_t)$, which is also demanded by employed households in youth. For simplicity, we assume a depreciation rate of one for real capital.

Any unemployed young-age household, denoted by superscript U, consumes $c_t^{1,U}$, saves s_t^U and receives from the government an unemployment benefit $\varsigma_t > 0$ to be able to finance its consumption and savings: $c_t^{1,U} + s_t^U = \varsigma_t$.

In old age, the employed household supplies inelastically $K_{t+1}^S/L_t(1-u_t) = I_t^D/L_t(1-u_t)$ to firms, and $B_{t+1}^S/L_t(1-u_t) = B_{t+1}^D/L_t(1-u_t)$ to young households in period $t+1$. Thus, the per capita savings of employed people are invested as follows: $s_t^E = K_{t+1}^S/L_t(1-u_t) + B_{t+1}^S/L_t(1-u_t)$. Similarly, the per capita savings of the unemployed household are invested as follows: $s_t^U = K_{t+1}^S/L_t u_t + B_{t+1}^S/L_t u_t$. In old age, both employed and unemployed households consume their gross return on assets: $c_{t+1}^{2,E} = q_{t+1}K_{t+1}^S/L_t(1-u_t) + (1+i_{t+1})B_{t+1}^S/L_t(1-u_t)$, respectively $c_{t+1}^{2,U} = q_{t+1}K_{t+1}^S/L_t u_t + (1+i_{t+1})B_{t+1}^S/L_t u_t$, where $c_{t+1}^{2,E}$, and $c_{t+1}^{2,U}$, represent the consumption of the employed, respectively unemployed, in old age, q_{t+1} denotes the gross rental rate on real capital, and i_{t+1} denotes the real interest rate on government bonds in period to remain as simple as possible, we assume that rental and interest income are not taxed.

A log-linear intertemporal utility function slightly generalized in comparison to Diamond ([2], p. 1134]'s leading example represents the intertemporal preferences of all two-period lived households. As usual, this simple specification aims at closed-form solutions for the intertemporal equilibrium dynamics (see e.g. [13, pp. 181–184]).

The typical younger, employed household maximizes the following intertemporal utility function subject to the budget constraints of the active period (i) and the retirement period (ii):

$$\text{Max} \rightarrow \varepsilon \ln c_t^{1,E} + \beta \ln c_{t+1}^{2,E}$$

subject to:

$$(i)\ c_t^{1,E} + I_t^{D,E}/L_t(1-u_t) + B_{t+1}^{D,E}/L_t(1-u_t) = w_t h_t(1-\tau_t),$$

$$(ii)\ c_{t+1}^{2,E} = q_{t+1} K_{t+1}^{S,E}/L_t(1-u_t) + (1+i_{t+1}) B_{t+1}^{S,E}/L_t(1-u_t),$$

$$K_{t+1}^{S,E} = I_t^{D,E}, B_{t+1}^{S,E} = B_{t+1}^{D,E}.$$

Here, $0 < \varepsilon \leq 1$ depicts the utility elasticity of employed household's consumption in youth, while $0 < \beta < 1$ denotes the subjective future utility discount factor. For the log-linear utility function above, a unique, interior solution of the optimization problem exists. Hence, one may solve the old-age budget constraint for $B_{t+1}^{S,E}/L_t(1-u_t)$ and insert the result into the young-age, employed budget constraint of (i), and thus obtain:

$$c_t^{1,E} + c_{t+1}^{2,E}/(1+i_{t+1}) + [1 - q_{t+1}/(1+i_{t+1})] K_{t+1}^{S,E}/L_t(1-u_t) = w_t h_t(1-\tau_t). \quad (1)$$

A strictly positive and finite solution to maximizing the intertemporal utility function subject to the constraint (1) requires that the following no-arbitrage condition holds:

$$q_{t+1} = 1 + i_{t+1}. \quad (2)$$

The no-arbitrage condition (2) implies that $K_{t+1}^{S,E}/L_t(1-u_t)$ is optimally indeterminate, and the first-order conditions for a maximum solution read as follows:

$$c_t^{1,E} + c_{t+1}^{2,E}/(1+i_{t+1}) = (1-\tau_t) w_t h_t, \quad (3)$$

$$(\beta/\varepsilon) c_t^{1,E} = c_{t+1}^{2,E}/(1+i_{t+1}). \quad (4)$$

Solving equations (3) and (4) for $c_t^{1,E}$ and $c_{t+1}^{2,E}$ yields the following optimal consumption for employed people in youth and old age:

$$c_t^{1,E} = [\varepsilon/(\varepsilon+\beta)](1-\tau_t) w_t h_t, \quad (5)$$

$$c_{t+1}^{2,E} = [\beta/(\varepsilon+\beta)](1+i_{t+1})(1-\tau_t) w_t h_t. \quad (6)$$

Since$s_t^E = K_{t+1}^{S,E}/L_t(1-u_t) + B_{t+1}^{S,E}/L_t(1-u_t)$, we find for the utility-maximizing savings:

$$s_t^E = [\beta/(\varepsilon+\beta)](1-\tau_t) w_t h_t. \quad (7)$$

The typical younger, unemployed household maximizes the following intertemporal utility function subject to the budget constraints of the active period (i) and the retirement period (ii):

$$\text{Max} \rightarrow \varepsilon \ln c_t^{1,U} + \beta \ln c_{t+1}^{2,U}$$

subject to:

$$(i)\ c_t^{1,U} + I_t^{D,U}/L_t u_t + B_{t+1}^{D,U}/L_t u_t = \varsigma_t,$$
$$(ii)\ c_{t+1}^{2,U} = q_{t+1} K_{t+1}^{S,U}/L_t u_t + (1 + i_{t+1}) B_{t+1}^{S,U}/L_t u_t,$$
$$K_{t+1}^{S,U} = I_t^{D,U}, B_{t+1}^{S,U} = B_{t+1}^{D,U}.$$

Again, $0 < \varepsilon \leq 1$ denotes the utility elasticity of consumption in unemployed youth, while $0 < \beta < 1$ depicts the subjective future utility discount factor and ς_t denotes the unemployment benefit per capita unemployed. As above, the log-linear intertemporal utility function ensures the existence of a unique, interior solution for the above optimization problem. Hence, one may again solve the old-age budget constraint for $B_{t+1}^{S,U}/L_t u_t$ and insert the result into the young-age, unemployed budget constraint of (i), and thus obtain:

$$c_t^{1,U} + c_{t+1}^{2,U}/(1 + i_{t+1}) + [1 - q_{t+1}/(1 + i_{t+1})] K_{t+1}^{S,U}/L_t u_t = \varsigma_t. \tag{8}$$

The no-arbitrage condition (2) implies that $K_{t+1}^{S,U}/L_t u_t$ is optimally indeterminate, and the first-order conditions for a maximum solution read as follows:

$$c_t^{1,U} + c_{t+1}^{2,U}/(1 + i_{t+1}) = \varsigma_t, \tag{9}$$

$$(\beta/\varepsilon) c_t^{1,U} = c_{t+1}^{2,U}/(1 + i_{t+1}). \tag{10}$$

Solving equations (9) and (10) for $c_t^{1,U}$ and $c_{t+1}^{2,U}$ yields the following optimal consumption in youth and old age:

$$c_t^{1,U} = [\varepsilon/(\varepsilon + \beta)] \varsigma_t, \tag{11}$$

$$c_{t+1}^{2,U} = [\beta/(\varepsilon + \beta)](1 + i_{t+1}) \varsigma_t. \tag{12}$$

Since $s_t^U = K_{t+1}^{S,U}/L_t u_t + B_{t+1}^{S,U}/L_t u_t$, we find for the utility-maximizing savings:

$$s_t^U = [\beta/(\varepsilon + \beta)] \varsigma_t. \tag{13}$$

All firms are endowed with an identical (linear-homogeneous) Cobb–Douglas production function which reads as follows:

$$Y_t = M(h_t N_t)^{1-\alpha} (K_t)^\alpha, \ 0 < \alpha < 1, M > 0. \tag{14}$$

Here, Y_t denotes aggregate output or GDP, $M > 0$ stands for total factor productivity, N_t represents the number of employed laborers, while K_t denotes the input of capital services, all in period t, and $1 - \alpha$ (α) depicts the production elasticity (= production share) of labor (capital) services.

Maximization of $Y_t - w_t h_t N_t - q_t K_t$ subject to Cobb–Douglas production (14) implies the following first-order conditions:

$$(1 - \alpha) M [K_t/(h_t N_t)]^\alpha = w_t, \tag{15}$$

$$\alpha M [K_t/(h_t N_t)]^{(\alpha - 1)} = q_t. \tag{16}$$

However, since the number of employed workers is $N_t = L(1 - u_t)$, we can rewrite the profit maximization conditions (15) and (16) as follows:

$$(1-\alpha)M[K_t/(h_tL(1-u_t))]^{\alpha} = w_t, \tag{17}$$

$$\alpha M[K_t/(h_tL(1-u_t))]^{(\alpha-1)} = q_t. \tag{18}$$

Finally, the GDP function can be rewritten as follows:

$$Y_t = M(h_tL(1-u_t))^{1-\alpha}(K_t)^{\alpha}. \tag{19}$$

As in Diamond [2], the government does not optimize, but is subject to the following constraint period by period:

$$B_{t+1} = (1+i_t)B_t + \Delta_t + L_tu_t\varsigma_t + \Gamma_t - \tau_t(1-u_t)w_th_tL, \tag{20}$$

where B_t denotes the aggregate stock of real public debt at the beginning of period t,Γ_t denotes human capital investment (HCI) expenditures, and Δ_t denotes all non-HCI expenditures of the government exclusive of government's unemployment benefits $L_tu_t\varsigma_t$ per period.

In line with Glomm and Ravikumar [8] human capital in period t is determined by the human capital of the generation entering the economy in period $t-1$, and by the government's HCI spending in period $t-1$, Γ_{t-1}:

$$h_t = H_0(h_{t-1})^{\mu}(\Gamma_{t-1}/L)^{1-\mu}, H_0 = \underline{H} > 0, 0 < \mu < 1, \tag{21}$$

whereby $\underline{H}$ indicates a level parameter, μ depicts the production elasticity of human capital, and $1-\mu$ denotes the production elasticity of public HCI spending. The macroeconomic version of equation (21) is obtained by multiplying it on both sides by L:

$$Lh_t \equiv H_t = H_0(Lh_{t-1})^{1-\mu}(\Gamma_{t-1})^{\mu} \equiv H_0(H_{t-1})^{1-\mu}(\Gamma_{t-1})^{\mu}. \tag{22}$$

The economy grows, even in the absence of population growth and exogenous progress in labor efficiency. Using the GDP growth factor $G_t^Y \equiv Y_{t+1}/Y_t$ as well as equations (19) and (22), the GDP growth factor can be written as follows:

$$G_{t+1}^Y = \frac{H_{t+1}}{H_t}\frac{(1-u_{t+1})^{1-\alpha}}{(1-u_t)^{1-\alpha}}\frac{(k_{t+1})^{\alpha}}{(k_t)^{\alpha}}, k_t \equiv \frac{K_t}{H_t}. \tag{23}$$

As Magnani [7], Morishima [6], Salotti and Trecroci [14] rightly states, aggregate investment in Solow [1]'s neoclassical growth model is not micro- but macro-founded since it is determined by aggregate savings. The same holds in Diamond [2]'s OLG model of neoclassical growth where perfectly flexible aggregate investment is also determined by aggregate savings of households. Deviating from those neoclassical growth models, Morishima [6] and more recently Magnani [7] and Salotti [14] claim that "investments are determined by an independent investment function." This function is specified in discrete time as follows:

$$I_t^D = \phi H_t(1+i_t)^{-\theta}, \phi > 0, \theta \geq 0. \tag{24}$$

The positive parameter ϕ reflects "Keynesian investors' animal spirits" [7, 14] while θ denotes the interest-factor elasticity of aggregate investment demand I_t^D.

In addition to the restrictions imposed by household and firm optimizations and the government budget constraint, markets for labor, capital services and assets, ought to clear in all periods (the market for the output of production is cleared using Walras' Law[1]).

$$L_t(1-u_t) = N_t, \forall t. \tag{25}$$

$$K_t^{S,E} + K_t^{S,U} = K_t^S = K_t, \forall t. \tag{26}$$

$$B_t^{D.E} + B_t^{D,U} = B_t^{S,E} + B_t^{S,U} = B_t, \forall t. \tag{27}$$

3. Temporary equilibrium and intertemporal equilibrium dynamics

As a first step, the unemployment rate in period t (= temporary unemployment rate) is derived. To this end, we use the output market-clearing identity:

$$\begin{aligned} &P_tL_t(1-u_t)c_t^{1,E} + P_tL_{t-1}(1-u_{t-1})c_t^{2,E} + P_tL_tu_tc_t^{1,U} + P_tL_{t-1}u_{t-1}c_t^{2,U} \\ &+P_tI_t^{D,E} + P_tI_t^{D,U} + P_t\Gamma_t + P_t\Delta_t = P_tY_t. \end{aligned} \tag{28}$$

Starting with identity (28), we insert equations (19), equation (5) and constraint (ii) from the employed household's optimization problem for period t as well as equation (11) and constraint (ii) from unemployed household's optimization problem for period t. In addition, we also insert equation (24), with $I_t^D = I_t^{D,E} + I_t^{D,U}$ and add the market clearing conditions (26) and (27). In this way, the following equation for $P_t = 1, \forall t$ is obtained:

$$\begin{aligned} M(h_tL(1-u_t))^{1-\alpha}(K_t)^\alpha &= \varepsilon/(\varepsilon+\beta)(1-\tau_t)w_th_tL_t(1-u_t) \\ &+\varepsilon/(\varepsilon+\beta)\varsigma_tL_tu_t + q_tK_t + (1+i_t)B_t + \phi H_t(1+i_t)^{-\theta} + \Gamma_t + \Delta_t. \end{aligned} \tag{29}$$

[1] The proof of Walras' law proceeds as follows: Denote by $P_t > 0$ the nominal price (level) of production output (GDP). Then, the current period budget constraint of employed households in youth can be rewritten as follows: $P_tL_t(1-u_t)c_t^{1,E} + P_tI_t^{D,E} + P_tB_{t+1}^{D,E} = (1-\tau_t)P_tw_th_t(1-u_t)L_t$. (F.1) The budget constraint of households in old age employed in youth reads as follows: $P_tL_{t-1}(1-u_{t-1})c_t^{2,E} = P_tq_tK_t^{S,E} + P_t(1+i_t)B_t^{S,E}$. (F.2) The budget constraint of young unemployed households in period t is as follows: $P_tL_tu_tc_t^{1,U} + P_tI_t^{D,U} + P_tB_{t+1}^{D,U} = L_tu_t\varsigma_t$. (F.3) Moreover, the budget constraint of the household in old age in period t, which was unemployed in youth, reads as follows: $P_tL_{t-1}u_{t-1}c_t^{2,U} = P_tq_tK_t^{S,U} + P_t(1+i_t)B_t^{S,U}$. (F.4) In addition, maximum profits are zero, which implies: $P_tY_t = P_tw_tN_t + P_tq_tK_t$. (F.5) Finally, government's budget constraint is rewritten as follows: $P_tB_{t+1} = P_t(1+i_t)B_t + P_t\Delta_t + P_t\Gamma_t + P_tL_tu_t\varsigma_t - P_t\tau_tw_th_tL_t(1-u_t)$. (F.6) Adding up the left- and right-hand side of equations (F.1), (F.2), (F.3) and (F.4) yields: $P_tL_t(1-u_t)c_t^{1,E} + P_tI_t^{D,E} + P_tL_tu_tc_t^{1,U} + P_tI_t^{D,U} + P_tL_{t-1}(1-u_{t-1})c_t^{2,E} + P_tL_{t-1}u_{t-1}c_t^{2,U} = (1-\tau_t)P_tw_th_t \times \times (1-u_t)L_t - P_tB_{t+1}^{D,E} - P_tB_{t+1}^{D,U} + L_tu_t\varsigma_t + P_tq_tK_t^{S,E} + P_t(1+i_t)B_t^{S,E} + P_tq_tK_t^{S,U} + P_t(1+i_t)B_t^{S,U}$. (F.7) Considering (25), (26) and (27) in (F.7), gives: $P_tL_t(1-u_t)c_t^{1,E} + P_tL_{t-1}(1-u_{t-1})c_t^{2,E} + P_tI_t^{D,E} + P_tL_tu_tc_t^{1,U} + P_tL_{t-1}u_{t-1}c_t^{2,U} + P_tI_t^{D,U} = P_tw_tN_t - \tau_tP_tw_tN_t - P_tB_{t+1} + P_tq_tK_t + P_t(1+i_t)B_t$.(F.8) Considering labor market clearing condition (24) when inserting (F.6) into (F.8), and taking account of (F.5) in (F.8) yields: $P_tL_t(1-u_t)c_t^{1,E} + P_tL_{t-1}(1-u_{t-1})c_t^{2,E} + P_tL_tu_tc_t^{1,U} + P_tL_{t-1}u_{t-1}c_t^{2,U} + P_tI_t^{D,E} + P_tI_t^{D,U} + P_t\Gamma_t = P_tY_t$, which is production-output market clearing. Since this equation is always true, P_t is indeterminate and can be fixed as $P_t = 1$.

On dividing equation (29) into both sides by Y_t, this equation turns into the following equation:

$$\begin{aligned}1 = \varepsilon/(\varepsilon+\beta)(1-\tau_t)w_t h_t L_t(1-u_t)/Y_t + \varepsilon/(\varepsilon+\beta)\varsigma_t L_t u_t/Y_t \\ +q_t K_t/Y_t + (1+i_t)B_t/Y + \phi H_t(1+i_t)^{-\theta}/Y + \Gamma_t/Y + \Delta_t/Y.\end{aligned} \quad (30)$$

Rewriting profit maximization condition (15) as

$$w_t h_t L(1-u_t) = (1-\alpha)(K_t)^{\alpha}(h_t L(1-u_t))^{1-\alpha} = (1-\alpha)Y_t, \quad (31)$$

and using the definitions $v_t \equiv K_t/Y_t$,$b_t \equiv B_t/Y_t$, $\delta_t \equiv \Delta_t/Y_t$, $\gamma_t \equiv \Gamma_t/Y_t$ and $\xi_t \equiv (\varsigma_t u_t L_t)/Y_t$, equation (30) can be rewritten as follows:

$$\begin{aligned}1 = \varepsilon/(\varepsilon+\beta)(1-\tau_t)(1-\alpha) + \varepsilon/(\varepsilon+\beta)\xi_t \\ +q_t v_t + (1+i_t)b_t + \phi(1/k_t)(1+i_t)^{-\theta}v_t + \gamma_t + \delta_t.\end{aligned} \quad (32)$$

The capital-output ratio v_t is related to the real-capital to human-capital ratio k_t as follows:

$$v_t = \frac{K_t}{M(H_t)^{1-\alpha}(1-u_t)^{1-\alpha}(K_t)^{\alpha}} = \frac{(K_t)^{1-\alpha}}{M(H_t)^{1-\alpha}(1-u_t)^{1-\alpha}} = \frac{(k_t)^{1-\alpha}}{M(1-u_t)^{1-\alpha}}, \quad (33)$$

which implies:

$$q_t = \alpha/v_t. \quad (34)$$

By use of the no-arbitrage condition (2) as well as of equations (33) and (34) equation (32) turns out to be:

$$\begin{aligned}1 = (\varepsilon/(\varepsilon+\beta)(1-\tau_t)(1-\alpha) + (\varepsilon/(\varepsilon+\beta)\xi_t + \alpha[1+b_t/v_t] \\ +\phi(\alpha/v_t)^{-\theta}M^{-1/(1-\alpha)}(1-u_t)^{-1}v_t{}^{-\alpha/(1-\alpha)} + \gamma_t + \delta_t.\end{aligned} \quad (35)$$

Next, it is apt to specify how the government determines its intertemporal policy profile. To this end, we assume that government consumption expenditures per GDP, δ_t, government human capital investment expenditures per GDP, γ_t, and unemployment benefits per GDP, ξ_t, are time-stationary, i.e., $\delta_t = \delta_{t+1} = \delta, \gamma_t = \gamma_{t+1} = \gamma, \forall t$ and $\xi_t = \xi_{t+1} = \xi, \forall t$. As in Diamond ([2], p. 1137) we furthermore assume that the government runs a 'constant-stock' fiscal policy: $b_{t+1} = b_t = b$. The budget constraint of the government written in per GDP terms reads as follows:

$$\begin{aligned}\frac{B_{t+1}}{Y_{t+1}}\frac{Y_{t+1}}{Y_t} \equiv bG_t^Y = (1+i_t)B_t/Y_t + \Gamma_t/Y_t + \frac{\Delta_t}{Y_t} + \frac{L_t u_t \varsigma_t}{Y_t} - \frac{\tau_t(1-u_t)w_t h_t L}{Y_t} \\ \equiv \alpha b/v_t + \gamma + \delta + \xi - \tau_t(1-\alpha).\end{aligned} \quad (36)$$

Equation (36) implies that the wage-tax rate ought to become endogenous and is determined by the following equation:

$$\tau_t = \left[(\alpha/v_t - G_t^Y)b + \gamma + \delta + \xi\right]/(1-\alpha). \quad (37)$$

Inserting τ_t from equation (37) into equation (32), leads to the following result:

$$1=(\varepsilon/(\varepsilon+\beta)\left[1-\alpha(1+b/v_t)-\gamma-\delta-\xi+bG_t^Y\right]+(\varepsilon/(\varepsilon+\beta)\xi \\ +\alpha[1+b_t/v_t]+\gamma+\delta+\phi(\alpha/v_t)^{-\theta}M^{-1/(1-\alpha)}(1-u_t)^{-1}{v_t}^{-\alpha/(1-\alpha)}. \tag{38}$$

Collecting terms and simplifying the resulting expression yields the following equation for $(1-u_t)$:

$$(1-u_t)=\left\{(\varepsilon+\beta)\phi\alpha^{-\theta}M^{-1/(1-\alpha)}{v_t}^{[\theta(1-\alpha)-\alpha]/(1-\alpha)}\right\} \\ /\left\{\beta[1-\gamma-\delta-\alpha(1+b/v_t)]-\varepsilon bG_t^Y\right\}. \tag{39}$$

In terms of the transformed variables, the growth factor of human capital reads as follows:

$$\begin{aligned}\frac{H_{t+1}}{H_t}&=H_0(H_t)^{\mu-1}(\gamma)^{1-\mu}(Y_t)^{1-\mu}\\ &=H_0(H_t)^{\mu-1}(\gamma)^{1-\mu}M^{(1-\mu)}(K_t)^{\alpha(1-\mu)}(H_t)^{(1-\alpha)(1-\mu)}(1-u_t)^{(1-\alpha)(1-\mu)}\\ &=H_0M^{(1-\mu)/(1-\alpha)}(\gamma)^{1-\mu}(v_t)^{\alpha(1-\mu)/(1-\alpha)}(1-u_t)^{(1-\mu)}.\end{aligned} \tag{40}$$

The GDP growth factor in terms of the capital-output ratio can be rewritten as follows:

$$\begin{aligned}G_t^Y&=\frac{H_{t+1}}{H_t}\left(\frac{v_{t+1}}{v_t}\right)^{\alpha/(1-\alpha)}\frac{(1-u_{t+1})}{(1-u_t)}\\ &=H_0M^{(1-\mu)/(1-\alpha)}(\gamma)^{1-\mu}(v_{t+1})^{\alpha/(1-\alpha)}(v_t)^{-\alpha\mu/(1-\alpha)}(1-u_{t+1})(1-u_t)^{-\mu}.\end{aligned} \tag{41}$$

By using the intertemporal equilibrium condition $K_{t+1}^S=I_t^D$, one obtains the following equation for the dynamics of the capital-output ratio:

$$v_{t+1}G_t^Y=\phi\frac{H_t}{K_t}\frac{K_t}{Y_t}{q_t}^{-\theta}=\phi\frac{1}{k_t}v_t{q_t}^{-\theta}=\alpha^{-\theta}\phi M^{\frac{-1}{(1-\alpha)}}(v_t)^{\frac{\theta(1-\alpha)-\alpha}{(1-\alpha)}}(1-u_t)^{-1}. \tag{42}$$

The final steps needed to arrive at the equation of motion for the capital-output ratio entail; first, inserting the GDP growth factor equation (41) into equation (42). This procedure yields:

$${v_{t+1}}^{1/(1-\alpha)}(1-u_{t+1})=\left[\phi/(\alpha^\theta H_0)\right]\gamma^{\mu-1}M^{(\mu-2)/(1-\alpha)}{v_t}^{[\theta(1-\alpha)-\alpha(1-\mu)]/(1-\alpha)}(1-u_t)^{\mu-1}. \tag{43}$$

Next, after inserting the growth factor equation (41) into equation (39) and rearranging, we arrive at the following intermediate result:

$${v_{t+1}}^{\alpha/(1-\alpha)}(1-u_{t+1})=(\varepsilon bH_0)^{-1}\gamma^{\mu-1}M^{(1-\mu)/(\alpha-1)}(1-u_t)^{\mu-1}{v_t}^{(\alpha\mu)/(1-\alpha)} \\ \times\left\{\beta(1-u_t)[1-\alpha(1+b/v_t)-\gamma-\delta]-(\beta+\varepsilon)\phi M^{-1/(1-\alpha)}{v_t}^{[\theta(1-\alpha)-\alpha]/(1-\alpha)}\right\}. \tag{44}$$

Solving equation (44) for $1-u_{t+1}$ and inserting the result into equation (43) then yields, after re-arranging, the first equation of motion:

$$v_{t+1}=\frac{\varepsilon b}{\beta\phi^{-1}\alpha^\theta M^{1/(1-\alpha)}[1-\alpha(1+b/v_t)-\gamma-\delta](1-u_t){v_t}^{[\alpha-\theta(1-\alpha)]/(1-\alpha)}-\beta-\varepsilon}. \tag{45}$$

Reinserting the dynamic equation (45) into equation (43) and solving for $1 - u_{t+1}$ generate the second equation of motion:

$$u_{t+1} = 1 - \phi(\alpha^{\theta}H_0)^{-1}\gamma^{\mu-1}(\varepsilon b)^{-1/(1-\alpha)}M^{(2-\mu)/(\alpha-1)}{v_t}^{[\theta(1-\alpha)-\alpha(1-\mu)]/(1-\alpha)}(1-u_t)^{\mu-1}$$
$$\times\left\{\alpha^{\theta}\beta\phi^{-1}M^{1/(1-\alpha)}(1-u_t)[1-\alpha(1+b/v_t)-\gamma-\delta]{v_t}^{[\alpha-\theta(1-\alpha)]/(1-\alpha)} - (\beta+\varepsilon)\right\}^{1/(1-\alpha)}. \tag{46}$$

4. Existence and dynamic stability of steady states

The steady states of the equilibrium dynamics depicted by the difference equations (45) and (46) are defined as $\lim_{t->\infty} v_t = v$ and $\lim_{t->\infty} u_t = u$. Explicit steady state solutions are not possible. Thus, we are in need to resort to an intermediate value theorem to prove the existence of at least one feasible steady-state solution $v_{\min} < v < \infty$ and $0 < u < 1$.

To this end, for given structural and policy parameters (except b), the maximally sustainable debt to GDP parameter is defined as $b^{\max}$, and the minimal capital-output ratio as $v_{\min}$ which ensure full employment. On inserting G^Y from the steady-state version of equation (41) into the steady-state version of equation (42) with $u = 0$, $v_{\min}$ can then explicitly be determined as follows:

$$v_{\min} = \left[\alpha^{-\theta}\gamma^{\mu-1}\phi(H_0)^{-1}M^{(\mu-2)/(1-\alpha)}\right]^{(1-\alpha)/[1+\alpha(1-\mu)-\theta(1-\alpha)]}. \tag{47}$$

Using the steady-state version of equation (39) with $u = 0$, $b = b^{\max}$ can be calculated as follows:

$$b^{\max} = \left[\beta(1-\alpha-\gamma-\delta) - \alpha^{-\theta}(\beta+\varepsilon)\phi M^{-1/(1-\alpha)}{v_{\min}}^{[\theta(1-\alpha)-\alpha]/(1-\alpha)}\right]$$
$$/\left[\alpha\beta(v_{\min})^{-1} + \varepsilon H_0 M^{(1-\mu)/(1-\alpha)}\gamma^{1-\mu}(v_{\min})^{\alpha(1-\mu)/(1-\alpha)}\right], \tag{48}$$

Whereby, to ensure a strictly larger than zero $b^{\max}$, it is assumed that: $\beta(1-\alpha-\gamma-\delta) > \alpha^{-\theta}(\beta+\varepsilon)\phi M^{-1/(1-\alpha)}{v_{\min}}^{[\theta(1-\alpha)-\alpha]/(1-\alpha)}$.

For the proof of the existence of at least one $0 < u < 1$ and $v_{\min} < v < \infty$ the steady-state versions of equations (45) and (46) are used. This results in:

$$v = \frac{\varepsilon b}{\alpha^{\theta}\beta\phi^{-1}M^{1/(1-\alpha)}[1-\alpha(1+b/v)-\gamma-\delta](1-u)v^{[\alpha-\theta(1-\alpha)]/(1-\alpha)} - \beta - \varepsilon}. \tag{49}$$

$$1-u = \phi(\alpha^{\theta}H_0)^{-1}\gamma^{\mu-1}(\varepsilon b)^{-1/(1-\alpha)}M^{(2-\mu)/(\alpha-1)}v^{[\theta(1-\alpha)-\alpha(1-\mu)]/(1-\alpha)}(1-u)^{\mu-1}$$
$$\times\{\alpha^{\theta}\beta\phi^{-1}M^{1/(1-\alpha)}(1-u)[1-\alpha(1+b/v)-\gamma-\delta]v^{[\alpha-\theta(1-\alpha)]/(1-\alpha)}$$
$$-(\beta+\varepsilon)\}^{1/(1-\alpha)}. \tag{50}$$

By substituting $\alpha^{\theta}\beta\phi^{-1}M^{1/(1-\alpha)}(1-u)[1-\alpha(1+b/v_t)-\gamma-\delta]v^{\alpha/(1-\alpha)} - \beta - \varepsilon$ in (50) for $\varepsilon b/v$, equation (50) can be reduced to the following simpler equation:

$$1-u = \alpha^{-\theta}\gamma^{\mu-1}\phi{H_0}^{-1}M^{(\mu-2)/(1-\alpha)}(1-u)^{\mu-1}v^{[\theta(1-\alpha)-\alpha(1-\mu)-1]/(1-\alpha)} \tag{51}$$

Using the short cut $1 - u \equiv w$, the two equations (49) and (50) can be explicitly solved for w as follows:

$$w_1 = \frac{\alpha^{-\theta}\phi M^{-1/(1-\alpha)} v^{[\theta(1-\alpha)-\alpha]/(1-\alpha)}[\beta + \varepsilon(1+b/v)]}{\beta[1-\alpha(1+b/v)-\gamma-\delta]}, \tag{52}$$

$$w_2 = \left[\alpha^{-\theta}\gamma^{\mu-1}\phi H_0{}^{-1} M^{(\mu-2)/(1-\alpha)} v^{[\theta(1-\alpha)-\alpha(\mu-1)-1]/(1-\alpha)}\right]^{1/(2-\mu)}. \tag{53}$$

Hereby, w_1 represents the solution of equation (49) for w, while w_2 exhibits the solution of equation (50) for w. A steady state solution exists if $w_1(v) = w_2(v)$ for at least one $v_{\min} < v < \infty$.

Proposition 1. Suppose there exist $\eta > 0$ and $v^{\max} > 0$ such that $w_1(v^{\max}) = w_2(v^{\max}) + \eta$. Then, the solution of $w_1(v) = w_2(v)$ for at least one $v_{\min} < v < v^{\max}$ exists and represents a steady state of the equilibrium dynamics (45) and (46) with $0 < w < 1, (0 < u < 1)$.

Proof. For $b = b^{\max}$ it is known from above that $v = v_{\min}$ and $u = 0$. Thus, let be $b < b^{\max}$. Using this assumption, we may then show that $0 < u < 1$ and $v_{\min} < v < v^{\max}$. From both $b < b^{\max}$, $dw_1/db = \{[\varepsilon(1-\gamma-\delta) + \alpha\beta] \times \alpha^{-\theta}\phi M^{-1/(1-\alpha)} v^{[1-2\alpha+\theta(1-\alpha)]/(1-\alpha)}/\{\beta[\alpha b - (1-\alpha-\gamma-\delta)]v\}^2 > 0$ and from equations (52) and (53), it follows that $0 < w < 1, (0 < u < 1)$. Now an intermediate value theorem is applied to demonstrate that $w_1(v) = w_2(v)$ for $v_{\min} < v < v^{\max}$. To this end, notice first that for $b = b^{\max}$, $w_1(v_{\min}) = w_2(v_{\min})$. Under $b < b^{\max}$ and $dw_1/db > 0$ it is clear that $w_1(v_{\min}; b) < w_1(v_{\min}; b^{\max})$. Since $w_2(v)$ does not depend on b, it follows that $w_2(v_{\min}; b) = w_2(v_{\min}; b^{\max})$ for all feasible b. Hence, $w_1(v_{\min}; b) < w_2(v_{\min}; b), \forall b < b^{\max}$. At the upper boundary of feasible values for v, at $v = v^{\max}$, the assumption employed in Proposition 1 above ensures that $w_1(v^{\max}; b) > w_2(v^{\max}; b)$. Since the two functions $w_1(v; b)$ and $w_2(v; b)$ are continuous on $v_{\min} < v < v^{\max}$, the intermediate value theorem implies at least one $v_{\min} < v < v_{\max}$ such that $w_1(v) = w_2(v)$ and $0 < w < 1, (0 < u < 1)$.. Moreover, for a broad set of feasible parameters the solution is unique. Q.E.D.

The next step is to investigate the local dynamic stability of the unique steady-state solution. To this end, the intertemporal equilibrium equations (39), (41), and (42) are totally differentiated with respect to $v_{t+1}, w_{t+1}, G_t^Y, v_t, w_t$. Then, the Jacobian matrix $J(v, w)$ of all partial differentials with respect to v_t and w_t is formed as follows:

$$J(v,w) = \begin{bmatrix} \frac{\partial v_{t+1}}{\partial v_t}(v,w) & \frac{\partial v_{t+1}}{\partial w_t}(v,w) \\ \frac{\partial w_{t+1}}{\partial v_t}(v,w) & \frac{\partial w_{t+1}}{\partial w_t}(v,w) \end{bmatrix}, \tag{54}$$

with

$$\frac{\partial v_{t+1}}{\partial v_t} \equiv j_{11} = -\frac{\varepsilon b G^Y[\alpha - \theta(1-\alpha] + (1-\alpha)\beta b q + [\alpha - \theta(1-\alpha](\beta+\varepsilon)G^Y v}{(1-\alpha)\,\varepsilon b\, G^Y},$$

$$\frac{\partial v_{t+1}}{\partial w_t} \equiv j_{12} = -\frac{v[\varepsilon b + (\beta+\varepsilon)v]}{\varepsilon b w} < 0,$$

$$\frac{\partial w_{t+1}}{\partial v_t} \equiv j_{21} =$$

$$\frac{w\{[\alpha - \theta(1-\alpha)](\beta+\varepsilon)G^Y v + (1-\alpha)\beta b q + \alpha\varepsilon b G^Y[\alpha - \theta(1-\alpha) + \mu(1-\alpha)]\}}{(1-\alpha)^2 \varepsilon b G^Y v},$$

$$\frac{\partial w_{t+1}}{\partial w_t} \equiv j_{22} = \frac{\varepsilon b[\alpha + \mu(1-\alpha)] + (\beta+\varepsilon)v}{\varepsilon b(1-\alpha)} > 0.$$

The sign of j_{12} is unambiguously smaller than zero, while the sign of j_{22} is always larger than zero. The signs of j_{11} and j_{21} depend on whether $\theta > \alpha/(1-a)$ or

$\theta \leq \alpha/(1-a)$. In the former case the sign of j_{11} is smaller than zero, whereby the sign of j_{21} is larger than zero. In the latter case, the signs of these entries of the Jacobian (54) are in general ambiguous. To evaluate the dynamic stability of the equilibrium dynamics in the neighborhood of the steady-state solution, the eigenvalues of the Jacobian matrix (54) are needed. To this end, the trace $\mathrm{Tr}J(v,w)$, the determinant $\mathrm{Det}J(v,w)$ and $1-\mathrm{Tr}J(v,w)+\mathrm{Det}J(v,w)$ need to be calculated.

$$\mathrm{Tr}J(v,w) = \theta + \mu - \frac{q\beta}{\varepsilon G^Y} + \frac{(\beta+\varepsilon)(1+\theta)v}{\varepsilon b}, \tag{55}$$

$$\mathrm{Det}J(v,w) = \frac{\beta(1-\mu)q}{\varepsilon G^Y} + \theta\mu\left[1+\frac{(\beta+\varepsilon)v}{\varepsilon b}\right] > 0, \tag{56}$$

$$1-\mathrm{Tr}J(v,w)+\mathrm{Det}J(v,w) = (1-\theta)(1-\mu) + \frac{q\beta(2-\mu)}{\varepsilon G^Y} - \frac{(\beta+\varepsilon)[1+\theta(1-\mu)]v}{\varepsilon b}. \tag{57}$$

The sign of the trace turns out to be, in general, indeterminate, while the determinant of the Jacobian (54) is larger than zero. Moreover, the sign of $1-\mathrm{Tr}J(v,u)+\mathrm{Det}J(v,u)$ is in general ambiguous. However, for a broad set of feasible parameters, all of which are following the assumptions used thus far, the trace is larger than zero (larger than 2) and $1-\mathrm{Tr}J(v,u)+\mathrm{Det}J(v,u)<0$.

Proposition 2. Suppose the assumptions of Proposition 1 hold. Then, the calculation of the eigenvalues λ_1 and λ_2 of Jacobian (54) at the steady-state solution $0<w<1$, $(0<u<1)$ and $v_{\min}<v<v^{\max}$ shows that for a broad set of feasible parameter combinations with $b<b^{\max}$, $\lambda_1>1$ and $0<\lambda_2<1$.

In other words, the steady-state solution in the present endogenous growth model with involuntary unemployment represents a non-oscillating, monotone saddle point with v_t as a slowly moving variable and w_t (u_t) as jump variables. With $v_0=\underline{v}>0$ historically given, w_0 (u_0) jumps onto the saddle-path along which both variables converge monotonically towards the steady-state solution.

5. Comparative steady-state effects of a higher public debt to GDP ratio

Being assured of the existence and dynamic stability of a steady-state solution it is now apt to investigate how a larger government debt to GDP ratio impacts the steady-state GDP growth rate and the steady-state unemployment rate. A comparable OLG model with endogenous growth and full employment [9] finds that the GDP growth is raised by a higher government debt to GDP ratio if the GDP growth rate is larger than the real interest rate in the initial steady state. If the real interest rate is higher than the GDP growth rate in the initial steady-state, larger government debt to GDP ratio lowers the GDP growth rate. Because of these interesting results, it will be expedient to explore whether in our model with an independent aggregate investment function the GDP growth rate effect of more government debt will also depend on the difference between the initial GDP growth rate and the initial interest rate. In addition, of particular interest is how a larger public debt to GDP ratio affects the unemployment rate which could not be investigated by Lin [9].

To proceed, we now consider the intertemporal equilibrium equations (37), (39), (41) and (42) in a steady-state and differentiate the resulting static equation system totally with respect to τ, G^Y, v, w and b. The following linear equation system with respect to the total differentials $d\tau, dG^Y, dv, dw, db$ is then obtained:

$$d\tau(1-\alpha) = \left(q - G^Y\right)db - bdG^Y - qb\,dv/v, \tag{58}$$

$$\frac{dG^Y}{G^Y} = (1-\mu)\left(\frac{\alpha}{(1-\alpha)}\frac{dv}{v} + \frac{dw}{w}\right), \tag{59}$$

$$\frac{dG^Y}{G^Y} + \frac{dw}{w} + \frac{[1-\theta(1-\alpha)]}{(1-\alpha)}\frac{dv}{v} = 0, \tag{60}$$

$$G^Y v\frac{dw}{w} + \left[\frac{\alpha - \theta(1-\alpha)vG^Y + (1-\alpha)bq}{(1-\alpha)}\right]\frac{dv}{v} + \frac{(1-\alpha)\varepsilon}{(\beta+\varepsilon)}d\tau = qdb. \tag{61}$$

Solving simultaneous equations (58) and (61) for $d\tau$ and dG^Y, and inserting the result for dG^Y into equations (59) and (60) we obtain a two-dimensional linear equation system comprising the variables dw and dv. The solution of this equation system for dv/db and dw/db reads as follows:

$$\frac{dv}{db} = \frac{(2-\mu)\left[\varepsilon\left(G^Y - q\right) + (\beta+\varepsilon)q\right]v}{\varepsilon G^Y b(1 - \mathrm{Tr}J + \mathrm{Det}J)}, \tag{62}$$

$$\frac{dw}{db} = -\frac{[1-\theta(1-\alpha) + \alpha(1-\mu)]\left[\varepsilon\left(G^Y - q\right) + (\beta+\varepsilon)q\right]w}{(1-\alpha)\varepsilon G^Y b(1 - \mathrm{Tr}J + \mathrm{Det}J)}. \tag{63}$$

The right-hand side of the differential quotient (62) shows that a higher public debt to GDP ratio affects the capital-output ratio unambiguously negatively if dynamic inefficiency prevails, i.e. the GDP growth factor is larger than the real interest factor since $1 - \mathrm{Tr}J + \mathrm{Det}J < 0$ for a broad set of admissible parameters. Under dynamic efficiency, i.e. the real interest factor is larger than the GDP growth factor the response of the capital-output ratio to higher public debt to GDP ratio becomes in general ambiguous.

The term on the right-hand side of equation (63) shows the response of one minus the unemployment rate to a higher government debt to GDP ratio. It transpires that when dynamic inefficiency prevails and moreover $\alpha > \theta(1-\alpha)$ holds, the response of one minus the unemployment rate is unambiguously positive and thus a higher public debt to GDP ratio reduces the unemployment rate. A glance at the output market equilibrium equation (38) makes clear why this is so. It shows that one minus the unemployment rate balances the inflexible investment to GDP ratio with the other aggregate demand to GDP ratios. E.g., with a higher debt to GDP ratio wealth of old consumers rises which induces a higher consumption demand of older consumers. With a relatively inflexible investment to GDP ratio, a higher consumption demand to GDP ratio can be maintained only if the unemployment rate falls. Moreover, higher public debt raises the real interest rate which necessitates a decline of the capital-output ratio due to profit maximization which additionally increases labor demand and thus diminishes unemployment.

The calculation of the marginal change of the steady-state wage tax rate and the GDP growth factor from equations (62) and (63) brings forth the following result:

$$\frac{d\tau}{db} = \frac{(\beta+\varepsilon)[1+\theta(1-\mu)]\left[G^Y v - q(b+v)\right]}{(1-\alpha)\varepsilon b(1 - \mathrm{Tr}J + \mathrm{Det}J)}, \tag{64}$$

$$\frac{dG^Y}{db} = -\frac{(1-\theta)(1-\mu)G^Y\left(\varepsilon G^Y + \beta q\right)}{(1-\alpha)\varepsilon G^Y b(1 - \mathrm{Tr}J + \mathrm{Det}J)}. \tag{65}$$

Debt to GDP ratio	Capital-output ratio	GDP growth factor	One minus unemployment rate	Wage tax rate	Interest factor
$b = 0.024$	0.14450	1.51422	0.905413	0.44784	2.07608
$b = 0.03$	0.134872	1.5212	0.941195	0.45870	2.22433

Table 1.
Steady solutions before and after the policy shock.

A glance on the right-hand side of equation (64) shows that the response of the wage tax rate to a higher debt to GDP ratio is in general ambiguous. If, however, the GDP growth factor is sufficiently larger than the interest factor (precisely if $G^Y > (1 + b/v)q$) then higher public debt decreases the wage tax rate. On the other hand, the right-hand side of equation (65) reveals that a larger public debt to GDP ratio is conducive for GDP growth provided that $\theta < 1$. Interestingly, for $\theta = 1$ more public debt does not enhance GDP growth.

Because in the case of dynamic efficiency the response of the unemployment rate to higher public debt is in general ambiguous, we use a numerical parameter set that implies dynamic efficiency before the policy shock and which is in line with the assumptions of Proposition 1. To this end, the following parameter combination not untypical because of medium-term econometric parameter estimations is assumed: $\beta = 0.6, \varepsilon = 0.45, \alpha = 0.3, A = 7, H_0 = 3, \mu = 0.5,$ $\gamma = 0.04, \delta = 0.2, \xi = 0.06, \phi = 2.5, \theta = 0.8$. For the policy shock, it is assumed that b is raised from 0.024 (= 72% p. a) towards 0.03 (= 90% p. a.). The calculation of the steady-state solutions for the capital-output ratio v, the GDP growth factor G^Y, the wage tax rate τ, 1 minus the unemployment rate w and the real interest factor q before and after the policy shock is depicted in the following **Table 1**.

Although under the present parameter set dynamic efficiency prevails (= the interest factor is larger than the GDP growth factor in **Table 1** with $b = 0.024$), a larger public debt to GDP ratio, i.e. $b = 0.03$ diminishes the capital-output ratio, enhances the GDP growth factor, reduces the unemployment rate and raises the wage tax rate and the interest factor. Thus, the qualitative responses of main macroeconomic variables to higher public debt are similar to those under dynamic inefficiency. As can be shown by variations of main parameters (see Farmer [10] and Farmer [12] in a similar model context), these results are not constrained to the specific parameter set presented above but hold for a broader set of structural and policy parameters.

6. Conclusions

This chapter aims to incorporate involuntary unemployment in an OLG growth model with internal public debt and human capital accumulation. Deviating from new-Keynesian macro models in which involuntary unemployment is traced back to inflexible wages, output prices and interest rates vis-à-vis market imbalances, real wages and real interest rates are perfectly flexible in our Diamond-type growth model with involuntary unemployment. Involuntary unemployment occurs in line with [6, 7] aggregate investment is inflexible due to investors' animal spirits.

After presenting the model set-up temporary equilibrium relations and the intertemporal equilibrium dynamics are derived from intertemporal utility maximization, atemporal profit maximization, government's budget constraint and the market-clearing conditions in each period. To arrive at determinate equilibrium dynamics, it is assumed that the government holds constant over time: the public debt to GDP ratio, the HCI-expenditure ratio, the non-HCI expenditure ratio and the unemployment benefit to GDP ratio. As a consequence, the wage tax rate becomes endogenous.

Due to the complexity of the intertemporal equilibrium relations, an explicit steady-state solution is not possible. Thus, the simplest mathematical existence theorem, the intermediate value theorem is applied to prove the existence of a steady-state solution with a strictly positive capital-output ratio and an unemployment rate larger than zero and smaller than one. Contrary to intuitive expectations, there exists a finite limit to the public debt to GDP ratio even in the economy with involuntary unemployment. Public debt to GDP ratios higher than that limit implies negative unemployment rates which are infeasible. As Farmer [10] shows in a similar model context maximum public debt in a growth model with involuntary unemployment is not a purely theoretical notion but turns out to be empirically relevant in a numerically specified growth model with involuntary unemployment.

Besides the existence of a steady-state solution for the intertemporal equilibrium dynamics, its dynamic stability was shown. It turns out that for a broad set of feasible structural and policy parameters the dynamics is saddle-point stable. With the capital-output ratio as a sluggish variable historically given, the unemployment rate jumps initially suddenly onto the saddle-path along which both variables converge monotonically (non-oscillating) towards their steady-state values.

Being assured of the existence and dynamic stability of the unique steady-state solution we shocked it by a higher public debt to GDP ratio mimicking the pandemic-related larger public debt to GDP ratios in almost all countries of the world economy. In line with Keynesian policy expectations, we were able to show analytically that in case of dynamic inefficiency, i.e., the GDP growth rate is larger than the real interest rate, a higher public debt to GDP ratio (below the maximum debt to GDP ratio) unambiguously reduces both the capital-output ratio and the unemployment rate while raising the GDP growth rate in a dynamic market economy with perfectly flexible real wage and interest rates. In the case of dynamic efficiency, the responses to the policy shock become in general ambiguous. However, in a numerically specified version of the presented model, it was shown that qualitatively similar comparative steady-state effects occur even in the case of dynamic efficiency. The main reason for these results is that under inflexible aggregate investment higher public debt creates a positive wealth effect with old-age consumers which raises aggregate demand and hence reduces unemployment.

The limitations of the present research are obvious: First, micro-foundations for the aggregate investment function are lacking. Here, stock-market foundations for the aggregate investment function in line with Farmer [15]'s investor's belief function should be provided to overcome the purely macro-foundation of the aggregate investment function. Second, there is no impact of larger public debt to GDP ratios on aggregate investment. Here, Salotti [14]'s an empirical specification of a negative relationship between public debt and aggregate investment may be incorporated in a future version of the present model. Both subjects are left to future research.

Author details

Karl Farmer[1,2]

1 Carl-Francis-University Graz, Graz, Austria

2 Babes-Bolyai-University Cluj-Napoca, Cluj-Napoca, Romania

*Address all correspondence to: karl.farmer@uni-graz.at

References

[1] Solow RM. A contribution to the theory of economic growth. The Quartely Journal of Economics. 1956;**70**:65-94

[2] Diamond P. National debt in a neoclassical growth model. American Economic Review. 1965;**55**:1126-1150

[3] Hicks JM. Keynes and the "classics": A suggested interpretation. Econometrica. 1937;**5**(2):147-159

[4] Keynes JM. The General Theory of Employment, Interest, and Money. London: Macmillan; 1936

[5] Dixon H. New Keynesian economics: Theory and evidence. In: Backhouse R, Salanti A, editors. Theory and Evidence in Macroeconomics. Oxford: O. U. P; 2000. pp. 203-214

[6] Morishima M. Walras' Economics: A Pure Theory of Capital and Money. New York: Cambridge University Press; 1977

[7] Magnani R. The Solow Growth Model Revisited. Introducing Keynesian Involuntary Unemployment [Internet]. 2017. Available from: https://hal.archives-ouvertes.fr/hal-01203393 [Accessed: December 8, 2017]

[8] Glomm G, Ravikumar B. Public versus private investment in human capital: Endogenous growth and income inequality. Journal of Political Economy. 1992;**100**:818-834

[9] Lin S. Government debt and economic growth in an overlapping generations model. Southern Economic Journal. 2000;**66**(3):754-763

[10] Farmer K. Are there limits to public debt in neo-classical growth models with involuntary unemployment? In: Bélanger A, editor. Public Debt. Impact, Management and Challenges. New York: Nova Science Publishers; 2020. pp. 115-162

[11] Farmer K, Enhancing GDP. Growth and employment: From unproductive public expenditures towards human capital investment. In: Tavidze A, editor. Progress in Economic Research. New York: Nova Science Publishers; 2014. pp. 80-100

[12] Farmer K, Kuplen S. Involuntary unemployment in an OLG growth model with public debt and human capital. Studia Universitatis Babes-Bolyai Oeconomica. 2018;**63**(2):3-34

[13] De la Croix D, Michel P. A Theory of Economic Growth. Dynamics and Policy in Overlapping Generations. Cambridge: Cambridge University Press; 2002

[14] Salotti S, Trecroci C. The impact of public debt expenditure and taxes on aggregate investment and productivity growth. Economica. 2016;**83**:356-384

[15] Farmer REA. Confidence crashes and animal spirits. The Economic Journal. 2012;**122**(559):155-172

Chapter 8

Youth Unemployment and Productivity-Pay in the GCC Countries

Wasseem Mina

Abstract

Although the total youth unemployment rate in the Gulf Cooperation Council countries is less than in other high-income countries, the female youth unemployment rate is more than quadruple the male youth unemployment rate compared to equal rates in high-income countries. The gender bias in youth unemployment is attributable to the generous social contract GCC nationals enjoy as well as the largely conservative GCC culture that perceives a more important role of women in the household than in the job market. The generous social contract is also a key factor in the duality of the GCC labor markets with one segment for national labor and the other for foreign labor. Foreign labor constitutes most of the labor force, and the link between pay and productivity is strong in the foreign labor segment indicating labor market efficiency. This chapter investigates whether the presence of strong pay-productivity links in both labor market segments reduces the national youth unemployment rates in the GCC countries. Empirical evidence shows that linking pay to productivity robustly reduces the total and female youth unemployment rates. The influence is strongest on the female youth unemployment rate, however. Productivity-pay helps reduce youth unemployment and the associated gender bias.

Keywords: youth unemployment, female youth unemployment rate, male youth unemployment, labor markets, productivity-pay, GCC

1. Introduction

The oil-rich Gulf Cooperation Council (GCC) countries are high-income countries. They include Bahrain, Kuwait, Oman, Qatar, Saudi Arabia, and the United Arab Emirates (UAE). Over the past two decades (2000–2020), Qatar, UAE, and Bahrain had the highest population growth rates of 8.2 percent, 5.9 percent, and 4.8 percent, respectively, followed by Oman, Kuwait, and Saudi Arabia at rates of 4.1 percent, 3.8 percent, and 2.6 percent.[1] The corresponding population growth rates for the Arab world, high income countries, and the world total are 2.2 percent, 0.6 percent, and 1.2 percent, respectively.

Despite the high population growth rates of the GCC countries, youth unemployment rates were lower than the rates in other high-income countries. High youth unemployment can constrain long-term growth and reduce economic, social,

[1] Figures are based on the World Bank's World Development Indicators (WDI).

and political stability [1].[2] As **Table 1** shows, the total youth unemployment rate in 2007–2017 averaged 28.5 percent, 12.5 percent, and 11.9 percent in Saudi Arabia, Oman, and Kuwait, respectively.[3] In comparison, the rate amounted to 6.9 percent, 5.3 percent, and 1 percent in the UAE, Bahrain, and Qatar, respectively.[4]

Compared to other high-income countries, the total youth unemployment rate in the GCC countries is lower. In 2007–2017, the total youth unemployment rate amounted on average to 11 percent in the GCC countries compared to 18 percent in a sample of 44 high-income countries.[5] The difference is even larger for the male youth rate: The male youth unemployment rate is 8.5 percent in the GCC countries compared to 18.1 percent in the other high-income countries. The GCC countries therefore fared well relative to other high-income countries with respect to the total and male youth unemployment rates.

Female youth unemployment is a serious issue in the GCC countries, however.[6] The female youth unemployment rate is 20.6 percent compared to 8.5 percent for the male youth unemployment rate, resulting in a ratio of female-to-male youth unemployment rate of 4.5.[7,8] In the sample of 44 other high-income countries, the male and female youth unemployment rates are almost equal (18.1 percent).

In addition, the GCC countries experience female youth unemployment rate heterogeneity. The female youth unemployment rate is higher in Saudi Arabia (53 percent), Oman (24.6 percent) and Kuwait (16.7 percent) compared to Bahrain (12.8 percent), UAE (11.2 percent), and Qatar (5.5 percent). This is perhaps not unusual given the pattern of the total youth unemployment rate in the two groups of countries.

However, the ratio of female-to-male youth unemployment rate is highly pronounced in Qatar and Bahrain. Despite enjoying low total youth unemployment rate, Qatar and Bahrain have the highest female-to-male youth unemployment rate

---

[2] Youth unemployment refers to the labor force ages 15–24 without work but is available for and seeking employment. Youth unemployment rate measures the extent of youth unemployment. The youth unemployment rate is measured as the number of youth unemployed relative to the total labor force between ages 15–24.

[3] This rate includes both male and female youth unemployment.

[4] The GCC countries can be therefore perceived as two heterogenous groups with respect to the total youth unemployment rate.

[5] The sample of high-income countries include Australia, Austria, Barbados, Belgium, Brunei Darussalam, Canada, Chile, Croatia, Cyprus, Czech Republic, Denmark, Estonia, Finland, France, Germany, Greece, Hong Kong, Hungary, Iceland, Ireland, Israel, Italy, Japan, Korea, Latvia, Lithuania, Luxembourg, Malta, Netherlands, New Zealand, Norway, Panama, Poland, Portugal, Singapore, Slovak Republic, Slovenia, Spain, Sweden, Switzerland, Trinidad and Tobago, UK, US, and Uruguay.

[6] Another useful metric of an active (female) labor force is the (female) labor force participation rate. This metric accounts for ages 15 and above and is not restricted to (female) youth. It is calculated as the sum of all (female) workers who are employed or actively seeking employment divided by the total noninstitutionalized, civilian (female) working-age population.

[7] Based on WDI data, the period average female labor force participation rate is 39.9 percent, which is less than half the male labor force participation rate (86.9 percent). The period average female labor force participation rate is lowest in Saudi Arabia (20 percent), Oman (28.4 percent), and Bahrain (43.1 percent). See the Appendix for information on the individual GCC countries labor force participation rate for both genders. In the other high-income countries, the period average female labor force participation rate amounts to 53.8 percent. The lowest rates are in Malta (38 percent) and Italy (39 percent).

[8] International Labor Organization data suggests regional female labor participation rate is lower in earlier years [2]. Female labor participation rate for Arab states was 12.8 percent in 2000 and dropped to 9.5 percent in 2011. The Arab states include Bahrain, Iraq, Jordan, Kuwait, Lebanon, Occupied Palestinian Territory, Oman, Qatar, Saudi Arabia, Syrian Arab Republic, United Arab Emirates, and Yemen.

	Total (%)	Male (%)	Female (%)	Female-to-Male Ratio
Bahrain	5.3	2.6	12.8	4.9
Kuwait	11.9	9.9	16.7	1.7
Oman	12.5	10.2	24.6	2.4
Qatar	1.0	0.4	5.5	13.6
Saudi Arabia	28.5	21.7	53.0	2.5
UAE	6.9	5.9	11.2	1.9
Total	11.0	8.5	20.6	4.5
Memo item				
Other high-income countries	18.01	18.06	18.09	1.02

Table 1.
Youth unemployment rates in the GCC countries (2007–2017; period average).

ratio of nearly 14 and 5, respectively. The average female youth unemployment rate is nearly 14-fold the male youth unemployment rate in the case of Qatar and five-fold in the case of Bahrain.

The purpose of this chapter is to explain youth unemployment in the GCC countries. I start by discussing the reasons for the gender bias in female youth unemployment (Section 2). The presence of generous existing social contract for GCC nationals as well as cultural factors are offered as explanations for the gender bias. The social contract is key to understanding the dual nature of GCC labor markets. To be able to reduce the youth unemployment rate, it is important to understand the degree of labor market efficiency. I discuss GCC labor markets efficiency and posit that it reflects more the foreign labor segment (Section 3). I conjecture that having a strong pay-productivity link in *both* the national and foreign labor segments can reduce the female and consequently the total youth unemployment rate (Section 4). This conjecture is based on a graphical analysis of the relationship between youth unemployment and the pay-productivity link in 124 non-GCC countries as well as in the six GCC countries. To explain youth unemployment empirically, I specify and estimate an empirical model (Section 5). The empirical results show that linking pay to productivity reduces the female and total youth unemployment rates (Section 6). I conclude with a policy recommendation (Section 7).

2. Social contract and labor market segmentation

The generous implicit social contract the GCC states have extended to its nationals is believed to have shaped their expectations and decisions to work. The social contract includes highly paid and protected government jobs as well unemployment benefits [3–5]. It also includes free education, health care, and child support. At retirement, generous public pensions are provided.

The highly paid government jobs have created high expectations about jobs in the private sector including high reservation wages. Thus, national youth on the labor supply side may offer their labor services at high wage rates. On the labor demand side, at high wage rates the demand for national youth labor services is normally low especially if unaccompanied by high productivity. The interaction of the supply and demand for labor leaves a surplus of national youth unemployed. The high reservation wages and unemployment benefits may reduce job search and increase the duration of unemployment.

With oil revenues financing the generous (implicit) social contract and economic activities in the GCC economies, the hiring of foreign labor was inevitable given the economic growth following oil exploration and production, and the limited indigenous population, labor force or human capital.[9] The stipulated benefits in foreign labor (explicit) contracts do not on average match those of GCC nationals. Accordingly, the GCC labor markets are segmented *de facto*.

In addition to the social contract and the resulting labor market segmentation, and the relatively less costly foreign labor, cultural factors weigh in towards more female youth unemployment. The GCC culture is largely conservative as suggested by gender segregation at public schools and universities. Many females prefer to remain at the household as opposed to working or remaining on the job market.[10] It should be noted however that the literacy rate gender parity index for youth shows that both genders are at par.[11]

3. Labor market efficiency: Pay and productivity

The World Economic Forum's Global Competitiveness Index (GCI) assesses labor market flexibility and efficiency. The assessments are based on executive opinion survey. Businesses included in the survey represent the sectors they operate in. These comprise agriculture, manufacturing industry, non-manufacturing industry, and services. The number of businesses surveyed depends on the contribution of the sector to GDP.[12] Surveyed businesses are in principle not necessarily large corporations. They may be small or medium in size.

Linking pay to productivity, performance-based pay, or performance-pay for short, is a labor market efficiency indicator. Given the segmented nature of the GCC labor markets and the significant presence of foreign workers in the GCC countries, the indicator tends to reflect the strength of the relationship between productivity and pay in the foreign labor segment.[13] Although the pay-productivity link is perceived as strong relative to the other high-income countries, labor is non-unionized and collective bargaining is absent. This may partially explain the link strength.[14]

Table 2 presents the 2007–2017 period average of the linking pay to productivity indicator for each of the GCC countries. A score of 1 indicates that the two are completely unrelated, while a score of 7 indicates they are strongly related. The table shows that Qatar and the UAE have the highest average scores, while Kuwait has the lowest. It also shows that the GCC countries, as a group, have a higher average than other high-income countries.

[9] The average annual growth rates for Bahrain is 3.77 percent (1981–2020), Kuwait 4.57 percent (1993–2019), Oman 8.38 percent (1966–2019), Qatar 8.43 percent (2001–2020), Saudi Arabia 4.86 percent (1969–2020), and UAE 4.86 percent (1976–2019). The rates are mathematical averages of annual growth rates obtained from the World Bank's World Development Indicators (WDI) over the specified periods.

[10] If they decide accordingly not to search for jobs, they should not be considered as part of the labor force. In cases of divorce, females may start searching for jobs, however.

[11] This is based on the WDI 2017 literacy rate gender parity index for youth for Bahrain, Kuwait, Oman, Qatar, and Saudi Arabia and the 2015 index for the UAE.

[12] Non-manufacturing industry includes mining and quarrying, electricity, gas and water supply, and construction.

[13] There is no collective bargaining in the GCC labor markets though.

[14] The strength of the link may depend on business professional management in case of large businesses.

Country	Average
Bahrain	4.53
Kuwait	3.84
Oman	4.19
Qatar	5.09
Saudi Arabia	4.57
UAE	5.03
Total	4.54
Memo item	
Other high-income countries	4.27

Table 2.
The pay-productivity link (2007–2017; period average).

4. The relationship between labor market efficiency and youth unemployment

Several IMF working papers find that labor market flexibility reduces unemployment [6–8]. Labor market flexibility, in particular hiring and firing policies and hiring costs, was found to reduce over unemployment, youth unemployment and long-term unemployment [6]. It was also found to reduce unemployment in Algeria, a resource-rich, labor-abundant North African country [7]. Flexible labor markets were also found to help fending off financial crises [8].

Does labor market *efficiency*, measured by the pay-productivity link, influence the youth unemployment rate? And what is the nature of the relationship? To answer these two questions, I undertake in this chapter a graphical analysis of this relationship in 124 high-income, upper- and lower-middle income, and low-income

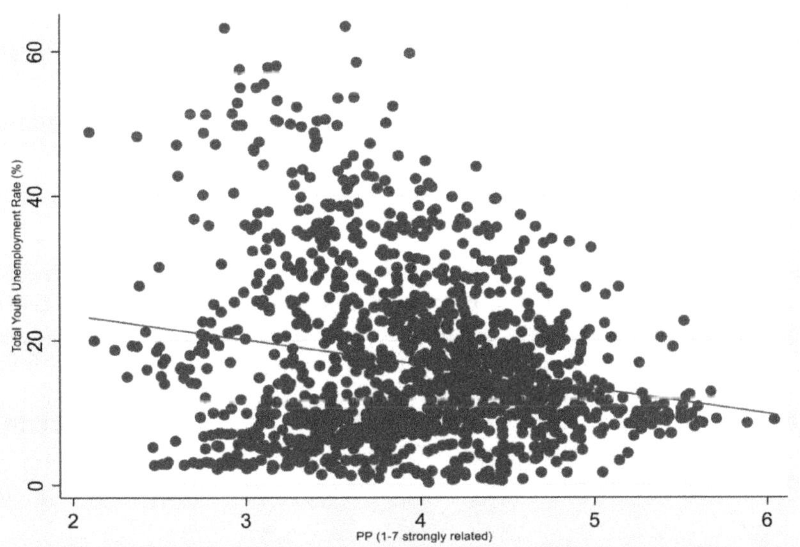

Figure 1.
Total youth unemployment rate and performance-pay: Large country sample evidence.

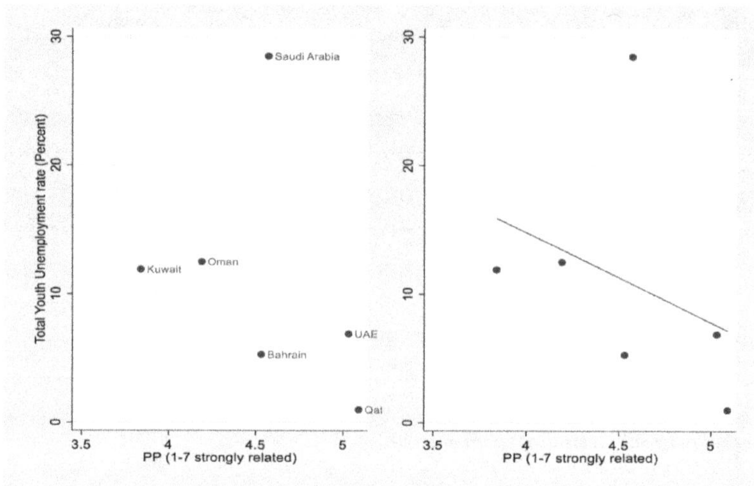

Figure 2.
Total youth unemployment rate and performance-pay in GCC countries.

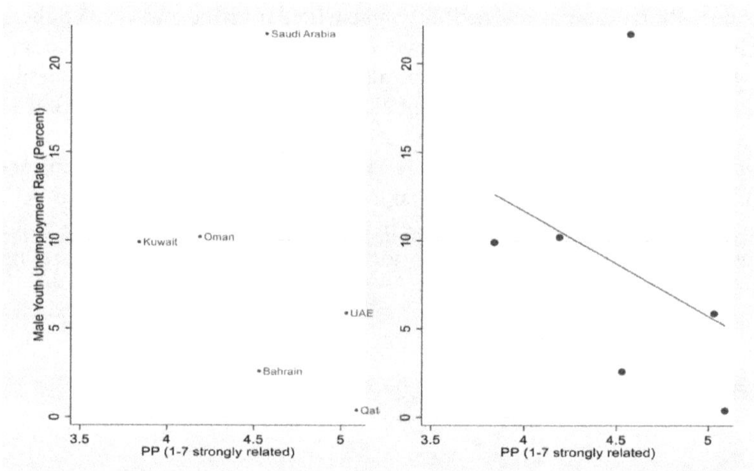

Figure 3.
Male youth unemployment rate and performance-pay in GCC countries.

countries as well as in the six high-income GCC countries. **Figure 1** suggests the presence of a negative relationship between the total youth unemployment rate and the pay-productivity link in a large sample of non-GCC countries.[15] This relationship still holds if I instead examine the influence of lagged pay-productivity link on the total youth unemployment rate.

Figures 2–4, which are based on 2007–2017 period averages, also suggest the presence of a negative relationship in GCC countries for the total, male, and female youth unemployment rates.[16]

[15] Graphical analysis also shows the youth unemployment rate negatively influences the pay-productivity link. Figure is available from the author.

[16] The figures are based on 2007–2017 period averages.

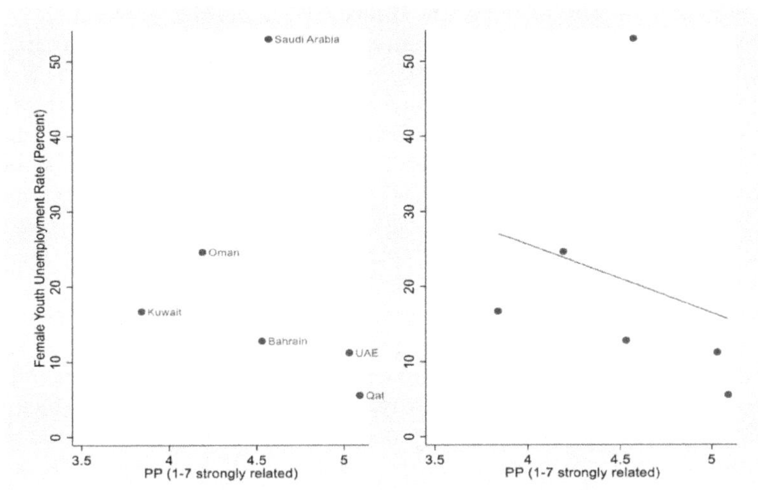

Figure 4.
Female youth unemployment rate and performance-pay in GCC countries.

Labor economics theory explains this relationship in terms of the substitution effect of higher wages on labor supply. Higher wages associated with more productivity encourage workers to increase their work hours. Alternatively, higher wages encourage workers to reduce their leisure hours in response. At the macro level, when youth observe that work effort and productivity are rewarded, they search for jobs and take employment. This in turn reduces the youth unemployment rate.

Therefore, I conjecture that having a strong pay-productivity link in *both* the national and foreign labor segments can reduce the female and consequently the total youth unemployment rate. In explaining the different youth unemployment rates – total, male, and female, I will assume in the next section that the strength of pay-productivity link is equal in both labor market segments.

5. Explaining youth unemployment in the GCC countries - the empirical model

The negative relationship between the different youth unemployment rates and productivity-pay observed in the above graphs is investigated empirically. Building on [9] who examines the relationship between labor market flexibility and youth unemployment, the empirical model includes the pay-productivity link as an explanatory variable.[17] In this chapter, I explain the different youth unemployment rates (total, male, or female). The empirical model is now expressed as:

$$UR_{it} = \beta_0 + \beta_1 PP_{it} + \beta_2 GROWTH_{it} + \beta_3 GFINANCE_{it} + \beta_4 URBAN_{it} + \varepsilon_{it}$$

where *UR* is youth unemployment rate. *PP* is the pay-productivity link indicator (log). *GROWTH* is economic growth, a proxy for the expansion in

[17] In [6], control variables include an output gap measure to control for business cycle fluctuations, the size of government, the degree of trade openness, the rate of urbanization, population density, a crisis dummy, and the lagged level of unemployment rate(s).

job opportunities. It is measured by the annual GDP per capita growth rate. *GFINANCE* is government fiscal expenditures, which account for the major employment role the GCC governments play in hiring nationals. *GFINANCE* is measured by the general government final consumption expenditures (as a percentage of GDP). *URBAN* is the degree of urbanization in the economy. It accounts for the geographic concentration of business in urban areas and is measured by the percentage of urban to total population. ε is the error term. The subscripts i and t are country and time indexes.

Data on *PP* are obtained from GCI. Data on the other variables are obtained from WDI. The data covers the period 2007–2017.

Panel data models are used in estimation. I account for both the GCC country- and time-specific effects. Country-specific effects may include factors such as culture and traditions, which do not change by time at least in the short and medium terms. Time-specific effects are related to global factors, such as oil prices or foreign direct investment, which are not country-specific and may impact the GCC countries at specific years.

6. Empirical results

Table 3 provides the 2007–2017 period average for the model variables. The table shows four interesting observations. First, Qatar and the UAE have the strongest pay-productivity links, as indicated by their scores. Second, Saudi Arabia and Oman have the highest level of fiscal expenditures relative to GDP. Yet they have the highest youth unemployment rates. Third, more than three quarters of the GCC population live in urban areas. Finally, the GDP per capita growth rates are negative for Kuwait, Oman, Qatar, and UAE.

The correlation between the different variables reveals interesting initial relationships, as **Table 4** shows. *PP* is negatively and statistically correlated with the total and male youth unemployment rates.[18] Government expenditures, *GFINANCE*, are positively correlated with all youth unemployment rates, while the degree of urbanization, *URBAN*, is negatively correlated with them all. The correlation between the GDP per capita growth rate, *GROWTH*, and the different youth unemployment rates is very low.

Country	*UR*			*PP*	*GROWTH*	*GFINANCE*	*URBAN*
	Total	Male	Female				
Bahrain	5.1	2.5	12.5	4.5	0.3	14.3	88.7
Kuwait	11.2	10.0	13.7	3.9	−3.3	16.8	100.0
Oman	12.4	10.4	22.2	4.3	−0.8	20.4	76.8
Qatar	1.2	0.5	6.2	5.1	−0.1	14.0	98.5
Saudi Arabia	29.2	22.3	53.8	4.6	1.2	22.1	82.3
UAE	7.0	6.0	11.2	5.0	−2.8	9.8	84.4
Total	11.0	8.6	19.9	4.6	−0.9	16.2	88.5

Table 3.
Empirical model variables (2007–2017; period averages).

[18] Pairwise correlated at the 5 percent statistical significance level.

	PP	*UR*-Total	*UR*-Male	*UR*-Female	*GROWTH*	*GFINANCE*	*URBAN*
UR-Total	**−0.275**	1	**0.986**	**0.965**	0.090	**0.655**	**−0.454**
UR-Male	**−0.313**	**0.986**	1	**0.915**	0.053	**0.617**	**−0.445**
UR-Female	−0.180	**0.965**	**0.915**	1	0.136	**0.684**	**−0.481**
GROWTH	0.147	0.090	0.053	0.136	1	0.105	−0.101
GFINANCE	**−0.396**	**0.655**	**0.617**	**0.684**	0.105	1	−0.241
URBAN	−0.055	**−0.454**	**−0.445**	**−0.481**	−0.101	−0.241	1

Notes: Bold fonts indicate statistical significance at the 5 percent level.

Table 4.
Correlation matrix.

6.1 Fixed effects model estimates

Empirical results are presented in **Table 5**. As mentioned above, the estimation methodology accounts for both country and time effects. Thus, the table provides estimates by country and year.

	Total	Male	Female
PP	**-13.235a**	**-12.796a**	**-21.837a**
	(2.030)	(2.856)	(7.391)
GROWTH	**−0.068b**	−0.035	**−0.215b**
	(0.026)	(0.027)	(0.087)
GFINANCE	0.044	−0.115	0.299
	(0.098)	(0.132)	(0.283)
URBAN	**−0.487a**	**−0.507a**	0.683
	(0.138)	(0.147)	(0.439)
Kuwait	**9.507a**	**11.709a**	**-10.992b**
	(1.418)	(1.367)	(4.449)
Oman	0.469	1.844	**14.534b**
	(2.095)	(2.299)	(6.719)
Qatar	2.420	**4.384b**	**-10.414b**
	(1.556)	(1.696)	(5.062)
Saudi Arabia	**20.998a**	**17.753a**	**44.035a**
	(1.455)	(1.816)	(4.476)
UAE	**1.113b**	**1.961a**	**4.513a**
	(0.491)	(0.619)	(1.318)
Year−2007	**-2.203a**	-2.004c	−1.744
	(0.669)	(1.054)	(2.452)
Year-2008	**-1.617b**	−1.873	−0.161
	(0.786)	(1.127)	(2.398)
Year-2009	**-1.631b**	−1.333c	−0.825
	(0.661)	(0.765)	(1.940)
Year-2010	−1.195c	−1.079	−0.096

	Total	Male	Female
	(0.611)	(0.733)	(2.256)
Year-2011	−1.194c	−1.369	0.356
	(0.682)	(0.874)	(1.813)
Year-2012	**−1.207b**	**−1.790b**	1.014
	(0.552)	(0.763)	(1.703)
Year-2013	−0.902c	−1.207c	0.032
	(0.502)	(0.667)	(1.540)
Year-2014	−0.223	−0.372	0.087
	(0.428)	(0.574)	(1.563)
Constant	68.707a	69.584a	−19.331
	(13.730)	(14.933)	(44.733)
Observations	54	54	54
R-squared	0.996	0.987	0.987

Notes: Robust standard errors in parentheses. a, b and c indicate significance at the 1%, 5%, and 10% levels, respectively.

Table 5.
Fixed effects model estimates (LSDV estimation).

The results confirm the negative relationship between productivity-pay and youth unemployment observed in **Figures 2–4**. In the three columns, the *PP* coefficients are negative suggesting a negative influence of the productivity-pay link on the three youth unemployment rates. However, the absolute coefficient value is biggest for the female youth unemployment rate. The coefficient indicates that a one percent improvement in the strength of the pay-productivity link reduces the total, male, and female youth unemployment rates by 0.13 percentage point, 0.12 percentage point, and about 0.22 percentage point, respectively. These coefficients suggest therefore that the influence on the female youth unemployment rate is almost double the influence on the male youth unemployment rate. The pay-productivity link plays a relatively more significant role in reducing female youth unemployment in the GCC countries.

GROWTH also has a negative influence, as we would normally expect. It is statistically significant in the total and female youth unemployment rate models. Interestingly, both *PP* and *GROWTH* have equal coefficients: A one percentage point increase in GDP per capita growth rate reduces the female youth unemployment rate by 0.22 percentage point. In contrast to [1], *GFINANCE* does not have a statistically significant influence on the different unemployment rates. The degree of urbanization, *URBAN*, reduces the total and male youth unemployment rates but not the female youth unemployment rate.

The coefficients of the country dummies – the country-specific effects - suggest that the country effects do not reduce total or male youth unemployment. This is obvious in Kuwait, Saudi Arabia, UAE and Qatar. Only in Kuwait and Qatar, the country-specific effects reduce the female youth unemployment rate.

The coefficients of the time dummies are negative and statistically significant in the total youth unemployment rate model. The time dummies are statistically significant at least at the 5 percent level in 2007–2009 and 2012. The increase in the world oil prices in 2006–2016, as **Figure 5** shows, may provide an explanation for this outcome. The oil price increase possibly feeds through GDP growth rate reducing the total youth unemployment rate.

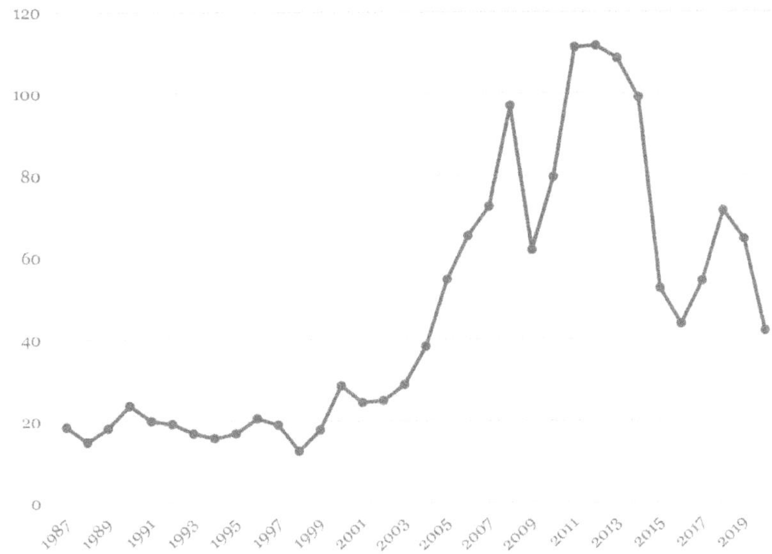

Figure 5.
World crude (Brent) oil prices (1987–2020; $/barrel).

6.2 Feasible generalized least squares estimates

Although the GCC countries seem alike, they may be different from each other in how the youth unemployment rate is explained by the empirical model. Thus, I test for panel-level heteroscedasticity. I also test for autocorrelation in the error term. If either or both empirical issues are present, I plan to adopt a feasible generalized least squares (FGLS) estimation methodology.

Since the likelihood ratio $\chi 2$ test rejects the null hypothesis of panel-level homoscedasticity at the one percent level for the three youth unemployment rates, as **Table 6** shows, I adopt FGLS accounting for panel heteroskedasticity. The Wooldridge F test for autocorrelation fail to reject the null hypothesis of no panel-level autocorrelation in the case of total youth unemployment rate. However, the test rejects the null hypothesis at the five percent level in the case of male and female youth unemployment rates. I account for serial correlation in FGLS estimation of these two youth unemployment rates.

FGLS estimation results are presented in **Table 7**. Results confirm the negative influence that linking pay to productivity has on the total and female youth unemployment rates but not on the male youth unemployment rate. An improvement in the pay-productivity link strength by one percent reduces the total and female youth unemployment rate by 0.23 percentage point and 0.21 percentage point, respectively.

UR	Heteroscedasticity test	Autocorrelation test
Total	**116.74a**	3.679
Male	**147.77a**	**13.108b**
Female	**152.68a**	**6.581b**

Notes: The null hypothesis for the heteroscedasticity test is panel-level homoscedasticity. The null hypothesis for the autocorrelation test is the absence of (across) panel autocorrelation. a, b and c indicate significance at the 1%, 5%, and 10% levels, respectively.

Table 6.
Panel heteroscedasticity and autocorrelation tests.

	(1)	(2)	(3)
	Total	**Male**	**Female**
PP	**-22.693a**	−4.018	**-20.603a**
	(6.102)	(2.850)	(4.633)
GROWTH	−0.123	−0.019	**-0.108c**
	(0.098)	(0.032)	(0.058)
GFINANCE	**0.437a**	0.080	**0.399a**
	(0.157)	(0.051)	(0.098)
URBAN	**-0.318a**	−0.028	**-0.326a**
	(0.082)	(0.079)	(0.095)
Constant	64.853a	15.790	67.470a
	(14.247)	(9.790)	(13.569)
Observations	54	54	54
Number of countries	6	6	6
Wald test	**42.76a**	4.72	**47.32a**
Panel heteroskedasticity	Yes	Yes	Yes
Panel autocorrelation	No	Yes	Yes

Table 7.
FGLS estimation results.

In contrast to the results of **Table 5**, empirical evidence shows that government expenditures increase the youth unemployment rates. A one percentage point increase in the share of government consumption expenditures in GDP increases the total and female youth unemployment rate by 0.44 percentage point and 0.4 percentage point, respectively. This result is in line with [1], who finds that an increase in government consumption expenditures (percentage of GDP) by one percentage point increases the total youth unemployment rate.

It might be the case that through consumption expenditures that the GCC governments put incomes in the hands of households, which discourage youth from searching for and taking jobs. From labor economics theory perspective, this is the negative (positive) income effect on work (leisure) hours. An increase in incomes discourage youth from increasing their labor supply. Alternatively, an increase in incomes encourage youth to take more leisure hours.

In contrast to the positive influence of government finance and like the result of **Table 5** for total youth unemployment, the degree of urbanization reduces the total youth unemployment rate. It also reduces the female youth unemployment rate. In addition, the GDP per capita growth rate reduces only the female youth unemployment rate but only marginally statistically.

7. Conclusion and policy recommendation

The empirical analysis of the two estimation methodologies supports the beneficial influence of linking pay to productivity on the total and female youth unemployment rates. Labor market efficiency can help reduce youth unemployment. This suggests that having an equal link strength in both labor market segments rewards the national youth, especially females.

The adoption of policies that increase labor market flexibility and efficiency to reduce (youth) unemployment is not unusual. Spain, for example, in 2010 and

2012 relaxed contract termination, reduced severance pay, notice period, and business social security contributions [1, 10].[19] The strength of collective bargaining was reduced, and enterprise-level agreement increased [10]. Firms have been able to withdraw from collective bargaining agreements one year from the agreement expiry date. Despite increasing labor market flexibility, youth unemployment remained high due to the *downward rigidity* of nominal wages, among other reasons [1]. The implicit GCC social contracts result in downward nominal wage rigidity.

The chapter recommends the adoption of labor efficiency policies and practices. Paying labor its economic value establishes efficiency in both labor market segments and encourage national youth to search for and take jobs not just in the government and state-owned enterprises – the traditional employer of nationals, but also in the private sector. Estimation results suggest that the magnitude of influence on female youth unemployment is relatively strong. GCC policy makers should be well-versed about the importance of the pay-productivity link and its implications for human resource management at the organization level. The obtained results suggest that national female youth are motivated by pay rewards.

Besides, efficiency helps clear the negative perceptions about labor market segmentation and the ensuing pay unfairness, and the gender bias. Labor efficiency helps in the efficient use of available domestic labor resources and in less reliance on foreign labor. By encouraging nationals of both genders to seek opportunities in the private sector, the adoption of labor efficiency policies and practices can help nationals of both genders develop a gamut of work-related skills including entrepreneurship. Entrepreneurship can help in job creation and reducing youth unemployment.

Finally, although this chapter makes the case of linking pay to productivity to *reduce the youth unemployment challenge*, I should point out though there is no one-solution-fit-all if the goal of reduction of the youth unemployment rates is regarded as merely political. GCC policymakers may consider alternative solutions to youth unemployment in changing economic, political, social environment. The remaining reality, however, is that each adopted solution has pros and cons that should be considered.

Acknowledgements

I would like to thank, without implication, Mark Gellerson and Jorge Martinez for their challenging and thoughtful comments on this chapter.

Conflict of interest

The author declares no conflict of interest.

Author note

The author is also a Research Fellow of the Economic Research Forum, Cairo, Egypt and an affiliated Associate Professor at the International Center for Public Policy, Andrew Young School of Policy Studies, Georgia State University, Atlanta, Georgia, US.

[19] Severance pay was reduced by more than 50 percent from 45 to 20 days. Notice period was reduced from 30 to 15 days regardless of length of employment.

Appendix

Labor Force Participation Rates.

Country	Male	Female
Bahrain	86.9	43.1
Kuwait	85.4	47.3
Oman	83.9	28.4
Qatar	94.6	53.9
Saudi Arabia	76.7	20.0
UAE	93.9	46.5
Total	86.9	39.9
Memo item		
Other high-income countries	68.7	53.8

Author details

Wasseem Mina
United Arab Emirates University, Al Ain, UAE

*Address all correspondence to: wmina@uaeu.ac.ae; wmina2004@aol.com

References

[1] Sacht, S. On the efficiency of labor market reforms: How to solve the Spanish puzzle? Economics: The Open-Access, Open-Assessment E-Journal. 2015:9(2015-44):1—28. http://dx.doi.org/10.5018/economics-ejournal.ja.2015-44.

[2] International Labor Organization. Global Employment Trends for Youth 2020: Technology and the Future of Jobs. Geneva: International Labor Office; 2020.

[3] Mina, W. Do GCC market-oriented labor policies encourage inward FDI flows? Research in International Business and Finan*ce.* 2020:51. DOI. org/10.1016/j.ribaf.2019.101092.

[4] Hertog, S. Arab Gulf states: An Assessment of nationalisation policies". GLMM – Research Paper 1, 2014, Gulf Labour Markets and Migration Programme, Badia Fiesolana, Italy.

[5] Hertog, S. A comparative assessment of labour market nationalization policies in the GCC. In: Hertog, S. editor. The Gulf Region: Economic Development and Diversification, 4. Gerlach Press, Berlin, Germany. ISBN 9783940924001.

[6] Bernal-Verdugo, LE, Furceri, D, Guillaume, D. Labor market flexibility and unemployment: New empirical evidence of static and dynamic effects. IMF Working Paper WP/12/64.

[7] Bernal-Verdugo, LE, Furceri, D, Guillaume, D. Crises, labor market policy, and unemployment. IMF Working Paper WP/12/65.

[8] Furceri, D. Unemployment and labor market issues in Algeria. IMF Working Paper WP/12/99.

[9] Mina, W. Labor market policies and youth unemployment in the GCC countries. The Empirical Economics Letters. 2020:19(2). ISSN 1681-8997.

[10] Horwitz, L, Myant, M. Spain's labour market reforms: The road to employment—or to unemployment? Working Paper 2015-03. European Trade Union Institute.

Section 3

The Financial System and Macroeconomic Performance

Chapter 9

Perspective Chapter: International Financial Markets and Financial Capital Flows - Forms, Factors and Assessment Tools

Nemer Badwan

Abstract

This paper/chapter empirically examines the reaction of international financial markets and financial capital flows across many developing and emerging market economies, with a particular focus on the dynamics of capital flows across emerging market economies. Using daily data from (2000 to 2020) and controlling for a range of local and global macroeconomic and financial factors and global financial crisis, we use a fixed-effects panel approach quantitative and descriptive approach combined to show that emerging markets have been affected more than advanced economies. In particular, emerging economies in Asia and Europe have experienced the strongest impact on stocks, bonds and exchange rates in recent times, as well as sudden and large capital inflows. Our findings suggest that very large fiscal stimulus packages, as well as quantitative easing by central banks, helped restore overall investor confidence by lowering bond yields and boosting stock prices. Our findings also highlight the role that global factors and developments in the world's leading financial centers play in financial conditions in emerging markets and developing countries. More importantly, the impact of quantitative easing measures related to the global financial crisis by central banks in developed countries.

Keywords: international financial markets, financial capital flows, financial development, economic growth, developing counties, emerging markets, global financial crisis

1. Introduction

International financial markets and emerging markets, financial capital flows play an important role in the economies of developing and developed countries alike, as they are one of the financial policy tools used to mobilize domestic savings and an attractive tool for foreign investments, in addition to their active role in financing economic development plans. With the growing deficit of the public budgets of some countries, these countries have started to search for non-sovereign financial resources to finance their development plans, so the financial markets have become one of the important tools used for such development goals.

 IntechOpen

The international financial markets and financial capital flows have witnessed tremendous developments in recent years, whether in terms of new financial instruments or terms of structural changes in market divisions, the creation of new markets and the development of regulations related to trading, settlement and clearing, which has called for the various countries of the world to make intensive efforts to keep pace with these changes due to the effects of this, positive on the liquidity and depth of financial markets [1, 2].

Moreover, the main factors for this development are global economic growth and the continent's growing integration into international financial markets. The capital yield at the Johannesburg Stock Exchange (JSE) was 43% in (2005), in third place after Seoul and Warsaw.

The increasing capital flows in the international financial markets and emerging markets, developed countries have raised various concerns worldwide. One main concern is the impact of the sharp decline of capital flows so-called sudden stops on financial markets and the stability of banking systems and the economy [3].

The sudden stops and banking crises have been identified as the two main features of most financial crises, including the recent Asian Financial Crisis and Global Financial Crisis.

However, how capital flows and banking crises are connected remains unanswered. Most current studies on capital flows are empirical work, which faces various challenges. The challenges include how data has been collected and measured in each country and how sensitive the results are to the data and the adopted methodologies [4].

Moreover, the links between capital flows and banking systems have been neglected. This book helps provide some insight into the challenges faced by empirical studies and the lessons of the recent crises.

The book develops theoretical analysis to deepen our understanding of how capital flows, banking systems and financial markets are linked with each other and provides constructive policy implications by overcoming the empirical challenges [5].

However, the problem remains only about (87000) Africans, i.e., less than 0.01% of the total population, benefit from this kind of growth. At present, more than half of the people on the continent survive on less than 1.9 USD a day. The World Bank (2007:79) predicts that by (2030), more than three-quarters of the population of sub-Saharan Africa is likely to be among the world's poorest [6].

The effects of poverty and wealth are not independent processes, but interrelated. Those talking about poverty cannot remain silent about wealth. An important correlation between poverty and wealth concerns financial markets, and in the move towards globalization, this is getting to be even more important [7].

The depth and global ramifications of the East Asian financial crisis which broke out in (1997) have confounded analysts and forecasters, and have been a major cause of more recent periods of extreme volatility in international financial markets. Expectations that the crisis would be confined to the region and that recovery would be relatively rapid have been repeatedly belied by events [6].

By the middle of (1998), it was clear that it was sharply reducing growth rates not only in the directly affected countries but also in most other developing and transition economies. The international liquidity crisis set off by the currency collapse and debt default in the Russian Federation raised the possibility that the full global implications might not yet have been realized [8].

On the other hand, the relatively benign response of financial markets to the later Brazilian currency crisis and the continued rapid growth of some major industrial countries suggest that the repercussions may still be restricted largely to developing countries [9, 10].

Subsequently, to the real economy, which means production and trade financial markets had a secondary or subservient position. The three market segments were largely separated from one another. Before the (1970s), financial markets were mainly national markets, thus concentrating on the prevailing national economy. Foreign trade is only related to monetary transactions and foreign investments [11].

Moreover, until the (1970s) international financial markets were regulated politically by the Bretton Woods system, which at its core promoted stable rates of exchange between important currencies and the control of capital transactions. This system provided a relatively stable general framework for the world economy, as well as considerable growth [12].

Financial markets were not limited in terms of individual national economies, but were opened internationally and globally. At the same time, business size and variety grew by scales. Proportions between the real economy and financial systems became inverted, which led to the economic dominance of the financial markets, creating the trigger, Centre and motor for the present wave of globalization [12, 13].

2. Introduction to international financial markets and financial capital flows

2.1 The emergence of international financial markets and financial capital flows

The most important financial markets and financial capital flows known to economic history in Europe, and indeed in the world - and in which they were dealt with bills of exchange, promissory notes, and precious metals are the markets of Venice and Genoa in Italy and the Frankfurt market, and these markets were among the most important European financial markets dealing with the Middle East, which witnessed in that period a huge commercial activity as a center of communication between the far East and Europe.

With the development of capitalist economic thought that calls for specialization and division of labor, and with the emergence of the industrial revolution, the importance of individual investments that require large financial resources that exceed the capabilities and capabilities of individuals has increased [13].

As a result, joint-stock companies appeared which opened a wide field for the participation of a larger number of shareholders in the ownership of companies, thus ensuring the necessary financing for them. On the other hand, the number of banks has developed and their importance has increased in various countries [4].

All these factors and conditions, as well as the expansion of investment projects and commercial transactions, contributed greatly to the emergence of financial markets as an effective tool for mobilizing the resources and savings needed for commercial and investment financing [14].

The first financial markets to appear were in the seventeenth century (17th century) in Amsterdam, then in the eighteenth century (18th century) in Venice, and the nineteenth and twentieth centuries (19th and 20th century), respectively, witnessed the emergence of the British and international financial centers American [15].

Stock exchanges appeared in the nineteenth century (19th century) for trading goods, products, and securities and concluding deals. The emergence of stock exchanges was the result of many economic factors, the most important of which are [16, 17]:

- Increasing the financial activity of large institutions that use huge funds, such as banks, insurance companies, and transport and communications companies;

- Increasing international trade exchanges, which saw the movement of commodities and raw materials from the colonized countries to the colonized countries.

- The financial markets in developed countries have developed in conjunction with the changes and developments taking place at the technological level, and the volume of production and large business units has grown faster than the available means of financing.

The activity of the financial markets has increased dramatically. The number of financial markets in the United States of America has reached fourteen at present, the most important and largest of which is the New York Stock Exchange. In Britain, too, all financial markets have merged since (1913) into one system, which is the London Stock Exchange [18].

In Japan, eight stock exchanges are currently operating, led by the Tokyo Stock Exchange. This is the case in Germany, where there are also eight stock exchanges, the most important of which is the Frankfurt Stock Exchange. As for France, there are seven stock exchanges headed by the Paris Stock Exchange [1].

2.2 The functions of international financial markets and financial capital flows

Financial markets and financial capital flows play an important role in economic life, and if we try to present the most important functions that they can perform, they can be summarized as follows:

1. Developing savings by encouraging investment in securities, and directing savings to serve the national economy.

2. The stock market encourages the development of the habit of investment saving, especially for small savers who cannot carry out independent projects with their little money, and therefore they prefer to buy securities according to their money, and this helps to serve the purposes of development and reduce inflation, as it helps direct Savings towards appropriate investments (either in stocks or bonds) according to price trends.

3. Assistance in transferring funds from groups that have surpluses (the lenders) to groups that have deficits (borrowers), and the lenders reduce their current consumption expenditures in exchange for higher incomes in the future when the maturity dates of those loans come, and when the borrowers use that borrowed money to buy and rent the factors of production, they will produce higher incomes, thus increasing the standard of living not only for the borrowers but for all segments of society [9].

4. Contribute to financing development plans by offering government securities in that market. The emergence of the importance of securities issued by joint-stock companies was accompanied by the increasing recourse of governments to public borrowing from members of the people, to meet their increasing expenditures and to finance development projects, by issuing bonds and bills issued by the public treasury with different terms. It is less important than other aspects of employment [10].

5. Contribute to the support of internal and external credit. As the buying and selling currencies on the stock exchange is a manifestation of internal credit, if the manifestations of this credit increased to include securities traded in global stock exchanges, it became possible to accept these securities as a cover for contracting financial loans.

6. Contribute to achieving high efficiency in directing resources to the most profitable areas; this is accompanied by economic growth and prosperity. This requires the availability of several features in the stock market, which can be summarized as follows:

    a. Efficient pricing: meaning that prices reflect all available information.

    b. Operational efficiency: meaning that the cost of transactions is minimized compared to the return that these transactions can yield.

    c. Market justice: meaning that the market provides an equal opportunity for everyone who wants to conclude deals.

    d. Safety: It means the necessity of providing means of protection against the risks that result from the relations between the parties dealing in the market, such as the risks of fraud, fraud and other unethical practices that some parties intend.

7. Determining the prices of securities realistically based on sufficient knowledge and a high degree of fairness.

8. The prices of securities are determined through negotiation or auction (public auction), which more closely reflects the opinion of dealers on the appropriate price of the security under the prevailing market conditions, in addition to what companies and economic authorities do in publishing all data related to companies, their instruments, profits and financial positions; This prevents creating an unrealistic price for the security. This price represents the best price for the seller (highest bid) and the buyer (Lowest Offer) [15].

9. A stock market is an important tool for evaluating companies and projects. It contributes to increasing investors' awareness and insight into the reality of companies and projects, and is judged on success or failure.

10. The drop in stock prices for a company is conclusive evidence of its lack of success or the weakness of its financial position; which may lead to making some adjustments in its leadership or in its policy in the hope of improving its position [15].

2.3 The components of international financial markets and financial capital flows

The money market requires the availability of several basic components to become an effective market capable of achieving the objectives for which these components are established, which can be summarized as follows:

1. Adopting a liberal economic philosophy based on confidence in the capabilities of market forces to move economic activity in light of considerations of economic efficiency and rational behavior of both producer and consumer, exporter and importer and other individuals and organizations based in economic activity, that private capital plays a leading role in accumulating private savings And re-allocate them to the faces of economic activity that achieve the highest possible rate of return in light of the lowest possible level of risks [2, 10].

2. The necessity of having a sufficient volume of savings, both national and foreign, offered and at the same time corresponding to sufficient demand for them so that there is no surplus in demand without being matched by the available supply of savings that undertakes to cover it, or an excess of supply that does not have the demand capable of employing it in the various financial investments [11].

3. Existence of sufficient investment opportunities capable of attracting short and long-term capital offered and looking at the same time for attractive investment opportunities.

4. Finding effective legislative and regulatory frameworks through their flexibility and ability to continuously develop and adapt to national and international economic changes.

5. Availability of effective and diversified banking and financial institutions to play their required role in accumulating national and foreign savings on the one hand and creating and generating investment opportunities and preparing them in the form of investment projects and promoting them on the other hand.

6. These financial or banking institutions play a prominent role in the mediation process between savings and those who join to find the required convergence between the supply and demand for savings and the presentation and demand for investment opportunities.

7. Having a good and diversified portfolio of securities that contains many different advantages to be able to attract dealers in the financial market and at the same time provide them with great opportunities to choose.

It is also noticeable that the term "Internationalization" has spread in international securities after (H2), due to the huge measures that were followed in the major advanced industrial countries to liberate the movement of capital from the restrictions imposed on them and the great role played by the information revolution, which made the international financial markets more like with a single financial village with interconnected parties and able to find diverse and attractive investment opportunities for those wishing to invest around the globe.

In addition to opening the door for international commercial and specialized banks to find the appropriate purpose to add the money that they accumulated in particular in the period (1947–1990) as a result of the phenomenon of accumulation of petrodollar surpluses, and the great development what the European currency markets witnessed is in addition to the success achieved by the central banks of the advanced industrial countries in controlling the inflationary phenomenon in the era of the eighties, thus opening the way for these countries to adopt flexible interest rate policies that enabled them to reduce their interest rates, which in turn contributed to an increase in the demand for high-quality securities [6, 19].

Fixed interest rates (International Bonds) and this development has created great popularity in the field of international financial investments and prepared the way for capital movements across international borders, in addition to the great role played by the policy of reducing and removing restrictions between international markets [20].

3. Investing in international financial markets and financial capital flows

3.1 The mechanism of dealing in international financial markets and financial capital flows

Securities are issued either denominated in real currencies traded in a country, and this is mostly either "Arithmetic" or "Compound" monetary units that are not traded, but are used only as units of measurement, because of the advantages of real currencies to avoid the fluctuations that may occur on the currency that may it harms the interests of dealers in the financial market and is dealt with in these markets according to indicators in the light of which the trends practiced by investors, speculators and financial analysts in the financial markets are determined which are:

1. Economic indicators: The movement of stock and bond prices in the financial market is affected by economic indicators, which in turn reflect the validity of speculations and expectations in the market, such as the case of announcing a huge financial budget or an ambitious investment approach, which means expecting prices to rise in general, and pumping additional funds. The market would reflect on the state and conditions of stock exchanges in developing countries, and so on in adopting statistics on industrial production, national product or disposable income as indicators in stock markets in developed countries [4].

2. Monetary and financial indicators: They are one of the most important indicators to know price trends in the financial market, as the rise in interest rates leads to investors moving towards depositing in banks, and selling their shares in the market, so the supply of them increases and their prices decrease, while the funds are heading towards the financial market in the event of falling prices interest in banks or transferred to the bond market [6, 21].

3. Increasing the money supply, whether in the economies of developing or developing countries, leads to a rise in stock prices, and conversely, a decrease in the growth rates of money supply will lead to a decrease in stock prices, and therefore the intervention of central banks in expanding or reducing the money supply is reflected in the shift in money prices, the interest is to rise or fall, and then influence the price trends in the financial market accordingly [21].

4. Trading volume in the stock exchange: The number of shares and bonds traded in the financial market determines the strength of the market and the expectations of its rise or fall in the future, as the intensity of trading volume means the optimism of investors and their willingness to invest in the market and the subsequent rise in prices as a result.

5. The individual nature of these markets, makes the investor face strong parties in the aspect of issuance and marketing, represented by public bodies and major companies, which can enter the international market [2].

6. It is difficult for the investor to have sufficient knowledge of the prevailing conditions in the markets in general, as well as the conditions of the bodies in which he invests his securities. Often the investor relies in this regard either on a few general information or on the advice and instructions of stock traders. This is if we know that the majority of investors resort to the services of specialists due

to the conditions and fees imposed by them that are rarely related to the quality and effectiveness of performance.

7. Securities holders, especially bond holders, need to tighten their protection not from risks in the normal market resulting from changes in interest rates, exchange rates or credit of securities, but rather the risks resulting from the failure of debtors (especially in the bond market) to perform their obligations, represented by the difficulty of obtaining On foreign currencies when paying or delaying the payment of interests and installments, or imposing exchange control or imposing taxes, such as taxes on transfers and so on.

Therefore, if the market achieved progress or supply and was not accompanied by heavy trading, then the prices remain unchanged or tend to decline due to the relative stagnation of participation, and thus investors are directed towards liquidating their investments as prices continue with downward trends. Hence, it becomes clear to us that the intensity of trading and the increase in prices is what generates the demand, which is followed by the occurrence of successive increases after that; therefore, demand is not the only thing that leads to an increase in prices in the financial markets [22].

Thus, this market has characteristics that differ from what it is in the investment markets and consumer goods markets, which reflect the effectiveness of the investment process mechanism in those markets, represented by the following [23]:

3.2 Analysis of the reality of Investment in International Financial Markets and Financial Capital Flows

The global economy, in view of the increasing importance of capital in the financial services industry with its banking and non-banking components, has become a tool driven by indices and symbols of global stock exchanges (Dow Jones, Nasdaq, Nikkei, DAX, Kick) which leads to the transfer of in-kind wealth from one investor's hand to another. Without hindrances or even across geographical borders, where the continuous movement of capital looking for a profit in front of its accumulated surpluses, providing guarantees to the owners of these funds and diversifying them through the mechanisms provided by financial instruments and controlling the different markets [24].

For example, World Bank reports indicate that the volume of transactions at the global level reached about (300) billion dollars for the (Euro-Dollar) market in one working day, which is approximately (75) trillion dollars per year, while the volume of trade in the sector did not exceed Goods and services (3) trillion dollars until it became a threat to the economies of the world [6].

The experiences of the nineties of the last century proved that this movement of huge amounts of capital often led to the occurrence of costly financial crises and shocks (in Mexico, the Asian tigers, Brazil, Russia) represented in [23]:

- Risks arise from sudden fluctuations in investments in international financial markets, especially short-term ones.

- Risks of exposure to speculation in the market.

- Risks of flight of national funds.

- Risks of entering dirty money (Money Laundering).

Weakening control over national policies in the areas of monetary and fiscal policy.

Thus, the great powers of investment accounted for the wealth and markets of the world, helped by the flourishing of communication networks and the transfer of information provided by the tremendous technical progress in linking global financial markets, allowing investors to respond to developments in the markets in a timely and immediate manner [25].

Because of the phenomenon of monetary inflation, which is one of the structural characteristics of modern economic life in various countries of the world, which in turn led to the rise in the costs necessary for investment, in addition to the need for capital to expand its activities and the inability of savings on the other hand to meet the volume of required investments, there is no other way but the financial markets to obtain the necessary funds to meet that demand for the implementation of investments, through which transactions are conducted through the investors selling their shares or increasing them by buying [26].

Thus the financial market became active as a new financial tool, and the accompanying calls for the abolition of legal and legislative regulations that stand in the way of promoting market economies and the practice of banking and financial operations on a large scale, and then accelerating the movement of capital flows across borders, which created an expansion in the scope of dealing in different types of securities, turning parts of the volume of traded capital into speculation globally in the currency markets, stock exchanges, securities, stocks, bonds and short sales, which made dealing in the international financial markets requires a continuous review of the concepts, effects, and even strategies followed [27].

Often, dealing in these markets is within a deliberate process driven by capitalist forces to achieve their interests, including trade liberalization and opening international markets to the free movement of goods and services through the main players. These international markets that lead investment operations, sales procedures, brokerage, and financial speculation [28].

3.3 Large transnational corporations and international financial markets, financial capital flows

In the wake of the economic boom following the end of the Second World War, the phenomenon of the spread of the so-called multinational corporations or transnational corporations (most of these corporations are American, European, or Japanese) has emerged [1].

Big companies seek to support and promote the global free market, where the largest and strongest player in the image of giant multinational corporations and major players in international financial markets. From here, the art of the game becomes clear in the international financial markets through these companies and as follows:

1. The escalation of trends and movements of Western capital and companies of this type with the help of the communications and information network, illustrates the huge sources of power that allow giant monopolies to penetrate global markets, including stock markets through movements, activities and interactions to increase their ability to maneuver in dealing in these markets by following the method of encouraging speculation in the stock exchanges on stocks and bonds in order to operate the huge moving financial masses of money with banking assets, whose value exceeds the total value of world trade by at least thirty times (of visible and invisible goods and services), and this means that if the total value of merchandise trade at the level of the world is three trillion dollars (as we have shown), the volume of investments offered in the field of stock exchanges, bonds, and electronic money or credit cards that they deal

in in those markets is not less than (100) trillion dollars, which in turn are far from the control of the richest central banks in the world [6, 29].

2. The movements and activities of Western commercial, industrial, information and media monopolies with terrifying capabilities were taking place in the direction of an attempt to cross or cross borders and affect the national sovereignty of countries and societies and what is known as (Trans border Trends), such actions and in the manner dictated by these companies, to facilitate the tasks of the movements of the great powers to dominate the economies of the world through major companies as one of the important methods for controlling the flows of capital and investments, and controlling the tracks of the stock markets in the world, including the stock and bond markets; In this case, it is considered the beneficiary of these markets, especially with regard to the capital invested in financial operations, which is reflected in the work mechanism in the international financial markets, which is most powerfully reflected in the giant transnational companies and players in the international financial markets [6, 30].

3. The role of currency laundering operations (Money Laundering), money laundering means the investment of illegally obtained currency by a third party to obscure the identity of its source, knowing that the source of these funds is a criminal act. These funds are exploited in the areas of accepting deposits, bank transfers, issuing bank payment methods, guarantees, and financial obligations Trading for third parties or for own account, external transfer, cash brokerage, cash portfolio management, owning and managing financial bonds, and other banking activities [6]. Preliminary data indicate that there are (−0.9) trillion dollars of world production spent in what is known as the "Shadow Economy" or transactions that are not subject to taxation and are not recorded in the official books, which includes the unrecorded legal income of cash-paid transactions from the unrecognized income side. Legal activities of smuggling, drug and other activities [21, 31].

Money laundering takes place in three stages:

The First Stage: Employing illegal funds in the form of deposits with banks and financial institutions, or buying shares and bonds.

The Second Stage: Concealing the true source of funds by conducting a series of financial transactions.

The Third Stage: Repositioning the illegal money after it has been laundered.

The international financial markets are considered one of the most important areas that enable this type of funds to operate, as it is difficult to follow up, control, or even besiege them in this market due to its integration into the network of traditional financial and banking activities.

Payment via the Internet, and money launderers do not care about the economic feasibility of investment as much as they are interested in employment that allows the return or continuity of money circulation, which poses a risk to the investment climate, especially in the financial markets represented in the stock markets of stocks and bonds, as the movement of money required to be laundered without taking into account profitability within the space of these markets will lead to confusion in the market and promote the process of speculation among dealers in the market and create a state of unequal competition with investors, as the money-laundering process, due to its large amounts, affects interest rates and exchange rates, and this reflects the rapid variation in the prices of stocks and bonds, and its changes, thus falling into the trap of losses, withdrawal from the market, or the bankruptcy of some investors; In view of the large size that laundered money occupies in the international financial markets, especially since there are gangs, networks and international organizations with huge potentials specialized in the processes of creating dirty money, and laundering it - its laundering - thanks to financial globalization through the movement of people, bank transfers and the transfer of capital [21].

The United Nations profits generated from organized crime amount to one trillion US dollars annually and a fifth of this huge amount is re-laundered in the global economy or about (200) billion dollars annually [6].

Among the most prominent of these dealings is what is happening in the field of financial markets and financial institutions that practice secret financial and banking accounts, where money is laundered and laundered through the means of entering into stock and bond purchases (a series of buying and selling operations) and the negative effects of such operations on trading operations, and dealing in those markets and the matter becomes more dangerous if we know that dirty money laundering networks employ a large number of economic and financial legal advisors and brokers to manage and follow up the transactions, especially through financial institutions and (Off Sure) banks that issue forged invoices and end-use certificates to hide the source of these funds, and what follows from the Confusion in the international financial markets as a result of sudden and rapid changes in the prices of stocks and bonds and the value of exchanges in general [32, 33].

This is the state of the international financial markets, financial capital flows and the cases of unequal competition, speculation, and manipulation in investment operations in them, which makes them under the weight of the alarming movements of financial blocs and capital flows and the growing ability of the most powerful actors on the global capital level, to form the empire of monetary capital independent of industrial and commodity capital and thus is done Monopolizing the resources and returns of the international financial markets through investment and speculation operations in those markets [34].

4. The main players in the international financial markets and financial capital flows

4.1 The most important international financial centers and their indicators of the financial capital flows

4.1.1 American stock exchange - New York stock exchange

New York is currently the most important market or international financial center, due to the large volume of capital traded in it, and the importance of pressure and influence exerted by the Wall Street Stock Exchange on the rest of the international financial centers in the world, which increased the importance of the American financial market as well, the situation The dollar's distinction in the international monetary system [23].

New York emerged as an international financial center after World War II, when in (1954) two-dollar loans were issued to Belgium and Australia, amounting to (55) million dollars, and the New York Stock Exchange developed during this period. In the mid-sixties, long-term investments in foreign bonds amounted to (5.7) billion dollars, and most of them were directed to European foreign banks [23].

In (1962), the total amount of bonds issued by the American stock market reached a record high of (1146) million dollars, and this amount exceeded the sum of foreign loans issued in England, Switzerland, Germany, the Netherlands, and Austria, all combined. In (1972), the volume of trading in the New York Stock

Exchange amounted to about (71.2) billion pounds, and this exceeds the total trading in (London, Tokyo, and Zurich) combined [16, 35].

During the period (1981–1987), the foreign capital employed in the American financial markets amounted to about (920) billion dollars, the majority of which was invested in US government bonds - to contribute effectively to covering the ongoing public budget deficit.

The American stock exchanges have become the most important markets in the world, as the value of the total financial investment tools registered in the American financial market represents from 30–60% of the value of capitalization in global stock exchanges, whether for stocks or bonds [36].

4.1.2 Characteristics of the US financial market

The rules of dealing in the New York Stock Exchange and the American stock market require that all sales and purchases be done by public auction and with a loud and audible voice, hence the prohibition of secret exchanges completely, in addition to the fact that the broker may not complete the purchase or sale requests received by him from His customers without displaying them in the hall by way of public auction [37].

American financial markets are characterized by a set of characteristics, the most important of which are [17, 38]:

- The presence of a sophisticated and efficient information system;
- The superior ability to continuously communicate with all financial markets in the world, by linking them to a multilateral electronic system;
- Allowing the sale of securities to foreigners, either through the secondary market, or by concluding transactions outside the official financial market;
- Continuous development and modernization at the level of American capital markets in order to achieve high efficiency.

4.2 British stock exchange - London stock exchange

London is the most important European financial center and ranks second after New York in the world. The activity of the London Stock Exchange dates back to the seventeenth century (17th century) when the British government and some major commercial companies began to raise capital through the sale of shares and bonds. With the increase in the volume of financial investments, a type of dealer appeared that plays the role of mediation between sellers and buyers of securities, and stock dealers - after they met in London cafes - moved to a private building to practice their activities [39].

London began to gain its importance as an international financial center during the nineteenth century (Q19) when British overseas investment reached its limits. After the First World War, the fame of the British financial market was affected by the great competition from the New York Stock Exchange, in addition to the negative impact of the economic crisis of (1929) on the role of London [40].

After World War II, London was able to return to the international financial arena by providing loans in Euro-Dollars. The London Stock Exchange plays two main roles, as it represents a source of capital for the British and foreigners, and it is considered a global center for dealing in securities. The British net revenues from financial services witnessed during the second half of the twentieth century, and the following table represents the development of this development during the period (1970–1980) [6, 41].

Statistics and studies indicate that the number of securities registered on the London Stock Exchange is more than (6000) shares, estimated at 50% of the total securities registered in the European financial markets, of which (2000) shares are for international and European companies. This area, because most of the bonds issued in the international financial market are registered in the London market [42].

The London financial market is characterized by a special system related to the means and methods of carrying out operations. It is not an auction market like other international financial markets but rather deals with negotiation and bargaining.

The broker in the London Stock Exchange is limited to mediating between the client and the jobbers, which is similar to the wholesaler in the commodity markets, as the jobber does not deal with the public, but sells and buys securities for his account, even if he works in the name and under the responsibility of one of the stock brokers [36].

The jobbers are a group of members of the London Stock Exchange, where they perform the function of "Market Makers", and their number is thirteen (13) traders dealing with stockbrokers.

Several characteristics also characterizes the London Stock Exchange, namely [3, 29]:

- Experience in financial transactions;
- Stability of the foreign exchange market;
- Low taxes on stock dividends.

The London Financial Market is also divided into the stock market, bond market, futures market, and foreign exchange market.

The Paris Stock Exchange and the Tokyo Stock Exchange, the Cairo Stock Exchange,and the United States of America Stock Exchange.

4.3 Paris stock exchange

Before the First World War, France played an important role in the international financial market, because the large amounts of capital accumulation and the limited use of it in the productive areas inside France helped French banks to assume their position in financing international trade operations and providing loans to other countries. The French financial market began to gain more importance during the second half of the twentieth century, due to the high rates of economic growth and capital accumulation within France [36, 43].

This is despite the fact that the Paris Stock Exchange faced some obstacles that limited the expansion of its financial activity, such as restrictions imposed on foreign direct investments in France and control over the issuance of foreign securities and loans obtained by French companies from abroad [44].

This is despite the fact that the Paris Stock Exchange faced some obstacles that limited the expansion of its financial activity, such as restrictions imposed on foreign direct investments in France and control over the issuance of foreign securities and loans obtained by French companies from abroad. In the French financial market, most dealing is done in bonds, and the government sets the conditions and criteria for registering foreign securities and the way they are traded in the market. That is why French financial markets are known as governmental management and decision [45].

4.4 Tokyo stock exchange

The Japanese financial market occupies third place after the financial market of America and the financial market of Britain, and the first financial markets were established in Japan in (1878 AD), namely the "Tokyo" market and the "Osaka" market. The Japanese financial market played an important role in the process of financing the industry resulting from the wave of economic development in Japan during the nineteenth and twentieth centuries, which made the Japanese government interested in developing and modernizing the Japanese financial markets, taking advantage of the American experience in this field, until the Tokyo Stock Exchange became one of the largest Competitors of the New York Stock Exchange in the second half of the twentieth century [35, 36].

Among the most important characteristics of the Japanese financial market [1]:

a. Diversity of investment tools traded in it and low risk;

b. Great openness to the registration and trading of securities of foreign companies;

c. The development of information systems and the ability to continuously communicate with international financial markets;

d. Characterized by high liquidity.

4.5 Cairo stock exchange

It occupies the first place in the Arab world, with its experiences in this field, as it is the oldest Arab stock exchange, and alongside the Palestinian stock exchange, it is considered the most important and active Arab stock exchange [12, 13].

The most important indicators used in international financial centers:

- The movement and direction of stock prices in the stock markets is measured through a number of indicators. Each index includes a group of companies that reflect the market movement, its degree of efficiency, and the rate of increase or decrease in share prices.

- The most important indicators that characterize international financial centers are the Dow Jones Index and the Standard & Poor's (500) Index in the American financial market, the Financial Times Index in the British financial market, the Nikkei index in the Japanese financial market, in addition to the CAC (40) index in the French financial market.

4.6 United States of America stock exchange

In (1887) Charles Dow developed two of the most widely used indexes, the Industrial Corporations Index, and the Railroad Industries Index, which includes (20) of the largest such corporations in the United States of America. These are now known as the Dow Jones Industrial Average and the Dow Jones Transportation Index [13, 14].

- The Dow Jones Index is one of the oldest and most famous indicators used in the financial markets, as it was first published in the Wall Street Journal on July 3, (1884).

- This index includes three sub-indices and a major index that represents the entire financial market.

- Standard & Poor's (500) (S&P 500): contains five hundred securities representing 80% of the market value of shares traded on the New York Stock Exchange (400) industrial companies, (40) public utility companies, (20) transportation companies, (40) companies in the field of finance, banking and insurance.

- England (FT-30): This index brings together thirty of the most important securities on the London Stock Exchange.

- (FTSE-100): the most popular index, containing (100) securities representing 70% of the total stock exchange capitalization.

- France (CA-C40) Index: It consists of (40) securities of the most important companies on the Stock Exchange Paris.

- Germany (DAX) Index: contains (30) securities representing 70% of the stock market capitalization

- Japan Nikkei Index: Contains (225) securities representing about 70% of the capitalization of the Tokyo Stock Exchange.

4.7 The European dollar market "Eurodollar"

The reasons for the emergence of these European dollars go back to the (the 1950s), when some countries, because of the conditions left by the Cold War between the two camps, deposited their dollar assets in Western European banks to avoid the (USA) from freezing them if they were employed in them [21, 22].

4.7.1 The concept of the European dollar

The European dollar is the same as the (US) Dollar, which is in the form of deposits in banks outside the United States of America. It is necessary to know another idiomatic expression, "Eurodollar", which originally meant dollar deposits in European banks, including branches of American banks in Europe as well [27, 44].

4.7.2 Characteristics of the euro-dollar market

Deposit operations with banks in Euro-dollars have led to the emergence of a new international financial market that is completely different from the national markets, and its operations are conducted in dollars through the intermediary of banks spread outside the (EU) [21, 35].

4.7.3 The most important characteristics of this market

1. The Eurodollar market, as part of the international financial market, does not have specific national borders, and therefore it is not subject to the control of any country or system. The supervisory authorities in a country are unable to influence the activity of this market effectively, and their capabilities are limited in this area with their foreign currencies.

2. This market is based on deposit and lending operations, and therefore it is considered a market for loaned funds.

3. The very large and growing volume of the Eurodollar market operations greatly affects the monetary and credit conditions of the entire capitalist system.

4. The affiliation of creditors and debtors in this market to different countries.

5. This market enjoys relative independence and a special interest rate policy that is completely different from the internationally applicable rates.

6. The Eurodollar market consists of two parts of operations:

   - Interbank transactions: They take the form of current and term deposits with certain interest rates.

   - Interbank and other dealers' operations: When banks make loans to their customers.

4.7.4 Reasons for the development of the Eurodollar market

The emergence and development of the Eurodollar market are due to several reasons, the most important of which are [33, 34]:

- Strictly limiting the credit interest rates paid by (US) banks to their depositors by the central banks or the so-called (K) or (Q) rule, which led to a large number of non-resident dollar deposit holders and some residents investing their money outside the country (MI) to evade the provisions of the aforementioned rule, and thus obtain higher interest rates in Europe.

- The chronic deficit in the (US) balance of payments, as well as the method of financing this deficit.

- The caution imposed on British banks since (1957) by using the pound sterling as a foreign currency for transfers, and for conducting monetary transactions between countries outside the sterling area, has forced the banks in London to replace the dollar with the sterling and thus obtain all the necessary dollars from outside England.

- The (USA) interest equalization tax has reduced the demand for loans by (non-US) residents (due to the high cost of these loans), forcing them to resort outside the (USA) to obtain the necessary financing.

- European insurance companies working for the (USA) found that it is in their interest to maintain their dollar reserves in the European dollar market, which brings them profitability and great financial returns.

- It should be noted that the Eurodollar market originated in the European foreign exchange market, as the latter includes several currency markets.

4.8 The European bond market

The financial services business in Europe as a whole is undergoing fast transformations because of numerous primary driving forces. The most obvious example is

(EMU), but liberalization continues apace, and technology is entering an exponential transition phase that may well allow for substantial disintermediation of many aspects of the financial system. The paper's first section provides an outline of the specific changes that appear to be most likely to alter the market structure within which the (ECB) will have to operate its monetary policy. Naturally, the first set of modifications were those necessary to run a monetary union with a population of 300 million people [16, 34].

Several other fundamental causes have been at work in the background at the same time, with the full implications only becoming apparent in the medium term. Nonetheless, the implications have the potential to have a significant impact on monetary policy implementation; therefore, they should be closely monitored [46].

The (ECB's) Technical Actions the (ECB) made several technical steps as part of its (EMU) preparations to ensure that its monetary policy could be implemented effectively. Some of these improvements may have happened spontaneously over time, as technology became more widely available, causing cost-cutting pressures to force market participants to adopt these techniques. Nonetheless, (EMU) sped up the following critical steps [17]:

1. Cross-border payments in real-time were required. Market players must be able to arbitrage any geographical price disparities in money to create a unified pan-European money market. The efficiency of payment systems will determine the perfection of that arbitrage, so large amounts of money will need to be moved quickly. A real-time system was the logical choice if central banks wanted to avoid potentially enormous credit exposure to payment banks – and technology had just made it possible. As a result, the target system was created [38, 47].

2. Once the decision to avoid central bank credit exposure had been established, real-time securities settlement became a need. The ability to settle very large volumes of securities flows immediately was required to carry out a monetary policy via securities transactions. Furthermore, the requirement for collateral movement as part of the payment mechanism suggested the same thing. The starting pistol for a major re-structuring of the entire settlement chain had been fired once the (ECB) decided it would require these settlement systems to be constructed for the limited purposes of monetary policy execution. Furthermore, the (ECB's) depositary minimum norms underscored the need for action. With this limited process in place, market players were bound to apply risk reduction and cost savings to all aspects of their business [38].

3. The creation of methods for dealing with the (ECB) prompted a broader expansion in the use of collateral. Tier One (high credit quality, marketable debt instruments) and Tier Two (National Instruments) appear to be broad enough to cover new securities that may emerge when market participants develop new products to appeal to (pan-EU) investors. The significance of the (ECB's) eligibility rules, however, should not be overstated. In March, the (ECB) had 600 billion euro in total collateral out of a pool of 6300 billion euro in eligible assets (2000). By a minimum issue size of 3.000 million euro at the end of March, Salomon Smith Barney forecasts a size of 500 million euro in (2000) markets that are easily accessible to institutional investors (2000). Given the broad eligibility criteria, it would be astonishing if a newly issued asset was not (ECB) eligible, and there appears to be a little price premium for "eligibility" at issue – or even in secondary trading, even in the repo market itself [48].

4. Improving collateral's legal certainty is an obvious step, and the Giovaninni Group published a paper on the subject in October (1999). It advised Member States to employ a broad interpretation of Article 9 (2) of the Settlement Finality Directive so that the protection of legal certainty was not overly limited to the ECB and payments systems. Instead, they should eliminate legal risk for all (EU) settlement system participants [49].

5. The (ECB's) basic duty of monitoring payment networks includes retail cross-border payment systems. In late (1999), a new Directive was enacted for retail systems, although it may not be enough to produce cross-border systems that are as efficient (fast and cheap) as domestic systems (2002) [34].

6. Citizens will be unimpressed if they are unable to move "Single Money" around to take advantage of pricing differences. Indeed, people may wonder what the aim of a single currency was on a technological level. Any resulting loss of popular enthusiasm for "Europe" at a time when (IGC) approval is on the table to allow enlargement to take place might have major political ramifications [50].

4.9 Issuance of bonds that have been underwritten

The increase in corporate issuance was a prominent trend in the new euro markets, and it is made up of various factors [34, 45]:

a. The (M&A) tsunami has resulted in a substantial increase in the need for finance, but it is unclear which came first: the chicken or the egg! The rules of the game have altered since Olivetti was able to raise funds for its offer for Telecom Italia, and Vodafone's hostile bid for Mannesmann could result in a new round of bond issuance. Vodafone's 30-million-euro bank facilities are estimated to be (364) a day, thus a large portion of it will need to be refinanced over a longer period. If European (M&A) activity maintains its pace of 1200 billion-euro announcements in (1999), and only 10% is refinanced in the bond market, it would equal the entire corporate bond issuance in that year (1999) [8].

b. In the investment-grade sector, (US) corporations exerted a significant effect last year, owing in part to (FAS) 133, but also to finance companies' aim to extend their investor base. Both of these trends are likely to persist this year. We feel that issuance relating to (FAS) (133) may easily quadruple.

c. Asset-backed securities (ABS) denominated in the euro have just begun to scratch the surface of potential issuance despite reaching 43 billion euro in (1999). The potential scale of the market that could result from the securitization of European credit is most obvious when considering the second-largest component of this volume – banks issuing Collateralized Loan Obligations (CLOs) to reduce their need for regulatory capital. The 9 billion euro issued in (1999) only amounted to less than 0.5% of the banking system's aggregate balance sheet [6].

d. Finally, the high yield market has developed very strongly as European institutional investors have stepped up their credit research capabilities much faster than many observers recognize. During the year, 7 billion euro was issued and more than half of that was in the fourth quarter alone – driven by the telecom/cable companies. Therefore, the capital markets are financing a vital part of Europe's technological development [23].

4.10 Markets for government bonds

a. The success of the Euro (MTS) – the electronic broking system established from the platform used to trade Italian government bonds – was possibly one of the most significant breakthroughs in (1999). It was launched in April and has quickly expanded to include (9) of the Euro-11 government markets, with a market share of around 30–40 percent of inter-dealer volumes. The decision in December to incorporate (P) fandbriefe as an initial move into the non-government sector - but still focused on the liquid component - underlines this success. A minor tightening of the spread on 10-year Portuguese bonds after their benchmark bond was listed on November 17 exhibited enhanced investor trust in liquidity and pricing transparency [3, 49].

b. Furthermore, Euro (MTS) has announced the availability of a service for arranging anonymous repos using the London Clearing House as the principal counter-party. These events highlight the growing relevance of liquid benchmark issues and the potential to construct a secure money market that comes with them. The need to ensure legal certainty for this type of business across the (EU) is a vital component, underscoring the necessity for a broad interpretation of the Finality Directive [30, 42].

c. Throughout (1999), debt re-structuring was a constant feature as debt managers worked to increase the liquidity of their issues. For example, the Dutch Treasury said in June that debt re-structuring was a constant theme during (1999), as debt managers tried to build up their liquid benchmarks to a typical level of 10 billion euro through a 19-billion-euro exchange offer program [42].

d. Government bond markets continue to evolve rapidly as debt managers respond to the new environment of low issuance and rising technology. Finland led the technological way with an 11-year bond that was partly sold via the Internet.

e. Bond issuance decreased by 21% in the first quarter, and we estimate a further drop of 12% in the second quarter. However, we expect just a little decrease in issuance for the year as several states alter their financing patterns to longer maturities [30].

f. As a result, issuance in the 30-year sector is likely to increase by roughly a third. Now that there is a defined yield curve in euros, more debt managers may be willing to experiment with such extended maturities in the future. The inversion of yield curves in the (UK) and now the (US) demonstrates actuarially driven investors' demand for long bonds. The euro curve is already flattening, which may pique the interest of debt management. Surprisingly, the issue of 30-year bonds in Euroland would account for about a third of the whole portfolio of long-dated (UK) government bonds, whose yield pattern has been severely warped by significant pension fund demand. This has resulted in minimal government issuance, even with the help of the (UK) government's fresh borrowing plans. With the introduction of the euro, Europe's capital markets can be consolidated into a single, global size market that can facilitate the movement of savings to a wide range of end-users [34, 37].

As the intermediary, the financial services industry has both a difficulty and an opportunity because of the same combination of increased savings flows and new technologies. The speed with which the European sector is consolidating shows that the transformation is already begun. However, because a merger takes time to complete, there may be a period before the new services are put out and advertised to the final client [51–53].

Other Stock Exchange operations could be eliminated, leaving only the certainty of settlement as the most important activity. Shorter settlement durations (eventually shifting to real-time) are lowering even that role as the scale of settlement risk grows. One strategy to change is the rise of clearing houses, such as for futures exchanges [33].

Trading functions must continue to be carried out by suitably funded and regulated exchanges, clearinghouses, and financial intermediaries as more exchanges become computerized and distant trading becomes available. This is critical for the financial markets' systemic stability. Allowing unregulated and undercapitalized software or technology firms to supply important procedures in electronic securities transactions (for example, trading software or electronic links) introduces new dangers [54].

By offering asset management services as an "institutional investor" or as a direct execution agent, the financial services industry is attempting to position itself as this intermediary. Nonetheless, as traditional Stock Exchanges compete with Over The Counter (OTC) traders and Alternative Trading Systems, the execution infrastructure is changing dramatically (ATS). Electronic Crossing Networks are becoming more common (ECNs) [36].

5. A comparative analysis of the effects of the global financial markets and global financial crisis on Arab economies

Arab economies were exposed to the global financial crisis and the consequent stagnation in the economies of the majority of developed and developing countries during the years (2008 and 2009) [2].

The main channels through which the effects of the crisis spread to the Arab countries varied, according to the nature of their economies, the degree of openness and their connection to the global economy. For analysis, the Arab countries, which are characterized by financial systems, can be classified into three groups. The first group, (Emirates, Bahrain, Saudi Arabia, Oman, Qatar and Kuwait), which is the Gulf Cooperation Council (GCC) countries, is open and trade with high exposure to global financial markets, and its close connection with both the global financial system and global markets for commodities, especially oil and gas Petrochemicals were the main channels for the global crisis to spread to, so the local financial markets in them are not directly linked to the global markets, except for their economies [4].

As for the second group, (Algeria, Sudan, Libya and Yemen), their economies depend on oil revenues, and therefore global demand and global oil prices affect the financial policy significantly. The practices followed in these countries and keeping with the global economic cycle, that is, government expenditures rise with the increase in oil revenues and decrease with the decrease in those revenues, in most of those countries [4].

They are countries in which the banking and financial sector depends on domestic lending resources, and thus the third group (Palestine, Jordan, Tunisia, Syria, Lebanon, Egypt, Morocco and Mauritania) whose economies are not directly affected by the fluctuations of global financial markets [4].

External shocks, on the other hand, are communicated to their economies through their tight trade ties with developed country markets and their key trading partners in the European Union and the United States. In terms of commodity transactions, these countries' exports are heavily reliant on developed-country markets. This is in terms of service transactions like tourism receipts, worker remittances, and foreign direct investment flows.

The fluctuations of the economic cycle and growth rates in developed countries, in light of the stagnation resulting from the crisis, lead to the risks of slowing growth in the third group countries, through the decline in the performance of their export sectors with high exposure to the markets of developed countries, and the decline in financial flows to them through the decline in revenues and the volume of tourism and remittances Overseas workers and foreign direct investment [10].

Regarding a comparative analysis of the effects of the crisis on Arab economies according to the three groups mentioned, the extension of the crisis is attributed to two main things, the first of which is financial factors related to the degree of exposure of the banking and financial sector in the economy to global financial markets, and the second is the commercial factors that are related to the main trading partners of Arab countries [11].

5.1 First group countries

The most important conduits for the crisis to extend to the economy of the Gulf Cooperation Council countries were financial factors connected to exposure to global financial markets. The (GCC) countries saw a boom in financial resources in the years leading up to the crisis, owing to large increases in oil income and foreign capital flows to finance significant projects in a number of these countries, as well as an expansion of bank credit to the private sector.

The financial surpluses of the (GCC) states shrank, as did the cash liquidity of the banking and business sectors, as well as the outflow of foreign financial flows, which entered the Gulf financial markets for speculative purposes, and as a result, investor confidence declined.

These circumstances coincided with a lack of liquidity in global markets, leading several (GCC) countries to reduce their reliance on external financing for major projects in their countries, as well as the fact that many loans owed to international financial institutions during the crisis needed to be refinanced, resulting in several (GCC) countries reducing their reliance on external financing for major projects in their countries. Several public and commercial sector enterprises and institutions were at risk of being reinstated (as happened in the Dubai debt crisis) [8].

The rescheduling of outstanding debt, the rise in financing costs, and the fall in investments in financing real estate development projects and the purchase of real estate projects have all contributed to the postponement of many real estate development projects. According to international reports, the total projects that were under implementation at the end of (2009) were expected to be around $575 billion, compared to the entire projects that were under implementation at the end of (2008), which were anticipated to be around $5.2 trillion (2008) [9].

This resulted in a drop in local demand for real estate, as real estate values fell, significantly affecting the value of real estate assets held in Gulf banks' investment portfolios. Because of these developments, the climate of uncertainty grew, and commercial banks implemented risk-reduction and capital-base-supporting policies, prompting banks to tighten lending conditions, resulting in a dramatic drop in bank credit growth [8, 9].

Declining growth in the non-oil and business sectors, also confirmed by the decline in the money meter (money and quasi-money). After the money stock recorded a growth rate of about 10 percent in the period (2002–2005), its growth accelerated during the economic boom period (2006–2008) to reach about

19 percent, but the growth rate of the money stock declined sharply after that and until the end of (2009) [4].

The repercussions of the global crisis were evident in the wake of the bankruptcy of the investment bank (Brothers Lehman) in September (2008), as global stock market indices declined as a result, and the impact was evident for the stock markets in the (GCC) countries. Losses in the market value of the Gulf markets are estimated at 41 percent or more. The equivalent of $400 billion during the period September–December (2008). The Gulf stock market indices were subjected to several fluctuations, and the Gulf stock market contagion with the global crisis became visible. (P500 & S) Before and during the crisis the trend of the correlation coefficient shifts from an inverse relationship before the crisis to a parallel (Direct) relationship during the crisis [8].

Gulf banks, on the other hand, were able to post reasonably solid financial performance towards the end of (2009), after absorbing some of the crisis' losses. As a result, the banking sector in all GCC countries maintained high capital adequacy rates before and during the crisis, and the increase in non-performing loans as a percentage of total loans had no significant impact on the banking sector's financial results at the end of (2009), as the sector achieved net profits, albeit at a much lower level than before the crisis [4].

The Gulf banking sector has also dealt with the systemic risks arising from the crisis, in addition to the implementation of quick practical measures by the official authorities in the (GCC) countries to support the safety and stability of the local banking and financial sector. Some of these measures came to support the banking and financial sector's liabilities side, by injecting capital in the balance sheets of banks, as was the case in the Emirates and Qatar, where the value of paid-up capital amounted to 2 percent and 3.7 percent of (GDP), respectively [11].

The monetary authorities in the (GCC) states have provided facilities and loans to the banks operating in them, in addition to the official authorities in Qatar supporting local banks with "Assets", by purchasing investment portfolios with local banks, whose value has fallen sharply in light of the decline in the Doha Securities Market indices [22, 30].

The total purchase value amounted to about 6 percent of the Qatari (GDP). Supporting the "asset" side of these banks aims to improve the quality of their assets and provide the necessary liquidity with local banks, in addition to restoring confidence in the local stock market. In addition, the Emirates, Qatar and Kuwait took decisions to guarantee deposits with local banks. This is in addition to the monetary authorities in the (GCC) countries in general facilitating the use of monetary policy tools to enhance liquidity in the banking sector by reducing the mandatory reserve ratios [12].

Within the framework of stimulating economic activity, Saudi Arabia took the initiative to implement a plan to stimulate and revive the national economy, by approving investments worth $400 billion over the next five years. It is worth noting in this regard that the allocations for the stimulus program are among the highest allocations in the stimulus programs applied by the Group of Twenty (G20) countries. Several other (GCC) countries have also backed infrastructure spending to boost aggregate demand, which helped support the non-oil sector's development in (2009), albeit at a slower pace than in prior years [6].

5.2 Second group countries

The local banking and financial sector in the countries of the second group (Algeria, Sudan, Libya, and Yemen) was unaffected by the global financial crisis because it was more closed and not directly linked to it, as (Algeria and Sudan) were not exposed to market value fluctuations due to the small volume of trading and the lack of a stock market in the countries of the group, the number of companies listed in it [4].

However, the economies of the group's countries were affected by the decline in demand for oil resulting from the stagnation in the global economy because of the global financial crisis. In addition, both (OPEC) members Algeria and Libya reduced their production quotas during (2008_and_2009), in implementation of the (OPEC) decision to reduce production quotas. Because of these factors, the volume of oil exports to the group's countries declined by 28 percent on average in (2009), compared to a decrease of 2 percent in the year (2008) [51–53].

On the other hand, the economies of the second category have seen a significant increase in non-oil sector activity, particularly in Algeria and Libya. In the case of Algeria, the non-oil sector grew at a healthy rate, owing to a large increase in the agricultural crop of cereals, as well as the continuation of high public spending on infrastructure development under the National Infrastructure Development Program, and the accumulation of oil surpluses before the onset of the crisis. The non-oil economy in Libya has grown rapidly because of increased government spending on infrastructure projects and increased foreign direct investment in Libya to implement infrastructure and construction projects [4].

As for Sudan and Yemen, the non-oil sector recorded high growth rates, similar to Algeria and Libya during the oil boom, albeit at a slower pace, in light of the availability of oil revenues before the outbreak of the crisis [55].

However, the decline in oil revenues due to the drop in international oil prices had a negative impact on non-oil economic activity. In Sudan, for example, the non-oil economic activity declined from a growth rate of 8 percent during the period (2006–2008) to about 8.3 percent in (2009).

This is attributed to the decline in foreign investments to Sudan, in addition to internal factors, some of which are related to the state implementing Measures to reduce import demand in light of the sharp decline in external reserves resulting from the decline in international oil prices.

5.3 Third group countries

The limited exposure to the global financial markets of the local banking and financial sector in the third group countries (Palestine, Jordan, Tunisia, Syria, Lebanon, Egypt, Morocco and Mauritania) has reduced the direct effects of the global financial crisis on these countries.

However, the economies of the group's countries are closely linked, the economic activity and demand in the developed countries, in terms of commodity transactions, represented in the concentration of export trends of a number of the group's countries to the markets of the European Union and the United States, as well as on the side of service and capital transactions represented in remittances of their workers abroad, tourism revenues and the flow of foreign direct investment [4, 6].

Therefore, the contraction in demand in the countries of the European Union and the United States, and the entry of the global economy into a period of stagnation, had a negative impact on the exports of the third group countries, and on the flow of foreign direct investment to them [34].

In general, the local banking and financial sector in the group's countries was able to avoid the severe negative effects that several emerging economies witnessed during the global financial crisis, because the foreign transactions of local banks in the majority of the group's countries are subject to restrictions on the freedom of capital flows.

The private sector has specific ceilings for investment abroad to reduce the exposure of its foreign assets to high investment risks, such as what the global financial markets witnessed during the crisis.

On the borrowing side, most of the group's countries' banks and financial sectors rely on domestic savings and financial resources. Even before the crisis, the stock markets of the third group countries were unaffected by global stock market fluctuations because the vast majority of local stock market investors are individuals from the group's countries, with only a small amount of institutional foreign investment in a few high-liquidity markets [31].

However, the developments in the global stock markets since the exacerbation of the global crisis in the last quarter of (2008) negatively affected the stock markets of a number of the third group countries due to the fluctuations in the international markets.

Including European in particular. For example, the trend of the correlation coefficient of the stock market indices of the group countries with the French stock market index (CAC40) shifted from an inverse relationship before the crisis to a parallel relationship during the crisis [2].

In terms of external financing, given the scarcity of global liquidity and the resulting rise in the cost of the loan in global markets, several third-group countries were able to fund their budgets from domestic financial sources, where domestic liquidity grew at a rather fast rate. The government's borrowing from the local market corresponded with a drop in the growth of bank loans to the private sector, which can be linked to global demand and supply dynamics [4].

Because of the reduction in foreign demand and the decline in global trade, demand for bank lending has decreased. Furthermore, the uncertainty created by the global crisis in local markets prompted commercial banks to adopt a precautionary policy, which entailed not squandering the resources at their disposal to avoid an increase in the number of cases of default and failure to repay, despite the availability of liquidity [21].

The repercussions of the global crisis on bank lending to the private sector were more visible in Palestine, Jordan, and Egypt, which saw a considerably greater decrease in bank credit to the private sector during the crisis (2008 and 2009). Following the implementation of the monetary authorities' strategy that supports stabilizing the value of the shekel and the dinar versus the dollar, the economy in Palestine and Jordan was subjected to interbank liquidity pressures [4, 21, 31].

The Palestinian and Jordanian financial markets have been affected by the exacerbation of the global crisis since the last quarter of (2008). As for Egypt, the growth rates of bank credit to the private sector were weak before the crisis, in light of the restructuring of the banking sector its assets and reducing the proportion of non-performing loans. With the decline in economic activity due to the crisis, the growth of bank credit to the private sector stopped, recording a negative rate at the end of (2009) [4, 6].

Given the early structural reforms in the banking sector implemented by the third group countries before the crisis's repercussions, the banking sector in a number of the group's countries was able to achieve good performance before the crisis by increasing the adequacy of risk-weighted capital and lowering the average ratio of non-performing loans to total loans.

The banking sector in these countries canceled numerous problematic loans whose value was fully covered by provisions, resulting in increased efficiency and profitability in a number of them, as it achieved relatively good returns on assets and shareholders' equity. In general, the banking sector's performance in the group's nations was unaffected by the crisis (2008 and 2009) [4, 6, 21].

However, the economic activity in the third group countries was affected by the decline in external demand, as their exports declined the remittances of workers abroad and the flow of foreign direct investment declined, while the tourism sector witnessed a slight improvement.

The intertwining of the export sector with the rest of the production and service sectors, including the banking sector, reflected in the pace of economic activity in the group's countries, necessitating the intervention of the authorities in the group's countries to take quick measures to facilitate the management of monetary policy and increase public spending through economic stimulus programs and revitalization [6, 21].

In this regard, it is possible to shed some light on the efforts made in several countries in this group. In the field of monetary policy, Jordan, Tunisia, Egypt and Morocco reduced the interest rates approved by monetary policy, to urge commercial banks to increase lending to the private sector. For example, the monetary authorities in Egypt reduced the overnight deposit rate six times during the period February–September (2009), bringing the cumulative reductions to 325 basis points [2, 4].

The monetary authorities in Jordan reduced the monetary policy interest rate three times during (2009), by 50 basis points each time. All the countries of the group have reduced the mandatory reserve ratio, opened new lending facilities, provided more liquidity to the banks operating in them, and provided guarantees for bank deposits [6, 21].

In the field of fiscal policy, Tunisia and Egypt implemented a comprehensive package of measures to increase public spending and stimulate economic growth, as represented by investing in infrastructure and education projects, providing support to private sector institutions that generate new jobs and supporting exports by increasing the guarantees available for exports [2, 9, 10].

Palestine, Jordan, Syria and Morocco increased public spending on investment in several development projects.

5.4 Lessons learned from the global financial markets, global financial crisis and the potential for action to restore macroeconomic stability and sustainable growth in Arab countries

The severity of the effects of the crisis on the performance of Arab economies varied. The economic performance of the countries of the first and second groups was affected more than the performance of the economies of the third group, because of the sharp decline in the (GDP) growth of the oil sector in them following the decline in global oil prices. It is worth noting that the growth in the non-oil sector (GDP) was the main driver for achieving growth rates in the (GDP) at constant prices in the first and second groups [4, 9].

Among the lessons learned, it became clear that the swiftness in the authorities in several Arab countries managing the consequences of the global crisis on their economies through the adoption of financial and monetary policies and procedures to address the negative effects of the crisis has succeeded in reducing the outcome of these effects on Arab economies. In general, the authorities were also able to intervene to activate various [10].

The existence of favorable conditions and space for policy alternatives (Space Policy), as well as the production and service sectors of the economy, which allows the employment of required policy tools to restore the national economy. For example, before the global financial crisis, the accumulation of financial surpluses stemming from increased oil income enabled a number of (GCC) countries Gulf Cooperation Council to pump funds into the local banking system and address systemic problems [6, 21].

Policy options were available to the authorities in a number of the third group countries, in addition to the economic reforms that they implemented early in the past years, as a number of the third group countries achieved macroeconomic stability, and the chronic deficit in the public budget turned into a surplus in countries such as Morocco, the cumulative external reserves rose to levels not seen in these economies before [9].

When the crisis hit the economies of the countries in the third group that had implemented economic reforms, some of them rushed to implement economic stimulus programs based on the adoption of expansionary fiscal and monetary policies that allow supporting domestic economic activity and maintaining growth and economic recovery trends without resorting to, for example, implementing a program to correct balance-of-payments imbalances and the required monetary stimulus.

On the other hand, the global crisis slowed the pace of economic reform in several countries that had already adopted reforms in prior periods.as the circumstances generated by the crisis led to the postponement of the implementation of new reforms that were planned before the crisis, such as Egypt's postponement of introducing reforms to the value-added tax system, expanding its tax base, and rationalizing the applicable rates to increase the efficiency of allocating productive resources in the economy [2, 10].

It also concerns the postponement of the introduction of the tax on real estate and the reduction of subsidies for some primary commodities. It remains for these countries to choose the appropriate conditions for the resumption of the process of economic reforms that they have implemented during the past years.

Undoubtedly, other lessons can be drawn from the crisis, but it is important in this context to explore the efforts that can be taken to strengthen the national economy's resilience in dealing with future crises, and to make recommendations related to economic policy regarding the possibilities of working within the framework of each of the three groups and the expected role of resuming the process of economic reform in light of the recovery of Arab economies from the global markets and crisis [2, 4].

5.5 The possibilities of working within the framework of the countries of the first group

The Gulf Cooperation Council countries sought to mitigate the effects of the global financial and economic crisis by stepping in quickly to pump monetary liquidity, simplify monetary policy management, and boost public spending to stimulate the national economy. The ability of the banking and financial sectors in the (GCC) countries to contain the systemic risks stemming from the crisis has improved because of the government's support [4].

Despite the lack of bank credit to the private sector, the non-oil economy continued to thrive. Given the projected oscillations in the world economy following the crisis, it is expected that the full recovery of the economies of the (GCC) countries from the effects of the global financial and economic crisis will take some time before they achieve sustainable growth rates.

The crisis exposed the dangers of rapid and sometimes excessive growth in bank lending in some (GCC) countries during the years of economic boom resulting from increased oil revenues, as well as the heavy reliance on foreign financing and the increasing exposure of many Gulf banks' assets to the real estate and securities sectors, with resorting to the use of hot and short-term funds deposited with them to finance projects and long-term liabilities [7, 8].

Due to its intertwining with the global banking and financial system, the regulatory role of the banking and financial system in various (GCC) nations was also found to be unable to keep up with the rapid advancements in the local banking and financial market.

The consequences of the global crisis, on the other hand, revealed the dangers of the oil sector's dominance in the national economy and reliance on oil revenues, necessitating a step up in the (GCC) countries' reform efforts over the last two decades to diversify the economy's base, increase non-oil revenues, expand the contribution of the private sector to economic activity, and preserve savings and to adopt an expansionary fiscal policy counter to the economic cycle during periods of economic stagnation and mitigate the dangers of reliance on the oil sector with income from oil revenues [9].

To continue the direction of the Gulf Cooperation Council countries to reform the economic conditions resulting from the crisis and restore the economy's ability to achieve sustainable growth, the banking sector is called upon to restore its role in financing economic development after Gulf banks rebuild their capital bases and get rid of the losses incurred by some banks due to their excessive risks [2, 4].

Likewise, the (GCC) states are called upon to intensify their efforts in developing the regulatory and supervisory role on the local banking systems to keep pace with the rapid developments in light of the intertwining of local systems with the global banking system.

On the economic policy side, there is a need for more coordination between monetary and fiscal policies in several (GCC) countries, using macroeconomic management tools that help slow down the transition of the oil cycle to the economy, in light of the limited independence of monetary policy by virtue of the linkage and stability of a number of Gulf currencies in dollars. In addition, the establishment and development of debt bond markets may help diversify the investment portfolios of investors away from the scope of the traditional role for banks in a way that contributes to enhancing financial depth [4].

To diversify the economy and increase the contribution of the private sector to economic activity, (GCC) states are being urged to improve their economies' competitiveness by developing financial market regulatory bodies and removing rentier restrictions on practices that stifle competition, as well as attracting local and foreign direct investment that creates jobs and supports the diversification strategy.

5.6 The possibilities of working within the framework of the countries of the second group

The countries of the second group, namely Algeria, Libya, Sudan and Yemen, were affected by the drop in world oil prices and their oil revenues declined, which led to a decrease in the surpluses in the public budget and the current account balance for Algeria and Libya and a deterioration in the deficit in them for Sudan and Yemen. As for the local banking sector in all the countries of the group, it was not affected because it is not exposed to the global financial markets [21].

Which requires continuing to implement reforms aimed at achieving efficiency in the "Fiscal Policy" from the side of public spending to allow it to keep pace with the economic cycle, up and down, and to maintain a sustainable financial position. Sustainability Fiscal, without resorting to making major adjustments in the expenditure components, pain, or the revenue-decreased oil [6].

In addition, non-oil economic activity in the second group of countries requires structural reforms to improve performance by simplifying business procedures, increasing the private sector's contribution to diversifying the production base and creating productive jobs, and attracting foreign direct investments that include the transfer of knowledge and modern technology and the creation of added value in the national economy.

To strengthen the role of monetary policy in dealing with future external shocks, monetary authorities in the second group are being urged to deepen banking reform by restructuring and liberalizing public sector banks, ending competition between specialized public sector banks and other commercial banks, and subjecting them to central bank standards for maintaining liquidity and exercising lending conditions on clearance [6, 21].

5.7 The possibilities of working within the framework of the third group countries

The minimal exposure of the local banking and financial sectors to global financial markets has helped to prevent the global financial crisis from spreading directly to the economies of the third group. The stalling of global demand, on the other hand, caused a slowdown in the group's exports, a drop in private sector investments, and a drop in the demand for bank credit. Despite this, the banking sector's performance in the majority of the group's countries was unaffected, thanks in large part to the efforts undertaken by these governments.

Countries to reform and liberalize the banking sector, within the framework of comprehensive economic reform programs that they pursued at an early date. These countries have been able to restructure the local banking system, which has led to an increase in capital adequacy rates and a reduction in the ratio of non-performing loans to total loans, while improving the quality of credit portfolios with banks. These reforms also contributed to strengthening the banking sector's resilience to external shocks. The economies of these countries have been achieved [6, 21].

Average growth rates are estimated at 5.4 percent in (2009), compared to average growth rates of about 6 percent during the period before the global financial and economic crisis, rates that exceed those recorded by many emerging economies. In the field of monetary policy, the monetary authorities in the third group countries have made unremitting efforts to reduce the effects of the global crisis on economic activity by using the policy tools available to them, and the return of this policy has been good on the banking and financial sector with the decline of inflationary pressures in the economy. Countries such as Tunisia, Egypt and Morocco are working to create the appropriate conditions for implementing the Policy Targeting Inflation to achieve price stability [4, 21].

However, the global financial crisis showed the need for the monetary authorities in a number of the group's countries to continue to deepen the structural reforms of the banking sector, such as continuing to reduce the proportion of non-performing loans and working to implement (Basel II) standards for the adequacy of risk-weighted capital, and to increase banking transparency in front of investors and depositors regarding the risks that may be exposed. It has commercial banks and the strengthening of the supervisory role on the local banking systems to avoid systemic risks [18, 31].

It is also important to continue to pursue and deepen economic reform in the group's countries to support the resilience of the national economy is facing the new challenges brought about by the global crisis.

In light of the decline in exports resulting from the contraction of external demand and the decline in remittances of workers abroad, the current account balance of the third group countries has deteriorated, and these countries hastened to develop and implement a package of measures to increase public spending and stimulate domestic economic activity [9, 10].

Thus, the budget deficit has worsened and the financial performance indicators that these countries have committed themselves to achieve within the framework of their implementation of economic reform programs have deteriorated.

Despite the high ratio of the budget deficit to the gross domestic product of a number of the group's countries, the outstanding debt balance as a percentage of the (GDP) was not significantly affected, in addition to the fact that some countries of the group [2, 4].

Other countries in this category were able to finance their budget deficits with a minor rise in the return on new treasury notes by relying on the liquidity available with local commercial banks using the external reserves they had built during the pre-crisis economic boom. Although, international financial institutions expect global demand and growth to recover in the future, continued volatility in global financial markets and uncertainty in developed country economies may foreshadow further negative repercussions in the future [12, 36].

The private sector's reluctance to risk investing may continue and the growth of bank credit to the private sector will remain weak.

Thus, the government in the countries of the group may continue to pursue an expansionary fiscal policy and countercyclical economic stagnation and to continue the stimulus measures for economic activity, such as providing tax incentives for some production and export activities [2].

However, the adoption of expansionary financial measures may have an impact on the medium-term sustainability of the financial position, necessitating efforts to return to the pre-crisis financial metrics that ensured macroeconomic stability.

As a result, it is necessary to resume structural reforms in the areas of public spending rationalization, financial transparency, and revenue reform, to increase tax revenues and their contribution to total revenues on the one hand, while lowering administrative costs and removing distortions in economic incentives on the other.

5.8 The global financial markets and the interconnection with global financial crisis and Arab economies

The global crisis showed the existence of a link between the Arab economies with each other, as a number of the third group countries Palestine, Jordan, Lebanon and Syria are closely linked to the economies of the Gulf Cooperation Council countries, through exports, workers' remittances, tourism and foreign direct investment and capital flows [2, 26].

Preliminary data on intra-regional trade for these countries indicate that its value did not decrease during (2009), but the value of remittances of Egyptian workers in the (GCC) countries, for example, decreased slightly 6.1 percent in the same year. As for Gulf tourism to Lebanon, Syria and Egypt only, it continued to grow during (2008 and 2009). As for the Arab Maghreb countries, tourism to Tunisia from the Maghreb countries played an important role in keeping Tunisia's tourism revenues at their level before the crisis, as the arrival of tourists from Algeria and Libya contributed to Compensating for the decline in the volume of European tourism and thus the revenue generated by it [9, 10, 12].

Finally, it can be summarized that the repercussions of the global crisis on the Arab region indicate the importance of the role that Arab economic integration can play to mitigate the negative effects of global economic crises on Arab economies.

6. Conclusions

The international financial markets and financial capital flows illustrate the need for concerted efforts to enhance the mobilization of domestic financial resources and global financial crisis in emerging markets countries, and to reduce exposure to international portfolio capital and financial contagion. The volume of capital outflows also makes the case for reviving discussions on managing capital outflows and on developing a global financial safety net.

In the end, it can be summarized that the development of the financial market is one of the main keys to achieving long-term economic growth. The financial market can lead to economic growth if it can provide a suitable environment for the optimal allocation of resources and increase the efficiency of capital, as we mentioned earlier.

Therefore, the governments of all countries, including the governments of developing countries, must work to create the appropriate atmosphere to attract local and foreign investments and to enhance interaction the stock exchange.

In addition, the local community, and disseminate information through all available means. An informational and promotional effort must be made to promote the culture of investment in all stocks by the relevant authorities.

Monitoring stock market operations, given those Stocks is a new product separate from itself. The rest of the securities in the stock market, to attract money fleeing from Dealing in traditional tools, as an alternative to them, by providing market indicators Stocks is similar to stock market indices, which activates the trading market, and is reflected in the positively on the issue markets.

The government must be working to follow up efforts in the field of deepening the market, increasing its efficiency and liquidity, and spreading the culture of investment, especially the development of its website.

Paying more attention to the issue of corporate governance rules and standards in the financial markets, which is what keeps us away from falling into financial crises, and leads us to enjoy efficiency and work on diversifying the available tools.

The existence of a stock market with a strong infrastructure based on a set of rules and Clear and specific regulatory and supervisory procedures, and the Governments should make their stock market completely governed by principles and provisions and Legitimacy to avoid falling into crises, it helps it reach higher levels of efficiency.

Urging and working to continue developing the technology infrastructure of the stock exchange to serve all dealers in the stock exchange. The International stock exchanges must keep pace with technological developments to create an efficient stock exchange.

The necessity of establishing specialized educational institutes and training centers and holding conferences and scientific centers International, to qualify the human cadres necessary to work in the emerging financial markets.

7. Policy recommendations

This paper presents an empirical analysis of the impact of the international financial markets and financial capital flows through the period of the global financial crisis on global economic growth and development especially in developing countries such as Arab countries, and dynamics in emerging markets and the Middle East. We investigate the impact on sovereign and bond markets, as well as currency rates and capital flows, against the backdrop of globally interconnected financial markets.

Our research allows us to make a comparison between advanced and emerging economies. Our findings show that international financial markets and financial capital flows have had the greatest impact on global economic growth and development, as well as global financial markets in Europe and Asia, after controlling for a large number of domestic and global financial and macroeconomic factors.

Moreover, outflows of stocks and bonds from emerging markets appear to be directly linked to the international financial markets and financial capital flows given investors' risk aversion and flight to safety. Sovereign bond markets in emerging market and developing countries appear to be the hardest hit by the coronavirus, compared to the magnitude of the effects on stock prices and exchange rates.

Additionally, while the international financial markets and financial capital flows will eventually recede, our findings show that global markets may face some Long-Term marginal effects.

Our findings show that government-sponsored fiscal stimulus packages, along with comprehensive central bank stabilization measures, have helped to reduce the negative effects of international financial markets and financial capital flows on financial market and capital flow dynamics. In particular, our findings highlight the key role of central banks in stabilizing financial markets globally during the international financial markets and financial capital flows crisis, through interest rate cuts, quantitative easing, and international swap lines.

More importantly, the impact of expansionary monetary policy in developed countries, which helped lower sovereign bond yields and bolster stock markets at home, also extended to emerging and small market countries, particularly about stable capital flow dynamics. This, combined with the influence of global factors such as (EPU) and (VIX), underscores the interdependence of the global financial system, and the impact of developments in the world's leading financial centers on financial conditions in emerging market countries.

The heightened uncertainty due to the international financial markets and financial capital flows pandemic has clearly affected the financial markets in emerging market and developing countries more harmful than in advanced economies.

However, emerging market economies appear to be strong performers in their policy responses to the pandemic. While fiscal stimulus packages have restored confidence in domestic markets, many central banks in Europe and the Middle East have embarked on quantitative easing for the first time.

Our results indicate that these monetary policy measures were effective in the case of Asian emerging markets, as they supported stock prices. More importantly, these measures also helped stabilize capital inflows.

Furthermore, given the size of bond and equities capital outflows from emerging, small and medium markets, our findings highlight the importance of strengthening the local investor base to be less dependent on international portfolio investments, supporting the findings of [12].

Acknowledgements

The author extends their appreciation for their support for scientific research at the Palestine Economic Policy Research Institute (MAS) in Palestine to support this research and encourage the author in particular, in addition to that the authors send a special thanks and a great appreciation to the jury staff Reviewers, and to the Editorial Board at IntechOpen.

Author's contribution

The Sole Author Designed, Analyzed, Interpreted and Prepared the Chapter.

Conflict of interest

The author has declared that no competing interests exist.

Data availability statement

The data and materials that support the findings of this study are available from the corresponding author upon request. Datasets are derived from public resources and made available with the authors. Data analyzed in this study were a reanalysis of existing data, which are openly available at locations cited in the reference section.

JEL classification codes

E22, E44, E58, F32, F41, F62, G01, G1, G15

Author details

Nemer Badwan
Palestine Economic Policy Research Institute (MAS), Jerusalem, Ramallah, State of Palestine

*Address all correspondence to: therock2031@gmail.com; nemer.badwan@mail.ru

References

[1] Bahaj S, Reis R. Central bank swap lines: Evidence on the effects of the lender of last resort. The Review of Economic Studies. London, United Kingdom: Oxford Academic; 2021:rdab074. DOI: 10.1093/restud/rdab074

[2] Bahaj S, Reis R. How coronavirus almost brought down the global financial system, The Guardian. 2020b. pp. 1-68. Available from: https://www.theguardian.com/business/2020/apr/14/how-coronavirus-almost-brought-down-the-global-financial-system

[3] Arslan Y, Drehmann M, Hofmann B. Central Bank Bond Purchases in Emerging Market Economies. BIS Bulletin No. 20. Basel: Bank for International Settlements; 2020

[4] Asian Development Bank. An Updated Assessment of the Economic Impact of COVID-19. ADB Briefs No. 133. Manila: Asian Development Bank; 2020

[5] Bahaj S, Reis R. Central Bank swap lines during the Covid-19 pandemic. Covid Economics. 2020a;**2**:1-12

[6] World Bank. Global economic prospects. World Bank, Washington: Managing the next wave of globalization; 2007

[7] Baker SR, Bloom N, Davis SJ, Kost KJ, Sammon MC, Viratyosin T. The Unprecedented Stock Market Impact of Covid-19. NBER Working Paper. Vol. No. 26945. Cambridge, MA: National Bureau of Economic Research; 2020

[8] Barro RJ, Ursúa JF, Weng J. The Coronavirus and the Great Influenza Pandemic: Lessons from the "Spanish Flu" for the Coronavirus's Potential Effects on Mortality and Economic Activity. NBER Working Paper No. 26866. Cambridge, MA: National Bureau of Economic Research; 2020

[9] Becchetti L, Ciciretti R, Trenta U. *Modelli di Asset Pricing I: Titoli Azionari*, in Il Sistema Finanziario Internazionale, Michele Bagella, a cura di. Torino: Giappichelli; 2007

[10] Beirne J, Renzhi N, Sugandi E, Volz U. Financial market and capital flow dynamics during the COVID-19 pandemic. In: ADBI Working Paper 1158. Tokyo: Asian Development Bank Institute; 2020. Available from: https://www.adb.org/publications/financial-market-capital-flow-dynamics-during-covid-19-pandemic

[11] Beirne J, Gieck J. Interdependence and contagion in global asset markets. Review of International Economics. 2014;**22**(4):639-659

[12] Belke A, Volz U. Capital flows to developing and emerging market economies: Global liquidity and uncertainty versus push factors. Review of Development Finance. 2019;**9**(1):32-50

[13] Boissay F, Rungcharoenkitkul P. Macroeconomic Effects of Covid-19: An Early Review. BIS Bulletin No. 7. Basel: Bank for International Settlements; 2020

[14] Boissay F, Rees D, Rungcharoenkitkul P. Dealing with Covid-19: Understanding the Policy Choices. BIS Bulletin No. 19. Basel: Bank for International Settlements; 2020

[15] Caballero RJ, Simsek A. A Model of Asset Price Spirals and Aggregate Demand Amplification of a "Covid-19" Shock. NBER Working Paper No. 27044. Cambridge, MA: National Bureau of Economic Research; 2020

[16] Milesi-Ferretti GM, Strobbe F, Tamirisa N. Bilateral Financial Linkages and Global Imbalances: A View on the eve of the Financial Crisis. IMF Working Paper 10/247, November. Vol. 2010, No. 257 [Google Scholar], Washington DC,

United States of America: International Monetary Fund; 2010

[17] Phillips-Simpson Keynes PL. The Politics of Aristotle. Chapel Hill: University of North Carolina Press; 1997

[18] Campbell JY, Lo WA, Mackinlay AC. *The Econometrics of Financial Markets*. Princeton New Jersey: Princeton University Press; 1997

[19] Cornell B, Reinganum M. Forward and Futures Prices: Evidence from the Foreign Exchange Markets. Graduate School of Management, UCLA, Working Paper 7-80. Vol. 36, No. 5. New York, United States of America: The Journal of Finance, The Journal of the American Finance Association [Wiley Online Library]; 1981. pp. 1035-1045

[20] Correia S, Luck S, Verner E. Pandemics Depress the Economy, Public Health Interventions Do Not: Evidence from the 1918 Flu (June 5, 2020). Washington DC, United States of America: SSRN; 2020. Available from: https://ssrn.com/abstract=3561560 or http://dx.doi.org/10.2139/ssrn.3561560

[21] International Monetary Fund. The Great Lockdown. World Economic Outlook. Washington, DC: International Monetary Fund; 2020

[22] Gallagher KP, Gao H, Kring WN, Ocampo JA, Volz U. Safety First: Expanding the Global Financial Safety Net in Response to COVID-19. GEGI Working Paper 37. Boston, MA: Global Development Policy Center, Boston University; 2020

[23] Zhang D, Hu M, Ji Q. Financial markets under the global pandemic of COVID-19. Finance Research Letters. 2020;**36**:1-2 101528

[24] Garrett TA. Economic Effects of the 1918 Influenza Pandemic: Implications for a Modern-Day Pandemic. Darby, PA: Diane Publishing Company; 2013

[25] Georgieva K. Confronting the Crisis: Priorities for the Global Economy, 9 April 2020. Washington DC, United States of America: International Monetary Fund; Available from: https://www.imf.org/en/News/Articles/2020/04/07/sp040920-SMs2020-Curtain-Raiser

[26] Gourinchas P-O, Rey H, Truempler K. The financial crisis and the geography of wealth transfers. NBER working paper No. 17353, August. Published in 2012 as global financial crisis. Journal of International Economics. 2011;**88**:266-283. DOI: 10.1016/j.jinteco.2012.05.008. [Crossref], [Web of Science ®], [Google Scholar]

[27] Habermas J. 1992, the Structural Transformation of the Public Sphere: Inquiry into a Category of Bourgeois Society. Cambridge: MIT Press; 1989

[28] Haddad V, Moreira A, Muir T. When Selling Becomes Viral: Disruptions in Debt Markets in the COVID-19 Crisis and the Fed's Response. NBER Working Paper No. 27168. Cambridge, MA: National Bureau of Economic Research; 2020

[29] Hartley J, Rebucci A. An Event Study of COVID-19 Central Bank Quantitative Easing in Advanced and Emerging Economies. NBER Working Paper No. 27339. Cambridge, MA: National Bureau of Economic Research; 2020

[30] Hofmann B, Shim I, Shin HS. Emerging Market Economy Exchange Rates and Local Currency Bond Markets amid the Covid-19 Pandemic. BIS Bulletin No. 5. Basel: Bank for International Settlements; 2020

[31] Hördahl P, Shim I. EME Bond Portfolio Flows and Long-Term Interest Rates during the Covid-19 Pandemic. BIS Bulletin No. 18. Basel: Bank for International Settlements; 2020

[32] Ishay MR. The Human Rights Reader: Major Political Essays, Speeches

and Documents from Ancient Times to the Present. 2nd ed. New York: Routledge; 2007

[33] Jackson JK, Weiss MA, Schwarzenberg AB, Nelson RM. Global Economic Effects of COVID-19. Congressional Research Service R46270. Washington, DC: Congressional Research Service; 2020

[34] Jordà Ò, Singh SR, Taylor AM. Longer-Run Economic Consequences of Pandemics. Federal Reserve Bank of san Francisco Working Paper No. 2020-09. San Francisco, CA: Federal Reserve Bank of San Francisco; 2020

[35] McKibbin W, Fernando R. The Global Macroeconomic Impacts of COVID-19: Seven Scenarios. CAMA Working Paper No. 19/2020. Australia, Canberra: Centre for Applied Macroeconomic Analysis, Crawford School of Public Policy, Australian National University; 2020

[36] Tooze A. Is the Coronavirus Crash Worse than the 2008 Financial Crisis? Foreign Policy, 18 March 2020a

[37] Klein LR. Lectures in Econometrics. Amsterdam, North-Holland; 1983 [Google Scholar]

[38] Schrimpf A, Shin HS, Sushko V. Leverage and Margin Spirals in Fixed Income Markets during the Covid-19 Crisis. BIS Bulletin No. 2. Basel: Bank for International Settlements; 2020

[39] Kubelec C, Sá F. The Geographical Composition of National External Balance Sheets: 1980-2005. Working Paper No. 384, April. [Google Scholar]; London, United Kingdom: Bank of England; 2010

[40] Landier A, Thesmar D. Earnings Expectations in the COVID Crisis. NBER Working Paper. Vol. No. 27160. Cambridge, MA: National Bureau of Economic Research; 2020

[41] Leontief WW, Bródy A. Money-flow computations. Economic Systems Research. 1993;**5**:225-233. DOI: 10.1080/09535319300000019 [Taylor & Francis Online], [Google Scholar]

[42] Maliszewska M, Mattoo A, van der Mensbrugghe D. The Potential Impact of COVID-19 on GDP and Trade: A Preliminary Assessment. World Bank Policy Research Working Paper No. 9211. Washington, DC: World Bank; 2020

[43] Tsujimura K, Mizoshita M. Asset-liability-matrix analysis derived from flow-of-funds accounts: The Bank of Japan's quantitative monetary policy examined. Economic Systems Research. 2003;**15**:51-67. DOI: 10.1080/0953531032000056936 [Taylor & Francis Online], [Google Scholar]

[44] McKibbin W, Sidorenko AA. Global macroeconomic consequences of pandemic influenza. In: CAMA Miscellaneous Publications. Canberra: Centre for Applied Macroeconomic Analysis, Crawford School of Public Policy. Sidney, Australia: Australian National University; 2006

[45] Ramelli S, Wagner AF. Feverish Stock Price Reactions to COVID-19. Swiss Finance Institute Research Paper Series. Vol. No. 20-12. Zurich: Swiss Finance Institute; 2020

[46] Organization for Economic Co-operation and Development (OECD). OECD Factbook 2015-2016: Economic, Environmental and Social Statistics. Paris, France: OECD Publishing; 2016. DOI: 10.1787/factbook-2015-en

[47] Schumann H. Staatsgeheimnis Bankenrettung. Economic Systems Research. 2019;**31**(3). Der Tagesspiegel, February 24. [Taylor & Francis Online], [Google Scholar]

[48] Chiruhula D, Mburu H, Omurwa J. An evaluation of foreign exchange risk

management effects on the firm performance of commercial banks in the democratic republic of congo. Journal of Finance and Accounting. 2019;**3**(3): 188-212. Retrieved from: https://stratfordjournals.org/journals/index.php/journal-of-accounting/article/view/334

[49] Stigum M. The Money Market: Myth, Reality and Practice. Homestead, II: Dow Jones-Irwin; 1978

[50] Stone R. The social accounts from a Consumer's point of view. Review of Income and Wealth. 1966;**12**:1-33. DOI: 10.1111/j.1475-4991.1966.tb00709.x [Crossref], [Google Scholar]

[51] Sunshine Mining Fashions Silver-Backed Certificates to Garner Big Savings. Business International Money Report. 1980. pp. 93-94

[52] Upper C, Worms A. Estimating Bilateral Exposures in the German Interbank Market: Is there a Danger of Contagion? Frankfurt, Germany: Economic Research Centre of the Deutsche Bundesbank, Discussion Paper 09/02. [Google Scholar]; 2002

[53] Verikios G, Sullivan M, Stojanovski P, Giesecke J, Woo G. The Global Economic Effects of Pandemic Influenza. General Paper G-224, Centre of Policy Studies. Melbourne: Monash University; 2011

[54] The Currency Deals behind the Market's Spree. Business Week. 1978. p. 152

[55] Tsujimura M, Tsujimura K. Balance sheet economics of the subprime mortgage crisis. Economic Systems Research. 2011;**23**:1-25. DOI: 10.1080/09535314.2010.523414 [Taylor & Francis Online], [Web of Science ®], [Google Scholar]

Chapter 10

Indicators of Banking Fragility of Participation Banks in Turkey

Ayşegül Aytaç Emin

Abstract

This study examines the significant variables of banking fragility of participation banks in Turkey. For this aim, a model is constructed by employing probit model over the time period 2008 and 2018. The results suggest that asset growth, capital adequacy ratio, financing to total deposits ratio (FDR), return on asset and cost to income ratio are significant banking level indicators of the banking fragility of participation banks in Turkey.

Keywords: banking sector fragility, participation banks, banking crises, Probit model, Islamic finance

1. Introduction

With the increasing integration and interaction of the financial markets, the number of financial crises has considerably increased especially since 1990s. With the contagion effect, on the other hand, the impacts and consequences of the financial crises go beyond the national level by causing significant international costs. In this context, an important part of those crisis is stem from the problems experienced in the banking sector, which is one of the leading sectors that have significant impact on the world economy.

As the importance of the banking sector on economies increases, the risk factors that has to managed by the sector has also increased considerably. Laeven and Valencia [1] emphasized that there were 151 banking crises worldwide between 1970 and 2017 where the duration of these crises is different with respect to the income levels of the countries. Accordingly, while the banking crises in high-income countries are considerably consistent and continue for 5 years or more, in low- and middle-income countries, banking crises continue for 4 years or less. In term of its outcomes, on the other hand, banking crises have devastating effects such as persistent output losses, economic activity, welfare, asset prices, unemployment, government debt, tax revenue [1–4].

As one of the fastest growing sectors of the global financial industry, participation banking sector accelerated its development especially as of the 1990s and become an important part of the banking sector for significant number of countries worldwide. Furthermore, the financial crisis experienced in 2008 shed doubts on the conventional banking system and draw attention to participation banking. The financial crisis of 2008 is considered to be the second most serious breakdown since the 1930s. The crisis, started in the USA, spread to many other countries in a short time and turned to a global crisis. As a consequence, the banking sector in those countries has adversely affected. In this regard, the interest in participation banks has increased, as they were more resistant to the financial crisis compared to conventional banks in terms of profitability, liquidity and asset quality [5, 6].

The breakdown of 2008 also triggered the efforts to investigate the impact of banking crisis on participation banks. However, most of these efforts aim to compare the impact of the crisis on participation banks and conventional banks, or investigate the performance of participation banks before/during/after the global financial crisis [7–10]. Despite those attempts, there is no prior study investigates the early warning indicators of banking fragilities of participation banks. Early warning indicators are crucial since they provide opportunity to detect the fragilities of the banking system and take precautions against a forthcoming banking crisis. In this regard, although there are number of studies in the literature on the significant indicators of banking crisis in Turkey, there have been no attempts to examine the indicators of banking fragilities of the participation banks. For instance, Tosuner [11] developed an early warning system to investigate the banking crisis in Turkey. The author reveals that domestic credit, M2, international reserves, real exchange rate and international trade are leading indicators of banking crisis of Turkey. To identify the causes of bank crises and determine the crisis indicators, Tunay [12] develop an early warning model for Turkey. The results show that exchange rate position, terms of trade, capital adequacy, interest rate risk and market risk are important factors of the banking crisis in Turkey. In addition, Cergibozan and Arı [13] develops a model specific to Turkey to examine the determinants of banking crisis over the time period 1990 and 2013. According to the results, increasing inflation and interest rate, depreciation rate, excessive fiscal deficit, increasing bank loans and bank short positions, liquidity mismatch and decreasing bank reserves are important determinants of banking crisis of Turkey. Furthermore, research on the subject on the participation banks and crisis has been mostly restricted to analyzing the financial performance of participation banks or limited comparisons of the financial performance of conventional banks and participation banks [14–16].

Motivated by the literature, this study constructs a model specific to participation banks in Turkey to identify the leading indicators fragility towards banking crisis. In addition, apart from the existing literature, this study considers banking level explanatory variables over a recent time period 2008 and 2018. This paper has been divided into five sections. The first part of this study gives the introduction. The second section presents an overview of the Islamic financial system and development of participation banks in Turkey. The third part highlights the key concepts of banking sector fragility. The fourth section is concerned with the data and methodology employed for this study. The fifth section presents the results of the study and the last section concludes the study.

2. Overview of the Islamic financial system

The Islamic financial system is constructed on the basis of Shari'ah principles (Islamic Law). In other words, Islamic financial system can be defined as a system in which all financial activities and transactions are carried out within the framework of Islamic rules. The main motive behind the emergence of Islamic financial system is the demand for a system that are based on Islamic principles. In other words, Islamic financial system has primarily arisen to stimulate the unused funds of Muslims with high religious sensitivity to evaluate their investments and further enabling the capital movements between countries. The fundamental resources of Islamic Law are the Holly Qur'an and Sunnah. One of the most important features of Islamic finance is the control of commercial activities and financial transactions with certain standards, moral principles and prohibitions in order to avoid injustice and unjust enrichment. The main prohibitions of Islamic finance can be given as follows:

- Prohibition of Riba (Interest)
- Prohibition of Gharar (Uncertainty)
- Prohibition of Maysir (Gambling)

One of the key principles of Islamic religion is the prohibition of riba. According to majority of Muslim jurist, all forms of interest is forbidden by Islam [17]. According to Islamic terminology, riba arises in two forms as riba on loans (Riba al-nasiah) and Riba al-fadl (riba on sales). In this regard, riba al nasiah addresses to "riba in money to money exchanges, where the exchange is delayed or deferred and gives rise to an additional charge" that also called as Riba al-Jahiliyyah [18]. According to Qur'an, riba al nasiah is strictly forbidden. According to Özsoy [19], riba al-Fadl, on the other hand, is involved in a transaction through the combination of the followings:

- An exchange of goods and money in cash.
- Exchange between two goods or money of the same kind.
- The goods are among the interest classes mentioned in the hadith or belonging to these classes although they are not included in the hadith.
- Excess of one of the goods compared to the other.

Most of the Muslim scholars argue that there is not a specific definition of riba in Qur'an. They support the idea that there is only a certain type of riba, Riba al-Jahiliyyah, in the period when the Qur'an was revealed. The riba, which is forbidden in a very harsh manner in the Quran, is based on an exorbitant increase in nature, and the jahiliyya riba, in which the principal is folded many times. Moreover, the supporters of this view argue that, it is not riba if an addition is made to the original amount in return for maturity from the very beginning of lending. Therefore, it is supported that the prohibited riba, riba-Jahiliyah, is different from the loan with interest transactions that stipulates the increase from the very beginning [19]. In this context, Rahman [20] explains that riba is the increase in capital, which raises the principle amount several folds by continuing redoubling. As stated, it is initially a situation that a part of wealth is loaned on interest for a certain period of time. If this loan cannot be paid on the expiration date then the extension of maturity leads to high increase in the principle amount where big sums involved. This situation ends up with the debtor pays the interest alone in installment but they cannot pay the usury interest nor the principle amount [21]. From this point of view, they differentiate the interest in current economic transactions with the interest prohibited by the Qur'an. They claimed that what is meant in the verse of the Qur'an is exorbitant interest, thus, the current interest practices are legitimate since these transactions are different from the interest prohibited in the verses and hadiths. They argue that the interest given by banks is not unlawful and should be excluded from the scope of riba.

Accordingly, they claim riba, which is forbidden in the Quran, is the usury rather than interest. For instance, Metwally [22] states that riba is closely related with usury. The author explains usury is interpreted as riba and it can be defined as the excess or addition over the principal capital lent. In other words, among some scholars and jurists, riba and usury is used for different terms where usury does not refer to interest [23]. Moreover, Ahmad and Hassan [24] argue that riba is involved in loan transactions that is used for consumption purposes. However, it is not prohibited by Islamic law if it is used for production purposes or the empowerment of micro and small enterprises [20]. Nevertheless, the majority of Islamic scholars state that there are no differences in the meaning and the scope of riba and any transaction that involves a predetermined return is riba and strictly prohibited by Islamic law [19].

Maysir means gamble or game of chance in Arabic. It can be explained as taking risk for increasing wealth by chance. Furthermore, maysir is also seen as speculation and price manipulation [25]. According to Mihajat [26], the activities are considered as gambling if the following three elements are in question:

- The existence of betting subject matter/asset from both sides of the gambler.
- The existence of the game that use to determine who is the winner and who is loser.
- The winner will take the property that being bet, while the loser will lose his bet property.

In games of chance, the win is one-sided. Namely, the gain of one party depends on the loss of the others. Maysir includes all gambling, speculative and chance contracts and it also contains the obligations and benefits that were not fully disclosed by either party at the time the contract was concluded [27]. If the risk involved in a game is not controllable and none of the players can affect the probability of the money paid back, such a game is a game of chance. In maysir, all deviations in actual earnings versus expected earnings are a result of the luck element and is prohibited by Islam [28]. In Islamic finance, maysir means "any transaction conducted by the two parties to posses the ownership of a particular asset or service which obtain benefit to one party and harm to others by linking a particular transaction with an act or event." [26]. According to Kamali [29], maysir is prohibited since it causes an unclean and immoral inducement with a hope of making profit by the loss of the others.

The second fundamental principle of Islamic finance is the prohibition of gharar in mutual contracts. Iqbal and Molyneux [30] states that gharar is one of the most challenging issue in the Islamic law. The types of gharar is divided into excessive, medium and minor gharar by The Accounting and Auditing Organization for Islamic Financial Institutions [30, 31]. In this regard, excessive gharar is existed in a transaction if:

a. it is involved in an exchange-based contract or any contract of that nature.

b. If it is excessive in degree.

c. If it relates to the primary subject matter of the contract.

d. If it is not justified by a Shari'ah-recognizable necessity.

The principles of gharar as can be categorized as follows [32]:

- Gharar in the terms and essence of the contract includes:
    - Two sales in one.
    - Downpayment ('Arbun) sale.
    - "pebble", "touch" and "toss" sales.
    - Suspended (Mu'allaq) sale.
    - Future sale.
- Gharar in the object of the contract includes:
    - Ignorance about the genus.
    - Ignorance about the species.
    - Ignorance about attributes.
    - Ignorance about the quantity of the object.
    - Ignorance about the specific identity of the object.
    - Ignorance about the time of payment in deferred sales.
    - Explicit or probable inability to deliver the object.
    - Contracting on a nonexistent object.
    - Not seeing the object.

When the historical development of Islamic finance is examined, it is seen that although the first practices of interest-free banking dates back to antient times, the foundations of modern Islamic banking began to emerge in the mid-1940s with the establishment of the Patni Cooperative Credit Society and the Muslim Fund Tanda Bavli in India. However, it was only at the end of the 1960s that interest-free banks emerged in a comprehensive manner by establishment of Mit Ghamr Savings Bank in Egypt. Following this, Nasser Social Bank, established in Egypt in 1971, is the first interest-free commercial bank based on Islamic laws. With the 1970s, there has been an increase in the number of institutions providing banking services that have adopted Islamic rules in many countries. For instance, in 1975 Dubai Islamic Bank is established in United Arab Emirates. In the same year, Islamic Development Bank (IsDB) is established in order to support the economic and social development of member countries and Muslim minorities within the framework of Islamic rules. In addition, the first academic meeting in the field of Islamic economics, the International Conference on Islamic Economics, was held in Mecca in 1976. In 1977, Kuwait Finance House, The Faisal Islamic Bank of Egypt, Establishment of The Faisal Islamic Bank of Sudan are established. In addition, to promote the coordination between Islamic banks, International Association of Islamic Banks is established in the same year. In 1978, the first attempt towards establishment an Islamic bank in Europe is occurred with the Islamic Finance House established in Luxembourg. These developments have also triggered the spread of Islamic banking in other

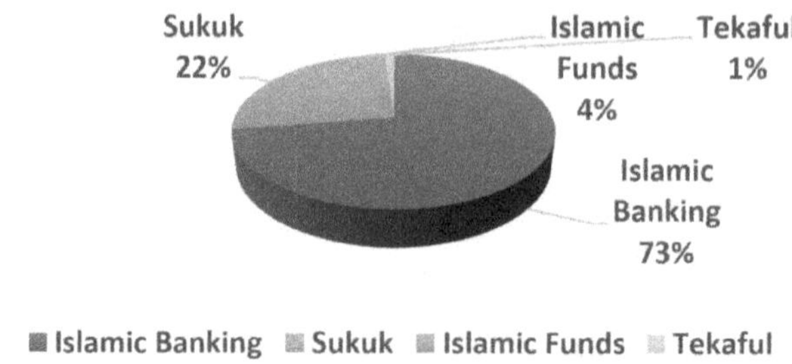

Figure 1.
Islamic finance industry, 2019 [33].

countries and between 1975 and 1990, Islamic finance gained rapid global momentum and spread to many countries such as UK, US and Switzerland. As a result of the increasing volume and growth of the Islamic finance industry, it has brought with it the need to establish and regulate standards in the field of Islamic finance. For this reason, Accounting and Auditing Organization for Islamic Financial Institutions (AAOIFI) is established in 1990. In 2000s, Islamic finance continue its growth globally and spread to countries such as Thailand, Singapore, Kazakhstan, Umman and Germany.

As of 2019, the global Islamic finance assets reach US$2.88 trillion by 14% increase with respect to 2018 [33]. **Figure 1** represents the segmental composition of the Islamic finance industry. According to the figure, the Islamic finance industry is comprised of Islamic banking, Sukuk, Islamic funds and Tekaful.

According to the figure, the Islamic banking is accounted for 72.4% of the industry and has the largest component of the Islamic finance industry. The total Islamic banking assets in 2019 reach US$ 2 trillion and there exist 526 Islamic banks globally [33]. According to IFSI [34], in 2019 the global Islamic banking assets increase by 13% compared to 2018. According to the report, the main reason of the increase in the Islamic banking assets in the GCC region with the considerable mergers of the Islamic banks. Sukuk,[1] on the other hand, account for 22% of the global Islamic finance industry and is the second largest component of the sector. In 2019, the total sukuk outstanding value reach to US$538 billion with a 15% increase compared to 2018. In 2019, there are 308 murabaha, 293 ijara, 235 mudaraba, 229 other sukuk, 225 hybrid sukuk and 156 salam is issued globally. The value of total Islamic funds outstanding is US$140 billion in 2019. It is comprised of mutual funds (US$1555), pension funds (US$86), insurance funds (US$76) and exchange traded funds (US$29). Global Tekaful assets[2] increase by 10% and account for US$51 billion. In 2019, Turkey is the fastest growing market in tekaful assets [33].

3. The development of participation banks in Turkey

In line with the global developments, for the purposes of merging the idle funds into the economy and providing funds to the country, participation banks[3] have

[1] Sukuk is the "certificates of equal value representing undivided shares in ownership of tangible assets, usufruct and services or (in the ownership of) the assets of particular projects or special investment activity" ([31], p. 468).

[2] Islamic insurance.

[3] In Turkey hosts dual banking system where both conventional banking and Islamic banking operate in the same banking sector. The banks that adopt Islamic banking practices are called as "participation banks". The term participation is chosen to emphasize the profit and loss sharing principle of the banks.

begun to established in Turkey by considering the needs of those who oppose the conventional banking system that operate based on interest. The financial liberalization process experienced in the 1980s has a significant role in terms of improving the efficiency of the Turkish banking system and encouraging the competition in the sector. With this process, the legal, structural and institutional arrangements made significant contributions to the development of the Turkish banking sector. In this respect, interest rates and exchange rates were liberalized, new entrances to the banking system were allowed and various arrangements were made for foreign banks to come to Turkey or open branches. Foreign banks were allowed to operate and open branches in Turkey. **Table 1** presents the historical development of the participation banks in Turkey. In this regard, the first attempt towards establishing a participation banking is made with by introduction of the Special Finance Houses (SFHs) in 1983. The operations of SFHs started in 1985 by providing financial products and services within the framework of Islamic principles and prohibitions. Following those arrangements, Albaraka Turk Special Finance House and Faisal Finance Special Finance House Were established in 1984 and 1985 respectively. Additionally, Kuveyt Turk Special Finance House in 1989, Anadolu Special Finance House in 1991, İhlas Special Finance House in 1995, Asya Finance Inc. in 1996 were established and stated their operations in the sector. By the Law no. 5411 article 3, SFHs was replaced with "Participation Banks" in 2005. In 2015, the government was attempted to participate in participation banking with the establishment of Ziraat Participation Bank, Vakıf Participation Bank and Emlak Participation Bank were introduced into industry between 2015 and 2019. As of 2021, Turkey is hosting a dual banking system, where both Islamic and conventional banks operate in the banking sector, with six participation banks as Kuveyt Turk Participation Bank Inc., Albaraka Turk Participation Bank Inc., Turkiye Finance Participation Bank Inc., Turkey's Ziraat Participation Bank Inc., Vakıf Participation Bank Inc. and Emlak Participation Bank (**Table 1**).[4]

Table 2 presents the share of total assets of participation banking in total banking assets. According to the table, while the share of participation banking in total banking system is 6.3% in 2019, it reached to 7.1 in 2020. Furthermore, the annual

1983	Establishment of Special Finance Houses (SFHs)
1984	Establishment of Albaraka Turk Special Finance House
1985	Establishment of Faisal Finance Special Finance House
1989	Establishment of Kuveyt Turk Special Finance House
1991	Establishment of Anadolu Special Finance House
1995	Establishment of İhlas Special Finance House
1996	Establishment of Asya Finance Inc.
2005	Establishment of Turkiye Finance Participation Bank
2015	Establishment of Ziraat Participation Bank
2016	Establishment of Vakıf Participation Bank
2019	Establishment of Emlak Participation Bank

Table 1.
The historical development of the participation banks in Turkey.

[4] As 2021, there are 54 banks operating in Turkish Banking Sector as deposit banks (34), development and investment banks (14), participation banks (6).

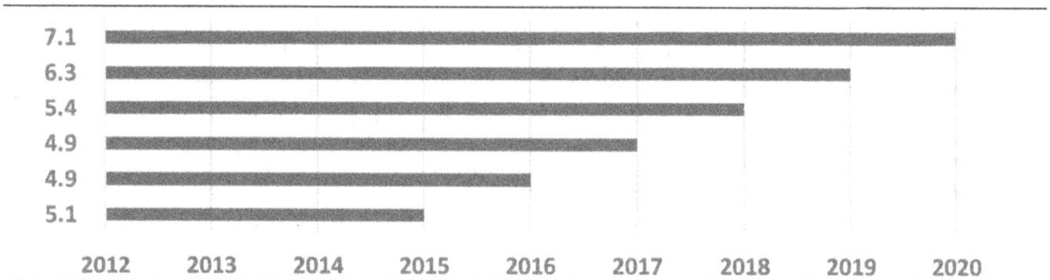

Table 2.
Share of total assets of participation banking in total banking assets.

	2019	2020	Change, %
Funds Collected	215.983	322.017	49.1
Funds Collected TL	91.145	102.620	12.6
Funds Collected FC	106.533	149.513	40.3
Precious Metals FC	18.305	69.884	281.8
Funds Allocated	149.475	240.133	60.7
Total Assets	284.45	437.092	53.7
Shareholder's Equity	21.762	27.603	26.8
Net Profit	2.433	3.716	52.4

Table 3.
Main indicators of the participation banks, TL million [30].

compound growth rate (CAGR) of the participation banking sector assets are 24.0% between 2015 and 2019.

The main indicators of the participation banks that operate in Turkey is presented in **Table 3**. According to the table, the funds collected in the participation banking sector in 2020 is increased by 49% compared to previous year. Furthermore, the total assets grew by 54% compared to 2019 and reached to TL 437 billion in 2020. The net profit of participation banks increased by 52.4% from TL 2.4 billion in 2019 to TL 3.7 billion in 2020. Total shareholders' equity, on the other hand, increased by 26.8% to TL 27.6 billion.

According to TKBB report, Kuveyt Turk Participation Bank has the highest net profit among participation banks in 2020, with TL 1400.3 million [30, 35]. In this context, Kuveyt Türk Participation Bank was followed by Türkiye Finance Participation Bank with 675.7 million TL, Vakıf Participation Bank with 666.9 million TL, Ziraat Participation with 638.6 million TL, Albaraka Turk Participation Bank with 255 million TL and Emlak Participation Bank with 80 million TL [30] (**Table 4**).

In 2020, the total number of domestic and international branches of 6 participation banks operating in Turkey is 1.255 which constitutes more than 10% of the total branch network of the banking sector. The total number of branches of participation banks increased by 83% in 2020 and reached to 1.255 compared to 2011. Accordingly, while the total number of employees in the participation banks in Turkey is 13.851 in 2011, it increased to 16.849 in 2020 with an increase of 22%.

4. Banking sector fragility

The banks are one of the leading financial institutions in Turkey. Therefore, the problems that may arise in the banking system have the potential to cause

Year	Total number of branches	Total number of employees
2011	685	13.851
2012	828	15.356
2013	966	16.763
2014	990	16.270
2015	1.080	16.554
2016	959	14.467
2017	1.032	15.029
2018	1.122	15.645
2019	1.179	16.040
2020	1.255	16.849

Table 4.
Total number of branches and employees of the participation banks in Turkey [36].

destructive social, economic, political and cultural outcomes. For this reason, the attempts towards revealing the vulnerabilities in the financial system to prevent to the costs of those crises or overcoming with the minimum cost where the crisis is inevitable, has gain considerable attention. Accordingly, banking sector fragility index (BSFI) is developed to detect the fragilities and vulnerabilities in the banking system, which is firstly introduced by Kibritçioğlu [37]. According to Kibritçioğlu [37], although banks are exposed to various risk factors, massive bank runs and withdrawals, huge amount of lending booms and increasing unhedged foreign liabilities of banks are the main banking crisis indicators. Accordingly, to monitor the fragilities of the banking sector, the author constructs a BSFI based on liquidity risk, credit risk and exchange rate risk. In this index, bank deposits (DEP), foreign liabilities of banks and credits the domestic private sector are considered as a measure of liquidity, exchange rate and credit risks respectively. The BSFI can be given as follows:

$$BSFI_{i,t} = \frac{\left(\frac{[(CPS_t - CPS_{t-1})/CPS_{t-1}] - \mu_{CPS}}{\sigma_{CPS}}\right) + \left(\frac{[(FL_t - FL_{t-1})/FL_{t-1}] - \mu_{FL}}{\sigma_{FL}}\right) + \left(\frac{[(DEP_t - /DEP_{t-1}] - \mu_{DEP}}{\sigma_{DEP}}\right)}{3} \tag{1}$$

In Eq. (1), the BSFI is the average of standardized values of CPS, FL and DEP, where μ and σ are the mean and standard deviation of the variables. Regarding the BSFI, the fragility episodes of the countries are divided into three as tranquil, medium and high fragility episodes. In this respect, the banking system is in tranquil episode if the index approaches the sample period average. The banking sector of the country is in medium fragility episode where BSFI is between 0 and −0.5. A high fragility episode is experiencing by the countries if BSFI is equal or lower than −0.5. In addition to this index, to investigate whether bank runs play a crucial role in triggering the banking crisis, Kibritçioğlu [37] also constructs an alternative index by excluding the liquidity risk factor:

$$BSFI_{i,t} = \frac{\left(\frac{[(CPS_t - CPS_{t-1})/CPS_{t-1}] - \mu_{CPS}}{\sigma_{CPS}}\right) + \left(\frac{[(FL_t - FL_{t-1})/FL_{t-1}] - \mu_{FL}}{\sigma_{FL}}\right)}{2} \tag{2}$$

According to the results, both indices reveal the similar results. This implies bank runs do not have a prominent role in explaining the banking crises in majority of the sample countries. Furthermore, to investigate the fragilities of Indian banks, Singh [38] developed a monthly BSFI following Kibritçioğlu [37]. The index is the weighted average of annual growth in real time deposits, real non-food credits, real investments in approved and non-SLR securities, real foreign currency assets and liabilities and the real net reserves of commercial banks. The author also constructs an alternative index, by excluding the bank deposits from the index, to show bank runs do not play a significant role for the fragility episodes of Indian banks.

By using the BSFI, Ahmad and Mazlan [39] aimed to monitor the trend and determinants of fragilities of locally and foreign-based commercial banks operating in Malaysia. Although the scholars consider BSFI of Kibritçioğlu [37], different proxies are employed to measure the liquidity, credit and exchange rate risks. The BSFI can be given as follows:

$$BSFI_{i,t} = \frac{\left(\frac{[(NPL_t - NPL_{t-1})/NPL_{t-1}] - \mu_{NPL}}{\sigma_{NPL}}\right) + \left(\frac{[(tier_t - tier_{t-1})/tier_{t-1}] - \mu_{tier}}{\sigma_{FL}}\right) + \left(\frac{[(DEP_t - /DEP_{t-1}] - \mu_{DEP}}{\sigma_{DEP}}\right)}{3} \tag{3}$$

As seen from the above equation, the credit risk factor is measure by using non-performing loans (NPL) and exchange rate/market risk is proxied by time-interest-earned ratio (tier). According to the results, bank specific variables and macroeconomic variables do not have any effect on the fragility of the foreign-based banks. Furthermore, asset quality, management quality and size of the bank asset are significant indicators for the bank fragility of local-based banks in Malaysia.

In addition to those efforts to investigate the fragilities of conventional banks, the BSFI index is also applied to Islamic banking to determine the banking fragilities as well. For instance, Kusuma and Asif [40] use the BSFI of Kibritçioğlu [37] to identify the fragility episodes of Indonesian Islamic banks by considering bank deposits and domestic credit proxies. The authors use the only macroeconomic variables such as ratio of M2 to reserve growth, credit growth, inflation rate and real effective exchange rate as explanatory variables of their model.

Wiranatakusuma and Duasa [41] constructs a monthly Islamic banking resilience index (IBRI) to examine the signaling macroeconomic indicators towards the resilience of Indonesian Islamic banks. The IBRI is constructed based on liquidity risk and credit risk factors. To measure liquidity risk, the authors use bank deposits. Furthermore, the credit risk factor is proxied by financing variable which is the various kinds of financings of Islamic banks. In the study, four macroeconomic variables, the ratio of M2 to international reserves, inflation rate, real effective exchange rate and credit growth, are investigated. The results of the study suggest that all of those macroeconomic variables are capable of explaining the vulnerabilities of Indonesian Islamic banks against the adverse external shocks.

5. Data and methodology

By year 2021, six participation banks are operating in Turkey. These banks are Kuveyt Turk Participation Bank, Albaraka Turk Participation Bank, Türkiye Finance Participation Bank, Turkey's Ziraat Participation Bank, Vakıf Participation Bank and Emlak Participation Bank. As explained in Section 1.2, Ziraat Participation Bank Inc., Vakıf Participation Bank Inc. and Emlak Participation Bank are established in 2015,

2016 and 2019 respectively. For this reason, regarding data availability and reliability, the analysis is conducted by considering the banks that are established before 2008. Therefore, Kuveyt Turk Participation Bank, Albaraka Turk Participation Bank, Turkiye Finance Participation Bank are included into the regression which represent 70% of the participation banking system in Turkey. Considering the fact that the origin of each banking crisis is stem from different reasons and vulnerabilities, there is lack of a standard number or list of explanatory variables in the literature. Nevertheless, there is some variables that are frequently used and found as statistically significant in the literature. Therefore, in this study, the banking level indicators are determined regarding the leading indicators of banking crisis literature.[5] Accordingly, the indicators of the fragility of participation banks towards a banking crisis are investigated by considering banking level variables:

Capital Adequacy: capital adequacy ratio, shareholders' equity to asset ratio.

Asset Quality: growth of total assets, the ratio of fixed assets to total assets.

Earning: Return on assets, return on equity.

Management: Cost to income ratio, total operating expenses.

Liquidity: Financing to total deposits ratio (FDR).

Sensitivity: the ratio of net open position in foreign currency assets to total regulatory capital, the ratio of total securities to total assets.

Namely, in this study it is investigated if capital adequacy, asset quality, management quality, earning ability, liquidity and sensibility to market risk variables are significant to explain the banking sector fragility of participation banks in Turkey.[6] The final data set covers the period between 2008 and 2018. The banking sector data is extracted from Bankscope, Fitchconnect and Datastream databases.

In this study, probit model is employed to investigate the significant indicators of fragilities of participation banks in Turkey. Probit model, as a binomial choice model, is seen one of the most powerful method regarding the early warning system literature [47–49]. In probit model, the dependent variable is a binary choice model and takes the values 0 and 1 with respect the occurrence of the certain event. Accordingly, in this study, the dependent variable, Y_(i,t), refers to the fragility episode (FE) of the participation banks in Turkey. In this study, the medium and high fragility episodes are considered as fragility episode. In this respect, FE take the value 1 if the participation banks are medium or high fragile to banking crisis. It takes the value 0 referring that the banks are experiencing a tranquil episode.

$\boldsymbol{FE_{i,t}}$= 0, if the participation banks are in a tranquil episode at time t.

$\boldsymbol{FE_{i,t}}$=1, if the participation banks are in a medium/high fragility episode at time t.

The $\boldsymbol{FE_{i,t}}$ relies on latent variable $\boldsymbol{y^*_{i,t}} = \boldsymbol{X_j\beta} + \boldsymbol{\varepsilon}$ where $\boldsymbol{\varepsilon} \sim \boldsymbol{N(0,1)}$. The regression equation to examine the relationship between the explanatory variables and the probability of fragility towards banking crisis can be given as:

$$\Pr(Y_{i,t} = 1|X_{i,t}) = \varphi\left(X'_{i,t}\beta\right) + \varepsilon_{i,t} \tag{4}$$

Where $X_{(i,t)}$ is the set of explanatory variables, β is the is a vector of the coefficients and φ is the cumulative distribution. *Pr* denotes the probability of experiencing fragility episode at time t. The binary dependent variable, $Y_{(i,t)}$ is regressed by using explanatory variables, banking level sector variables between the time period 2008 and 2018 by employing probit model.

---

[5] See Masood et al. [42]; Saeed et al. [43]; Paulet and Mavoori [44].

[6] To be able to specify the superior explanatory variable set regarding the statistical significances of the variables, they alternately included into analysis and various combinations of the variables are examined [45, 46].

Following Kibritçioğlu [37], the BSFI is constructed for identifying the indicators of fragilities of participation banks in Turkey. The index is comprised of credit risk, liquidity risk and exchange rate risk. In this regard, non-performing financing (NPF), bank deposits (DEP) and times interest earned ratio (tier) are used to measure credit risk, liquidity risk and exchange rate risk respectively. The BSFI can be given as:

$$BSFI1_{i,t} = \frac{\left(\frac{[(NPF_t - NPF_{t-1})/NPF_{t-1}] - \mu_{NPF}}{\sigma_{NPF}}\right) + \left(\frac{[(tier_t - tier_{t-1})/tier_{t-1}] - \mu_{tier}}{\sigma_{tier}}\right) + \left(\frac{[(DEP_t - /DEP_{t-1}] - \mu_{DEP}}{\sigma_{DEP}}\right)}{3} \quad (5)$$

The BSFI is transformed into a binary variable FE, defining the fragility episode. The participation banks in Turkey experiences three stages as high fragility, medium fragility and tranquil episodes with respect to the level of BSFI. Accordingly, banking system is experiencing a high fragility period if BSFI is less than -0.5. This states that Islamic banks at time t are highly fragile to banking crises. The system is in medium fragility episode if BSFI is between -0.5 and 0. On the other hand, an episode is classified as tranquil period if the BSFI exceeds 0. μ_{NPF}, μ_{tier} and μ_{DEP} represent the arithmetic mean of non-performing financings, foreign liabilities of banks and bank deposits respectively. In addition, σ_{NPF}, σ_{tier} and σ_{DEP} are the standard deviation of each of the variable. To investigate whether bank runs are crucial for the fragilities of participation banks in Turkey, an alternative index, BSFI2, is constructed as:

$$BSFI2_{i,t} = \frac{\left(\frac{[(NPF_t - NPF_{t-1})/NPF_{t-1}] - \mu_{NPF}}{\sigma_{NPF}}\right) + \left(\frac{[(tier_t - tier_{t-1})/tier_{t-1}] - \mu_{tier}}{\sigma_{tier}}\right)}{2} \quad (6)$$

As can be seen from Eq. (6), the alternative BSFI is designed by excluding bank deposits variable from the BSFI1. In this regard, defining and detecting the fragile and tranquil episodes towards banking crisis by observing the index value is crucial as the index reveals detailed information on the business cycles within the banking system.

6. Results

To examine the significant banking level indicators of fragility of participation banks in Turkey, first the BSFI is constructed. In this regard, the fragile and tranquil episodes are determined based on the index. **Table 5** presents the fragility and tranquil episodes in Turkey between 2008 and 2018. According to the table, the participation banks in Turkey experiences 20 fragility periods and 16 tranquil periods between 2008 and 2018.[7] It is observed that, majority of participation banks in Turkey experienced fragility episode in 2007, the year before the financial crisis. Furthermore, although it is argued that the participation banks are more resistant and perform better during the financial crisis in terms of profitability compared to conventional banks [15], the participation banks are in fragility episode in 2009 and 2010, in the following two years of the financial crisis. As the effects of the financial crisis spread rapidly to other developed and developing countries and took over the banking sectors in those countries, it is seen that participation banks in Turkey also

[7] Since the movement paths of BSFI1 and BSFI2 are similar, the crisis dates are the same for both of the indices.

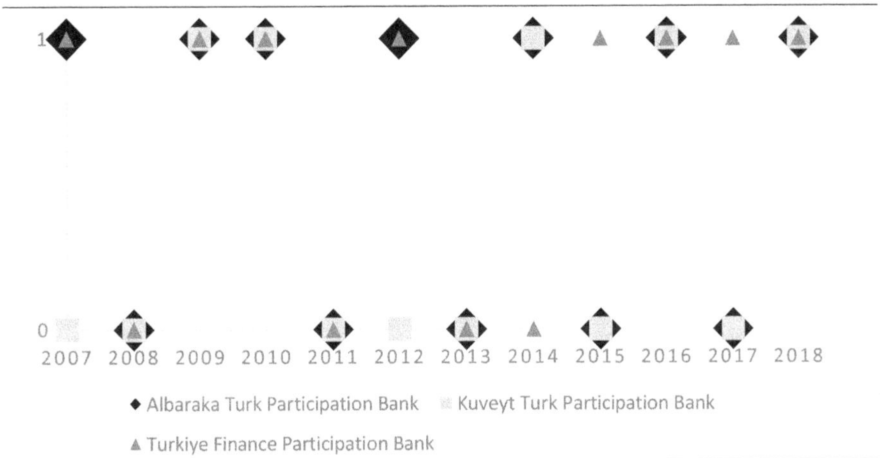

Table 5.
Fragile and tranquil episodes of the participation banks.

be affected by the outcomes of the crisis. In this regard, according to Hasan and Dridi [7], while the business models of the participation banks prevent the destructive outcomes of the 2008 crisis, the participation banks suffer from greater decline in profitability after 2009 because of their weak risk management practices. As the impact of the global financial crisis on the world economy continued in 2012, most of the countries such as USA and developed economies in the eurozone, have not been able to fully recover and overcome the negative outcomes of the crisis. With the deepened eurozone recession, debt ratios and unemployment increased in those countries. The slowdown in the global economy also affected Turkey. The GDP growth of Turkey slowed down. Furthermore, the external balance of the Turkish economy has deteriorated and the ratio of current account deficit to GDP reached 10%. In line with the global slowdown and deterioration of the Turkish economy, it is seen that the participation banking sector is adversely affected and majority of the banks in the sector experiences a fragile period in 2012. In 2014, developments such as the rapid decline in oil and natural gas prices, the inability of the European economy to recover from the recession, the slowdown in the Chinese economy and the uncertainties in the Middle East caused slowdown in the global economy. Parallel to these global developments and its continuing current account deficit problem, the Turkish economy also grow lower than expected. Accordingly, participation banking sector in Turkey experiences fragility episode in 2014. The political developments (i.e., Brexit, US Presidential elections) and concerns in the global economy (i.e., fluctuations inf energy prices, uncertainty in global interest rate, exchange rate depreciations) affect the financial markets worldwide in 2016. In this regard, the growth of the Islamic finance assets has also deceased. In this regard, the main reason of the slowndown is shown as the depreciation of exchange rate in Turkey, Indonesia, Malaysia and Iran [50]. Accordingly, the table show that in 2016, the participation banks in Turkey has experienced fragility episode in line with those global and domestic developments. In this regard, when the return on assets of the participation banks in Turkey are examined, it is seen that its value decreased by 11% on average in 2016 compared to 2015. Furthermore, since the global uncertainties and the impact of the foreign exchange risks become effectual in the global scale, the improvement of the Islamic finance sector slowed down in 2018 compared to 2017. As in 2016, the return on assets ratio of participation banks in Turkey decrease on average by 15% compared to previous year.

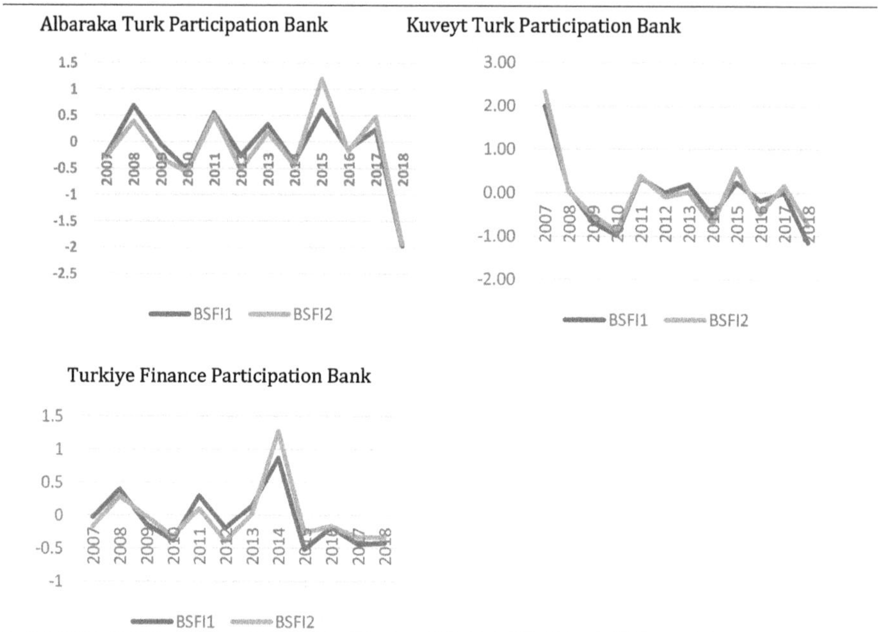

Table 6.
Banking sector fragility indices.

Table 6 present the BSFI1 and BSFI2 for the participation banks in Turkey. Accordingly, when the movement paths of the BSFI1 and BSF2 are compared in **Table 6**, it is observed that both indices follow a similar path. In this respect, bank deposits do not play a significant role in explaining the fragility episodes in Turkish participation banks as in conventional banks [37]. As Laeven and Valencia [4] suggest, the impact of bank runs on banking crises has decreased with the savings deposit insurance.[8]

To investigate the significant indicators of fragilities of participation banks in Turkey, probit model is employed over the time period of 2008 and 2018. To remedy a possible endogeneity, the explanatory variables of the regression of the fragility of Turkish participation banks are lagged one year. The final explanatory variable set for the analysis of the significant indicators of fragility of Turkish participation banks towards banking crisis is determined by following several steps. Firstly, to indicate the significances of the variables, each independent variable is analyzed separately. Secondly, those significant variables are divided into the categories with respect to CAMELS classification. Thirdly, probit model is conducted with respect to those groups. Finally, the explanatory variables that are significant in each step constitute the final explanatory variable set. Accordingly, the final explanatory variable set is comprised of capital adequacy ratio, return on assets, net interest margin, cost to income ratio and FDR. The dependent variable is the binary fragility variable that is regressed on the lagged variables by employing panel regression.

Table 7 presents the estimation results of the probit regression. According to the table, among capital adequacy indicators, the capital adequacy ratio has

[8] In Turkey, Savings Deposit Insurance Fund (SDIF) is a public legal entity and established to protect the rights of the account owners by compensating their losses.

Variables	Coefficient	Std. error	Z-stat.	Prob.
Capital adequacy ratio	−0.041	0.10	−3.03	0.002**
Asset growth	−0.021	0.008	−2.66	0.008**
Cost to income ratio	0.023	0.006	3.63	0.000***
FDR	−0.023	0.007	−3.31	0.001**
Return on assets	−0.035	0.007	−3.51	0.001***

*$p < 0.1$
**$p < 0.05$
***$p < 0.01$

Table 7.
Results of the probit regression.

significantly and negatively correlated with the probability of the fragility of participation banks in Turkey. The capital adequacy ratio, which is the ratio of the total regulatory capital to risk weighted assets, is considered as one of the most crucial indicators for the safe and stable banking system by indicating the financial strength [50]. In other words, the ratio shows whether the bank's capital is sufficient against the calculated risks that the bank may be exposed to during its operations. The ratio is related to banking crisis since it mirrors the risky assets and indicates financial health and stability of the banks. To prevent possible banking crises and ensure the healthy functioning banking system, various restrictions have been imposed on the risks taken by banks. In this context, the capital adequacy ratio constitutes an important part of the Basel Criteria. According to the Basel criteria, the minimum capital adequacy ratio must be higher than 8%. In addition to the standard level of 8%, the minimum ratio of 12% is set for the Turkish banks in 2006. It has been seen as one of the most effective measures to prevent Turkish banks from experiencing capital shortages during the financial crisis [38]. According to the TKBB [36], while the capital adequacy ratio of the participation banks in Turkey is 16% in 2018, the level increases to 18% in 2019 and 2020 based on the low non-performing financings ratio and high asset quality of the banks. In line with the related literature,[9] the results of the probit regression show that capital adequacy ratio is a significant indicator of the fragility of the Turkish participation banks to banking crisis.

Return on assets is a profitability ratio which is an important indicator for the financial performance of banks. The ratio shows the bank's ability to generate profit from its assets. In line with the related literature, the results of the analysis show that return on assets is significant indicator of the fragility of the participation banks [53]. Put differently, increasing return on assets reflects the strength and efficiency of participation banks and decreases the likelihood of experiencing a fragility towards banking crisis. Since the conventional banks operate based on interest, they have a fixed rate of return. However, as interest is prohibited by the Islamic law, the investments are based on mark-up and equity in participation banks. Furthermore, the pre-agreed return on deposits do not allowed, there is higher risks and uncertainties of return on investments [54]. For this reason, return on assets is crucial for the participation banks in Turkey.

According to the estimation results, cost to income ratio, which is measured as the operating expense as a percent of operating income, has significant impact on

[9] See Klomp and de Haan [51]; Korkmaz et al. [52].

the fragility of the participation banks. The indicator is frequently used in the literature to measure management efficiency [55]. Furthermore, low cost efficiency is an essential factor of low profitability of banks [56, 57]. In line with the literature, the estimation results suggest that lower values of cost to income ratio, increases the likelihood of participation banks to experience banking crisis. The cost to income ratio is crucial especially for participation banks since they are found as less cost efficient than conventional banks in the countries where both banks operates in the same banking sector [58].[10]

Asset growth is found as statistically significant indicator and decreasing value of this variable increases the fragility of the participation banks. As Al-Kayed et al. [59] investigate, optimal asset growth has a positive impact on the performance of the participation banks. In this regard, since the asset growth is originated from TPF, those funds should be allocated to public to obtain optimal margin income and revenue sharing [60].

As conventional banks and participation banks are different in terms of financing, the loan to deposit ratio in Shari'ah banking calculated as financing to deposit ratio (FDR) [61–63]. FDR indicates the ability of participation banks to repay funds withdrawn by customers, based on financing as a source of liquidity [64]. In other words, it is the ratio of financings outstanding to third party funds (TPF) [65]. According to the results, FDR is found as negatively correlated with the fragility of participation banks in Turkey. As Kinanti [66] states, FDR has a positive impact on the profitability of participation banks. Furthermore, increasing FDR ratio increases the bank's ability to channel financing, therefore, makes participation banks less prone to banking crisis. In addition, according to Widiwati and Rusli [67], since FDR demonstrates that the bank is able to adjust the amount of funds received and the murabaha financing distributed it has also positively related with the murabahah financing. Furthermore, TPF has also has a positive impact on murabahah financing as banks accept high amount of funds, the distribution of murabahah financing increases.

The estimation results reveal that, among banking level indicators, return on assets, FDR, capital adequacy ratio, asset growth and cost to income ratio are the leading indicators of banking sector fragility of participation banks in Turkey. In this respect, return on assets, FDR, capital adequacy ratio and asset growth are found as negatively related with the fragility of participation banks. Accordingly, increasing return on assets, FDR, capital adequacy ratio and asset growth make participation banks less prone to experiencing a banking crisis. Cost to income ratio, on the other hand is also found as statically significant and positively related with the banking sector fragility of the participation banks. Therefore, increasing cost to income ratio increases the likelihood of the participation banks in Turkey to experience banking crisis.

7. Conclusion

Turkish banking sector hosts dual banking system where both conventional banking and Islamic banking operate in the same banking sector. Furthermore, the banks that operates based on Islamic banking practices are called as "participation banks". Although the literature on the banking sector fragility indicators of conventional banks is vast, there are limited number of studies that focus on participation banks. For this reason, in this study, the significant banking level indicators of participation

[10] Islamic vs. Conventional Banking.

banks towards banking crisis is investigated. The estimation is employed by conducting probit model over the time period 2008 and 2018. According to the estimation results, asset growth, capital adequacy ratio, FDR, return on asset and cost to income ratio are significant banking level indicators of the banking fragility of participation banks in Turkey. Accordingly, increasing return on assets, FDR, capital adequacy ratio and asset growth decreases the likelihood of experiencing banking crisis. On the other hand, the results suggest that increasing cost to income ratio increases the probability of banking sector fragility of participation banks.

Following Kibritçioğlu [37], the BSFIs are constructed in order to investigate whether bank deposits are essential role in determining the banking sector fragility of the participation banks in Turkey. It is important to examine the role of bank runs in Turkish participation banking sector since they play a crucial role in majority of the banking crisis as Asian crisis and Argentina crisis in 1989 [4, 67]. However, it is found that both of the indices follow the same pattern, revealing that bank deposit are not crucial in determining the fragility of the participation banks. In line with the existing literature, with the adoption of deposit insurance, the role of bank runs in banking crisis become less effective [4, 68]. Although conventional banks and participation banks share similar objectives, they perform their functions in different manners which make their risk exposure idiosyncratic in terms of their funding methods, principles and prohibitions. As one of the fastest growing sectors of financial industry, participation banking has developed rapidly on a global scale. In addition to its rapid growth and its share in the banking sector, it attracted special attention with the financial crisis experienced in 2008. Although the participation banks are considered as they performed better compared to conventional banks during the financial crisis of 2008, a considerable amount of literature has been published after the crisis reveal that they have also experienced negative outcomes of the crisis, therefore, they are not completely safe against banking crisis [69, 70]. Furthermore, according to the results of this study, although the participation banking sector in Turkey experiencing a tranquil episode in 2008, the sector was in fragility episode in 2009, 2010 and also majority of the banks in 2007. Accordingly, by revealing the leading indicators of the banking sector fragility for participation banks, the results of this study are crucial and beneficial since policymakers may prevent potential future banking crises and take early precautions to minimize the losses by utilizing the results of this study.

Author details

Ayşegül Aytaç Emin
Social Sciences University of Ankara, Ankara, Turkey

*Address all correspondence to: aysegulaytac.emin@asbu.edu.tr

References

[1] Laeven L, Valencia F. Systemic banking crises database II. IMF Economic Review. 2020;**68**:307-361

[2] Hoggarth G, Reis R, Saporta V. Costs of banking system instability: Some empirical evidence. Journal of Banking and Finance. 2002;**26**:825-855. DOI: 10.1016/S0378-4266(01)00268-0

[3] Reinhart C, Rogoff K. This time is different: A panoramic view of eight centuries of financial crises. NBER Working Paper Series. No. 13882. 2009

[4] Lindgren C-J, Garcia G, Matthew IS. Bank Soundness and Macroeconomic Policy. 1st ed. Washington: International Monetary Fund; 1996. 232 p

[5] Ansari R, Rehman A. Comparative financial performance of existing Islamic banks and contemporary conventional banks in Pakistan. International Proceedings of Economics Development & Research. 2011;**22**: 45-49

[6] Zehri C, Abdelbaki A, Najla B. Effects of the current financial crisis on Islamic banks compared to conventional banks. Banks and Bank Systems. 2012;**7**: 83-93

[7] Hasan M, Dridi J. The effects of the global crisis on Islamic and conventional banks: A comparative study. Journal of International Commerce, Economics and Policy. 2010;**02**:163-200. DOI: 10.1142/s1793993311000270

[8] Setyawati I, Suroso S, Suryanto T, Nurjannah DS. Does financial performance of Islamic banking is better? Panel data estimation. European Research Studies Journal. 2017;**20**: 592-606. DOI: 10.35808/ersj/661

[9] Erfani R, Vasigh B. The impact of the global financial crisis on profitability of the banking industry: A comparative analysis. Economies. 2018;**6**:1-13. DOI: 10.3390/economies6040066

[10] Muhammad R, Triharyono C. Analysis of Islamic banking financial performance before, during and after global financial crisis. Jurnal Ekonomi & Keuangan Islam. 2019;**5**:80-86. DOI: 10.20885/JEKI.vol5.iss2.art5

[11] Tosuner A. Finansal Krizler Ve Kırılganlık: Türkiye İçin Bir Erken Uyarı Sistemi Denemesi. İktisat İşletme ve Finans. 2005;**20**:42-61

[12] Tunay B. Bankacılık krizleri ve erken uyarı sistemleri: Türk bankacılık sektörü için bir model önerisi. BDDK Bankacılık ve Finansal Piyasalar. 2010;**4**: 9-46

[13] Cergibozan A, Arı A. Türkiye'deki banka krizlerine yönelik ekonometrik bir yaklaşım: Markov rejim değişim modeli. Marmara Üniversitesi İktisadi ve İdari Bilimler Dergisi. 2017;**39**:47-64. DOI: 10.14780/muiibd.329728

[14] Sarıdoğan HÖ. Katılım bankalarının performansını etkileyen faktörler: küresel kriz bağlamında bir dinamik panel veri analizi. Bartın Üniversitesi İktisadi ve İdari Bilimler Fakültesi Dergisi. 2020;**11**:149-167

[15] Kendirli Çağıran H, Kendirli S, Aydın Y. Küresel kriz çerçevesinde katılım bankalarının ve ticari bankaların mali performanslarının TOPSIS yöntemiyle analizi. İktisadi ve İdari Bilimler Dergisi. 2020;**33**:137-154

[16] Canbaz M, Dur A. Katılım bankalarının performansının konvansiyonel bankalar ile karşılaştırılması: 2008 kriz dönemi örneği. İşletme Araştırmaları Dergisi. 2019;**11**:1744-1756. DOI: 10.20491/isarder.2019.702

[17] Ayub M. Understanding Islamic Finance. 2nd ed. Chichester: Wiley; 2007. 544 p. DOI: 10.1002/9781119209096

[18] Iqbal Z, Mirakhor A. An Introduction to Islamic Finance: Theory and Practice. 2nd ed. Chichester: Wiley; 2011. 544 p. DOI: 10.1002/9781118390474

[19] Khan M, A. Islamic economics: Annotated Sources in English and Urdu. 1st ed. Leicester: The Islamic Foundation; 1983. 221 p

[20] Rahman Z, A. Contracts and the Products of the Islamic Banking. 1st ed. Kuala Lumpur: CERT Publication; 2010. 218 p

[21] Rahman F. Riba and interest. 1st ed. Chicago: University of Chicago Press; 1982. 182 p

[22] Metwally M, M. Economic consequences of applying Islamic principles in Muslim societies. Journal of Islamic Banking and Finance. 2006;**23**: 11-33

[23] Vogel F, Hayes L. Islamic law and finance; religion, risk, and return. Journal of Law and Religion. 2000;**15**: 475-479

[24] Ahmad AUF, Hassan M. Riba and Islamic banking. I Journal of Islamic Economics. 2008;**3**:9-42

[25] Uddin A. Principles of Islamic Finance: Prohibition of Riba, Gharar and Maysir. Munich Personal RePEc Archive No. 2015;**67711**:1-8. DOI: 10.13140/RG.2.2.36029.20969

[26] Mihajat MIS. Contemporary practice of riba, gharar and maysir in Islamic banking and finance. International Journal of Islamic Management and Business. 2016;**2**: 1-19

[27] Al-Omar FA, Abdel-Haq NK. Islamic Banking: Theory, Practice and Challeges. 1st ed. London: Zed Books; 1996. 137 p

[28] Al-Suwailem S. Towards an objective measure of Gharar in exchange. Islamic Economic Studies. 2000;7:62-100

[29] Kamali MH. Islamic Commercial Law. 1st ed. Cambridge: Islamic Text Society; 2000. 253 p

[30] Participation Banks Association of Turkey (TKBB). Participation Banks [Internet]. 2020. Available from: https://tkbb.org.tr/Documents/tkbb-publications-97/TKBB_FR20_ENG-KOD_ENG.pdf [Accessed: July 01, 2021]

[31] The Accounting and Auditing Organization for Islamic Financial Institutions (AAOIFI). AAOIFI Sharia Standards [Internet]. 2017. Available from: https://aaoifi.com/shariaa-standards/?lang=en [Accessed: September 02, 2021]

[32] Al-Dareer S. Al Gharar in Contracts and Its Effect on Contemporary Transactions. 1st ed. Jeddah: Islamic Research and Training Institute; 1997. 79 p

[33] Thomson Reuters. Islamic Finance Development Report [Internet]. 2020. Available from: https://icd-ps.org/uploads/files/ICD-Refinitiv%20IFDI%20Report%2020201607502893_2100.pdf [Accessed: December 02, 2021]

[34] Islamic Financial Services Board (IFSI). Islamic Financial Services Industry Stability Report http://www.ifsb.org 2020 [Internet]. 2020. Available from: https://www.ifsb.org/sec03.php [Accessed: October 17, 2021]

[35] Iqbal Z, Molyneux P. Thirty Years of Islamic Banking. 1st ed. London: Palgrave Macmillan; 2005. 190 p. DOI: 10.1057/9780230503229

[36] Banking Regulation and Supervision Agency. Annual Report [Internet]. 2020. Available from: https://www.bddk.org.tr/KurumHakkinda/EkGetir/5?ekId=22 [Accessed: August 24, 2021]

[37] Kibritçioğlu A. Monitoring banking sector fragility. The Arab Bank Review. 2003;**5**:51-66

[38] Singh TR. An ordered probit model of an early warning system for predicting financial crisis in India. IFC Bulletin Chapters. 2011;**34**: 185-201

[39] Ahmad N, Mazlan NF. Banking fragility sector index and determinants: A comparison between local based and foreign based commercial banks in Malaysia. International Journal of Business and Administrative Studies. 2015;**1**:5-17

[40] Kusuma W, Asif A. Building an Early Warning System for Islamic Banking Crisis in Indonesia: Signal Approach Model [Internet]. 2012. Available from: https://www.ibs.edu.jo/files/Building.pdf [Accessed: August 15, 2021]

[41] Wiranatakusuma DB, Duasa J. Building an early warning towards the resilience of Islamic banking in Indonesia. Al-Iqtishad: Journal of Islamic Economics. 2017;**9**:1-35

[42] Masood O, Ghauri K, Aktan B. Predicting Islamic banks performance through CAMELS rating model. Banks and Bank Systems. 2016;**11**: 37-43. DOI: 10.21511/bbs.11(3).2016.04

[43] Saeed H, Shadid A, Tirmizi MA. An empirical investigation of banking sector performance of Pakistan and Sri Lanka by using CAMELS ratio of framework. Journal of Sustainable Finance & Investment. 2020;**10**: 247-268. DOI: 10.1080/20430795.2019.1673140

[44] Paulet E, Mavoori H. Cross-regional analysis of banking efficiency drivers. Applied Economics. 2021;**53**:2042-2065. DOI: 10.1080/00036846.2020.1855312

[45] Vidal-Abarca AO, Ruiz AU. Introducing a New Early Warning System Indicator (EWSI) of banking crises. BBVA Working Paper. 2015; **15**(02):1-40

[46] Coudert V, Idier J. Reducing model risk in early warning systems for banking crises in the euro area. International Economics. 2018;**156**: 98-116. DOI: 10.1016/j.inteco.2018.01.002

[47] Frakel J, Rose A. Currency crashes in emerging markets: An empirical treatment. Journal of International Economics. 1996;**41**:351-366

[48] Kumar M, Moorthy U, Perraudin W. Predicting emerging market currency crashes. Journal of Empirical Finance. 2003;**2002**:427-454

[49] Davis E, Karim D. Comparing early warning systems for banking crises. Journal of Financial Stability. 2008;**4**: 89-120

[50] Dincer H, Hacıoğlu U, Yuksel S. Performance assessment of deposit banks with CAMELS analysis using fuzzy anp-moora approaches and an application on Turkish banking sector. Asian Journal of Research in Business Economics and Management. 2016;**6**: 32-56

[51] Klomp J, de Haan J. Bank regulation and financial fragility in developing countries: Does bank structure matter? Review of Development Finance. 2015; **5**:82-90. DOI: /10.1016/j.rdf.2015.11.001

[52] Korkmaz Ö, Erer D, Erer E. Bankacılık sektöründe yoğunlaşma ile finansal kırılganlık arasındaki ilişki: Türkiye örneği (2007-2014). Muhasebe

ve Finansman Dergisi. 2016;**69**:127-146. DOI: 10.25095/mufad.396665

[53] Ismawati K, Istria PC. Detektor fınancıal dıstress perusahaan perbankan Indonesıa. Jurnal Ekonomi Bisnis Dan Kewirausahaan. 2015;**4**:149-167

[54] Van Greuning H, Iqbal Z. Risk Analysis for Islamic Banks. 1st ed. Wahington, D.C.: World Bank; 2007. 310 p. DOI: 10.1596/978-0-8213-7141-1

[55] Borio C, Gambacorta L, Hofmann B. The influence of monetary policy on bank profitability. International Finance. 2017;**20**:48-63

[56] Molyneux P, Thorton J. Determinants of European bank profitability: A note. Journal of Banking and Finance. 1992;**16**:1173-1178

[57] Kok C, More C, Pancaro C. Bank profitability challenges in euro area banks: The role of cyclical and structural factors. Financial Stability Review. 2015; **1**:134-145

[58] Beck R, Jakubik P, Piloiu A. Non-performing loans: What matters in addition to the economic cycle? European Central Bank Working Paper Series. 2010;**1515**:1-32

[59] Al-Kayed T, Zain SRS, Duasa J. The relationship between capital structure and performance of Islamic banks. Journal of Islamic Accounting and Business Research. 2014;**5**:158-181

[60] Rachmadita D, Nindito M, Hasanah N. The influence of savings, equity, non performing financing and profit sharing on the financing of islamic banks in Indonesia. In: Proceedings of the IBEA International Conference on Business, Economics, and Accounting; 20-23 March 2013; Bangkok. Indonesia: IBEA; 2013. pp. 243-252

[61] Alamsyah H, Zulverdi D, Gunadi I, Idris R, Pramono B. Banking disintermediation and its implication for monetary policy: The case of Indonesia. Buletin Ekonomi Moneter dan Perbankan. 2005;**4**:499-521. DOI: / 10.21098/bemp.v7i4.122

[62] Haque A, Osman J, Ismail AZ. Factors influences selection of Islamic banking: A study of Malaysian customer preferences. American Journal of Applied Sciences. 2009;**6**:992-928. DOI: 10.3844/ajassp.2009.922.928

[63] Ebrahim M, Joo T. Islamic banking in Brunnei Darussalam. International Journal of Social Economics. 2001;**28**: 314-337. DOI: 10.1108/ 03068290110357708

[64] Kartika R, Jubaedah S, Astuti AD. The influence of financing to deposit ratio, return on assets and non performing finance on profit sharing finance of sharia banks in Indonesia. Advances in Economics, Business and Management Research. 2019;**123**: 136-140

[65] Nugroho L, Badawi A, Nugraha, Putra YM. What determines Islamic performance ratio of Islamic banking in Indonesia: An analysis using financing deposit to ratio as moderator. Jurnal Ekonomi dan Keuangan Islam. 2021;**10**: 104-123. DOI: 10.22373/share. v10i1.9314

[66] Kinanti RA. Influence of third-party funds, car, npf and fdr towards the return on assets of Islamic banks in Indonesia. Jurnal Ilmiah Bidang Akuntansi dan Manajemen (JEMA). 2017;**14**:135-143

[67] Radalet S, Sachs JD. The East Asian financial crisis: Diagnosis, remedies. Prospects. Brookings Papers on Economic Activity. 1998;**29**:1-90

[68] Midiwati R, Rusli D. The Influence of Third Party Fund, Financing to Deposit Ratio, Capital Adequancy Ratio, and Non Performing Financing on

Murabaha Financing Studies on Sharia Commercial Banks in Indonesia Period 2015–2019 [Internet]. Indonesia: Sekolah Tinggi Ilmu Ekonomi Indonesia; 2020. Available from: http://repository.stei.ac.id/2063/2/NASKAH%20PUBLIKASI%20INGGRIS_11160000150_RASKIM%20WIDIWATI%20pdf.pdf [Accessed: July 11, 2021]

[69] Claessens S, Kose MA. Financial crises explanations, types, and implications. IMF Working Papers. 2013;**13**:1-65. DOI: 10.5089/9781475561005.001

[70] Amba MS, Almukharreq F. Impact of the financial crisis on profitability of the Islamic banks vs conventional banks —Evidence from GCC. International Journal of Financial Research. 2013;**4**: 83-93. DOI: 10.5430/ijfr.v4n3p83

Chapter 11

Exchange Rate Volatility and Monetary Policy Shocks

Gbalam Peter Eze and Tonprebofa Waikumo Okotori

Abstract

The study investigated the influence of innovations in monetary policy on the rate of exchange volatility in Nigeria. The research adopted vector error correction model as well as impulse response function and forecast error variance decomposition function in the estimation using two models derived in the study. Monthly data between the periods 2009 and 2019 were adopted for the research. Our findings show that in the long run; all the monetary policy variables have a significant long run correlation with volatility in the exchange rate; but that money supply and the rate of exchange seem to have significant short run impact on volatility in the exchange rate, the other variables such as liquidity ratio or monetary policy rate did not show a significant short run relationship with the volatility in the exchange rate. Further findings on the volatility impulse response and the forecast error variance decomposition suggest a significant link between volatility in the exchange rate and money supply though the link was much more pronounced. The use of monthly data shows that the managed exchange rate regime by the CBN seems to have the desired effect in exchange rate volatility and thus having a critical impact on inflationary spikes.

Keywords: exchange rate volatility, monetary policy, central Bank of Nigeria, exchange rate regime, vector error correction model, impulse response function, forecast error variance decomposition

1. Introduction

1.1 Background of study

Exchange rate and price instability seems to have a negative effect on producers economic well-being, on upcoming investors as well as the situation of current consumers alike as it results in unpredictability, which has a negative impact on commitments that are of longer run; that reduces the chances of attaining self-reliant growth in output, income, and employment. The foregoing has led both the monetary and fiscal authority to develop policies or moves that aim at the attainment of the exchange rate and price stability. One of the key goals of the monetary authority in Nigeria (Central Bank of Nigeria (CBN)) is the attainment of price and stability of the rate of exchange. The CBN's policy on the rate of exchange regime over the years can be placed in two categories, (1) The Pre-SAP (1960–1986) period, (2) Post SAP (1986–present). The pre SAP period was characterized by: direct foreign exchange control, in that the authorities simply maintained overvalued exchange rates. These policies led to the fall in the value of the naira as it made imports cheaper. It also led to a weak balance of payments position subsequently. The Post SAP period was characterized by free float exchange rate, which also led to the steep depreciation of the naira.

Emefiele [1] observed that for the Nigeria economy, a depressed GDP growth, which having grown by nearly 7% in previous years culminated in the 2016 recession, rising inflation, did rise to the level of 18.7% by the end of January, 2017 from 9.6% a year earlier, depreciation of the foreign exchange from N155/1 US dollar as at June, 2014 to a peak of N525/1 US dollar in February, 2017. There seems to be a nexus linking shocks from monetary policy to exchange rate volatility for an economy such as Nigeria that is import-dependent [2]. Thus, maintaining an effective and stable exchange rate is a realistic proposition for the Nigerian economy. Exchange rate regimes differ from country to country, and the level of financial development is the basis for whatever policy position a country might adopt. The important attention given to price stability is said to be derived from "new developments in monetary theories and empirical evidence which show that sustainable growth can only be achieved when the price level is stable" [3].

Liberalization of the financial system in Nigeria is still ongoing; hence the anticipated impact of these monetary policy variables in dictating trends in the financial markets such as the foreign exchange market raises a query about their empirically verified effects on the various financial markets. The most pressing issue is the identification of: (a) monetary authority's policy tools and their actual effect on the naira rate of exchange to the US Dollar, (b) the aggregate impact of these tools on the Naira exchange rate, and (c) determining if financial liberalization undertaken in Nigeria has yielded the anticipated results. The main targeted goal this research sought to attain is to ascertain the extent of the volatility of the rate of exchange due to monetary policy shocks. Amato et al. [4] observed that based on "the implications of exchange rates for monetary policy, several questions are particularly relevant these are; what is the appropriate response of volatility in the exchange rate to broad money supply, treasury bills rate, statutory liquidity ratio, exchange rate and the external reserve changes"?

The theoretical postulations of Mundell-Fleming known as the impossible trilemma states that every country has three policy options, and these are: (i) unfettered mobility of capital, (ii) rate of exchange that is fixed, and (iii) ability to embark on monetary policy that can be considered independent. That any country's monetary authority can only apply two of the three policy options simultaneously at any point in time. What is revealed from the Nigerian experience is that in its adopted regime on the rate of exchange, the Central Bank of Nigeria has taken a middle ground approach as regards its regime on the rate of exchange by using a managed float exchange rate regime, thus making the exchange a monetary policy tool. The CBN has also allowed the operation of three different exchange rates in Nigeria. The foregoing was though not factored into the policy prescriptions of Mundell-Fleming.

The rest of the study is subdivided into: 2—review of relevant literature; 3—methodology, 4—data presentation, analysis, and discussion; 5—summary.

2. Review of relevant literature

2.1 Conceptual framework

2.1.1 Exchange rate volatility

The rate of exchange refers to that rate at which the currency of one country is converted to another currency from a different country. There is volatility in the exchange rate when the rate of such exchange rate change happens rather randomly or in rapidity. Ozturk [5] defined exchange rate volatility as being associated with exchange rate movements that are unexpected. Exchange rate volatility has been a serious concern for those in the academia, policymakers, and participants in the financial markets for all economies across board in the world [6]. The volatility of the exchange rate has inflationary tendencies; hence the attempts by the central banks to watch exchange rate volatility.

2.1.2 Monetary policy

Monetary policy is the pathway through which the Central Bank of Nigeria or the monetary authority in any country decides on amount of supply of money for that given country. It has been the "fundamental instrument over the years in attaining macroeconomic stability and as a prerequisite to attaining sustainable output growth" [7, 8]. Mathai [9] saw monetary policy as the regulating amount of the supply of money in a country's economy in order to attain an optimal mix of output and inflation goal realization. Jimoh [10] observed that it is generally believed that an exchange rate is an important variable that has a significant impact on the overall outcome of macroeconomic performance as it concerns internal and external balances. But Pattnaik et al. noted that a specific regime of the rate of exchange cannot be one solution fit it all remedy for the world, noting the real scenario can change at any time. Exchange rates can thus serve as "automatic stabilizers" for the macroeconomy in any nation [11].

2.2 Exchange rate regimes

2.2.1 The free float rate of exchange regime

The rate of exchange regime that is free floating depends on market forces in the determination of the exchange rate. Alade [12] opined that in a rate of exchange regime that is free float, "the monetary authority does not intervene in the foreign exchange market and that monetary policy is therefore independent of the exchange rate regime and can be used to steer the domestic economy". Okoli et al. [13] did observe that the "high level of exchange rate volatility in the world market, particularly the Naira/Dollar exchange rate especially in the recent past is not only alarming but economically threatening".

2.2.2 The fixed rate of exchange regime

In the fixed exchange rate regime, the exchange rate of the local currency is pegged to the amount of another country's currency or a basket of currencies or the Special Drawing Right (SDR). The monetary authority adjusts this peg in the scenario where misalignment becomes a threat to the economy. Fixed exchange rates are to "promote certainty and orderliness in foreign exchange markets and of course in international trade transactions" [13, 14]. Alade [12] opined that the fixed rate of exchange regime can achieve stability and the ability of the local currency to compete when the peg is credible, though noting that "the regime is prone to currency crises if the country is open to international capital market (free capital mobility) because of the limited shock absorptiveness capacity".

2.2.3 Managed float rate of exchange regime

In the managed float exchange rate regime, there is active intervention from the monetary authority in the market that deals on exchange of the domestic currency with foreign currencies, and this is not subject to any preannounced path for the policy as regards the adopted rate of exchange regime. Under the managed float exchange rate regime, the monetary policy is said to be relatively independent. Monetary policy here serves to move the economy in the desired direction; hence exchange rate can be used as an instrument of monetary policy. Alade [12] observed that the limited flexibility of managed float "permits partial absorption of adverse shocks and that it can also maintain stability and competitiveness if the regime is credible, as it is less vulnerable to currency crises". But in practice, "no exchange rate is 'clean or pure float,' that is a situation where the exchange rate is left completely to be determined by the market forces of demand and supply"; yet the existing regime is a managed float, in which a country's monetary authorities get involved the dynamics in country's foreign exchange market in an attempt to accomplish very important economic objectives [15, 16]. According to Heipertz [17], "exchange rate is adjusted by the central bank like the use of the interest rate as an operating instrument."

2.3 Theoretical review

The exchange rate channel is certainly effective in a given economy with a shallow money market, as well as a deep market for foreign. Overall, random changes in the rate of exchange were observed for Nigeria, specifically in all the years for the period 1980–1990 [2].

2.3.1 Purchasing power parity (PPP)

Mordi [18] opined that the purchasing power parity (PPP) presupposes "those exchange rates between two currencies at a given period are equal if the ratio of the level of price in a certain amount of products produced" and flowing in two countries and the rate of exchange among those two countries are equal. Adeoye and Saibu [2] observed that purchasing power parity hypothesis is the most useful reason proffered as regards the stability in the long term as well as persistence of the rate of exchange in bilateral relations and that testing for PPP in the long term; this is useful for a lot of purposes: following many monetary models [19], that this rests on the reliability of the PP theory in the long run, in addition to a lot of models that describe the macroeconomy by adopting the PPP to express the nexus to foreign and local development; mostly when examining market economy such as Nigeria. Adenekan et al. [20] did observe that the "PPP theory was criticized for not considering the impact of international capital movements, and suffers from the choice of an appropriate price index used in price calculations." There is thus the need for theoretical postulations that can be all encompassing in application.

2.3.2 Mundell-Fleming theory

The Mundell–Fleming model is also called the IS-LM-BOP model (or IS-LM-BP) model based on the independent research of Mundell [21] and Fleming [22]. Though the Mundell-Fleming model is an offshoot of the IS-LM model, the original IS-LM model expresses the situation in a closed economy (autarky), this model expresses the situation that exists in an economy that is not closed, but small and open. The impossible trilemma of this theoretical model is the premise for the position that in an economy that is open, a country cannot follow the path of: a fixed rate of exchange, free mobility of capital, and the application of monetary policy that is independent simultaneously. The operation of a managed float was not specifically captured at the beginning of this model, yet managed float is an imperfect free float or fixed exchange rate regime. The model states that two and not three of the trilemma can be operated simultaneously at any point in time.

Aizenman [23] observed that the financial crises of 1990 have "induced emerging markets to converge to the trilemma's middle ground—managed exchange-rate flexibility, restricted financial integration, and an effective but less prominent monetary independence" and that the crisis of flight of capital has led to financial stability becoming an additional goal in the operation of the trilemma's targeted goals. Hence, the present scenario goes beyond the textbook description unveiled by the trilemma. This encapsulates the theoretical foundations of our present study.

2.4 Empirical review

Ndung'u [24] assessed if the rate of exchange of Kenyan currency is influenced by the monetary authority's policy moves and whether the observed impact transient or consistent. The findings of this research reveal that the rate of exchange in nominal terms for the period 1970–1994 was impacted upon by income increase in real terms, the inflation rate, expansion in the supply of money, the circular movements in the volatility in the real rate of exchange, the cointegrating vectors, and the shocks. A similar research by Ubok-Udom [25] did study the nexus linking the total GDP growth rate in annual terms, GDP attributable to the non-oil sector, and the variations in the rate of exchange spanning 1991–1995. The results of this study further indicate that the rates of growth for total GDP and GDP from non-oil sources seem to reduce or rise with drops or spikes in the rate of exchange in nominal terms. Pattnaik et al. disclosed that the study shows that monetary policy has been useful achieving sustained factors in the exchange rate market revealing the pass-through via the exchange rate to the local inflation rate.

Similar studies such as Adebiyi [26] investigated the influence of the monetary authority's involvement in Nigeria's currency exchange market. The research did not focus on the link that connects shocks from monetary authority's policy moves and changes in the rate of exchange but looked at whether these involvements of the local monetary authority in the foreign exchange market are sterilized or not. The research by An and Sun [27] investigated the linkage between monetary policy, the monetary authority's intrusion into the foreign exchange market, and the rate of exchange for Japan in the form of a unifying model. The results from the study firstly lend support to the hypothesis referred to as "leaning-against-the –wind" as well as the hypothesis referred to as "signaling," though the presence of the "signaling" postulation happens to be rather minimal. Another finding is that the impact of intervention is not effective, possibly even a negative effect. Lastly, normal monetary policy seems to exert a major impact on both the rate of exchange and interventions in foreign exchange.

Cagliarini and Mckibbin [28] used the G-Cubed model for analyzing several sectors in an economy for a cross-country data; examining the possible impact of three shocks on US monetary policy, risk premia, and productivity to determine major relative price movement for the period 2002–2008. A very important summary of the study experimental exercise was done by this study, and it shows that monetary authority's policy moves seem to impact prices in relative terms for as much four years due to the fact that a non-permanent in real interest rates varies across sectors. Asad et al. [29] studied the influence of rate of exchange(in real and effective terms) on inflation on the economy of Pakistan by utilizing secondary data on GDP (in real and nominal terms), effective real rate of exchange, prices, and the supply of money that covered 1973–2007. The results from their study show that the exchange rate (in real terms) has a significant influence on the rate of inflation as regards the economy of Pakistan; the nexus between the effective real rate of exchange and inflation was found to be positive and strong.

But Dickson [30] did study to examine the influence of volatility in the real rate of exchange on Nigeria's growth in output by adopting annual data from 1970 to 2009. The results of the study did reveal that the nexus between economic growth and rate of exchange volatility was positive in the short run; but in the long run, the relationship for both variables is negative. Adeoye and Saibu [2] analyzed that monetary policy shocks influence via movements in the policy instruments on volatility in the rate of exchange in Nigeria. Specifically the study focused on the relationship between volatility in the rate of exchange and shocks due to monetary policy in Nigeria. The short-run dynamics reveals that changes in monetary policy instruments correlate to the variations in the rate of exchange via process that is self-correcting without the involvement of the CBN. Furthermore, the findings from the test for causality that link the volatility in the rate of exchange and the monetary authority's policy tools indicate significant nexus between as regards historical values of the rate of exchange and monetary policy variables. It was observed that shifts in past values of policy tools result in changes in exchange rate volatility.

Nwachukwu et al. [31] modeled the long-run nexus that linked "the Bureau De Change rate of exchange and Nigeria's external reserves in a threshold vector error correction model (TVECM)" econometric methodology by utilizing daily data that spanned from 2014 to 2015. The study concluded that "the adjustment mechanism between the two variables flow from external reserves to BDC exchange rate." Ayomitunde et al. [32] examined the nexus that exists linking monetary authority's policy instruments and the rate of exchange rate Nigeria. The study adopted the Autoregressive Distributed Lag (ARDL) model to achieve the focused goal of the study. The results show that there was a negative nexus linking the Treasury bill rate, cash reserve requirement to the rate of exchange. On the other hand, the policy rate and money supply (broad) have a nexus with the exchange rate that is positive for Nigeria.

Miyajima [33] did carry out a study that was premised on an answer to the question "does the South African rand's relatively large volatility affect inflation?" The derived results indicate that when the volatility in the rate of exchange spikes, it leads to an increase in core inflation, though that impact is limited for the economy of the country under study.

The Nigeria experience shows that some research studies have been carried out on the nexus linking volatility in the rate of exchange and the actions of the Central Bank's stabilizing actions. The study is an attempt to determine the interventions in the markets for the buying and selling of foreign currency by the monetary authority; whether such intervention is sterilized or not sterilized has had the moderating impact on exchange rate volatility. The Nigerian experience from a few studies in the area of the interrelationship between exchange rate volatility and macroeconomic policies of the CBN have been carried out; yet the use of monthly data was not common in all these studies. This study did apply monthly data to reveal that nexus in a more timely manner.

3. Methodology

3.1 Study design

The study utilizes an ex-post facto research design, the events have already taken place before the analysis, and hence there is no way the data can be manipulated. The "ex post facto design in its application is causal comparative and used when the researcher aims to establish relationship between the independent and dependent variables with a view to establishing the causal link between them" [34, 35].

3.2 Population of study

The dataset is monthly time series data for Nigeria on the rate of exchange, money supply (M2), policy rate (nominal anchor), reserve requirement, treasury bills rate, and external reserve. These form the population of study.

3.3 Sample

The study sample is secondary data, retrieved after the occurrence of the event; hence the ability of the researcher to influence it is not possible. The sample period covered 2009–2019. The sample period covered over 48,180 days.

3.4 Sources of data

The data was extracted from the CBN's statistical bulletin, CBN website, World Bank, and IMF databases.

3.5 Model development and variable description

The research employs vector error correction (VEC) methodology to study the magnitude of the effect and the response to the impulse function of the rate of exchange concerning stock prices. This is done after determining the variables are cointegrated. Vector error correction model (VECM) is used to capture the evolution and the interdependencies between multiple time series, generalizing the univariate AR models. There is a symmetrical treatment of all the variables adopted for the VECM in the study via the addition in every one of the given equation in determining process on the bases of its lags as well as the lags of all other variables.

3.6 Model specification

Chen [36] did note that volatility in the rate of exchange volatility might be either for the description of a regime that is tranquil regime, and this rests how descriptive the adopted policy tools are (e.g. interest rate) utilized as a tool of stabilization instruments as follows:

Model 1

$$\mathrm{Erv} = f\ (\mathrm{MPR}, \mathrm{M2})$$
$$\mathrm{Erv} = \mathrm{MPR} + \mathrm{M2} + \mathrm{u_t} \tag{1}$$

Model 2

$$\mathrm{Erv} = f\ (\mathrm{TBR}, \mathrm{LQR}, \mathrm{EXR})$$
$$\mathrm{Erv} = \mathrm{TBR_t} + \mathrm{LQR} + \mathrm{EXR} + \mathrm{u_t} \tag{2}$$

3.7 Method of data analysis

Experience has shown in Nigeria that the monetary authority uses either the quantitative or qualitative measures of stabilizing the macroeconomic activities. But most often, money supply, interest rate, and inflation are the major quantitative measures employed by the Central Bank in maintaining a close watch of monetary balances in Nigeria. However, the exchange rate deepening experienced in the past prompted the monetary authority to strengthen the stock of money reserves to decelerate exchange rate volatility and watch the overall economy performance closely in terms of productivity. Based on the above argument, the empirical model for analyzing the effect of monetary policy shocks on generated exchange rate volatility series in Nigeria by considering the most employed monetary tools in formulating the error correction model is as follows:

Model 1

$$Erv_t = d_0 + d_1MPR_t + d_2M2_t + +u_t \tag{3}$$

Model 2

$$Erv_t = d_0 + d_1TBR_t + d_2LQR_t + d_3EXR + u_t \tag{4}$$

Here erv represents volatility in the rate of exchange, which is generated from the nominal rate of exchange of Nigeria's domestic currency the naira as measured in value against the US dollar by adopting the approach trough the standard deviation; mpr is the proxy for the nominal rate of interest, the monetary policy rate, which is the rate at which the Central Bank lends to the bank; ms is the broad money supply; tbr is the treasury bills rate; rsq is the reserve requirement; lqr is the liquidity ratio; and u represents the error term, and it describes the Markov models depiction transition from one regime to another. The dynamics linking monetary policy to volatility in the rate exchange for the Nigeria economy in the short run via the error correction mechanism model is investigated.

Since estimated regression results do not provide an answer to which variables cause changes in the other while ignoring the impact interaction. In terms of data requirement and sources, the paper uses a time-series data on the nominal exchange rate of naira vis-a-vis US dollar, minimum policy rate as a proxy for the interest rate, money supply, inflation rate, reserve requirement.

4. Presentation of data/results

4.1 Empirical analysis

This section elaborates on the empirical results and the analysis.

4.1.1 Unit root tests

The test for unit root reveals information on the stationarity properties of variables. The variables were tested at levels and their first differences. The results are given in **Tables 1** and **2** respectively.

The unit root test result for the variables at level are shown in **Table 1**, the ADF test statistic for exchange rate ($t = 0.29$, $p > 0.05$) is insignificant at the 5% level. From the foregoing, a unit root at the 5% significance level for the null hypothesis cannot be rejected. The rate of exchange is thus not stationary at level. Similarly, liquidity ratio ($t = -1.79$, $p > 0.05$), monetary policy rate ($t = -1.55$, $p > 0.05$), money supply ($t = -2.46$, $p > 0.05$), and Treasury bill rate ($t = -2.41$, $p > 0.05$) are nonstationary at levels. These variables were all tested determine their stationarity at their first differences.

Variable	ADF statistic	5% Critical value	Remarks
EXR	0.29	−2.89	Nonstationary
LQR	−1.79	−2.89	Nonstationary
MPR	−1.55	−2.89	Nonstationary
MS	−2.46	−2.89	Nonstationary
TBR	−2.41	−2.89	Nonstationary

Source: Results Extract from Eviews 11.0.

Table 1.
(augmented dickey-fuller unit root tests at levels (augmented Dickey-Fuller regression has an intercept as an addition, but not a linear trend).

Variable	ADF statistic	5% Critical value	Order of integration	Remarks
D (EXR)	−17.18	−2.89	I(1)	Stationary
D (LQR)	−11.15	−2.89	I(1)	Stationary
D (MPR)	−11.04	−2.89	I(1)	Stationary
D (MS)	−3.89	−2.89	I(1)	Stationary
D (TBR)	−16.64	−2.89	I(1)	Stationary

Note: Note: D denotes first difference of the variable.
Source: Results Extract from E views 11.0.

Table 2.
(augmented dickey-fuller unit root tests at first differences (augmented Dickey-Fuller regressions include an intercept but not a linear trend).

The results for the unit root test at first difference are given in **Table 2**; the findings indicate that at the 5% level of significance both the independent and dependent variables are all significant at first difference. This is because the ADF test statistics are all greater than the 5% critical values in absolute terms. Thus, we fail to accept the null hypothesis of a unit root at the 5% level.

4.1.2 Cointegration tests

Following the establishment of the time-series data's properties, the study carried out the multivariate Johansen cointegration test. The test was conducted for the two sets of the VEC models. The findings from the tests for exchange rate volatility, monetary policy rate, and money supply are reported in **Tables 3** and **4**, and those of exchange rate volatility, treasury bill rate, liquidity ratio, and exchange rate are presented in **Tables 5** and **6**.

As shown in **Tables 3** and **4**, the cointegration test based on the trace and maximum eigen statistics indicate that there is one cointegrating equation among exchange rate volatility, monetary policy rate, and money supply within significance level of the 5% level. The findings indicate that there exists a long run relationship among: exchange rate volatility, monetary policy rate, and money supply. Similarly, from **Tables 5** and **6**, the cointegration test based on the trace and maximum eigen statistics indicates that there is one cointegrating equation among exchange rate volatility, Treasury bill rate, liquidity ratio, and exchange rate at the 5% level. This shows that exchange rate volatility, Treasury bill rate, liquidity ratio, and exchange rate have a common long-run trend.

Hypothesized No. of CE(s)	Eigenvalue	T race statistic	0.05 critical value	Probability**
None*	0.186630	33.73461	29.79707	0.0167
At most 1	0.080373	9.979107	15.49471	0.2823
At most 2	0.002983	0.343533	3.841465	0.5578

Trace test indicates 1 cointegrating eqn(s) at the 0.05 level.
**denotes rejection of the hypothesis at the 0.05 level.*
***MacKinnon-Haug-Michelis [37] p-values.*
Source: Results Extract from Eviews 11.0.

Table 3.
Unrestricted cointegration rank test (trace).

Hypothesized No. of CE(s)	Eigenvalue	Max-Eigen statistic	0.05 critical value	Probability**
None*	0.186630	23.75550	21.13162	0.0209
At most 1	0.080373	9.635573	14.26460	0.2370
At most 2	0.002983	0.343533	3.841465	0.5578

Max-Eigenvalue test indicates 1 cointegrating eqn(s) at the 0.05 level.
**denotes rejection of the hypothesis at the 0.05 level.*
***MacKinnon-Haug-Michelis [37] p-values.*
Source: Results Extract from Eviews11.0.

Table 4.
Unrestricted cointegration rank test (maximum eigenvalue).

Hypothesized No. of CE(s)	Eigenvalue	T race statistic	0.05 critical value	Probability**
None*	0.233281	56.64510	47.85613	0.0060
At most 1	0.151818	26.09708	29.79707	0.1258
At most 2	0.046361	7.161141	15.49471	0.5590
At most 3	0.014692	1.702127	3.841465	0.1920

Trace test indicates 1 cointegrating eqn(s) at the 0.05 level.
**denotes rejection of the hypothesis at the 0.05 level.*
***MacKinnon-Haug-Michelis [37] p-values.*
Source: Results Extract from Eviews11.0.

Table 5.
Unrestricted cointegration rank test (trace).

Hypothesized No. of CE(s)	Eigenvalue	Max-Eigen statistic	0.05 critical value	Probability**
None*	0.233281	30.54803	27.58434	0.0202
At most 1	0.151818	18.93593	21.13162	0.0987
At most 2	0.046361	5.459013	14.26460	0.6831
At most 3	0.014692	1.702127	3.841465	0.1920

Max-Eigenvalue test indicates 1 cointegrating eqn(s) at the 0.05 level.
**denotes rejection of the hypothesis at the 0.05 level.*
***MacKinnon-Haug-Michelis [37] p-values.*
Source: Results Extract from Eviews11.0.

Table 6.
Unrestricted cointegration rank test (maximum eigenvalue).

4.1.3 Analysis of the estimated vector error correction models

The results of the first estimated VEC model are reported in **Table** 7.

The coefficient of determination (R^2) for exchange rate volatility short-run equation is approximately 0.26. This indicates that the regressors in the equation account for about 26% of the systematic variations in volatility of the rate of exchange on the short-run basis. Similarly, the adjusted R^2 shows all the independent variables in the first model account for about 21% of the systematic variations in exchange rate volatility in the short run. Thus, the overall goodness of fit of the exchange rate volatility short-run model is low.

From the exchange rate volatility short-run equation, its one-month previous volatility rate has a negative significant effect on its current rate, but its two-month previous volatility rate has an insignificant impact on its current rate in the short term. The two previous values of monetary policy rate have no significant effects on exchange rate volatility in the short run. However, the one-month lagged value of money supply has a negative significant effect on exchange rate volatility in the short run. The foregoing leads to a rejection of the acceptance of the null hypothesis that the monetary policy rate has no significant effect on the volatility in the exchange rate in Nigeria, whereas the null hypothesis on money supply not having a significant nexus with the volatility in the exchange rate is rejected as money supply has a significant impact on exchange rate volatility in Nigeria.

The results of the second estimated VEC model are reported in **Table 8**.

The coefficient of determination (R^2) for exchange rate volatility short-run equation is approximately 0.26. This indicates that the regressors in the equation account for about 26% of the systematic variations in exchange rate volatility in the short term. Similarly, the adjusted R^2accounts for about 21% systematic variations in exchange rate volatility in the short run. Thus, the overall goodness of fit of the exchange rate volatility short-run model is low.

From the exchange rate volatility short-run equation, its one-month previous volatility rate has a negative significant effect on its current rate, but its two-month previous volatility rate has an insignificant impact on its current rate in the short term. The two previous values of monetary policy rate have no significant effects on exchange rate volatility in the short run. However, the one-month lagged value of money supply has a negative significant effect on exchange rate volatility in the short run.

The results of the second estimated VEC model are reported in **Table 9**.

The coefficient of determination (R^2) for exchange rate volatility short-run equation is approximately 0.92. This indicates that the regressors in the equation account for about 92% of the systematic variations in exchange rate volatility in the short term. Similarly, the adjusted R^2 indicates that all the independent variables in the second model account for about 91% systematic variations in exchange rate volatility in the short run. The F-statistic (F = 139.33, p < 0.05) indicates the overall exchange rate volatility short-run model is significant at the 5% level.

From the exchange rate volatility short-run equation, its one-month previous volatility rate has a negative significant effect on its current rate while its two-month previous volatility rate has a positive significant impact on its current rate in the short term.

The two previous values of Treasury bill rate have no significant effect on exchange rate volatility in the short run. Also, the two lagged values of liquidity ratio have no significant effect on exchange rate volatility in the short run. However, the two lagged values of exchange rate have positive significant effects on

Cointegrating Eq:	CointEq1		
EXRV(−1)	1.000000		
MPR(−1)	−7817.859		
	(1584.61)		
	[−4.93362]		
MS(−1)	−1723.057		
	(784.802)		
	[−2.19553]		
C	119340.6		
Error Correction:	D(EXRV)	D(MPR)	D(MS)
CointEq1	−0.058246	2.23E-05	2.25E-06
	(0.02723)	(7.7E-06)	(3.3E-06)
	[−2.13889]	[2.87772]	[0.68702]
D(EXRV(−1))	−0.407297	−1.31E-05	9.58E-06
	(0.09440)	(2.7E-05)	(1.1E-05)
	[−4.31465]	[−0.48875]	[0.84535]
D(EXRV(−2))	0.018987	−4.17E-07	1.98E-05
	(0.09219)	(2.6E-05)	(1.1E-05)
	[0.20596]	[−0.01593]	[1.78598]
D(MPR(−1))	−271.3121	−0.145712	−0.039322
	(323.488)	(0.09193)	(0.03883)
	[−0.83871]	[−1.58495]	[−1.01274]
D(MPR(−2))	−228.4871	−0.225357	−0.013785
	(317.403)	(0.09021)	(0.03810)
	[−0.71986]	[−2.49827]	[−0.36183]
D(MS(−1))	−1777.983	0.497631	0.398358
	(762.661)	(0.21675)	(0.09154)
	[−2.33129]	[2.29592]	[4.35169]
D(MS(−2))	59.68383	−0.018873	0.321481
	(827.667)	(0.23522)	(0.09934)
	[0.07211]	[−0.08023]	[3.23605]
C	212.6540	0.109331	−0.051629
	(402.479)	(0.11438)	(0.04831)
	[0.52836]	[0.95583]	[−1.06872]
R-squared	0.260032	0.203020	0.371578
Adj. R-squared	0.212511	0.151838	0.331220
F-statistic	5.471951	3.966619	9.207182

Source: Extract from Eviews 11.0.
Notes: Standard errors are in ()and t-statistics are in [].

Table 7.
Estimated VEC model 1.

Cointegrating Eq:	**CointEq1**		
EXRV(−1)	1.000000		
MPR(−1)	−7817.859		
	(1584.61)		
	[−4.93362]		
MS(−1)	−1723.057		
	(784.802)		
	[−2.19553]		
C	119340.6		
Error Correction:	D(EXRV)	D(MPR)	D(MS)
CointEq1	−0.058246	2.23E-05	2.25E-06
	(0.02723)	(7.7E-06)	(3.3E-06)
	[−2.13889]	[2.87772]	[0.68702]
D(EXRV(−1))	−0.407297	−1.31E-05	9.58E-06
	(0.09440)	(2.7E-05)	(1.1E-05)
	[−4.31465]	[−0.48875]	[0.84535]
D(EXRV(−2))	0.018987	−4.17E-07	1.98E-05
	(0.09219)	(2.6E-05)	(1.1E-05)
	[0.20596]	[−0.01593]	[1.78598]
D(MPR(−1))	−271.3121	−0.145712	−0.039322
	(323.488)	(0.09193)	(0.03883)
	[−0.83871]	[−1.58495]	[−1.01274]
D(MPR(−2))	−228.4871	−0.225357	−0.013785
	(317.403)	(0.09021)	(0.03810)
	[−0.71986]	[−2.49827]	[−0.36183]
D(MS(−1))	−1777.983	0.497631	0.398358
	(762.661)	(0.21675)	(0.09154)
	[−2.33129]	[2.29592]	[4.35169]
D(MS(−2))	59.68383	−0.018873	0.321481
	(827.667)	(0.23522)	(0.09934)
	[0.07211]	[−0.08023]	[3.23605]
C	212.6540	0.109331	−0.051629
	(402.479)	(0.11438)	(0.04831)
	[0.52836]	[0.95583]	[−1.06872]
R-squared	0.260032	0.203020	0.371578
Adj. R-squared	0.212511	0.151838	0.331220
F-statistic	5.471951	3.966619	9.207182

Source: Extract from Eviews 11.0.

Table 8.
Estimated VEC model 2.

Cointegrating Eq:	**CointEq1**			
EXRV(−1)	1.000000			
TBR(−1)	1549.282			
	(1397.79)			
	[1.10838]			
LQR(−1)	−2231.369			
	(505.274)			
	[−4.41616]			
EXR(−1)	−213.4598			
	(86.0715)			
	[−2.48003]			
C	109208.8			
Error Correction:	**D(EXRV)**	**D(TBR)**	**D(LQR)**	**D(EXR)**
CointEq1	−0.010650	1.15E-05	4.67E-05	2.24E-05
	(0.00673)	(4.6E-06)	(1.7E-05)	(6.2E-05)
	[−1.58296]	[2.51205]	[2.70826]	[0.36361]
D(EXRV(−1))	−0.385805	−4.52E-05	0.000422	−0.002019
	(0.08789)	(6.0E-05)	(0.00023)	(0.00080)
	[−4.38984]	[−0.75693]	[1.87360]	[−2.51091]
D(EXRV(−2))	0.059607	1.05E-06	−7.54E-08	−0.000309
	(0.03030)	(2.1E-05)	(7.8E-05)	(0.00028)
	[1.96705]	[0.05102]	[−0.00097]	[−1.11294]
D(TBR(−1))	38.35665	−0.561259	−0.380656	−0.203570
	(147.432)	(0.10007)	(0.37770)	(1.34903)
	[0.26017]	[−5.60869]	[−1.00783]	[−0.15090]
D(TBR(−2))	40.87102	−0.210251	−0.382622	−0.232701
	(146.478)	(0.09942)	(0.37525)	(1.34030)
	[0.27903]	[−2.11474]	[−1.01963]	[−0.17362]
D(LQR(−1))	−20.11324	−0.021162	0.021844	0.056033
	(37.9020)	(0.02573)	(0.09710)	(0.34681)
	[−0.53066]	[−0.82260]	[0.22497]	[0.16157]
D(LQR(−2))	−22.85686	0.006525	0.031133	0.104535
	(37.2871)	(0.02531)	(0.09552)	(0.34118)
	[−0.61300]	[0.25780]	[0.32592]	[0.30639]
D(EXR(−1))	319.5856	0.001760	0.019157	−0.424650
	(10.4040)	(0.00706)	(0.02665)	(0.09520)
	[30.7176]	[0.24918]	[0.71874]	[−4.46070]
D(EXR(−2))	132.7066	0.014933	−0.149753	0.638002
	(29.8317)	(0.02025)	(0.07642)	(0.27296)
	[4.44852]	[0.73749]	[−1.95949]	[2.33731]
C	−401.4474	0.206492	0.398258	2.063144

Cointegrating Eq:	CointEq1			
	(138.532)	(0.09403)	(0.35490)	(1.26759)
	[−2.89787]	[2.19605]	[1.12217]	[1.62761]
R-squared	0.921381	0.239291	0.097537	0.242732
Adj. R-squared	0.914768	0.175306	0.021629	0.179037
F-statistic	139.3325	3.739801	1.284933	3.810822

Source: Extract from Eviews 11.0.
Notes: Standard errors are in ()and t-statistics are in [].

Table 9.
Estimated VEC model 2.

exchange rate volatility in the short run. The results lead to the acceptance of null hypothesis that the treasury bills rate and the liquidity ratio have no significant nexus with the volatility in the exchange rate in the, but the impact of exchange rate on exchange rate volatility is significant in the short run, thus rejection of the null hypothesis concerning this nexus.

4.1.4 Impulse response functions

The results of the Impulse Response Functions (IRFs) of the first VEC model in graphical form are reported in the **Figure 1**.

The impulse response function of exchange rate volatility in the VEC model to a shock in itself shows that exchange rate volatility reacted positively to its innovations all through the five months of forecast. Similarly, it responded positively to innovations in monetary policy rate throughout the five months of forecast. However, exchange rate volatility responded negatively to a shock in money supply all through the five months of forecast.

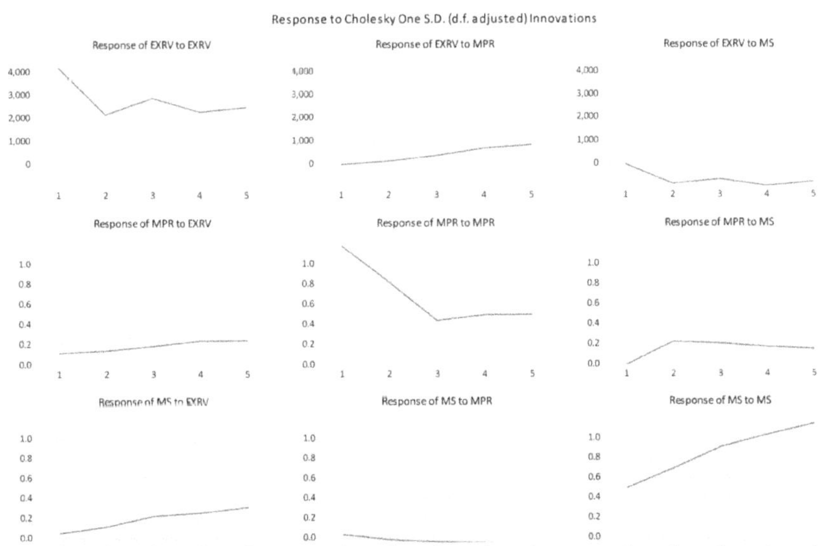

Figure 1.
Impulse response functions. Source: Results extract from E-views 11.0

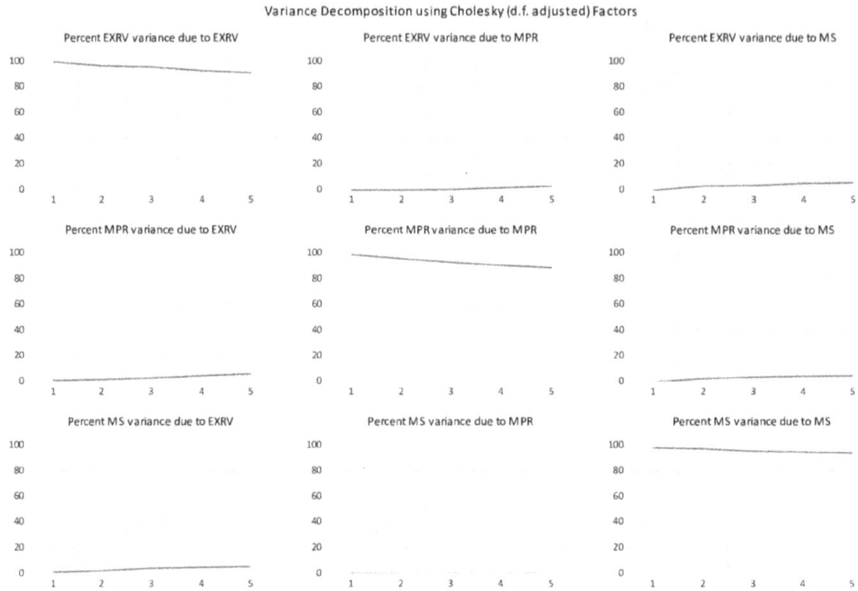

Figure 2.
Forecast error decomposition functions. Source: Results extract from E-views 11.0.

4.1.5 Forecast error variance decomposition functions

The estimation of a VAR model firstly requires the explicit choice of lag length in the equations of the model. In this study, graphs of the forecast error variance decomposition functions are presented in **Figure 2**.

As shown in **Figure 2**, it can be observed from the variance decomposition of exchange rate volatility that own shocks contributed most [100%] to its variations in the first month of forecast but declined marginally to 91% in the fifth month of forecast. The proportions of variations in exchange rate volatility, due to shocks in monetary policy rate and money supply, are minimal throughout the five months of forecast. The two variables accounted for less than 6% in the entire periods of forecast. Hence, the variance decomposition of exchange rate volatility shows that own shocks predominantly determined variations in its variations throughout the months of forecast. Monetary policy rate and money supply accounted for less than an average of 6% variations in exchange rate volatility all through the five months of forecast. The proportions of variations in exchange rate volatility due to money supply shocks are marginally higher than those of monetary policy rate during the periods.

4.1.6 Impulse response functions

The results of the Impulse Response Functions (IRFs) of the second VEC model in graphical form are reported in the **Figure 3**.

The impulse response function of exchange rate volatility in the VEC model to a shock in itself shows that exchange rate volatility reacted positively to its innovations all through the five months of forecast. However, it responded negatively to innovations in treasury bill rate throughout the 5 months of forecast. With respect to a shock in liquidity ratio, exchange rate volatility responded positively all through the 5 months of forecast. Similarly, exchange rate volatility responded positively to shocks in exchange rate within the 5 months of forecast.

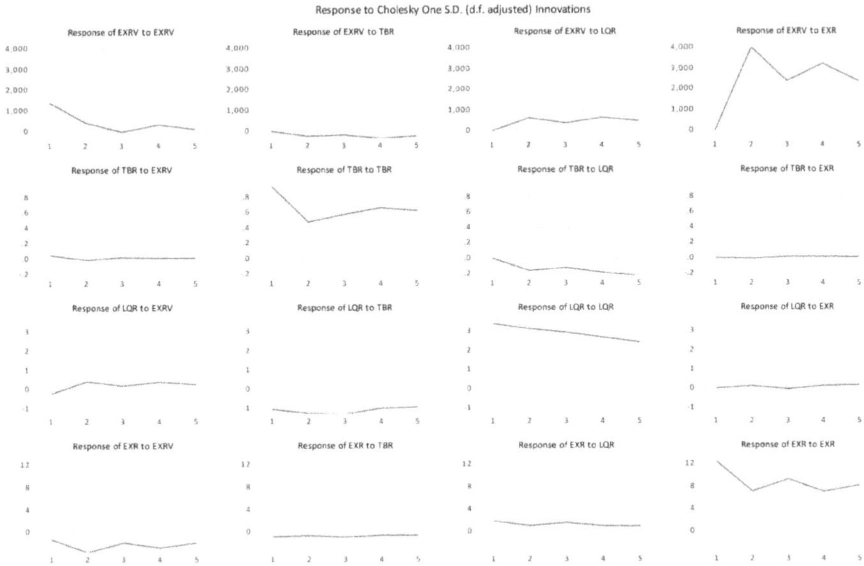

Figure 3.
Impulse response functions. Source: Results extract from E-views 11.0.

4.1.7 Forecast error variance decomposition functions

The graphs of the forecast error variance decomposition functions are presented in **Figure 4**.

As shown in **Figure 4**, it can be observed from the variance decomposition of exchange rate volatility that own shocks contributed most [100%] to its variations in the first month of forecast but declined drastically in the other months. The proportions of variations in exchange rate volatility, due to shocks in treasury bill

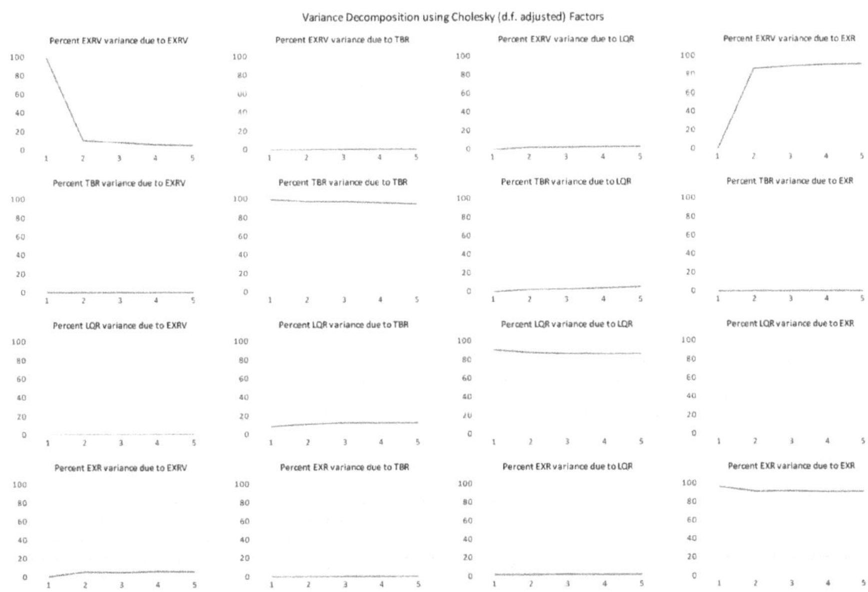

Figure 4.
Forecast error decomposition functions. Source: Results extract from E-views 11.0.

rate and liquidity ratio, are minimal throughout the 5 months of forecast. As revealed in the top panel of **Figure 4**, the variance decomposition function for exchange rate volatility due to own shock (top left corner) is the transpose of that due to exchange rate shock (top right corner). Thus, the percent exchange rate volatility variance due to a shock in exchange rate is minimum [0%] in the first month of forecast. However, in all other months of forecast, it rose drastically to an average of 90% ranging between 86% and 91%. To this end, the variance decomposition of exchange rate volatility shows that own shocks predominantly determined variations in the first month of forecast while exchange rate mainly accounted for volatility in exchange rate in the other periods. Treasury bill rate and liquidity ratio accounted for less than an average of 3% all through the five months of forecast.

5. Summary

The first model shows that the monetary policy rate did not have a significant relationship with volatility in the exchange rate not even with a two-month lagged period, but the money supply had a negative and significant short run nexus with the volatility in the exchange rate. Though, the monetary policy rate was not significant; yet the impulse response functions exchange rate volatility responded negatively to innovation in the MPR from what is revealed by **Figure 1**. The forecast error decomposition reveals that own shocks account for 100% of variation in the first month falling to only 91% in the fifth month; there were minimal variations for monetary policy rate and money supply for five months. The two variations account for less than 6% in the entire forecast period. Though, MS was marginally higher than MPR.

In the second model, the Treasury bill rate's two lagged values were not significant in the short run. The liquidity ratio's two lagged values of the liquidity ratio nexus with the volatility of the exchange rate were not significant in the short run. Exchange rate volatility responded negatively to innovations in Treasury bill rate throughout the 5 months of forecast. But a shock to liquidity ratio and exchange rate volatility responded positively all through the five months of forecasting exchange rate volatility and responded positively to shocks in exchange rate within the months of the forecast as shown in **Figure 3**. Shocks predominately determine variations in its variations, in the first month of forecast, while exchange rate and liquidity ratio accounted for less than average of 3% all through the five months of forecast as in **Figure 4**.

6. Conclusion

In the long run, monetary policy instruments tend to have significant long run nexus with the volatility in the exchange rate; yet looking at the critical short-run dynamics, we find that only the exchange rate and money supply that have significant short-run impact on volatility in the exchange rate. The nexus for money supply is negative as in a priori expectation; yet exchange rate had a negative but significant impact on the volatility in the exchange rate.

The study seems to justify the CBN's managed float exchange rate regime a well as reliance on monetary targeting as this tends to stabilize the volatility in the exchange rate, due to its inflationary impact (volatility in the exchange rate). The Mundell-Fleming trilemma never envisaged the existence of managed float exchange rate regime, and this has produced and unexpected reality as it exists in Nigeria. The impact on deposit money banks as a result of an unmitigated fall in the rate of exchange and the attendant inflationary spiral is something that should be of serious concern to the CBN and other regulatory institution. Inflation and exchange depreciation will impact negatively on the assets of DMBs and the ability of stable and useful global players; hence the ability of the CBN's managed float exchange rate regime to mitigate such volatility happens to be a great relief.

6.1 Recommendation

The fact that money supply and the exchange rate are dominant sources that introduce volatility in the exchange rate makes these instruments very important to Nigeria's monetary authority. The CBN should focus on this important nexus as the current experience of dwindling revenues from crude oil exports diminishes the possibility of other instruments of stability geared toward curtail instability that flows from instability due to exchange rate volatility.

Classification

JEL: D53, E44, E52, E58, G15

Author details

Gbalam Peter Eze[1] and Tonprebofa Waikumo Okotori[2]*

1 Department of Banking and Finance, Niger Delta University, Wilberforce Island, Bayelsa State, Nigeria

2 Faculty of Management Sciences, Department of Banking and Finance, Niger Delta University, Wilberforce Island, Bayelsa State, Nigeria

*Address all correspondence to: tonprebofa@gmail.com

References

[1] Emefiele GO. Address at the 2018 Annual Bankers' Dinner Lagos, 30 November 2018. Nigeria: Central Bank of Nigeria, Abuja; 2018. Available from: https://www.cbn.gov.ng/OUT/SPEECHES/2018/DINNER.PDF

[2] Adeoye BW, Saibu OM. Monetary policy shocks and exchange rate volatility in Nigeria. Asian Economic and Financial Review. 2014;**4**(4): 544-562

[3] Nnanna OJ. Monetary Policy and Exchange Rate Stability in Nigeria, Nigerian Economic Society. In: Proceedings of a One-day Seminar on Monetary Policy and Exchange rate Stability. Federal Palace Hotel, Lagos. 2002

[4] Amato J, Filardo A, Galati G, Peter GV, Zhu F. Research on exchange rates and monetary policy: an overview? Papers No 178). Basel, Switzerland. 2005. Retrieved from: http://jamesgoulding.com/Research_II/Federal%20Reserve,%20The/Fed%20(CBs%20and%20Exchange%20Rates)

[5] Ozturk I. Exchange rate volatility and trade: A literature survey. International Journal of Applied Econometrics and Quantitative Studies. 2006;**3**(1):85-102

[6] Rigobon R. Contagion, spillover and interdependence (European Central Bank Working Paper Series No.1975). 2016. Retrieved from: https://RePEc:ecb:ecbwps:20161975

[7] Okotori TW. Effect of monetary policy on inflation in Nigeria 2009–2014 [Masters' thesis]. Wilberforce Island Bayelsa, Nigeria: Niger Delta University; 2017

[8] Okotori TW. The Dynamics of monetary policy and inflation in Nigeria. IOSR Journal of Economics and Finance (IOSR-JEF). 2019;**10**(2):37-49

[9] Mathai K. Monetary policy: Stabilizing Prices and Output [Online]. Washington DC: International Monetary Fund; 2012. Available from: http://www.imf.org/external//monpol.htm

[10] Jimoh A. Exchange rate policy and economic management: A Theoretical nexus. Economic and Financial Review. 2014;**52**(4):13-28

[11] Gang Y. Monetary Policy Retrospective and Outlook. Vol. 3. China Finance; 2018

[12] Alade SO. Speech at the proceedings of exchange rate policy and economic management in Nigeria-Is there a need for CBN Executive Staff at Sheraton Hotel, April 27-30, 2015, Abuja. CBN Economic Review. 2015;**52**(4):9-12

[13] Okoli TT, Mbah SA, Agu OC. Exchange rate volatility and inflation: The Nigerian experience. Journal of Economics and Sustainable Development. 2016;**7**(10):6-15

[14] Obadan MI. Impact of external sector policies on Nigeria's economic development. Central Bank of Nigeria Economic Review. 1996;**34**(4):928-961

[15] Mordi NO. Challenges of exchange rate volatility in economic management in Nigeria. Central Bank of Nigeria Bullion. 2006;**30**(3):17-25

[16] Onuoha IP. Impact of exchange rate variation and inflation on the economic growth of Nigeria: An empirical approach. Research Journal of Finance. 2014;**5**:166-176

[17] Heipertz J, Mihov I, Santacreo AM. The exchange rate as an instrument of monetary policy. Federal Reserve of Paper 2017-028A. St Louis, USA; 2017

[18] Mordi CNO. Exchange rate and inflation: Is there a link? Economic and Financial Review. 2014;**52**(4):105-124

[19] Dornbusch R. Multiple exchange rates for commercial transactions. In: Edwards S, Ahamed L, editors. Economic Exchange Rate Changes in Developing Countries. Chicago: The University of Chicago Press, University of Chicago; 1986

[20] Adenekan AT, Sanni GK, Itodo AI. Investigating the impact of exchange rate volatility on naira exchange rate in Nigeria. Central Bank of Nigeria Economic and Financial Review. 2019; **57**(3):17-39

[21] Mundell RA. Capital mobility and stabilization policy under fixed and flexible rates. Canadian Journal of Economics and Political Science, XXIX. 1963;**4**:475-485

[22] Fleming M. Domestic financial policy under fixed and under floating exchange Rates. IMF Staff Papers. 1962; **9**:369-379

[23] Aizenman J. A modern reincarnation of Mundell-Fleming's trilemma. Economic Modelling. 2019;**81** (C):444-454

[24] Ndung'u NS. Monetary and exchange rate policy in Kenya. (AERC Working Paper No. 84). 1999. Available from: http://invenio.unidep.org/invenio//record/17200/files/ndungu.pdf .Nairobi:Kenya

[25] Ubok-Udom EU. Currency depreciation and domestic output growth in Nigeria: 1971-1995. The Nigerian Journal of Economics and Social studies. 1999;**41**(1): 31-44

[26] Adebiyi MA. An Evaluation of foreign exchange intervention and monetary aggregates in Nigeria (1986-2003). RePEcArchive. 2007. Retrieved from: https://mpra.ub.uni-muenchen.de/3817/1/MPRA_paper_3817.pdf. Munich-Germany

[27] An L, Sun W. Monetary policy, foreign exchange intervention, and the exchange rate: The case of Japan. International Research Journal of Finance and Economics. 2008;**15**: 271-283

[28] Cagliarini A, Mckibbin W. Global relative price shocks: The role of macroeconomic policies. RBA Research. 2009;**25**(4):581-607

[29] Asad I, Ahmad N, Hussain Z. Impact of real effective exchange rate on inflation in Pakistan. Asian Economic and Financial Review. 2012;**2**(8): 983-990

[30] Dickson OO. Exchange rate volatility and economic growth in Nigeria. Mediterranean Journal of Social Sciences. 2012;**3**(3):399-407

[31] Nwachukwu NE, Ali AI, Abdulahi IS, Shettima MA, Zirra SS, Falade BS, et al. Exchange rate and external reserves in Nigeria: A threshold cointegration analysis. CBN Journal of Applied Statistics. 2016;**7**(1b):233-254

[32] Ayomitunde AT, Akinwuyi AS, Omotayo OH, Abayomi OM. Impact of monetary policy on exchange rate test and ARDL approach. Acta Universitatis Danubius. 2019;**15**(4):234-243

[33] Miyajima K. Exchange rate volatility and pass-through to inflation in South Africa. IMF Working Paper, WP/19/277. Washington DC: International Monetary Fund; 2019. Available from: https:///C:/Users/USER1/Downloads/wpiea2019277-print-pdf%20(1).pdf

[34] Kerlinger FN. Foundations of Behavioural Research Technique in Business and Economics. New York: Holt, Rinehart; 1979

[35] Onwumere JUJ, Imo GI, Ugwuanya UB. 2012. Does Open Market Operations as Monetary Policy Tool Have Impact on Price Stability in Nigeria, Available

from: http://www.iiste.org/journals/index.php/RJFA/dowload/3359/3387

[36] Chen SS. Revisiting the interest rate-exchange rate nexus: A markov switching approach. 2004. Retrieved from: http://homepage.ntu.edu.tw/~sschen/profile/JDE_Chen_revised_f.pdf

[37] Mackinnon J, Haug A, Michelis L. Numerical distribution functions of likelihood ratio tests for cointegration. Econometrics. 1999;**14**(5):563-577

Chapter 12

Exchange Rate Volatility and Macroeconomic Performance in Nigeria

Kehinde Mary Bello, David Oluseun Olayungbo and Benjamin Ayodele Folorunso

Abstract

The study examined the asymmetric relationship between exchange rate volatility and macroeconomic performance in Nigeria covering the period between 1986Q1 and 2019Q4. The Non-linear Generalised Autoregressive Distributive Conditional Heteroscedasticity (GARCH) model was employed. The study was motivated as a result of periodic increase in exchange rate of naira to a dollar and instability of macroeconomic variables in the economy. The presence of Autoregressive Distributive Conditional Heteroscedasticity (ARCH) effect established the use of non-linear GARCH models which showed that volatility was persistent over the period of study. Consequently, the result revealed that exchange rate volatility exhibited a positive relationship with trade balance, industrial output and inflation in the study period. Thus, good news prevailed more over bad news in the foreign exchange market. The study therefore recommended that monetary authorities in Nigeria should regulate exchange rate and macroeconomic variables in order to control the general price level in the economy.

Keywords: Exchange rate volatility, non-linear GARCH, trade balance, industrial output, inflation, Nigeria

1. Introduction

The obligation of every responsible government is to ensure a balance among the different macroeconomic indicators which reveals the health of the economy. However, the major macroeconomic goal of a country is to achieve rapid growth. But persistent volatile exchange rate is a current impediment for successful macroeconomic policies [1] in any country. Consequently, the monetary authority (Central Bank of Nigeria) has engaged in different exchange rate adjustment policies in attaining macroeconomic objective of price stability. Still, all have proved abortive as greater flexibility in exchange rate is more important to attain equilibrium level and curtail shocks associated with transition from one regime to another. Though, the major objective of exchange rate policy in accordance to [2] is to regulate the domestic currency towards maintaining favourable financial balances and overall macroeconomic stability in order to attain sustainable growth. Subsequently, effort has been made over the years to achieve this objective via adoption of several policy options in foreign exchange market, specifically adoption of Structural Adjustment

Programmes (SAP) by developing countries which was initiated by World Bank and International Monetary Fund in 1986. This eventually resulted to instabilities in exchange rates and aggravated inflationary problems.

The [3] clarified the assertion that instabilities in macroeconomic variables cannot increase output, it could harm the economy wherein firms cannot perform effectively in incidence of high inflation. This indicates that the economy cannot grow unless the macroeconomic environment is stabilised. However, since the economy cannot exist in isolation, balance of trade with other countries is another important factor for macroeconomic performance. International trade is said to be sensitive to macroeconomic changes, in that if openness is positively related to growth, inflation which distorts the price of goods ought to be seriously monitored. However, it has been acknowledged that the breakdown of Bretton Woods system in 1973 rendered exchange rate of many countries unstable overtime. This has increased motivation in predicting exchange rate basically because it is an important price that links the world and domestic market for goods and assets. It as well designates competitiveness of a country's exchange rate with the global market. Its uncontrollable cases have brought about currency crisis in the financial market in terms of output and investment which disrupt macroeconomic performance in Nigeria.

Nevertheless, it is appropriate to examine the interaction that exist among volatility of exchange rate and macroeconomic variables (trade balance, industrial output and inflation) due to the role they play in the overall development of the economy. The three macroeconomic variables are selected because of their sensitivity to exchange rate and their determinant of the general price level in the economy. In relation to trade, it could result to trade surplus or trade deficit therefore distorting trade balance [4]. When trade deficit arises, government might find it difficult to finance the deficit which pose a challenge to the economy. In terms of surplus, it inhibits consequences for government revenue and foreign reserves by upsetting the flow of imports and exports [5]. However, inflation has been acknowledged as the major cause of macroeconomic instability [6]. It was observed that whenever there is an increase in inflation, volatility in exchange rate rises but reverses in periods of relative stability. This implies that increase in exchange rate leads to higher inflation, therefore, variations in exchange rate influences inflation which might prevail for a long time in the economy [7]. Lastly, in relation to output, exchange rate volatility can initiate uncertainty among profit maximisation traders, and thus deteriorates trade balance and alter economic growth [8].

In respect to various empirical studies: [9–11], it is inappropriate to liberalise trade in the periods of macroeconomic instabilities especially inflation and exchange rate volatility. In this regards, macroeconomic policies will destruct and bring about loss of consumers' and investors' confidence and in turn impairs trade in such country. In Nigeria, financial authorities have played an essential role in implementing trade policies and different strategies to regulate important macroeconomic variable that relates to exchange rate. Unfortunately, it has witnessed several economic adversities which have all proved to no avail as the major problem is that Nigerian economy is still an import dependent country. Exchange rate which is the most important variable is still on the increase periodically and this is detrimental to macroeconomic performance.

The main objective of this study is to examine the asymmetric relationship between exchange rate volatility and macroeconomic variables in Nigeria. To accomplish this, the article is structured as follows: the next section reviews empirical literature, followed by theoretical review and methodology. Afterwards, the article dwells on data interpretation and then conclusion.

2. Literature review

Macroeconomist in developed and developing countries have emphasised the impact of exchange rate volatility on macroeconomic performance. In developed countries, using ARCH and GARCH models, [12] examine the link between exchange rate volatility and trade. The result disclosed that bilateral exchange rate volatility lowered trade between countries but displayed positive contribution to trade. Also, asymmetric effect was found between trade-depressing effect and trade promoting effect which are larger for external volatility and swings in volatility. [13] estimated the effect of exchange rate volatility on trade between 1999 and 2009. It was found that upsurge in real exchange rate volatility exhibited negative impact on import and export in the long-run. [14] examined the relationship between exchange rate and inflation in UK and Turkey from 2005 to 2014. The result revealed that purchasing power parity does not occur in Turkey and this might be due to some related factors.

In developing countries, employing the ARCH and GARCH models, [15] examined the effect of exchange rate volatility on macroeconomic performance in Sudan. GARCH technique and two stage Least Square Methods with data series from 1979 to 2009 showed that Real Effective Exchange Rate (REER) volatility exhibited harmful effects on flow of Foreign Direct Investment (FDI) and economic growth. [16] estimated the direct effect of real exchange rate volatility on trade balance in Iran between 1993 and 2011. Result showed that REER had no significant effect on trade balance and trade balance is not affected by export but import. [17] used annual data from periods between 1980 and 2013 to examine the effects and cause of volatility of exchange rate on growth in Ghana. It was established that extreme volatility is dangerous for economic growth. However, decomposition of shocks to exchange rate indicated that three quarter of exchange rate volatility is self-driven. Considering sub-Saharan countries (SSA), [18] investigated the impact of exchange rate volatility on trade applying data spanning from 1993 to 2014. The result found no effect on import when pooled mean group estimators and GARCH model was used. However, negative effect of exchange rate volatility on export transpired in short-run while positive effect occurred in long- run. Considering seven (7) developing countries, [19] investigated effect of exchange rate volatility on FDI and trade along "One Belt and One Road". Panel data series from 1995 to 2016 in addition to techniques of Threshold Autoregressive Conditional Heteroskedasticity (TGARCH) was used. Result showed that exchange rate volatility affected FDI and trade in OBOR related countries.

In Nigeria, [20] reported the presence of overshooting volatility shocks while investigating consistency, severity and persistency of exchange rate volatility from 1986 to 2008. [21] focused on monthly data from 2000 to 2015 in examining impact of exchange rate volatility on trade balance in Nigeria, a long run relationship was found between exchange rate volatility and trade. [22] investigated the impact of exchange rate volatility and the role exchange rate policy plays in Nigerian economy. Data spanning from 1996 to 2017 showed causal relationship between GDP growth and exchange rate volatility are inversely related but a bidirectional relationship occurred between RGDP and exchange rate. [23] investigated relationship between exchange rate volatility and inflation. Quarterly data ranging from 1970Q1–2014Q4 was employed. Result showed there was no causal relationship between real exchange rate and inflation.

[24] examined the interaction among exchange rate volatility, interest rate and exchange rate pass-through in Nigeria. Monthly time series spanning from 1970 to 2008 was used. The result showed there exist positive relationship among the variables in long run but negative nexus existed between inflation and exchange rate

volatility in short-run. [25] examined exchange rate volatility and sectorial export oil and non-export sectors in Nigeria using annual data from 1980 to 2011. GARCH techniques was employed to measure volatility of exchange rate while Seemingly Unrelated Regression was used to estimate coefficient of two-system equation. The result suggested exchange rate was unpredictable whereas the SUR model showed existence of negative relationship between export performance and exchange rate volatility of non-oil and oil sector. [26] used ARCH model and extension (GARCH, Exponential Generalised ARCH (EGARGH) and Threshold (TGARCH)) to examine effect of exchange rate volatility on export of non-oil in Nigeria. Quarterly data spanning from 1986Q1–2014Q4 was used in conjunction with ECM technique. The result confirmed presence of exchange rate volatility and existence of negative impact on non-oil export.

In view of the empirical literature above, the gap identified is the issue of measurement of exchange rate volatility. Several methods have been employed in measuring volatility: moving average, ARCH and GARCH models. [21] are of the opinion that GARCH is the right model for modelling volatility in Nigeria. But because the measurement of volatility is of great importance to macroeconomic performance, there is need to employ non-linear GARCH model due to its advantages of positive variance irrespective of estimated parameters and its asymmetric effects on innovations [27]. Furthermore, according to [28], asymmetric GARCH have revealed better results than simple GARCH models.

3. Theoretical review and methodology

The study is based on Mundell-Fleming model (MFM) developed by [29, 30]. The model is based on the extension of IS-LM model. The traditional IS-LM model describes an economy under autarky (i.e., closed economy) but MFM describes an open economy. It designates the relationship between output (short run), nominal exchange rate and interest rate in an economy. Thus, Mundell-Fleming model is adopted in this study since Nigeria is attributed to an open economy. In that, Nigeria is small to influence the world market in terms of world prices and interest rate and then assumed to have a perfect capital mobility.

3.1 Model specification

The overall model to capture the broad objective of the study which is to examine the asymmetric relationship between exchange rate volatility and macroeconomic variables in Nigeria is stated in the equation below:

$$Y_t = f\left(ERV_t^*\right) \tag{1}$$

where '*Y*' is output and 'ERV' is exchange rate volatility.

The macroeconomic theory in relation to Mundell-Fleming framework implies that income, interest rate, exchange rate, price, net export and similar variables can be implicitly related.

$$Y_t = f(ERV_t, Z_t) \tag{2}$$

where 'Y_t' is output, 'ERV_t' is exchange rate volatility; Z_t is vector of macroeconomic variables.

The explicit equation of the above is presented below as:

$$Y = f(i, e, P, NX) \tag{3}$$

where 'i' is interest rate, 'e' is exchange rate, 'P' is price and 'NX' is Net Export.

Also, macroeconomic theory behind the Mundell-Fleming framework makes us believe that income, interest rate, exchange rate, price, net export variables can be implicitly related as follows:

The Mundell-Fleming Model

$$Y = C(Y - t(Y)), r - E(\pi) + I(r - E(\pi), Y_{t-1}) + G + NX(e, Y, Y^*) \tag{4}$$

where Y_t = Output; C_t = Consumption; I_t = Investment; R_t = Interest rate; in_t = Inflation rate; G_t = Government spending; TB_t = Trade balance; E_t = Exchange rate.

Therefore, the model formation of this study is illustrated below as:

$$Y = f(i, R, E, NX) \tag{5}$$

where 'i' is inflation rate; 'R' is interest rate; 'E' is Exchange Rate and NX is 'Net Export'.

3.2 Estimation of heteroskedasticity using non-linear GARCH model

The confirmation of the presence of ARCH in the model as presented in **Table 1** enabled the study to proceed to non-linear GARCH. The ARCH model comprises of two parts: the mean equation and the variance equation as proposed by [31]. The mean equation can be mathematically specified as:

$$Y_t = \alpha + \beta^! X_t + \mu_t \tag{6}$$

where Y_t is the vector of variables; α represents the constant term. $\beta^!$ is the vector of unknown parameter; X_t represents the vector of unknown variable; then μ_t is the random error term.

The variance equation is presented as:

$$h_t = \gamma_0 + \sum_{i=1}^{q} \gamma_1 \mu_{t-i}^2 \tag{7}$$

ARCH model is majorly a moving average (MA) and the variance is mainly responding to errors. It does not capture the autoregressive (AR) part of the model. This prompted the use of more comprehensive models like GARCH propounded by [32].

Consequently, the GARCH model also lack some important features. It cannot explain the effect of events and news which exhibit asymmetric effect on exchange rates. However, investors react in different ways to incidence of good and bad news in the financial market, wherein bad news leads to higher volatility. But the non-linear

F-Statistics	9.9019	Prob. F (1,133)	0.0020
Obs*R-squared	9.3544	Prob. Chi-Square (1)	0.0022
Scaled explained SS	276.1406	Prob. Chi-Square (1)	0.0000

Source: Authors computation 2021.

Table 1.
ARCH test.

GARCH (EGARCH) model is proficient in capturing events, news and incidence that lead to asymmetric impact and this gives preference to use EGARCH which is believed to be superior in accounting for asymmetric and non-linear effects [33].

The aim of achieving a robust result resulted in the consideration of EGARCH model for this study. To begin with, exchange rate returns was generated through the log of difference of exchange rate which is mathematically specified as:

$$d\log\left(EXR_t - EXR_{t-1}\right) \tag{8}$$

The EGARCH model as propounded by Nelson (1991) is specified in a general form as:

$$\log\left(h_t\right) = \gamma_0 + \sum_{i=1}^{p} \beta_i \left| \frac{\mu_{t-i}}{\sqrt{h_{t-i}}} \right| + \sum_{i=1}^{q} \gamma_i \frac{\mu_{t-i}}{\sqrt{h_{t-i}}} + \sum_{i=1}^{m} \alpha_i \log\left(h_{t-1}\right) \tag{9}$$

where γ_0 is constant term, β_i is a measure of ARCH effect, γ_1 is the leverage effect, α_i is the GARCH effect, positive value of μ_{t-i} with total effect as $(1+\gamma_i)|\mu_{t-i}$ denotes good news, negative value of μ_{t-i} with total effect as $(1-\gamma_i)|\mu_{t-i}$ denotes bad news. In this case, good news is assumed to have a greater effect on volatility compared to bad news. There is asymmetry if $\gamma_i \neq 0$ and symmetry when $\gamma_i = 0$.

3.3 Source of data and variable selection

This research employed secondary (quarterly) data spanning from 1986Q1–2019Q4. The data was sourced from CBN Statistical Bulletin (2018; 2019; 2020) and International Financial Statistics (2019) editions. The macroeconomic variables used in the study are trade balance, industrial output and inflation while interest rate was used as control variable in the model.

4. Data interpretation

The descriptive statistics is made up of statistical distribution of a total of 136 observation presented in **Table 2**. The result showed that almost all the variables demonstrated significant level of consistency within the minimum and maximum values. The closeness of the mean and median indicates the variables have a normal distribution. It was discovered that the mean and the median values are positive Also, the mean and the median falls within the maximum value. This suggest that the individual values are normally distributed. The large difference between the maximum and minimum exchange rate indicates the high volatile nature of exchange rate. The standard deviation which measures the amount of dispersion of a variable revealed that the standard deviation of the variables reported were very low except for trade balance and interest rate which are greater than two. This revealed that the values of the variables clustered around their average with little or no variability. For a normal distribution, the skewness is zero while positive and negative skewness indicates distribution with right and left tail respectively. The standard deviation, skewness and kurtosis greater than zero indicates that the distribution is not normally distributed. The positive skewness of exchange rate returns, industrial output and interest rate implies their distributions are skewed to the right. Then, the negative skewness of exchange rate, trade balance and inflation indicate their distribution are skewed to the left. Negative skewness denotes a tail towards the left side of the distribution while positive skewness signifies a tail towards the right side of the

Variables	NER	RNER	TDB	IDP	INF	INR
Mean	3.6888	0.0064	10.3603	11.4508	3.3763	11.9218
Median	4.4165	0.0012	10.9364	11.1563	3.7163	11.5400
Maximum	5.1945	3.6477	13.4853	15.0223	5.6339	25.9300
Minimum	−0. 3567	−1.4628	1.7574	9.8521	−0.0619	4.6000
Std. Dev.	1.4173	0.3781	2.4548	1.3104	1.6539	3.9657
Skewness	−1.1526	5.9230	−0.6673	1.0456	−0.6659	0.8533
Kurtosis	3.2353	68.1764	2.7179	3.6343	2.2620	3.9657
Jarque-Bera	30.4238	2468.11	10.5427	27.0588	13.1386	21.5339
Probability	0.0000	0.0000	0.0051	0.0000	0.0014	0.0000
Observations	136	136	136	136	136	136

Note: NER is exchange rate; RNER is the returns of exchange rate, TDB is trade balance; IDP is industrial output; INF is inflation, INR is interest rate.
Source: Authors computation 2021.

Table 2.
Descriptive statistics.

distribution. Lastly, the Jarque-Bera statistics which is used to test the normality in the distribution of the series. The result indicated that the probability of J-B is or less than 0.05. Therefore, the null hypothesis of normal distribution is rejected and the alternative hypothesis that the variables have a non-normal distribution is accepted. The implication of the non-normality of trade balance and inflation verified their responses to the volatile nature of exchange rate movement in Nigeria.

The result of the unit root test presented in **Table 3** was to verify the stationarity properties of the variables. The Augmented Dickey Fuller (ADF) and Phillips Peron (PP) test was used to determine the order of integration of the variables. The result revealed that exchange rate returns (RNER) and trade balance (TDB) are stationary at levels, i.e., I (0) while NER (exchange rate), industrial output (IDP), inflation (INF) and interest rate (INR) are stationary at first difference, i.e., I (1), hence the variables are integrated at levels and order one i.e., mixture of I (0) and I (1).

Variables	Levels			First difference		
	Intercept + trend			Intercept + trend		
	ADF	PP	STATUS	ADF	PP	STATUS
NER	−3.6811*	−3.2571*	—	−11.5112***	−11.6093***	I (1)
RNER	−11.5112***	−11.6093***	I(0)	—	—	
TDB	−5.7023***	−5.6849***	I(0)	—	—	
IDP	−1.6265	−1.6846	—	−12.7396***	−12.7625***	I (1)
INF	−2.3329	−1.3505	—	−3.8607**	−7.4348***	I (1)
INR	−4.5889***	−3.4472**	—	−8.1564***	−7.6674***	I (1)

*Note: ***, **, * at 1%, 5% and 10% respectively.*
Source: Authors computation 2021.

Table 3.
Unit root test.

4.1 Preliminary test

In order to verify the presence of heteroscedasticity in the model, ARCH test was carried out using Breush-Pagan-Godfrey method. Therein, the evidence of ARCH effect enables the study to proceed to estimating non-linear GARCH model. The ARCH effect result is presented in **Table 1** while **Figure 1** shows the evidence of volatility clustering. Therein, the null hypothesis states that there is no presence of heteroscedasticity in the return series. But since the probability is 1%, the null hypothesis is rejected while the alternative hypothesis of presence of ARCH effect is accepted.

4.2 Non-linear GARCH results

The result of EGARCH (1,1) model for dependent variable trade balance is presented in **Table 4**. The normal distribution analysis reveals that the effect of exchange rate volatility on trade balance is negative at −0.013%. The ARCH result is 1.32% at a significance level of 1%, this showed a positive relationship between exchange rate volatility and trade balance. The leverage term is −0.045% which is significant at 1%. The negative leverage term implied that bad news prevails over good news in the foreign exchange market. Likewise, the GARCH result at 0.81% indicate that present volatility positively predicts future volatility at 1% level of significance. The result of student-t distribution shows the marginal effect of exchange rate volatility on trade balance is −0.02%. The result of ARCH is 1.32% at 1% significance which indicates a positive relationship between exchange rate volatility and trade balance. The leverage term at 0.07% was significant at 1%. The positive leverage effect implies that good news prevails over bad news in the foreign exchange market. Also, the GARCH term was 0.81% which indicates that present volatility positively predicts the future volatility at 1% level of significance. Lastly, the generalised error distribution result show that the marginal effect of exchange rate volatility on trade balance is −0.04%. The outcome of the ARCH result is 1.29% and this implies a positive relationship between exchange rate volatility and trade balance. The leverage effect is at 0.183% and it show that goods news prevails over bad news in the foreign exchange market. The GARCH term is 0.80% and this implies that present volatility predicts the future volatility at 1% significance level. Nevertheless, the best model for the distribution is the generalised error distribution with minimum variance of Schwarz Criterion value at 3.5145 and log likelihood value of −212.7013.

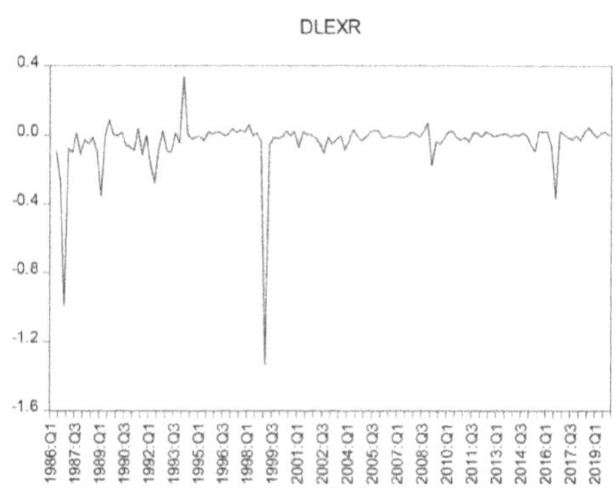

Figure 1.
Graphical representation of returns of exchange rate in Nigeria. Source: Authors computation (2021).

EGARCH (1,1)				
Normal Distribution				
Mean Equation				
Variables	Coefficient	Std. error	z-Statistics	Prob.
RNER	−0.0133	0,3492	−0.0380	0.9697
Constant	14.7341	1.0363	14.2186	0.0000***
Variance Equation				
Variables	Coefficient	Std. error	z-Statistics	Prob.
Constant	−0.9879	0.2023	−4.8832	0.0000****
Residual Square	1.3196	0.2863	4.6084	0.0000***
Leverage Term	−0.0453	0.1661	0.2809	0.7787
GARCH (−1)	0.8133	0.1125	7.2273	0.0000***
Log Likelihood	−210.7896			
Schwarz Criterion	3.4498			
Student.t Distribution				
Mean Equation				
Variables	Coefficient	Std. error	z-Statistics	Prob.
RNER	−0.0203	0.6953	−0.0292	0.9767
Constant	14.3965	1.0252	14.0427	0.0000***
Variance Equation				
Variables	Coefficient	Std. error	z-Statistics	Prob.
Constant	−0.9671	0.2068	−4.6753	0.0000***
Residual Square	1.3157	0.3035	4.3346	0.0000***
Leverage Term	0.0725	0.1764	0.4107	0.6813
GARCH (−1)	0.8131	0.1201	6.7663	0.0000***
Log Likelihood	−211.0528			
Schwarz Criterion	3.3623			
Generalized Error Distribution				
Mean Equation				
Variables	Coefficient	Std. error	z-Statistics	Prob.
RNER	−0.0442	0.4357	−0.1016	0.9191
Constant	12.1887	1.0669	11.4235	0.0000***
Variance Equation				
Variables	Coefficient	Std. error	z-Statistics	Prob.
Constant	−0.8419	0.2173	−3.8739	0.0001***
Residual Square	1.2879	0.4043	3.1854	0.0014***
Leverage Term	0.1832	0.2348	0.7800	0.4354
GARCH (−1)	0.7955	0.1201	6.6217	0.0000***
Log Likelihood	−212.7013			
Schwarz Criterion	3.5145			

****, ** and * represent 1%, 5% and 10% respectively.*
Source: Authors computation 2021.

Table 4.
EGARCH (1,1) result for dependent variable trade balance.

EGARCH (1,1)				
Normal Distribution				
Mean Equation				
Variables	Coefficient	Std. error	z-Statistics	Prob.
RNER	0.0441	0.0319	1.3777	0.1683
Constant	10.0803	0.0522	193.0716	0.0000***
Variance Equation				
Variables	Coefficient	Std. error	z-Statistics	Prob.
Constant	−0.8958	0.3099	−2.8902	0.0038***
Residual Square	0.9260	0.3001	3.0862	0.0020***
Leverage Term	0.0955	0.0996	0.9586	0.3378***
GARCH (−1)	0.9371	0.0546	17.1738	0.0000***
Log Likelihood	−12.3675			
Schwarz Criterion	0.5502			
Student.t Distribution				
Mean Equation				
Variables	Coefficient	Std. error	z-Statistics	Prob.
RNER	0.0439	0.0307	1.4310	0.1524*
Constant	10.0771	0.0508	198.4041	0.0000***
Variance Equation				
Variables	Coefficient	Std. error	z-Statistics	Prob.
Constant	−0.8767	0.3143	−2.7895	0.0053***
Residual Square	0.9198	0.3079	2.9866	0.0028***
Leverage Term	0.0843	0.1404	0.6007	0.5480
GARCH (−1)	0.9406	0.0549	17.1186	0.0000***
Log Likelihood	−12.2295			
Schwarz Criterion	0.5445			
Generalized Error Distribution				
Mean Equation				
Variables	Coefficient	Std. error	z-Statistics	Prob.
RNER	0.0437	0.0368	1.1870	0.2352
Constant	10.0819	0.0559	180.3712	0.0000***
Variance Equation				
Variables	Coefficient	Std. error	z-Statistics	Prob.
Constant	−0.9242	0.2920	−3.1645	0.0016***
Residual Square	0.9360	0.2763	3.3878	0.0007***
Leverage Term	0.0913	0.1163	0.7851	0.4324
GARCH (−1)	0.9332	0.0496	18.8167	0.0000***
Log Likelihood	−11.6548			
Schwarz Criterion	0.5360			

****, ** and * represent 1%, 5% and 10% respectively.*
Source: Authors computation 2021.

Table 5.
EGARCH (1,1) result for industrial dependent variable output.

EGARCH (1,1)				
Normal Distribution				
Mean Equation				
Variables	Coefficient	Std. error	z-Statistics	Prob.
RNER	−0.03225	0.0961	−0.3385	0.7350
Constant	−6.3262	0.2901	−21.8100	0.0000***
Variance Equation				
Variables	Coefficient	Std. error	z-Statistics	Prob.
Constant	−1.3526	0.2710	−4.9908	0.0000***
Residual Square	1.0013	0.2123	4.7158	0.0000***
Leverage Term	−0.4518	0.1698	−2.6609	0.0078***
GARCH (−1)	0.7986	0.0862	9.2690	0.0000***
Log Likelihood	−83.9817			
Schwarz Criterion	1.7712			
Student.t Distribution				
Mean Equation				
Variables	Coefficient	Std. error	z-Statistics	Prob.
RNER	−0.0326	0.0880	00.3705	0.7110
Constant	−6.5065	0.3386	−19.2155	0.0000***
Variance Equation				
Variables	Coefficient	Std. error	z-Statistics	Prob.
Constant	−1.3407	0.3640	−3.6829	0.0002***
Residual Square	1.0066	0.2210	4.5536	0.0000***
Leverage Term	−0.4374	0.2089	−2.0936	0.0363***
GARCH (−1)	0.8074	0.0936	8.6283	0.0000***
Log Likelihood	−83.9067			
Schwarz Criterion	1.6064			
Generalized Error Distribution				
Mean Equation				
Variables	Coefficient	Std. error	z-Statistics	Prob.
RNER	−0.0335	0.1022	−0.3277	0.7431
Constant	−6.3774	0.3362	−18.9700	0.0000***
Variance Equation				
Variables	Coefficient	Std. error	z-Statistics	Prob.
Constant	−1.3899	0.3633	−3.8261	0.0001***
Residual Square	0.9907	0.2116	4.6808	0.0000***
Leverage Term	−0.4797	0.1884	−2.5469	0.0109***
GARCH (−1)	0.7888	0.0865	9.1151	0.0000***
Log Likelihood	−83.8706			
Schwarz Criterion	1.6059			

****, ** and * represent 1%, 5% and 10% respectively.*
Source: Authors computation 2021.

Table 6.
EGARCH (1,1) result for dependent variable inflation.

The result of EGARCH (1,1) for dependent variable industrial output is presented in **Table 5**. The outcome of the normal distribution show that the effect of exchange rate volatility on industrial output is positive at 0.04%. The leverage term is 0.95% which indicates that good news prevails over bad news in the foreign exchange rate market. The positive outcome of ARCH is at 0.93% with a significant level of 1%, this shows the existence of a positive relationship between exchange rate volatility and industrial output. The GARCH result is 0.94% at 1% significance level and this indicates that present volatility positively predicts the future volatility at 1% level of significance. The student-t distribution result reveal that the marginal effect of exchange rate volatility on industrial output is 0.04% at 10% significance level. This indicate that exchange rate volatility exhibits a positive relationship with industrial output in Nigeria. The leverage effect is 0.08% which indicate goods news prevails over bed news in the foreign exchange market. The ARCH result of 0.08% infer that present volatility positively predicts the future volatility at 1% significance level. Moreover, the GARCH term at 0.94% infer that present volatility positively predicts the future volatility at 1% significance. The result of generalised error distribution showed that the effect of exchange rate volatility on industrial output is 0.04%. This designates a positive relationship between exchange rate volatility and industrial output in Nigeria. The leverage term at 0.09% indicate that good news prevails over bad news in foreign exchange market. In reporting the GARCH term at 0.93%, this infers that present volatility predicts future volatility at 1% significance. In relating the distributions in terms of goodness of fit, normal distribution is the best model to be considered with a minimum variance value of SC at 0.5102 and the log likelihood maximum value at −12.3675.

The EGARCH (1,1) result for dependent variable inflation is presented in **Table 6**. The normal distribution show that the effect of exchange rate volatility on inflation is negative at −0.03%. The ARCH result at 1.0% with a significant level at 1% infer that exchange rate volatility and inflation are positively related. The leverage term is −0.45% and indicates that bad news prevails over good news in the foreign exchange rate market. However, the GARCH effect is 0.79% which indicates that the present volatility predicts the future volatility at 1% significance level. The student-t result revealed that the marginal effect of exchange rate volatility on inflation is negative at −0.03%. The ARCH result is 1.01% and significant at 1% level indicate the existence of a positive relationship between exchange rate volatility and inflation. The leverage effect at −0.44% infer that bad news prevails over good news in the foreign exchange market. The GARCH term at 0.81% revealing that present volatility predicts the future volatility at 1% level of significance. Lastly, the generalised error distribution result showed that the marginal effect of exchange rate volatility on inflation is negative at −0.03%. The ARCH effect at 0.99% deduce there is a positive relationship between exchange rate volatility and inflation at 1% significant level. The leverage term at 0–0.48% indicate that bad news prevails over good news in the foreign exchange market. Then the GARCH result at 0.79% indicate that present volatility predicts future volatility at 1% level of significance. In choosing the best model for goodness of fit with minimum variance, the normal distribution with log likelihood value of 83.9817 and minimum variance of 1.7712 is selected.

5. Conclusion and policy implication

The study examined the asymmetric relationship between exchange rate volatility and macroeconomic performance in Nigeria through the period between 1986Q1 and 2019Q4 using the non-linear GARCH model. In order to employ the non-linear GARCH model (EGARCH), ARCH effect was verified to confirm the presence of heteroscedasticity. The preliminary test such as unit root test and ARCH test to verify the presence of heteroscedasticity revealed the evidence of volatility clustering. The outcome of the analysis revealed that volatility movement was very high and persistent over the period of study. Exchange rate volatility exhibited a positive relationship with trade balance and industrial output but a negative relationship with inflation. The leverage effect of exchange rate volatility on trade balance and industrial output indicated the prevalence of good news over bad news. But contrary to the aforementioned, the leverage effect of exchange rate volatility on inflation revealed the prevalence of bad news over good news in the foreign exchange market. On the other hand, the present volatility predicts the future volatility for all the variables. Also, the non-linear GARCH model confirmed that the normal distribution is the best model for traders in the financial market. The implication of the findings imply that exchange rate volatility is an important factor in the macroeconomic performance of the Nigerian economy. It is therefore recommended that government should procure a stable economy through the monetary authorities (CBN) by implementing policies to control and regulate exchange rate and macroeconomic variables in order to control the general price level. Also, investors and financial analyst should consider exchange rate volatility in predicting macroeconomic performance in the future by ensuring stability in the financial market. Furthermore, even though investors in financial markets are risk averse, it is recommended that they should be more sensitive to good news rather than bad news in the events of movement of exchange rate volatility on macroeconomic performance in Nigeria.

Appendix

- The probability density function of normal distribution is represented as:

$$f(x|\mu,\sigma) = \frac{1}{\sigma\sqrt{2\pi}} e^{\frac{-(x-\mu)^2}{2\sigma^2}} \tag{10}$$

- Its log likelihood function in GARCH term is:

$$-\frac{n}{2}\ln(2\pi) - \frac{n}{2}\ln(h) - \frac{1}{2h}\sum_{j=1}^{n}(x_j-\mu)^2 \tag{11}$$

- The probability density function for Student-t distribution is illustrated as:

$$f(y,v) = \frac{\Gamma\frac{v+1}{2}}{\sqrt{\pi(v-2)\Gamma\frac{v}{2}\left(1+\frac{v^2}{v-2}\right)^{\frac{v+1}{2}}}} \tag{12}$$

- The log likelihood function in GARCH term is depicted as:

$$\log\left[\Gamma\left(\frac{v+1}{2}\right)\right] - \log\left[\Gamma\left(\frac{v}{2}\right)\right] - \frac{1}{2}\log(\pi(v-2))$$
$$-\frac{1}{2}\sum_{j=1}^{n}\left[\log(h_t) + (v+1)\log\left(1+\frac{\varepsilon_t^2}{h_t(v-2)}\right)\right] \tag{13}$$

- The probability density function for generalised error distribution is mathematically represented as:

$$f(x|\mu,\sigma,k) = \frac{e^{-\frac{1}{2}|x-\mu|^{\frac{1}{n}}}}{2^{k+1}\sigma\Gamma(k+1)} \tag{14}$$

- Its log likelihood function in GARCH term is:

$$-\frac{1}{2}|x-\mu|^{\frac{1}{n}} - (k+1)\log(2) - \log(h) - \log(\Gamma) - \log(k+1) \tag{15}$$

JEL Classification

B22, C22, E31, E58, F14

Author details

Kehinde Mary Bello*, David Oluseun Olayungbo and Benjamin Ayodele Folorunso
Department of Economics, Obafemi Awolowo University, Ile-Ife, Nigeria

*Address all correspondence to: kennybello2008@gmail.com;
kbello@pg-student.oau.edu.ng

References

[1] Morina F, Hysa E, Ergun U, Panait M, Voica MC. The effect of exchange rate volatility on economic growth: Case of the CEE Countries. Journal of Risk and Financial Management. 2020;(13),177,1-17713.

[2] Central Bank of Nigeria. Exchange rate policy and macroeconomic management. https//www.cbn.gov.ng/intops/exchratepolicy. 2017. Retrieved 15-12-2017.

[3] Global Competitiveness Report.http://reports.weforum.org/globalcompetitiveness- index-2017-2018/ (accessed on 26 April 2018).

[4] Aubion M, Ruta M. The relationship between exchange rates and international trade: A review of economic literature. WTO Staff Working Paper, World Trade Organisation, Geneva. 2011;1-28.

[5] Taylor, BJB. The role of the exchange rate in monetary-policy rules. The American Economic Review. 2001; 91 (2), 263–267.

[6] Akpan OE, Atan JA. Effect of exchange rate movement and economic growth in Nigeria. CBN Journal of Applied Statistics. 2012; 2(2),1-14.

[7] Mordi, GNO. Exchange rate and inflation: Is there a relationship in Nigeria. Economics and Financial Review. 2014; 52(4), 105-123.

[8] Bahmani-Oskooee M, Aftab M. On the asymmetric effects of exchange rate volatility on trade flows: New evidence from US-Malaysia trade at the industry level. E*conomic Modelling.*2017; 63: 86–103.

[9] Zahonogo P. Trade and economic growth in developing countries: Evidence from sub-Sahara Africa. Journal of trade. 2016; 3,41-56.

[10] Odili O. Real exchange rate volatility, economic growth and international trade in an emerging market economy: Evidence from Nigeria. International Journal of Academic Research in Business and Social Sciences. 2015; 5(7),179-201.

[11] Semancikova J. Trade, trade openness and macroeconomic performance. Procedia: Social and Behavioral Sciences. 2016; 220, 407-416.

[12] Tunc C, Solakoglu MN, Hazar A, Babuscu S. Exchange rate volatility and trade: External exchange rate volatility matters. *MPRA Paper No*. 86401.2018; 1-25.

[13] Bakhromov N (2011). The exchange rate volatility and the trade balance: Case of Uzbekistan. Journal of Applied Economics and Business Research. 2011; 1(3), 149-161.

[14] Abudurehman AA, Hacilar S.The relationship between exchange rate and inflation: An empirical study of Turkey. International Journal of economics and Financial Issue. 2016; 6(4),1454-1459.

[15] Ebaidalla, ME. Impact of exchange rate volatility on macroeconomic performance in Sudan.Working Paper: No 789, 2013; 1-23.

[16] Lotfalipour MZ, Bahare B. The impact of exchange rate volatility on trade balance in Iran.Advances in Economic and Business. 2014; 2(8), 293-302.

[17] Alagidede P, Muaza I. On the causes and effect of exchange rate volatility on economic growth: Evidence from Ghana. Working paper. International Growth Centre. 2016, 1-27.

[18] Sanadza B. Diaba DD. Effect of exchange rate volatility on trade in Sub-Saharan Africa.Journal of African trade. 2017;(4), 20-36.

[19] Latif, R. and Lefen, L. The effect of exchange rate volatility on international trade and foreign direct investment (FDI) in developing countries along "one belt and one road". International Journal of Financial Studies. 2018; 6 (86), 1-22.

[20] Adeoye BM, Atanda AA. Exchange rate volatility in Nigeria: Consistency, persistence and severity analysis. Central Bank of Nigeria Journal of Applied Statistics. 2011; 2(2), 29-49.

[21] Dada JT, Olomola, PA. Exchange rate volatility and trade balance: Evidence from Nigeria.International Journal of Humanities and Social Science Research. 2017; 3(5), 4-10.

[22] Eneji MA, Nanwul DF, Eneji AI, Anga R, Dickson V. Effect of exchange rate policy and its volatility on economic growth in Nigeria. International Journal of Advanced Studies in Economics and Public Sector Management. 2018; 6(2), 166-190.

[23] Okoli T, Mbah SA, Agu OC. Exchange rate volatility and inflation: The Nigerian Experience. Journal of Economics and Sustainable Development. 2016;17(10), 6-15.

[24] Osabuohien E, Obiekwe E, Urhie E, Osabuohien R. Interest rate, exchange rate volatility and exchange rate pass-through interactions: The Nigerian experience. Journal of Applied Economic Sciences. 2018; 2(56), 574-585.

[25] Olufayo MB, Fagbite BA. Exchange rate volatility and sectorial export in Nigeria: Case of oil and non-oil sector. Journal of Economics and Sustainable Development. 2014;5(10), 66-75.

[26] Musibau HO, Babatunde SA, Halimah AA, Hammed AY. Exchange rate volatility and non- oil export in Nigeria: An empirical investigation. Journal of Global Economics. 2017; 5(2), 1-5.

[27] Baum, ARCH and GARCH models. *Applied Econometrics. 2013.*

[28] Khan, MS, Khan, KI, Mahmood S, Sheeraz M. Symmetric and asymmetric volatility clustering via GARCH family models: An evidence from religious dominant Countries.University of Central Punjab, Lahore. 2019;13(1), 20-25.

[29] Mundell, A. A theory of optimum currency area. The American Review. 1961; 51(4), 657-665.

[30] Fleming, JM. Domestic financial policies under fixed and under floating exchange rate. Staff Papers (International Monetary fund). 1962; 9 (3), 369-380.

[31] Engle R. Autoregressive conditional heteroscedasticity with estimates of the variance of United Kingdom inflation Econometrica. Journal of the Econometric Society. 1982; (50), 987-1007.

[32] Bollerslev T. Generalized autoregressive conditional heteroscedasticity. Journal of Econometrics. 1986; 31, 307-327.

[33] Olayungbo DO. Volatility effect of the global oil price on shock price in Nigeria: Evidence from linear and non-linear GARCH. Linear and Non-Linear Financial Econometrics Theory and Practice. IntechOpen 93497. 2021; 1-20.

www.ingramcontent.com/pod-product-compliance
Lightning Source LLC
LaVergne TN
LVHW081934200926
848484LV00009B/2425
* 9 7 8 1 8 3 9 6 9 8 8 1 1 *